Colorado Women in World War II

TIMBERLINE BOOKS

STEPHEN J. LEONARD AND THOMAS J. NOEL, EDITORS

Dr. Charles David Spivak: A Jewish Immigrant and the American Tuberculosis Movement
JEANNE ABRAMS

Enduring Legacies: Ethnic Histories and Cultures of Colorado
ARTURO J. ALDAMA, WITH ELISA FACIO, DARYL MAEDA,
AND REILAND RABAKA, EDITORS

Frank Mechau: Artist of Colorado, Second Edition
CILE M. BACH

Colorado Women: A History
GAIL M. BEATON

The Last Stand of the Pack, Critical Edition
ARTHUR H. CARHART WITH STANLEY P. YOUNG; ANDREW GULLIFORD AND
TOM WOLF, EDITORS

Ores to Metals: The Rocky Mountain Smelting Industry
JAMES FELL

Denver's Lakeside Amusement Park: From the White City Beautiful to a Century of Fun
DAVID FORSYTH

Colorado's Japanese Americans: From 1886 to the Present
BILL HOSOKAWA

The Gospel of Progressivism: Moral Reform and Labor War in Colorado, 1900–1930
R. TODD LAUGEN

The Beast
BEN B. LINDSEY AND HARVEY J. O'HIGGINS

Denver: An Archaeological History
SARAH M. NELSON, K. LYNN BERRY, RICHARD E. CARRILLO, BONNIE J. CLARK,
LORI E. RHODES, AND DEAN SAITTA

Denver Landmarks and Historic Districts, Second Edition
THOMAS J. NOEL AND NICHOLAS J. WHARTON

Helen Ring Robinson: Colorado Senator and Suffragist
PAT PASCOE

Season of Terror: The Espinosas in Central Colorado, March–October 1863
CHARLES F. PRICE

The History of the Death Penalty in Colorado
MICHAEL L. RADELET

The Trail of Gold and Silver: Mining in Colorado, 1859–2009
DUANE A. SMITH

A Tenderfoot in Colorado
RICHARD BAXTER TOWNSHEND

Colorado Women in World War II

Gail M. Beaton

Gail M. Beaton

UNIVERSITY PRESS OF COLORADO
Louisville

© 2020 by University Press of Colorado

Published by University Press of Colorado
1624 Market Street, Suite 226
PMB 39883
Denver, Colorado 80202

 The University Press of Colorado is a proud member of the Association of University Presses.

The University Press of Colorado is a cooperative publishing enterprise supported, in part, by Adams State University, Colorado State University, Fort Lewis College, Metropolitan State University of Denver, University of Alaska Fairbanks, University of Colorado, University of Denver, University of Northern Colorado, University of Wyoming, Utah State University, and Western Colorado University.

∞ This paper meets the requirements of the ANSI/NISO Z39.48-1992 (Permanence of Paper)

ISBN: 978-1-64642-032-2 (hardcover)
ISBN: 978-1-64642-558-7 (paperback)
ISBN: 978-1-64642-033-9 (ebook)
https://doi.org/10.5876/9781646420339

Library of Congress Cataloging-in-Publication Data

Names: Beaton, Gail Marjorie, author. | Noel, Thomas J. (Thomas Jacob), writer of foreword.
Title: Colorado women in World War II / Gail M. Beaton ; foreword by Thomas J. Noel.
Other titles: Timberline books.
Description: Louisville : University Press of Colorado, 2020. | Series: Timberline books | Includes bibliographical references and index.
Identifiers: LCCN 2020023720 (print) | LCCN 2020023721 (ebook) | ISBN 9781646420322 (cloth)| ISBN 9781646425587 (paperback) | ISBN 9781646420339 (ebook)
Subjects: LCSH: World War, 1939-1945—Women—Colorado. | World War, 1939–1945—Participation, Female. | Women—Colorado—History—20th century.
Classification: LCC D810.W7 B39 2020 (print) | LCC D810.W7 (ebook) | DDC 940.53092/5209788—dc23
LC record available at https://lccn.loc.gov/2020023720
LC ebook record available at https://lccn.loc.gov/2020023721

Cover illustration credits. Front, clockwise from top: WASP Archive, Texas Woman's University, Denton; Steelworks Center of the West, Pueblo, Colorado; Denver Public Library, Western History Collection. *Back cover, left to right:* Bernice Moran Miller Collection, University of North Carolina at Greensboro; Bancroft Library, University of California, Los Angeles; Diana Doyle; Auraria Library, Denver, CO.

In honor of,
and in dedication to,
the women who proudly served in the military,
worked in defense plants and government agencies,
nursed overseas and state-side,
farmed and ranched,
and volunteered on the home front during World War II

In memory of my mother and father,
Alice M. Beaton and Arthur P. Beaton

Contents

Foreword

Thomas J. Noel

Gail Beaton herself has been making Colorado women's history.

In 2018 she served on the Advisory Council that established the state's first Center for Colorado Women's History at the Byers-Evans House Museum, which is owned and operated by History Colorado. Gail is also the author of the leading book in the field, *Colorado Women: A History* (University Press of Colorado, 2012). In addition to having written articles and other publications, she is a popular public speaker for civic organizations, churches, retirement communities, philanthropic organizations, libraries, museums, historical societies, and classes (middle school, high school, college, adult learning). She has portrayed many prominent women, including "Gail Murphy: Colorado's Rosie the Riveter," "Sarah Platt Decker: National Women's Club Leader, Reformer, and Suffragist," and "Sadie Likens: Denver's First Lady Cop."

Gail's favorite role is Rosie the Riveter. Her favorite T-shirt proudly asserts the World War II slogan for women: "We Can Do It." Gail does do it with this book. She brings back to life the many, many women who served during World War II, both in the military and on the home front.

As a teacher at the high school and college levels, she is experienced and knowledgeable about how to make history appealing and relevant, as you will discover in these pages.

During World War II, women served in every branch of the military and the Merchant Marines. Some worked in untraditional jobs as riveters, welders, air

DOI: 10.5876/9781646420339.c000a

traffic controllers, bank tellers, inspectors, bullet makers, and chemists. Many, of course, served as nurses, others as technicians, drivers, code breakers, clerks, instructors, and mechanics, to name a few. Filing government forms may have been their biggest and most tedious job. The many roles women played during the war led to their much greater acceptance in subsequent years in many more occupations and at higher levels. Even women of color, Beaton finds, moved up the ladder—albeit temporarily—in terms of jobs and pay. Of the 300,000 who worked with the American Red Cross, women were probably a majority. Beaton explores many angles ranging from an army nurse landing on Normandy Beach to a Black Colorado woman's typing work for a federal agency to a Red Cross "doughnut girl" serving soldiers in Europe. She finds that because of Colorado's isolated inland position, far from any coastline, its wartime women have received little attention. This thoroughly researched, well-written, and comprehensive book fills that gap.

The Timberline Series of the University Press of Colorado, which takes pride in publishing the best new scholarship on Colorado as well as classic reprints, proudly adds Gail Beaton's *Colorado Women in World War II* to the shelf of important books on the Highest State.

Acknowledgments

Material for this book came from a variety of sources. One was personal interviews. In 2014, I had the pleasure of interviewing Leila Allen Morrison, a World War II Army Nurse Corps veteran. For nearly twenty years, I had been modifying and refining "Gail Murphy: Colorado's Rosie the Riveter." Through this composite character, I present the wartime roles of American women. My interview with Leila sparked a desire to learn even more about the contributions of Colorado women. Over the years I interviewed women who served in the military and the Cadet Nurse Corps, worked in defense plants and offices, and participated in home front activities. I met many of them when I presented "Gail Murphy" at retirement communities, civic and social organizations, church auxiliaries and senior groups, libraries, and historical societies. Women—and a few men—I interviewed warmly opened their homes to a stranger. They pulled out photo albums from closets, storage areas, and basements for me to pore over. I am eternally grateful to them and have enjoyed not only that initial interview but in many cases subsequent visits and phone conversations. They insisted that they had not done anything special; they "just did it."

I also had the pleasure of talking with family members of World War II women who had passed away. My gratitude is extended to Jay Alire, nephew of Pauline Apodaca; Lorelei Cloud, granddaughter of Sunshine Cloud Smith; Julie Geiser, daughter of Doris Bristol Tracy; Julie Jensen, daughter of Omilo Halder Jensen; Lee Kizer, son of Marie Kizer; John McCaffrey, husband of Peggy Moynihan

McCaffrey; and Charlene Grainger O'Leary, daughter of Roberta Grainger. Many of the interviewees themselves or family members were generous in allowing me to use photographs from the time of their military or civilian service during World War II. I know you will enjoy the ones in this book as much as I do.

In addition to interviews I personally conducted, I pored through written transcriptions and listened to oral interviews conducted by others. I am especially grateful to Monys Hagen who brought to light the experiences of members of the Women's Army Corps at Camp Hale, the training site for the heralded Tenth Mountain Division (United States Army). In Colorado, numerous institutions were invaluable. Although they are listed in the sources, I would like to specifically thank certain individuals: Victoria Miller, museum curator, manager and director Chris Schreck, and assistant Blake Hutton, the Steelworks Center of the West; Katie Adams, curator, Tread of Pioneers Museum; Tabitha Davis, special collections and museum services clerk, Pueblo Rawlings Library, who indexed "Our Boys and Girls in the Service" notebooks and newspaper articles, saving me hours of blinding microfilm viewing; Coi Drummond-Gehrig, Digital Image Sales and Research at Denver Public Library; Terry Nelson, senior special collection and community resource manager, Blair-Caldwell African American Research Library; Lesley Struc, curator, and Jessica Gengler, assistant archivist, the Archive at the Fort Collins Museum of Discovery; Anna Scott, archivist, Aspen Historical Society; and David Hays, archivist at University of Colorado's Norlin Library and Jennifer Sanchez in Archives for photo work/research help. Brad Hoopes, while not affiliated with an institution, has practically become one himself. He has done a remarkable job preserving stories of World War II veterans as the guiding force and tireless interviewer for the Northern Colorado Veterans History Project.

Across the nation, numerous institutions hold fascinating archival records. The Library of Congress's Veterans History Project collects thousands of oral interviews and materials from American veterans. I would like to thank the hundreds of volunteers who have conducted interviews and placed them at that repository. Megan Harris, reference specialist at the Library of Congress, provided me with materials on my research trip to Washington, DC. Texas Woman's University is the official caretaker of the Women Airforce Service Pilots records. Kimberly Johnson, director, special collections, and university archivist, was most helpful in providing me with information and photographs. The opportunity to visit the National WASP WWII Museum, Sweetwater, Texas, and speak with Carol Cain was enhanced by the wonderful hospitality of my good friend Nancy Speck. At the University of North Carolina at Greensboro, Beth Ann Koelsch (assistant professor and curator of the Betty H. Carter Women Veterans Historical Project, Hodges Special Collections and University Archives) promptly supplied me with information and photographs from their wonderful collection. I also appreciate the efforts of Michael Maire Lange, copyright and information policy specialist at the University of California, Berkeley. The Women in Military Service for America Memorial should be on everyone's list to visit. Their exhibits on women in the armed forces throughout time is a "must see." As is the Rosie the Riveter World War II Home Front Museum and Archives, which chronicles the contributions of women defense workers. Also on the grounds of the national park is the evocative Rosie the Riveter Memorial Park.

Other primary sources of information were newspapers and magazine articles, obituaries, census records, letters, and diaries. Research forays were productive as a result of help from Erin Barnes at the Carnegie Library of the Pikes Peak Library District; Sara Francis, archivist for the Glenwood Springs Historical Society and Frontier Museum; Doris Heath at the Fort Sedgwick Historical Society; Nicole LeBoeuf, electronic resources and discovery librarian at Adams State University Library; and Erin Johnson Schmitz, curator of collections and archives, and volunteer Marie Tipping at the Museums of Western Colorado.

As I conducted research and interviews, a number of people put me in contact with others who could help. Sara Beery told me about Thelma Morey Robinson after hearing her speak at a community event; Gerald Langston provided me with an introduction to Julie Geiser, daughter of Doris Bristol Tracy; and Janet and Don Bailey gave me contact information for Virginia Wilson Horn.

I am indebted to Maureen Christopher and Kathy Noll for their personal knowledge of navy nursing; Marcia Goldstein for her paper on the Denver Ordnance Plant; Sherrie Langston and Abbey Beaton for transcribing interviews; Andrew Manriquez for asking me to perform Gail Murphy at his "40s Forever" event at the Loveland–Fort Collins Airport where I met "my army nurse"; professor Dr. Fawn Montoya and students Lauren Knight and Alyssa Vargas Lopez for their research on the women workers at the Pueblo Ordnance Depot; WestPac Restorations' volunteer Pam Potter for teaching me to rivet; and Thelma Robinson (Cadet Nurse Corps), Lucile Doll Wise (WASP), and Julie Jensen (daughter of navy nurse Omilio Halder Jensen) for suggestions and corrections on those chapters.

Sherrie Langston and my mother, Alice Beaton, listened to countless drafts, summaries of research trips, and gleeful accounts of nuggets discovered. I am grateful to have been surrounded by friends and family who never failed to show their support for this project. Thank you.

I am grateful to the staff at the University Press of Colorado—Darrin Pratt, Laura Furney, Charlotte Steinhardt, Beth Svinarich, and Daniel Pratt—who brought their collective skills and energy to see this project from start to finish, repeatedly working with me to ensure that the experiences of these women would be shared. Once again, Cheryl Carnahan wielded an incisive and thoughtful editing pen to the manuscript. I appreciate all of your efforts.

There is a saying that when a person dies, it is as if a library burned. As the Greatest Generation ages, we continue to lose women and men whom I or others have interviewed. Each loss saddens me.[1] My hope is that this book will enlighten readers to the contributions of Colorado women in World War II and spark family conversations and remembrances. I encourage those who know a member of the generation that came of age during World War II to make a concerted effort to learn and preserve their stories so that, upon their passing, we will not lose stories from those "libraries." I offer *Colorado Women in World War II* in tribute.

Colorado Women in World War II

Introduction

Four months before the attack on Pearl Harbor, Mildred McClellan Melville, a member of the Denver Woman's Press Club, predicted that war would come for the United States and that its long arm would reach into the lives of all Americans. She warned club members that the coming war will not be "a man's war at The Front. It will be a civilian war reaching into every kitchen and nursery. It will be a war, not only of bombs, but also of butter; not only of Maginot Lines, but also of morale. It will be a war which leaves no room for hysteria and helplessness; snobbishness and intolerances."[2] And reach it did — in the huge numbers of drafted and enlisted loved ones, in the unprecedented number of women in the armed forces, in the availability of new job opportunities, and in the form of government mandates, restrictions, and regulations.

World War II "ushered in sudden dramatic changes for American women."[3] In a similar manner, the authors of one history book asserted that the Japanese bombing at Pearl Harbor "transformed Colorado more profoundly than any other single event except the 1859 gold rush."[4] In ways similar and dissimilar, Colorado women experienced significant changes—in their military service, civilian workforce participation, and home front roles—during World War II. Their wartime experiences impacted their lives. Some effects were immediate; others were seeds that bore the fruit of greater social and cultural transformations in the following decades.

Prior to 1941, very few women served in the US military. In the civilian labor force, Anglo women were clustered in domestic and personal service, laundry and

DOI: 10.5876/9781646420339.c000b   3

food establishments, pink-collar jobs in offices and telephone companies, agriculture, and the teaching and nursing professions. African American women were
largely employed in agriculture in the South and in domestic service throughout
the United States. The nation's Hispanics and Japanese Americans were predominantly agricultural workers.[5] Women in Colorado followed this general pattern. Prior to the war, the top three occupational categories for white women in
Colorado were domestic and personal service, professional service (teaching and
nursing), and clerical occupations. Colorado's Latinas and Japanese American
women were largely agricultural workers. Black women in Colorado were heavily
represented in the domestic and personal service category. There are two notable
exceptions—factors of Colorado's agricultural and mining economy—regarding
Colorado women's employment. Colorado women were not heavily represented in
manufacturing, the second-highest occupational category for American women.[6]
Unlike African American women in other states, Colorado Black women were seldom employed in agriculture, since over 95 percent of Blacks lived in Colorado's
urban centers (64 percent in Denver alone).[7]

After the Japanese attack on Pearl Harbor, the wheels of change for all Americans
kicked into high gear. Throughout the United States, military bases and forts
expanded and began training soldiers for battle. Over 16 million Americans
served in the armed forces, including approximately 140,000 Coloradans, some of
whom trained or served at expanded and newly established bases along the Front
Range.[8] As the war progressed, Fort Logan and Lowry Field were joined by Camp
Carson, Buckley and Peterson Fields, Camp Hale, and several auxiliary airfields.

Before the attack on Pearl Harbor, American industries had provided war
materiels to England through the Lend-Lease program. That production was
quickly dwarfed by the all-out effort of American industries, government agencies, organizations, and individuals after December 7, 1941. It is mind-boggling
to contemplate the human brain and brawn required to recruit, train, mobilize,
and supervise this effort. War materiel production totals are *staggering*. American
defense plants produced 2.4 million trucks, 300,000 fighter jets, 3.3 million rifles,
41 billion rounds of ammunition, and 47 million tons of artillery ammunition.
Seventy-five private and government shipyards and 400 other companies manufactured 70,000 vessels of all kinds.[9] In Colorado, well-established factories
enlarged their operations. New defense plants and depots produced and stored
ammunition, bombs and projectiles, and equipment for the military. Colorado
farmers and ranchers joined the nationwide blitz to sustain those on the battlefields and in the United States.

Prior to December 1941, Americans had been preoccupied with the lingering
effects of the Great Depression even as they cast wary eyes toward battles raging in Europe and Asia. Once the United States was "all-in," they rushed to support the war effort. About 7.5 million Americans, including 300,000 Coloradans,

volunteered for Red Cross activities. By war's end, the American public had contributed over $784 million in support of the organization.[10] Across the nation, Americans wrote Victory Mail letters to their sons and daughters in the military, bought war bonds (nearly $860 million worth), recycled metal and rubber items, entertained troops, and "did without" for the duration.

While they were not on the front line of the battlefields, American women were nevertheless central and active players in the American war effort. As author and woman's rights advocate Margaret Culkin Banning argued, "Women by themselves cannot win this war. But quite certainly, it cannot be won without them."[11] Over 350,000 women joined the military, a far cry from the 1,500 female nurses serving in the United States Army and Navy in 1940. During World War II, servicewomen were nurses, technicians, drivers, code breakers, clerks, instructors, and mechanics, to name a few. Some served stateside while others were sent overseas on the heels of fighting men.

Because of the dramatic increase in numbers, women in the civilian work force during World War II have specifically drawn the attention of historians. The war represents a significant break from previous trends in women's labor force participation in the United States. Notably, higher numbers of women, more women over age thirty-five, and more married women entered the labor force than ever before. Even the labor pattern for women of color, who had historically been in the workforce in greater percentages than white middle-class women, changed during the war years. Although they continued to face discrimination, Black women profited from upward job mobility during the war.[12] Nationally, the percentage of Black women in non-professional white-collar jobs rose from 1.7 percent in 1940 to 4.6 percent in 1944. In industry, the increase was from 5.8 percent to 17.6 percent, while agriculture decreased from nearly 21 percent to less than 11 percent. Domestic service experienced a similar decline (57 percent to less than 44 percent).[13] And some women worked in very untraditional jobs as riveters, welders, air traffic controllers, bank tellers, inspectors, bullet makers, and chemists, to list a very few.[14] Others diligently typed, filed, and processed hundreds of thousands of forms to expedite the war effort.

Colorado women played an equal role.[15] They enlisted in the military from every corner of the state—women who had been teachers, typists, salesclerks, domestic servants, farmers' daughters, and ranchers' nieces. They served in every branch available to them, including one in the Merchant Marines. In defense plants they riveted steel, made bullets, inspected bombs, operated cranes, and stored projectiles. Colorado women processed countless stacks of reports. Their work took them to European battlefields, the Pacific Theater of Operations, US territories, the nation's capital, and other states in the nation. Regardless of whether they worked outside the home, they wholeheartedly participated in the kaleidoscope of home front activities. Without their efforts, there "would have been no spring in 1945."[16]

In addition, although outside the scope of this book, the experiences of female family members, wives, and children of military personnel are significant. During World War II, almost 20 percent of American families contributed one or more family members to the armed forces.[17] The majority of draftees were single men; therefore, mothers were four times as likely as wives to experience a war death.[18] Sadly, many of them experienced the death of more than one son. Clara May suffered inconsolable grief the remainder of her life after her two sons were killed aboard the USS *Arizona* during the attack on Pearl Harbor.[19] Mothers, wives, and sisters exhibited a "particularly self-sacrificing kind of courage" as they navigated the war years.[20] They experienced the loneliness of missing loved ones and the pressures of maintaining home and family life. They handled constant uncertainty amid exhortations from practically everyone to remain cheerful and upbeat.

There were approximately 4 million wives of American military personnel.[21] Some of these women, with and without children in tow, became camp followers, moving across the country to live as close as possible to husbands stationed stateside. Others made the heart-rending decision to leave their children with family members as they followed their husbands. If and when the men were sent to the battlefronts, wives faced another difficult choice: stay in the last city in hopes of seeing their husbands again on furlough, or return home, wherever that might be. The first option meant being hundreds of miles away from relatives and friends; the second option usually ensured not seeing one's loved one until the end of the war.[22]

Similarly, the experiences of hundreds of thousands of children whose lives were disrupted and forever changed by wartime fears, dislocation, fathers' absences, and working mothers are beyond the scope of this book. As illuminated in William M. Tuttle's comprehensive study, wartime separations rearranged family roles and significantly changed the lives of American families as a unit and the lives of the separate individuals within those families.[23] Depending on the age of the child, the details of his or her wartime situation, and the level of support available, the stormy seas of war colored their lives as adults.

Coloradans, while experiencing many of the same events and situations as other Americans, had different wartime experiences because of certain features of the state. As a landlocked state, Colorado was 5,000 miles from the battlefields in the European Theater of Operations and 7,800 miles from the Pacific Theater of Operations; it was 2,000 miles from the industry-laden East and West Coasts and 1,300 miles from busy Detroit, Michigan, home of Henry Ford's Willow Run factory. For that reason, Coloradans did not experience an overwhelming crush of people seeking war work. Between 1940 and 1950, three counties in California underwent exponential growth. The population density of San Francisco, Alameda, and Los Angeles Counties—the sites of aircraft and shipbuilding industries—grew 3,000 percent, 307 percent, and 337 percent, respectively. In contrast, the population density of Denver, Arapahoe, and Jefferson Counties in Colorado—closest to the state's large war employer, the Denver Ordnance Plant—grew by 84 percent, 24 percent, and 15 percent, respectively.[24]

Minorities in Colorado also had different experiences than those in other states. Colorado's African American population numbers did not substantially decrease or swell as happened in other communities when countless numbers of Blacks left the repressive South to work in defense plants in California or the Midwest. Colorado Blacks who left to work in the nation's capital faced segregation in transportation that they had not encountered in their native state. Likewise, the state's Hispanic population did not boom as it did in California and Texas. While braceros were hired for Colorado farms, their numbers were significantly smaller. Whereas huge numbers of Latinas worked in California canneries, relatively few were hired in Colorado's—mostly because plants were located on the Western Slope. In contrast to other states, most notably California, Colorado's governor supported the state's Japanese American residents and welcomed Japanese Americans who were forcibly removed from the West Coast.

In sum, during World War II, Colorado women had similar yet not identical experiences to other American women because of factors specific to Colorado—its geographic location, the makeup of its population, and its relative lack of manufacturing. Colorado's experience with World War II was specific to itself—as were the wartime experiences of the coastal and Midwestern industrial areas. *Colorado Women in World War II* relates the experiences of Colorado women who contributed to the war effort at home and overseas and places them within the broader picture of American women during World War II. Adding Colorado stories enhances our understanding of the wartime experiences of all American women. They contributed to winning World War II and in the process were themselves changed. To view women's wartime experiences only through the eyes of those in highly industrialized areas is to pursue a historically incomplete picture. World War II did not occur only on European battlefields or Pacific islands; it did not occur only in the miles of Ford aircraft factories or the spread of Kaiser shipyards; it did not occur only in cabinet meetings or war rooms. It occurred at small steel companies in a landlocked state that produced parts for warships; it occurred in college classrooms dedicated to learning the enemy's language; it occurred in railroad canteens in small towns; it occurred in sugar beet fields far from bombing raids; it occurred in a Japanese relocation camp. It occurred in Colorado, and because of that, the state—and its women—were transformed.

Part I

Women in the Military

Nationwide, over 358,000 American women served in the military during World War II.[1] Women served as nurses, technicians, stenographers, Link Trainer instructors, machinists, air traffic controllers, pilots, and more. Women enlisted in the Army Nurse Corps, the Navy Nurse Corps, the Women's Army Auxiliary Corps (later the Women's Army Corps), the Naval Reserve, the United States Coast Guard, and the United States Marine Corps. Although never officially a part of any military branch during the war, the Women Airforce Service Pilots performed military duty and are included in this section as they rightfully received formal recognition of their service decades after the war.

1

The Army Nurse Corps

Lieutenant Leila Allen, Army Nurse Corps, gingerly stepped out of the Landing Ship, Tank (LST) and picked her way along Omaha Beach. Pausing to stare at the steep hill in front of her, Allen pondered the effort—and grieved at the loss of lives—it took for Allied soldiers to secure the beach head so that she and the other nurses could safely trudge their way through rubble that riddled the sand. A large artillery gun looked down on them menacingly, the bearer of death for thousands of Allied soldiers. As they scaled the infamous mountain, Allen saw strings of parachutes hanging from the trees—tragic testament to the fate of hundreds of paratroopers two months earlier. On that fateful day, Allen had been in Texas awaiting her overseas orders. And scant months before, she and several other young nursing school graduates had been approached by army recruiters exhorting them to enlist and relieve America's nursing shortage. If they did not, the recruiters warned them, the army might draft them, sullying the nursing profession's reputation. Allen and several others accepted their argument and enlisted. When they were given options for basic training, they chose Lowry Field in Colorado—naively thinking they would see American Indians. Now, as Lieutenant Allen trudged further inland, she was reminded of all the calisthenics and marching their frustrated drill sergeant had put them through. Although he had been relieved of his duties—the nurses thought perhaps their initial ineptness drove him to a Section 8—she was thankful for his attempts at making them "military."[2] Now, on the heels of those who had landed on the Normandy beaches on June 6, 1944, Lieutenant Allen and the other nurses would prove their mettle, too.

American women served as nurses during the Civil War and in the Spanish-American War but were not officially a part of the United States Army. In 1901, the US Congress created the Army Nurse Corps (ANC). During World War I, army nurses were the only women to serve with the American Expeditionary Force. They were sent overseas to Britain, Belgium, France, and Italy to serve on trains and transport ships. Female nurses provided medical care at six base hospitals attending to the huge number of casualties evacuated from the front lines. By March 31, 1918, over 2,000 American nurses were serving in France. After World War I, demobilization of American military personnel resulted in an Army Nurse Corps force of 851 women on active duty.

At the time of the Japanese attack on Pearl Harbor on December 7, 1941, the ANC numbered fewer than 1,000 nurses. Quickly understanding the future need for a substantial supply of nurses, the federal government issued quotas for each state. Colorado was required to enroll 500 nurses in the Red Cross Nursing Service (RCNS) and to certify their readiness to respond to military service. Nurses were classified and recruited through joint efforts of the RCNS and the National Nursing Council for War Service (NNCWS), an organization made up of six nursing organizations and directed by the Nursing Division Procurement and Assignment Service of the War Manpower Commission. Although women could directly join the Army or Navy Nurse Corps, these organizations worked together to compile an inventory of available nurses, coordinate recruiting campaigns, and contact women about service. First Lady Eleanor Roosevelt pleaded to the nation's nurses: "I ask for my boys [she had three in the service] what every mother has a right to ask—that they be given full and adequate nursing care should the time come when they need it . . . You must not forget that you have it in your power to bring back some who otherwise surely will not return."[3]

In the spring of 1943, the NNCWS's Retailers War Campaigns Committee worked with 180,000 major retailers across the United States to set up special recruitment displays and information booths manned by nursing students or graduates.[4] The largest recruitment aid was the Bolton Act (Public Law 146), which allocated nearly $5 million for nursing education in its first two years. Sponsored by US representative Frances Bolton (R-OH), it provided for refresher courses for graduate nurses, assistance to schools of nursing so they might increase their student body, postgraduate classes, preparation for instructors and other medical personnel, and training in midwifery and other specialties.

To join the Army Nurse Corps, a woman had to be a citizen of the United States or one of its Allies, a graduate of an approved nursing school, a registered nurse, and between the ages of twenty-one and forty (later changed to a maximum age of forty-five). At the start of the war, nurses had to be single. By November 1942, army nurses, married or not, were recruited for the duration of the war plus six months and were forbidden to resign.

In Colorado, Mary C. Walker, chairwoman of the State Committee on Supply and Distribution, sent letters to district presidents of the Colorado State Nurses Association (CSNA; after 1947, the Colorado Nurse Association) asking for help in meeting the state's federal quota of nurses. In 1942 Walker placed Mrs. Hazel Harlan and Mrs. Merle Byrne in charge of District 4, the Pueblo region. Their quota was fifty nurses. The three women met with nurses at Corwin and St. Mary's Hospitals and urged retired nurses to attend. Nurses were required to register at one of the area's hospitals on December 29, 1942. By 1944, forty-three nurses (thirty-six in the Army Nurse Corps, six in the Navy Nurse Corps, and one unspecified) were in military service.[5]

Nurses in other states also answered the call to service. Leila Allen was born in 1922 to William and Emma Allen of Blue Ridge, Georgia. Her mother passed away when she was very young. Leila always wanted to be a nurse, but her dad told her she was too spindly for the profession. Undeterred, she talked him into letting her attend Baroness Erlanger School of Nursing (now part of the University of Tennessee–Chattanooga).[6] After basic training at Lowry, Allen was assigned to Easter Field (Mississippi) where she received more training before being sent to Santa Ana Army Air Base (California) to treat cadets badly burned in airplane crashes.

By the time Allen joined the Army Nurse Corps, other nurses were completing their first year of duty in Europe. Helen I. Hyatt was born near Masonville, 46 miles north of Denver. As a teenager, Hyatt moved in with an aunt to attend Loveland High School, after which she found work as a housemaid prior to enrolling in the Nursing School at Springfield Baptist Hospital (Missouri). After graduation, she worked in a New York City hospital and at Stanford University Hospital, which is where she was on December 7, 1941. Hyatt joined a medical unit formed from medical staff at Stanford General Hospital and the University of California San Francisco Hospital. After reporting for duty in May 1942, Hyatt was sent to Fort Ord (California) for training: "We were placed under the training supervision of one of the surgeons, Dr. Roy Cohen. He really put us through punishing paces and routines as we hiked in full army regalia, including unopened gas masks and carriers, canteens filled with water, and steel pots, for miles over the scrub oak, carved hills, down the sand cliffs to the beach and back up at a good fast pace."[7]

Following summer training at Fort Ord, Hyatt's unit was moved across the United States by train in preparation for transportation to a war zone. At railroad depots, civilians gave nurses candy bars and gum. On December 11, 1942, the nurses embarked from Staten Island, New York. Serenaded by a band playing inspiring martial music, they walked up the gangplank onto the USAT *Uruguay*, a former passenger cruise ship. The next morning the *Uruguay* joined other ships

FIGURE 1.1. United States Army nurses and soldiers wave farewell as a troop ship leaves the pier. *Courtesy*, Library of Congress, Prints and Photographs Division, FSA/OWI Collection, LC-USW33-000375-ZC, Washington, DC.

in a convoy. After a couple of days at sea, they ran into a storm with extremely high waves, causing considerable seasickness among the troops. Hyatt nearly became a casualty when her supervisor told her to go below to the dental clinic to assist with a patient. The ship was rolling, the air in the room was hot and humid, and both the patient and the doctor turned green. After the dental officer asked a corpsman to open a porthole to let in some air, the ship rolled to that side and they were all deluged with seawater. Scrambling, they rushed to the deck level where they could get outside.

While nurses' staterooms had four to six berths bunk-style, the men were "shoe-horned in" to transport as many fighting men as possible across the Atlantic Ocean. Later, Hyatt and her good friend were assigned to a battle station in the bowels of the ship. "Abandon ship" drills were held periodically: "We couldn't believe the number of G.I.s pressed in the room to which we were assigned, lying on bunks probably eight to ten high or sitting on them with almost no head space . . . We were appalled at the number of men and the crowded living conditions and the absolute impossibility of any of us getting out of the place should we be attacked and sinking. The stairs to upper decks (this was far below decks) was metal, narrow and winding. Thank God we never had the occasion to learn what would truly happen in an emergency."[8]

After two weeks at sea, the *Uruguay* pulled into the harbor at Casablanca, French Morocco. Stationed some distance from the front, the nurses were not very busy for awhile. They took advantage of the situation to date American servicemen, wander the streets of the city, shop, sightsee, and lunch at restaurants and tearooms without fear. At some point they were issued olive drab (OD) service uniforms. Hyatt's hospital consisted of large, long OD tents set up as wards, with canvas folding cots lined up side to side on each side of the tent.

In mid-July 1943, Hyatt's unit was transported across North Africa by train to Bizerte, Tunisia, and then by ship to Palermo, Sicily, in August. They remained stationed there until May 1944. As Allied troops bogged down in Italy, medical units operated as station hospitals at Naples, Anzio, and Salerno, Italy. By August 1944, Hyatt's unit was shipped to France for the next eight or so months. In Epinal, Hyatt worked in the shock ward, receiving an unusually large number of casualties with head injuries as a result of shell bursts in forest areas. Called tree bursts, they were shells fired into the treetops that exploded aboveground, becoming shrapnel and numerous wood splinters that sliced areas of the body away—as likely as not the top of the head, causing the brain to be severely injured. Nurses positioned wastebaskets under the injured soldiers' heads as they lay on litters placed on sawhorses in her shock ward. There were so many of these injuries that a brain surgeon was assigned to the unit.

Hyatt was just one of hundreds of army nurses who served in North Africa and Italy. Ellen Belle Donnelly, born in Holyoke, Colorado, was one of five of the ten Donnelly children to serve in the armed forces during World War II. John and Margaret Donnelly, who farmed south of Julesburg, had three sons serving in the United States Navy and another son in the United States Coast Guard. Ellen, their oldest daughter, worked as a nurse for five years before enlisting in the Army Nurse Corps in 1942. In the fall of 1943 she was sent overseas to serve in Africa and New Caledonia.[9]

Wisconsin native Jeanne A. Wells trained at Bellin Memorial Hospital and enlisted in the Army Nurse Corps in 1942. After an early stint at Fort Sheridan (Illinois), Wells was assigned to the Twenty-first General Hospital unit and transferred to Fort Benning (Georgia), where soldiers' parachute training resulted in a lot of broken bones to mend. England was a way station before being sent to Africa. There, the Twenty-first General Hospital took over a spa north of Oran. Far from the front lines, hospital personnel and officers held dances on the roof of one of the buildings. Wells faced quite a different situation when she volunteered for detached service on the Anzio beachhead.

On January 22, 1944, six months after the Allied invasion of Sicily, American and British troops swarmed ashore at Anzio, roughly 30 miles south of Rome. The brainchild of Winston Churchill and dubbed Operation Shingle, the attack caught German troops stationed along the Italian coast largely by surprise; but after the

initial onslaught, the Germans dug in. The next four months saw some of the fierc-
est, most prolonged fighting in the European Theater of Operations as Canadian,
French, British, and American troops battled the enemy. Germans shelled the beachhead regularly in hopes of dislodging their enemies. As Wells related: "We were
taken there by a British hospital ship with red crosses all over it. Nevertheless, when
we reached the bay near Anzio the shells started coming all around us. This scared
us to death, but we finally got to the shore by small boat."[10] She soon discovered that
the shelling of hospital sites was neither sporadic nor accidental: "There was shelling
day and night. We were required to wear helmets all the time and fined if caught
without them. At night awakened during an air raid, I would wake Sally [her tent
mate] and she would reach down and put it [her helmet] over her head and go back
to sleep. I was not that relaxed and able to sleep."[11] One early morning she got out of
bed to see the activity outside. In her absence her cot was pierced by a piece of shrapnel.[12] Wells was luckier than six army nurses who were killed by German bombing
and strafing of the hospital areas on Anzio. As expected, Anzio was "depressing, as
we had to care for the wounded from the front lines. These patients had brain injuries, mental fatigue and almost every kind of injury possible. The surgeons would
spend hours doing brain surgery and the patient would die soon after."[13]

By 1944, nurses who had enlisted soon after the United States entered the war
were approaching their second and third year of deployment in Europe and were
scheduled to return home to the States. In England, medical teams that had served
in North Africa trained new arrivals who would follow the Allied troops' invasion
of continental Europe. The battle-hardened teams taught the new units how to set
up, receive, treat, and evacuate casualties from the front lines to hospitals in the
rear areas. Demonstrations included the best placement of wards in relation to
X-ray, laboratory, and operating-room facilities for the most efficient movement
of patients. Medical personnel discussed improvisation in patient care, special
methods of adding light to operating-room tents, and coping with the ubiquitous
mud on the OR floor.[14]

Unlike in North Africa, no field or evacuation hospital units went ashore with
the troops that stormed Normandy on June 6, 1944. However, minus their nurses,
two field hospital units followed the troops a day later and two more units the
following day. In the meantime, American nurses in England received casualties from the invasion. Irene DuBois was with the 305th Station Hospital, a mere
20 miles from the English Channel, while Eleanor Gingras Kruchten worked at
Netley Hospital, which the United States Army had taken over shortly before
D-Day. Janet A. Bachmeyer's unit was put on alert days before the invasion. They
added tents between the hospital buildings to house the anticipated large number
of casualties. As she tearfully related in an interview decades later, she heard the
drone of airplanes and awoke to the sight of "an air armada" of planes filling the
sky from horizon to horizon.[15]

FIGURE 1.2. Army nurse Jan Shimp doing laundry in a steel helmet in a Normandy cow pasture. *Courtesy*, Jewish Women's Archive, Brookline, MA.

On June 10, forty-two nurses with the 128th Evacuation Hospital were the first women to land in Normandy. They were followed in the next couple of months by other nurses and medical personnel. First Lieutenant Sally Burke Kelly, a wife for only six months, entered France on June 22, 1944. Her husband, Lieutenant Charles Kelly, was killed two months later.[16] By the end of August 1944, 35,000 medical personnel including 6,640 nurses had gone ashore right behind the troops.

Army nurse Lille Margaret Steinmetz (later Magette) arrived in Normandy in early July. She had always wanted to be a nurse, but her mother did not approve. Instead, she got married. However, a few months after their wedding, her husband took ill and died. At that point Steinmetz declared to her mother that she had been married and was a widow now on her own, and she was going to go into nurses' training. While she was attending St. Mary's College Nursing School, Pearl Harbor was attacked. Still grieving and not caring if she was killed, she enlisted in the Army Nurse Corps. Steinmetz and other nurses were instructed in the use of gas masks and regularly marched 15 miles or more as part of their training for overseas duty. She learned to pitch a tent and pack a duffle bag. In September 1943, Steinmetz boarded the *Mauritania* in Boston along with 20,000 troops. Sailing without a convoy, they crossed the Atlantic in thirteen days. Landing at Liverpool, the nurses were trucked to Malvern, England. There they took over a psychiatric hospital before being moved once again to Bristol to treat soldiers with physical wounds. On July 7, 1944, Steinmetz and the other nurses crossed the English

Channel to Utah Beach in landing craft.[17] She was just one of hundreds of nurses who spent a short time in England before sailing across the channel to land on the same beaches stormed by thousands of Allied soldiers on D-Day.

In the United States, Lieutenant Allen and fifteen other nurses were transferred to Camp Bowie (Texas) for additional training prior to boarding a train. Once the train veered to the east, the nurses were relieved to realize that they were going to the European Theater of Operations (ETO). They reasoned that the cold was going to be less of a hardship than the Pacific Theater's bugs and oppressive heat. Aboard the *Queen Elizabeth*, they sailed across the Atlantic and docked in northern Scotland, where the nurses rode a train to the small English town of Altrincham. The night they arrived, six German buzz bombs struck all around the house in which they were billeted. Exhausted, Allen simply stayed in her bed in the garret, not knowing where she should go and too tired to care. After a stop in Southampton, Lieutenant Allen boarded a LST (Landing Ship, Tank) to cross the English Channel, arriving just weeks after the Allied invasion.

Eileen Bradley took a more circuitous route to the ETO. A 1943 graduate of nurses' training, Bradley and two classmates took their army physicals at Kearney Air Base (Nebraska) before being sent to Camp Carson south of Colorado Springs for basic training, which included calisthenics and identifying airplanes. Hazel Pahler of Collbran and a graduate of Grand Junction High School remembered abandoning "pretend" ships and crawling on her stomach through the rifle range as soldiers shot blanks at the recruits. They were also "bombed" by sacks of flour.[18]

Camp Carson housed German prisoners of war (POWs). Bradley worked on a locked ward that held approximately thirty prisoners. After six weeks, she was transferred to Fort Warren in Cheyenne, Wyoming, before debarking from New York in September 1944. Unlike Allen and Steinmetz, who were stationed in England first and then traversed the English Channel, Bradley stepped directly from her American transport ship onto a British ship bound for France.[19]

Landing at Normandy was memorable for the nurses. Steinmetz, in fatigues and a helmet, was told that if she had not gotten seasick on the Atlantic journey, she surely would while crossing the English Channel. However, sporting a "cast iron stomach," the trip "never fazed" her.[20] Bradley was so worried about not being able to walk through the surf to the shore that she did not put on enough warm clothing. She struggled through the pouring rain and up a hill before being loaded into a truck that took her and the rest of her unit inland to their hospital. Leila Allen recalled that the nurses carried all their possessions, including a sleeping bag, onto the beach. Only twenty-two years old, she was extremely touched and "felt I was walking on sacred ground. We lost so many boys and here we were able to walk up and nobody was shooting at us. And then down on the Omaha beachhead, it was just straight up like the mountains here [in Colorado] . . . how our boys ever got up there . . ."[21]

As emotional as it was, nurses had no time to dwell on what had happened on those beachheads. Moving inland, they set up work in a number of hospital settings. Each type of hospital was designed to perform a different function in an evacuation chain that removed the wounded from the battlefields and into medical care as quickly as possible. Battalion surgeons, medics, and corpsmen manned the battalion aid station, the first link in the chain. Located close to front line combat but far enough away from small-arms fire, it was the first place surgeons tended to wounded soldiers. The aid station's main function was to stabilize and evacuate casualties to hospitals farther from the front.

The second link was collecting stations where medical personnel changed bandages, adjusted splints, administered plasma, and combated shock in preparation for the next step. At clearing stations—4 to 6 miles further back—medical personnel triaged wounded, maintained wards for the care of shock and minor sickness and injuries, and transferred men needing immediate surgery to adjacent field hospital platoons.

At field hospitals, surgeons, nurses, and medics stabilized the wounded and oversaw their recovery, after which the wounded were transported to evacuation hospitals 10 to 15 miles behind the front lines. They were generally staffed by 40 army nurses; 38 officers, including doctors; 218 medics, and auxiliary surgery teams. Allen's unit was headquartered near Neuchatel, France, before following US troops into Germany. Medics carried wounded from the field to a small tent where they were evaluated by a doctor. If it was determined that a soldier would not survive the trip to a station or a general hospital, the field hospital tended to them. Just beyond the doctor's tent was a larger one for shock and pre-op. Lieutenant Allen was its sole nurse. Most of her patients were hemorrhaging, in shock, or needing preoperative care. The staff gave "hundreds and hundreds of units of blood plasma."[22] Blood plasma was given because the demand for whole blood airlifted from England and later from the United States always exceeded the supply. This was especially true for hospitals close to the front. Nurses mixed powdered plasma with sterile water to administer the blood through IV tubes.

As battle lines shifted, collecting stations and evacuation hospitals were sometimes too close to the action. Twice, Allen's unit had to fall back. Each time the men worried about the nurses. They warned, "Oh, ma'am, you shouldn't be up this close. This is too close." The nurses replied that they were there to help save the soldiers. Lieutenant Allen promised herself to never show fear "because if I had been in their place, I wouldn't have wanted a nurse working on me, giving me IVs and what not with a shaky hand."[23] The one thing that made Allen jumpy was the German 88 gun. When the shells passed over the red-cross–labeled tent, the roof went "whoof, whoof," worrying the staff that it was going to fly off. Even now, decades later, a dropped dish or other sudden loud noise elicits the same response from her. One time when the medical unit crossed the Rhine River on pontoon bridges, the front

FIGURE 1.3. Lieutenant Leila Allen in front of her tent in Germany. Notice the laundry drying on the line. *Courtesy*, Leila Allen Morrison.

line did not advance as expected, forcing the medical personnel to re-cross the river and wait a few days. Cut off from the supply line, they lived on rations for awhile. The mess had not served gourmet food, but it was superior to C and K rations.

Mud was another problem. It seemed that every time Allen's unit moved, it rained. Lieutenant Bradley, too, recalled wearing galoshes and working in the mud. She roomed with five other nurse officers in a tent that held six cots and a pot-bellied stove. Every night they heated a big bucket of water to take sponge baths in their helmet liners, hoping to wash away some of the mud. Journalist Lee Miller, who had landed in Normandy to do a report on the Forty-fourth Evacuation Hospital, asked an off-duty nurse what plans she had for her free time. The nurse thought she would wash everything she owned as well as herself.[24]

The last two links in the medical chain were station hospitals and general hospitals. Both were housed in permanent buildings instead of tents. Located 30 to 50 miles from the front, station hospitals received patients who needed a longer term of treatment. After six months, patients returned to the States for recovery. Larger staffs specializing in orthopedic, thoracic, and facial reconstruction set up general hospitals 70 to 100 miles behind the front lines. But at times, these medical personnel also found themselves too close. During the Battle of the Bulge in December 1944, the Fifty-sixth General Hospital, hunkered down near Liege, Belgium, was forced to evacuate patients and nearly evacuated the nurses, including Steinmetz, before the Germans retreated. Casualties arrived so quickly that nurses gave blood transfusions, usually a physician's job.

As the war in Europe ground to a halt, nursing took on a different dimension. Patients were POWs, displaced persons (DP), soldiers who accidentally wounded themselves, and those stricken with illnesses. There was more time for R&R (rest and recuperation). Some nurses visited Paris; others, Mont St. Michel or the sights of Switzerland. However, some nurses visited more horrific sites. As the Allies liberated German concentration camps, hospital units were encamped nearby. At Buchenwald, a Czech survivor who had hidden in a pile of corpses to escape detection guided Lieutenant Allen and other army nurses through the camp. She witnessed survivors, saw the gas chambers, and walked by the crematorium. It is a memory that still shakes her.[25] Other women who bore early witness to the Holocaust were journalists Sigrid Schultz (*Chicago Tribune*), Helen Kirkpatrick (*Chicago Daily News*), and Marguerite Higgins (*New York Herald Tribune*). General George Patton was so enraged that he ordered MPs to round up German citizens and shepherd them through the camp. Photojournalists Margaret Bourke-White (*Life*) and Lee Miller (*Vogue*) chronicled their reactions.[26]

By 1945, the number of army nurses in the ETO had reached a peak of 17,345.[27] With the surrender of Germany in May, it was time for American troops and medical personnel to return to the United States. The military created a point system to determine which soldiers, nurses, and other female military personnel deployed in the ETO were eligible for early discharge. The Adjusted Service Rating (ASR) Scorecard was also used to determine which soldiers were earmarked for redeployment to the Pacific for an Allied invasion of Japan. Soldiers with high points could go home first, while those with low points were to be reorganized and trained for deployment in the Pacific. Just how high a man's points had to be to avoid redeployment was a source of endless speculation among the troops. After several years of battlefield fighting or front line nursing, it was understandable that most did not wish to join the soldiers and nurses already stationed in the Pacific Theater.

However, army nurses who were scheduled for deployment to the Pacific arena after V-E Day would not have been the first in that theater. At the outset of World War II, United States Army and Navy nurses were stationed at Sternberg General Hospital and other military hospitals around Manila. Captain Maude Davison and Second Lieutenant Josephine (Josie) Nesbit commanded the army nurses. Nesbit, one of ten children and orphaned by the time she was twelve, attended the Red Cross Hospital and Training School (Kansas City, Missouri), graduating in 1915. Recruited by the United States Army during the flu epidemic of 1918, she served at a variety of military installations including Denver's Recuperation Hospital. On December 7, 1941, Nesbit was serving her second tour of duty in the Philippines. Until that date, being stationed on the islands, with plenty of free time, mild weather, and nurses quarters furnished with bamboo and wicker furniture and mahogany ceiling fans, had been a desirable posting.[28] That changed instantly when the Japanese attacked Pearl Harbor. Nesbit, the acting chief nurse at Sternberg General Hospital, was stopped by several nurses who were worried about their friends stationed in Hawaii. As a veteran nurse, the forty-seven-year-old Nesbit knew her nurses would be needed in the days and months to come. She gently admonished them, "Girls, you have to get to sleep today. You cannot stay here and weep and wail over this because you have to go to work tonight."[29] The nurses settled down, although Nesbit doubted that they slept. On December 8, 1941, the Japanese attacked the Philippines, filling the hospital with patients. Army nurses were ordered to set up a hospital in the Bataan jungle. Without a building, the front line hospital served 6,000 patients in its eighteen wards. In extremely primitive conditions and often sick themselves, the nurses, later called the "Angels of Bataan," cared for wounded and sick GIs. Lieutenant Nesbit insisted that the nurses always "act as nurses, as army officers, and as a united group."[30] She cared for them, ordered those who were sick to go to bed, and located shoes and clothing for those who were without.[31] Just prior to the fall of Bataan, nurses were ordered to evacuate. When Colonel James Gillespie informed Nesbit that only American nurses were to be evacuated and that twenty-six Filipina nurses were to remain behind, Nesbit refused to leave unless all nurses were evacuated.[32] Aboard a zig-zagging motorboat, the American and Filipina nurses dodged enemy strafing.

Beginning on April 9, 1942, Corregidor nurses lived and worked in a maze of underground tunnels connected to the Malinta Tunnel. Although having a roof over their heads and a floor under their feet was a welcome respite from the Bataan jungle, working in the tunnels was literally sickening. The complex, organized in a series of narrow corridors called "laterals," was like a small, cramped city with sections for supply, mess, administration, ordinance, and a thousand-bed hospital staffed first by nurses from the Corregidor base hospital and then by the evacuated nurses from Bataan and some civilian volunteers. Secretly built many years before, the gray concrete tunnel had its own power and water supply.

Captain Davison and Lieutenant Nesbit commanded eighty-five army nurses, twenty-six Filipina nurses, one navy nurse, and dozens of civilian women. The hospital consisted of a central corridor a hundred yards long and open to the outside on one end. Eight smaller wards were connected to other passages in honeycomb fashion. Amenities included enamel bedside tables, iron beds, flush-type latrines, showers, spigots, filing cabinets, and refrigerators. Laterals held operating rooms, a dental clinic, laboratories, recovery and convalescent wards, kitchen and dining areas, a dispensary, and nurses' sleeping quarters. Although the Japanese had been bombing Corregidor since December, once they controlled Bataan, they intensified their siege until the Americans thought the tunnel was going to collapse. In addition to enduring reverberations from the bombs, tunnel dwellers developed serious respiratory diseases, fungus infections, and skin boils, or "Guam blisters," because of the stagnant air.

As the bombardment intensified, it became obvious that Corregidor, too, would fall to the Imperial Army. In late April, Lieutenant General Jonathan Wainwright, Allied commander in the Philippines, was informed that two navy seaplanes would slip through the Japanese blockade, deliver supplies, and evacuate some passengers including twenty nurses. Captain Davison had the unenviable job of choosing the evacuees. She selected nurses she did not believe had the fortitude and mental stability to withstand the horrors that were sure to follow, those seriously ill with tropical diseases, those wounded during the bombing of the Bataan hospital, and women in their late forties and early fifties. Lieutenant Nesbit, in her late forties, however, refused to leave her post.[33] After the initial group flew off, the quartermaster listed the shortages—no helmets, towels, handkerchiefs, blankets, raincoats, or tarpaulins. He grimly predicted that Corregidor would run out of power and water in thirty days.

In early May a second group was ordered to leave. Left behind with thousands of patients and troops trying in vain to hold on to Corregidor were Davison, Nesbit, fifty-four army and twenty-six Filipino nurses, an army dietitian, an army physical therapist, and twenty-one civilian women. On May 6, 1942, Wainwright surrendered the island to the Japanese. About 12,000 American and Filipino soldiers were herded onto a small concrete slab where a twelve-hour wait in the water line to refill a canteen was the norm.[34] By the end of June, the hospital was moved out of the tunnel, to the delight of the nurses. In early July the sick and wounded were transferred to Manila. The nurses, separated from their charges once again, were trucked to the University of Santo Tomas campus, which had been converted into the Santo Tomas Internment Camp (STIC), a prisoner-of-war facility.

Nurses, first housed in the Santa Catalina convent, were isolated from the rest of the nearly 40,000 internees. They were later moved into the main camp. Captain Davison and Lieutenant Nesbit, knowing that morale-crushing boredom would quickly set in, made out work schedules. Although a few nurses initially balked at serving civilian patients, the two officers held firm. As weeks turned into months and months into years, conditions at STIC grew progressively debilitating. The Japanese army provided less than 1 ounce of fish and meat per person daily. In September, the rice ration was cut from 400 grams to 300 grams per day. As Japanese military fortunes worsened under Allied counterattacks, command of the camp was transferred to the War Prisoners Department of the Japanese Imperial Army. The new camp commandant, Colonel S. Onozaki, shut down the package line, the internees' one link to the outside world and a source of extra food, clothing, and provisions. He promised to provide sufficient supplies. He lied.

As time wore on, the Japanese closed the rodent control center, library, soap shop, and textile department. In March 1944 they halved the bread issue and sugar rations. By summer they again cut rations. The main kitchen and hospital kitchen served only two meals a day, if the portions could be called meals. People

FIGURE 1.4. United States Army nurses from Bataan and Corregidor, freed after three years of imprisonment in Santo Tomas Internment Camp, climb into trucks as they leave Manila. *Courtesy*, United States Army.

in chow lines fainted from hunger. An internee survey reported that on average, men in the camp lost over 31 pounds and women nearly 18 pounds. Sixty-year-old Maude Davison, who entered Santo Tomas carrying 156 pounds on her 5-foot 2-inch frame, lost 76 pounds; Josie Nesbit lost 38 pounds, dropping from 187 to 149 pounds.[35] Malnutrition led to a variety of ailments: nerve inflammation, numbness in the hands and feet, blurred sight or double vision, and anemia. Protein and vitamin deficiencies caused small epidemics of measles, whooping cough, and bacillary dysentery and left almost everyone else dizzy with head-aches.[36] Lieutenant Nesbit grew concerned about her nurses: "Their eyes grad-ually sank deeper into hollowed cheekbones. Their gait slowed down more and more as their strength grew less. Even their shoulders drooped noticeably."[37] The nurses, however, continued to work four-hour shifts until liberated by American troops in February 1945. They had survived thirty-three months in captivity.

Other ANC nurses served in the Pacific Theater of Operations between the time of the fall of Corregidor and Bataan and the Japanese surrender. Althea Williams, born in Platteville, graduated from Bethel Nursing School in Colorado Springs. She was working at Poudre Valley Hospital in Fort Collins, Colorado, when Pearl

FIGURE 1.5. Althea Williams on the roof of Fitzsimons Army Hospital. *Courtesy,* the Archive at Fort Collins Museum of Discovery [H15038], Fort Collins, CO.

Harbor was attacked. At first, she and her co-workers did not believe the radio report, thinking it was "an Orson Welles activity" (like the radio broadcast of "The War of the Worlds" in 1938).[38] Williams was immediately placed on active duty and assigned to Fitzsimons Army Hospital. Soon, she was transferred to a surgical hospital in the California desert. Her 400-bed evacuation hospital unit was next ordered to the Pacific Theater of Operations. Without an armed escort, the ship changed its route every seven seconds to avoid enemy attack. For a year and a half, nurses and doctors treated US soldiers stricken with malaria, dengue fever, and scrub typhus. As the patients piled up, R&R was eliminated. By the end of the war, Williams had accumulated over three months' leave. But she had no complaints: "They asked us to serve, we served, and I was serving because of the fact that all of my friends, boyfriends, brothers, and all were serving. They had a right to have the best equipment and good nursing and medical care."[39]

Agnes Turnovec was in her thirties when she enlisted in the ANC, hoping to "see the world."[40] However, her first duty station was only 6 miles from her training hospital in the Bronx. After nearly a year, she was briefly sent to Seattle before sailing to Hawaii. It was on the troop train to the Northwest that she first set eyes on Colorado. After seven days at Oahu, the nurses boarded a ship for the thirty-day journey to Saipan. Half of the nurses remained there while others continued on to Guam. Temperatures were ideal during the day, but stifling nights forced Turnovec from her stilt-raised hut to a sleeping cot underneath. She spent her last four months at Iwo Jima before Japan surrendered to end World War II.

Wilma Vanden Hoek also served in the Pacific Theater of Operations. A native of Iowa, Vanden Hoek received her nurses training at Denver's Presbyterian Hospital. She enlisted in the Army Nurse Corps after graduation and was assigned to the Thirty-first General Hospital, whose first duty station was the mountainous Camp Hale near Leadville, Colorado. That convinced the nurses that they would be sent overseas to Europe. The army had other ideas, sending the unit to the Pacific Theater. Nurses were on detached orders, meaning they served with units that most needed them. Vanden Hoek spent a few months on New Caledonia and over a year on the Hebrides Islands. The island environment was a distinct change from frigid Camp Hale in the Rockies. Jungle rot was a common ailment for servicemen and nurses alike. "Flies had their pick of the food first," but one "simply looked the other way and ate anyway."[41] On the Hebrides Islands, nurses' quarters were wooden barracks open on all sides to catch cooling breezes. Mosquito netting covered the cots. As the Allies moved north toward Japan, the nurses trailed right behind them. Next stop: New Guinea and the Philippines. Because the Thirty-first General was always on the move, it was often months before Vanden Hoek's mail from the United States caught up with her. It was not until the Philippines that the nurses had one weekend off. Vanden Hoek's unit was "all packed and ready to go to Japan" when the war ended.[42]

While for many Americans the debate still rages over President Harry S. Truman's decision to drop atomic bombs on Hiroshima and Nagasaki, Althea Williams staunchly supported her president: "Oh, we were thrilled to death because we knew we were getting ready to go into Japan. If the atomic bomb had not been dropped, we knew we would be having thousands and thousands of casualties on both sides. I get very upset when the people are trying to revise history and trying to change what actually took place in those days. My brother was a B-29 pilot and he was on the island of Saipan. He had to go in and bomb Japan."[43]

While thousands of army nurses served overseas, others served stateside. Roberta Trexler completed a one-year training program and three weeks of basic training at Camp Swift (Texas). One particular experience in basic training convinced her that "women really don't have any part in some of the aspects of the army. You need muscles."[44] The unit was supposed to go on an overnight bivouac.

Carrying only half a tent and a bedroll each, the women embarked on the six-hour hike to the top of a hill in the pouring rain on "the muddiest road you ever saw." Many girls dropped out, and Trexler stopped a number of times to rest her pounding heart. The captain in charge abandoned her jeep and exhorted the girls to finish the hike. Once they were at the top, they put up tents, which were blown to the ground during the night. After basic training, Trexler was assigned to McCloskey General Hospital (Texas), an amputee and spinal injury center. Physical therapy was a relatively new field up until World War II. Water, heat, massage, stretching, and strengthening exercises were a therapist's primary tools. As one of thirty physical therapists, Trexler worked six days a week with Sundays off. They carried a patient load that was "way beyond what we could do." Similar to the experiences of nurses overseas, Trexler "never had any feeling that there was any self-pity" among her patients.[45]

Army Nurse Corps members served at Colorado bases and airfields. Beginning in the late 1930s, the number of military bases in Colorado increased.[46] Lowry Field and Fort Logan, established before World War II, were joined by Peterson and Buckley Fields and by auxiliary army airfields in Leadville, La Junta, and Pueblo, as well as Camp Hale and Camp Carson. Camp Carson—the home of the ANC Training Center beginning in October 1943—trained over 3,000 nurses.[47] Several of the bases were early-duty stations for army nurses before being shipped overseas—Lowry (Leila Allen), Camp Carson (Eileen Bradley and Puebloan Lieutenant Helen E. Kuhns), and Camp Hale (Wilma Vanden Hoek).[48] Other army nurses spent longer periods of time in Colorado. At Lowry, chief nurse and First Lieutenant Kathleen L. McNulty performed administrative and supervisory work. She assigned duties to staff nurses who supervised the ward, made rounds with the ward surgeon, gave medications, and was responsible for the ward's cleanliness and patient safety. To accommodate army nurses, civilian workers, WACs, and wives of officers and enlisted men, the base commander sponsored the Lowry Women's Club, believed to be the first of its kind in the nation. It served as a semi-official social center and meeting place for women at Lowry. The first floor housed a nursery, playroom, lounge, kitchen, and two Red Cross sewing rooms. Additional kitchen equipment, a room for fabricating surgical dressings and bandages, and restrooms filled the second floor.[49]

Betty Berry joined the Army Nurse Corps at the suggestion of the obstetrics doctor she worked for after her boyfriend, who was an instructor pilot, was killed in a training accident in San Antonio.[50] Berry was stationed at both Lowry and Buckley Fields, but only after serving as a flight nurse in the Pacific. In late 1942, the US Department of War authorized the 349th Air Evacuation Group to train surgeons, flight nurses, and enlisted personnel for aeromedical evacuation (aerovac) duty aboard troop and cargo carriers. In early 1943, the squadrons became the Medical Air Evacuation Transport Squadrons (MAES). Each squadron had

FIGURE 1.6. Betty Berry carrying gas mask and awaiting transport. *Courtesy,*
Betty Berry Godin Collection, Martha Blakeney Hodges Special Collec-
tions and University Archives, University of North Carolina at Greensboro
[WV0096.6.002].

a headquarters and four sets of medical crews. A flight surgeon led a crew of six
nurses and six technicians. A flight team included one nurse and one enlisted
technician. In early 1943, the first strategic aerovac flight transported five patients
from India to Washington, DC. In the spring of 1943, Berry attended the School of
Air Evacuation at Bowman Field (Kentucky). Although training for the first class
was rudimentary and brief, by the time Berry attended, the curriculum had been
expanded. Nurses spent Monday through Friday learning in classrooms; engag-
ing in practical demonstrations, swimming, physical training and drills; taking
exams; and participating in retreats and parades. Saturday mornings involved
more classwork and weekly inspections. Nurses sometimes had flying time or
field maneuvers on Saturday afternoons.[51] Berry was assigned to the 803rd MAES.
Between graduation and being sent overseas, the squadron completed an infiltra-
tion course in which nurses rolled, crawled, wriggled, and slithered under barbed

wire with machine gun fire overhead. Morris Kaplan, flight surgeon and commanding officer of the 803rd, concluded: "I felt that if all 25 girls could take that beating, then I could take them anywhere. I had just finished it myself through much less dust than they and had wanted to quit a dozen times. It was certainly the hardest physical work I had ever done." The squadron also spent the last weeks at Bowman Field gaining proficiency on the firing range and learning to drive jeeps and trucks. They also learned how to properly prepare a parachute.[52] Following graduation, Berry and the 803rd were sent to California to board the *George Washington*. Without escort ships, it zigzagged across the Pacific Ocean for two months. Berry, unfazed by the dangerous conditions, sat on the deck and did needlepoint when she was not attending mandatory daily lectures or doing calisthenics.[53] The ship stopped briefly in Hobart, Australia, before continuing on to Bombay, India. Transferring to a British ship, the HMS *Nevasa*, Berry and the other medical personnel sailed to Chabua, India, her staging area for the next year. Nurses lived in tents, wore their boots at night for protection against snakes and mosquitoes, and took Atabrine for malaria. Stationed just 100 miles from the war front, the staging area often experienced Japanese flyovers. One time, everyone was ordered into the slit trenches in the middle of tea patches for safety. When the nurses jumped in, they were greeted by a python. Fortunately, the air police, who were also hopping into the trench, shot and killed it. Once the Japanese danger had passed, they pulled the snake out of the trench. Berry asked to keep the python. After someone skinned it, she had it made into shoes and a purse.[54]

Chief nurse Audrey Rogers assigned specific nurses for individual flights. Each plane had a medical ambulance chest that included portable oxygen, blood plasma, bedpan and urinal, tourniquets and dressing supplies, catheters and lubricating jelly, stethoscope; blood pressure cuff and thermometer, alcohol, iodine, and aromatic ammonia. Aspirin, sedatives, quinine, sulfa tablets and powder, and nasal spray were the medicines. In addition, each flight nurse carried a small medical bag with more dressing supplies and medicines in a small musette bag and morphine in her pocket. Medical evacuation teams flew to sites in a C-47 cargo plane that may have had pigs, chickens, mules, ducks, rabbits, cans of gasoline, aircraft parts, and ammunition aboard to be delivered to the troops. Upon arrival, enlisted technicians made the C-47 ready for patients by snapping unneeded bucket seats back against the walls, securing metal arms or pulling webbing from the ceiling, and attaching the seats to the floor. Berry as flight nurse supervised the loading of patients, with those with head injuries placed forward in the most stable part of the plane; men in bulky casts low in the plane because of their weight, and those with injured limbs in the aisle for easy access.[55]

There were several satellite bases in India, so evacuation teams picked up patients at Ledo and flew them into Karachi (Pakistan), a four-day journey of 2,000 miles. At Karachi another squadron of flight nurses accompanied the patients—most of whom were battle casualties—on their way home. After the Allies controlled Burma, flights picked up patients and brought them to a general hospital for treatment.

By the end of 1944, the 803rd MAES were awaiting their orders to return to the United States as new flight nurses arrived to take over their duties. Berry was first assigned to Buckley, where she was in charge of the orthopedic ward. When that was closed, she was transferred to Lowry. There she met Gene Godin, whom she married in 1947.[56]

During the war, 32,500 members of the ANC served overseas. By the end of the war, the Army Nurse Corps had suffered 201 deaths, 16 directly from enemy fire.[57] Six were killed at Anzio, 6 died when the hospital ship *Comfort* was attacked by a Japanese suicide plane, and 4 flight nurses died in action. Thirteen other flight nurses died in weather-related crashes while on duty. Pueblo native Second Lieutenant Anna Pritekel was a casualty of World War II. A Corwin Hospital graduate, Pritekel was stationed at a Fort Bliss (Texas) hospital when she came down with an infection and died on December 24, 1942.[58]

Like their male counterparts, women serving overseas endured harsh weather conditions, ubiquitous mud and rain, and monotonous C and K rations. They saw their friends and comrades suffer illnesses, wounds, and death. They slept on cold cots and warded off rats and other creatures. They often did not receive mail for weeks and months on end. They moved at a moment's notice. During their twelve-hour shifts, nurses stayed at their patients' sides even as the sounds of "ack ack" deafened their ears and buzz bombs and 88s threatened their lives. They "didn't want to concentrate on that. We wanted to keep the few gray cells we had on business. Because it [caring for the wounded] was too important."[59] They became very partial to their helmets, which served them well as "hat, bucket, washtub, bathtub, basket, and chair, and in a pinch . . . as a shovel for digging an emergency foxhole."[60] Those they served were eternally grateful. On October 21, 1944, *Stars and Stripes* published an open letter to army nurses signed by hundreds of GIs: "To all Army nurses overseas: We men were not given the choice of working in the battlefields or the home front. We cannot take any credit for being here. We are here because we have to be. You are here because you felt you were needed. So, when an injured man opens his eyes to see one of you . . . concerned with his welfare, he can't but be overcome by the very thought that you are doing it because you want to . . . you endure whatever hardships you must to be where you can do the most good."[61]

The 59,000-plus nurses who served in the ANC during World War II had indeed shown their power to "bring back some who otherwise surely" would not have returned from the battlefields.[62] For the nurses, it was their honor and privilege to do so. They consistently remarked on the wonderful treatment they received from the soldiers. Lieutenant Allen thought the "wonderful fellas" had the greatest respect for the nurses. Both Allen and Steinmetz noted that the soldiers looked on them as mothers and sisters, even though they were often not any older than the men.[63] For many nurses, their stint in the ANC is their proudest accomplishment. Seventy-five years later, they often reflect on those who made the ultimate sacrifice: "I'll never, never forget them because when they play the National Anthem, I try to stand straighter; when we say the Pledge of Allegiance, I try to stand straighter and I have a lot, a lot of faces in front of me that gave everything for that privilege."[64]

Army nurses earned 1,619 medals, citations, and commendations. As Major General Jeanne Holm emphasized, "Of the women who served overseas during the war, the nurses deserve special recognition. Wherever the US forces could be found, there were nurses."[65] Those nurses also included members of the Navy Nurse Corps. Although they, too, served in the United States and overseas, their war experiences differed in many ways from those of the Army Nurse Corps. Because of their comparatively smaller numbers and the ban on serving on ships (except hospital ships), navy nurses were more likely to be administrators and instructors.

2

The Navy Nurse Corps

Ensign Jackie Jacquet, Navy Nurse Corps, pushed aside the mosquito netting and rose from her cot. In the light of the moon, she donned coveralls of green nylon and placed a matching baseball cap on her head. As quietly as she could so as not to wake her two bunkmates, Jacquet slipped out the door. Within minutes, precisely at 1:30 a.m., a jeep pulled up. Jacquet exchanged small talk with the driver until they arrived at the Guam airfield. As she boarded the R-5D aircraft, she greeted the pilot and the lone medical corpsman. After taxiing down the airstrip, Jacquet began a well-rehearsed ritual. She reviewed her equipment, made sandwiches for the wounded sailors and marines who would soon fill racks stacked four high on both sides of the plane, and prepared emergency lockers. With those tasks complete, she and the corpsman reviewed their evacuation plan. Once on the island—an eight-hour flight away—the medical team would have less than an hour to evacuate over thirty wounded men.[1]

The US Congress established the Navy Nurse Corps (NNC) in 1908. The "Sacred Twenty" were hand-selected as its first members and assigned to the Naval Medical School Hospital in Washington, DC. By the time of America's entry into World War I, the NNC had expanded to 160 women. Nurses trained navy corpsmen in addition to their regular hospital and clinical duties. During World War I, nurses served overseas on operating teams near combat front lines. Nineteen navy nurses died on active duty, over half of them from influenza. By the time of the armistice on November 11, 1918, over 1,550 nurses had served in

DOI: 10.5876/9781646420339.c002

naval hospitals and other facilities abroad and at home. As with the Army Nurse Corps, enrollment in the NNC decreased in the 1920s and 1930s. By 1940 it had only 440 nurses.[2]

Just as they had for the Army Nurse Corps, the Labor-Federal Security Appropriations Act of 1941, the Bolton Act of 1943, and the recruiting efforts of the American Red Cross bolstered the Navy Nurse Corps. The Red Cross joined with the General Federation of Women's Clubs (GFWC) and the National Nursing Council for War Service to promote women serving as nurses during the war. The GFWC distributed a booklet, "War Work with a Future: A Nursing Program," to clubs throughout the nation. It encouraged each club, district, and state to have at least one nursing program with local nurses as special guests. The brochure suggested that the chief nurse at a nearby army or navy hospital send a nurse to a club meeting to discuss the need for additional nurses. Clubs established rooms in their clubhouses for nurse's aide and home nursing classes. The GFWC suggested parties for military nurses, farewell parties for civilian nurses leaving for the Army or Navy Nurse Corps, publicity for women who won nursing scholarships, and service flags for club members' daughters serving as military nurses.[3] These coordinated efforts successfully persuaded women to enroll in nursing and nurse's aide programs and encouraged nurses to enlist. At peak strength in June 1945, the NNC had 11,086 active-duty members. Altogether, 14,178 women served in the corps.[4]

The Navy Nurse Corps set ages, education, and training requirements similar to those of the Army Nurse Corps. An applicant had to pass professional and mental examinations, as well as stringent physical requirements. Once appointed, a nurse served a six-month probationary period to determine her fitness for naval service. Most NNC nurses were white, middle-class women in their mid-twenties. Like their counterparts in the Army Nurse Corps, women joined the navy to help their country. Foreign travel, more education, and specialized training were also incentives.[5] Although one might assume that because both were in the military, army and navy nurses had similar war experiences. However, that was not the case for a couple of reasons. One, as for their male counterparts, the land versus the sea venue of their service resulted in different experiences. Second, while army nurses concentrated on nursing, many navy nurses were instructors during the war. Their contribution centered on their expertise in training naval corpsmen.

In the beginning, navy (and army) nurses were paid $70 per month. This was increased to $90 in June 1942. At the end of that year, nurses' pay was aligned with that of navy officers. Nurses in the relative rank of ensign received $150 per month. A lieutenant (junior grade) received $166.67, while a lieutenant (senior grade) received $200.[6]

At first, there was no formal naval indoctrination for nurses. However, it was soon discovered that with such a program, women would transition more

FIGURE 2.1. Navy nurse Jacqueline (Jackie) Jacquet in her white dress uniform. An overseas duty uniform of gray-and-white-striped seersucker, which did not need to be laundered as often, was created for nurses serving in the Pacific Theater of Operations. To have more freedom of movement, navy nurses assigned to hospital ships or air evacuation units purchased commercially available slacks and resorted to wearing male uniform khaki clothing because of its availability. These items also provided better protection against the sun and insects. *Courtesy*, Jackie Jacquet Melvin and Maureen Christopher.

smoothly from civilian nursing to military nursing. In November 1943, the first recruits were sent to the Naval Hospital in Portsmouth, Virginia. A two-week course familiarized them with naval terminology, etiquette, customs, procedures, and medical practices. Naturally, military drill was included.[7] Navy lingo is unlike that of other service branches or civilian life. The first and foremost rule is to never call a ship a "boat," as a boat is carried on a ship. A rope is a line; a wall is a bulkhead. The first time a naval officer referred to a wet floor with the phrase "the deck is awash in water," Ensign Jacqueline Jacquet was baffled.[8] Other unfamiliar naval terms were overhead (ceiling), hatch (door), head (bathroom), forward (ahead), and aft (rear).

Navy nurses served in North America, Brazil, the Caribbean and West Indies, Bermuda, parts of Europe (Italy, Sicily, and England), Algiers and Tunisia, and the South Pacific. Navy nurses were given numerous general assignments: ward supervision and administration, out-patient dispensary work, industrial clinics in connection with naval construction, naval or United States Marine Corps air base dispensaries, transport service, hospital ships, operating-room supervision, anesthetists, naval training station hospitals, foreign duty, Hospital Corps Training Schools as instructors, pediatric clinics, physical therapy, convalescent hospitals, dietetics, Officer Procurement Offices, family hospitals, first aid stations, and ammunition depots and dispensaries.

As casualties mounted, convalescent hospitals opened throughout the nation. In Glenwood Springs, chief nurse Irene Shelley supervised a unit of 12 nurses at the Naval Convalescent Hospital, a rehabilitation facility for sailors and marines. The staff also included 15 medical officers, 15 other staff officers, 142 corpsmen, 3 Women Accepted for Volunteer Emergency Service (WAVES), and 2 Red Cross

FIGURE 2.2. Because it was relatively isolated, Glenwood Springs was selected as a site for a convalescent hospital. Hotel Colorado offered a serene environment for recuperating seamen. Back row: Sterling, Gregor, Dodd, Burquist, Spooner, Parrish, Kelly Dicod, Willmarth, Pewitt, Blumstein; Center: Miss L. Paulson, Dr. G. E. Drewyer, Miss M. E. Parrish; Front row: Meager, Powers, Buchanan, Hansen, Woodall, Murph, Rosen, Wilson, Siefried, Russell. *Courtesy*, Glenwood Springs Historical Society, 366, Glenwood Springs, CO.

representatives.[9] When the hospital opened in Hotel Colorado in 1943, Shelley had been a nurse for over twenty years. The 250-room hotel, with its sweeping lawns and landscaped gardens, was originally built as a resort or hunting lodge for wealthy industrialists.[10] Although Glenwood Springs was accessible from Denver by train and automobile, it was well isolated from the standpoint of military objectives. Off the route of flying lanes and protected on all sides by the rugged Rocky Mountains, the site offered relaxation and recuperation for sailors suffering from combat fatigue and those who were in need of convalescence after surgery or medical treatment at other naval hospitals. Patients and nurses lodged in the hotel, which piped spring water into baths and steam rooms.[11]

In the spring of 1944, the hospital extolled the work of Ensign L. Paulson, whose work and Kenny method of treatment had gotten William H. Cornell back on his feet—literally. Cornell, who had contracted polio at Pearl Harbor, was wheeled into the hospital weighing a mere seventy-eight pounds. Ensign Paulson utilized all of the hotel's amenities to care for Cornell. He soaked in the natural hot springs and swam in the pool. At one end of the pool he laid on a table for massages. Nurse and patient used parallel bars for support as he learned to walk again. Over the course of months, Cornell gained forty-six pounds and learned to walk unaided.[12] At that point, Cornell returned to duty. Nurse Paulson had kept the promise of the navy medical corps: "To keep as many men at as many guns for as many hours as possible."[13]

A hospital ship was an important assignment for a navy nurse. At the outbreak of World War II, the United States Navy had two hospital ships: the USS *Relief* and the USS *Solace*. The latter was moored at Pearl Harbor at the time of the Japanese attack. Immediately, its nurses took on casualties. Chief nurse Grace B. Lally and her eleven nurses worked feverishly for days.[14] Later, the ship accompanied invasion forces in the Solomons, the Marianas, Iwo Jima, and Okinawa. The USS *Relief* joined the Pacific fleet in 1943.

During the war, the number of hospital ships was increased to fifteen. While nurses trained, ships were converted to hospital ships. However, because these ships were insufficient to handle the tremendous number of casualties from the American invasions of Pacific islands, six cargo ships were converted. They functioned as hospitals and medical supply ships, base hospitals, and warships. These newly converted ships provided space for over 800 patients. By 1945, twelve hospital ships were stationed in the Pacific Theater.[15] The vessels' mission was to transport casualties from rendezvous points to shore hospitals.

Aboard ships, nurses participated in evacuation drills and became adept at operating under blackout conditions. After the 1907 Hague Convention, hospital ships were always painted white with a wide green band around the hull and large red crosses for easy identification. They were fully lit at night. Onboard nurses had double duty, as they were also administrators. Most patients were treated for burns, combat wounds, or malaria. The nurses, under frequent alerts, kept life vests and gas masks readily available. During the Battle for Okinawa, hospital ships were targeted by Japanese kamikaze pilots and aircraft, making it necessary to enforce blackout restrictions.[16]

The proliferation of warships, bombs, torpedoes, and huge quantities of petroleum, diesel, and gasoline made burn wounds a common World War II injury. Margaret Gates, born in South Dakota, roomed with her aunt and uncle in Aberdeen to attend college. After graduation, she taught for a short time before restlessness drove her to Bremerton, Washington, where she worked in the shipyards for nearly a year. From there she returned to the Midwest to enlist in the navy. Although she went in as a hospital apprentice and passed the test for pharmacists' mate, Gates instead worked with a plastic surgeon at Oak Knoll Naval Hospital in California. She tended to burn patients from the war in the South Pacific. Experimental treatments were often employed to treat those horrendous wounds. That nursing experience stayed with Gates the rest of her life.[17]

Not all nurses were assigned military patients. Mary Edith "Meg" Goldcamp, graduated from St. Luke's School of Nursing in Cleveland, Ohio. In 1944, she and five girlfriends took a trip to Florida, where they decided to enlist in the navy. Three of them became navy nurses; the other two became members of the Army Nurse Corps. Goldcamp's first duty station was Norfolk Naval Hospital (Portsmouth, Virginia) for two years. Her second was the North Island Naval Hospital on Coronado Island. There she cared for mothers and newborns in the maternity ward.[18]

FIGURE 2.3. Flight nurse Lieutenant (jg) Omi Halder listens to Morse Code in a lighthearted off-duty moment aboard a NATS (Naval Air Transport Service) Skymaster evacuation plane. *Courtesy*, Omilo Jensen family.

The United States Navy and Marine Corps "island-hopped" through the Pacific Theater on their way to Japan. Naval medical personnel could not establish a series of land hospitals or medical facilities as the army had in Europe. For that reason, air evacuation units complemented hospital ships. Two navy nurses took air evacuation training in 1943 at the army's Bowman Field in Kentucky, but it was not until December 10, 1944, that the Naval School of Air Evacuation began its formal two-month training class. Lieutenant (jg) Mary Ellen O'Connor, a former United Airlines stewardess and registered nurse, hand-selected and supervised the training of navy flight nurses. The first class consisted of twenty-four navy nurses and twenty-four pharmacists' mates. Lectures and demonstrations covered survival training, air evacuation techniques, physiology of flight, first aid with an emphasis on shock, splinting/redressing wounds, and treatment of patients in non-pressurized cabins. Nurses studied the care of burn patients, hyperbaric medicine, ditching an aircraft, and evacuation of patients. Students learned about artificial horizons and altitude through flight simulation exercises. Following this training, they were given flight indoctrination on Naval Air Transport Service (NATS) hospital planes in the United States. An intensive eighteen-hour "watermanship" training simulated conditions of a water landing or crash scenario. Prospective flight nurses were required to swim 1 mile, tow or push a victim for 220 yards, swim 440 yards in ten minutes, and swim under water (to escape burning oil). Nurses were also trained in basic hand-to-hand combat.[19]

Only about one-fifth of the nurses who volunteered were accepted for flight nurse training. After training, nurses were assigned to one of three Naval Air Evacuation Service squadrons. The flight nurses were officially designated VRE-1 but were nicknamed "Hell's Angels" by the servicemen they aided. Each squadron consisted of twelve planes, twenty-four nurses, and twenty-four pharmacists' mates. Following graduation in January 1945, twelve of the first twenty-four flight nurses were sent to Naval Air Station Agana, Guam, to prepare for their first battlefield mission. The other twelve nurses were used to transport casualties in the continental United States and from Hawaii.

In war zones, the first hospital plane landed with medical personnel. The squadron flight surgeon established an evacuation clearing station, collected patients with the help of his corpsmen from first aid and holding stations, and screened them for transport. Then the second hospital plane landed with a flight nurse. Corpsmen loaded the plane with twenty-five to thirty-five patients in twenty to forty-five minutes. On March 6, 1945, a Naval Air Transport Service R4D airplane landed on Iwo Jima. It not only carried whole blood and medical supplies but also a twenty-two-year-old navy nurse, Jane "Candy" Kendeigh, the first navy flight nurse to land on an active Pacific battlefield. For the next fifteen days, Kendeigh and her sister flight nurses evacuated 2,393 marines and sailors from Iwo Jima.[20]

The second class of air evacuation nursing began in January 1945. Included in this class were Jacqueline (Jackie) Jacquet and two of her good friends, Pauline Dougherty and Dolores Metzger.[21] The three nurses had bonded when they were stationed at the US Naval Hospital in San Diego. It was there that a large piece of paper was hung in the nurses' quarters announcing the inaugural Naval School of Air Evacuation. If interested, a nurse signed her name to the paper. By the time Ensign Jacquet saw the bulletin, it was full of names. She folded the sheet over and added hers. Later, after returning from leave, she was called into the chief nurse's office, where she found her two friends also waiting. The three of them had been selected to attend the second class of flight nurse training. In a way, Jacquet felt as if life had come full circle. She had grown up with an older brother who had littered his bedroom ceiling with model airplanes. While he dreamed of being a pilot, she dreamed of becoming an airline stewardess. In the early years of commercial flights, stewardesses were required to be nurses, so Jacquet thought, "I'll be a nurse." She attended the School of Nursing at Ravenswood Hospital in Chicago. Her brother joined the Army Air Corps and became a pilot. Now

FIGURE 2.4. Checking over her kit of medical supplies is Ensign Jane Kendeigh, United States Naval Reserve (USNR), a navy flight nurse, as she flies from a base in the Marianas to the Iwo Jima battleground aboard a navy transport plane, March 6, 1945. Other flight nurses, such as Jackie Jacquet and Omi Halder, performed the same procedure for their air evacuation flights. *Courtesy, Naval History and Heritage Command.*

she, too, was going to be in military planes. Betty Lou Sullivan, her best friend and fellow nursing graduate of Ravenswood Hospital, convinced her to enlist at Chicago's Navy Pier because Betty Lou's father said the navy treated its nurses like gold. Unfortunately, Betty Lou failed the physical because of a bum knee.

While Jacquet hated to leave her friend behind on this new adventure, she soon found herself on a full train to San Diego. Surrounded by men in uniform, Jacquet sat on the only seat available—her luggage—and thought, "What am I doing?" Her first assignment was SOQ (Sick Officers Quarters), caring for a colonel's wife, a captain suffering from cancer, and many sick and wounded men. As was the custom, nurses rotated through a variety of wards and specialties. Penicillin, a new medicine in World War II, was generally scarce. However, the navy was able to acquire it for its wards. Jacquet was one of the nurses who administered it to her patients.

She and the other navy nurses lived in the old Exposition Building in Balboa Park. After being selected for flight nurse training, Jacquet and her two friends took a train north to Oakland and then a ferry to Alameda to begin their schooling. She was assigned a room with Metzger and Kay Balog. Her friend Pauline Dougherty was assigned elsewhere.[22]

By the time Ensigns Jacquet, Dougherty, Metzger, Balog, and twenty other nurses graduated, the Battle of Iwo Jima had been won and the Battle of Okinawa was raging. The newly graduated flight nurses were flown in a primitive airplane to Pearl Harbor, where they assembled the necessary clothing for battlefield conditions. Then they received their orders for the Pacific Theater. Admiral Chester W. Nimitz's airplane was heading to Guam empty, so it became the nurses' transport. Onboard, the nurses were fed steak and were allowed to order drinks. Thrilled to be in such a plush aircraft compared to the one they had flown in from Alameda, the nurses giggled the whole time. In Guam, they were temporarily housed in the captains' quarters which had been filled with cots. Once their Quonset huts were ready for occupancy, Jacquet, Metzger, and Balog roomed together. Each hut was divided into four rooms with three nurses to a room. Rooms were furnished with iron cots and a table. Jacquet did not recall sheets but concluded, "It's wartime. You were lucky to get a bed." They did have indoor plumbing. Some girls claimed they saw rats skittering around in the huts, but Ensign Jacquet never came across any herself. Because of the fear of Japanese soldiers in the jungle, nurses' huts were encircled with a barbed wire fence. An armed soldier escorted them on dirt paths to the mess hall, and an armed driver accompanied the nurses from their quarters to the hospital. When air raids occurred, the nurses jumped out of bed, put on their boots or shoes, and walked single file into the jungle. Perhaps it was nervousness that caused them to giggle as they made their way down to a cave for safety.[23]

The Battle of Okinawa accounted for 17 percent of the total United States Navy and Marine Corps casualties suffered in World War II—more than double those of Iwo Jima and Guadalcanal combined. Because of this, Okinawa was the largest combat casualty evacuation operation in US military history. It also marked the first time the navy evacuated more casualties by air than by sea. Evacuation planes traversed three major routes. The first was from the combat area to the fleet hospital at Guam; the second from Guam to Pearl Harbor, with an intermediate island stop such as at Kwajalein, an island in the Marshall Islands; and the third from Pearl Harbor to the United States.[24] In the words of servicemen stationed at Kwajalein, it was "enough to cure any Robert Louis Stevenson addict of any romantic ideas about life on an atoll." The island was 2.5 miles long and half a mile wide, just large enough for a few Quonset huts, a long runway, and fruitless palm trees. Once Japanese troops were driven off the island, the US military converted it to an island-hopping station for the Air Transport Command. "Kwajalein Lodge," the one-room passenger terminal, had a large chalkboard on which GIs scrawled "No liquor atoll—no wimmen atoll—no nothin' atoll" and "Spend a week and go home a freak."[25] Over a three-month period, crews evacuated nearly 10,000 wounded soldiers from Okinawa. Each plane hauled one nurse and one corpsman.

Ensign Jacquet was one of those evacuation heroes. After preparing her "air hospital," Jacquet tried to catch a catnap on a part of the aircraft floor away from the landing gear because that area was extremely noisy and rough. Having risen from her nurse's cot before 1:00 a.m., she needed all the rest she could squeeze in before landing and the tense but orderly evacuation of wounded men took place.[26]

On the island, a doctor separated the wounded into those who would be evacuated and those who would not. If the doctor determined that a man would not survive the trip, he was not evacuated. Following a diagnosis, evacuees were placed safely in a cave near the airfield to await the airplane. After the plane landed, corpsmen used litters to move the wounded into the plane, which had removable stretcher fittings. Generally, there were twenty-six men on litters. Ambulatory patients occupied six seats in the body of the plane. The land and air crews had only one hour in which to make the transfer of all patients. Jacquet sometimes saw the smoke from a nearby battle as the plane was loaded. She often heard and felt the rumbling of big guns firing. The air crew was as anxious to fly off the island as were the wounded. Once, a soldier pulled Jacquet aside and asked her if she wanted any souvenirs of Okinawa. Unsure, she followed him a few steps to a cave where he showed her some things left behind by the Japanese when they abandoned Okinawa. Jacquet chose a sake dish, a teak wood platter, and a larger dish. Without a bag, she stowed the three items in her flight jacket, boarded the airplane, and prepared for takeoff.[27]

Doctors on the island had given Jacquet a manifest of the names and injuries of the wounded. With her patients stacked four high along the sides of the plane, Jacquet repeatedly knelt and bent over to attend to some patients and stood extra tall for those in the top litters. She administered medicine, gave blood plasma, and changed dressings. She monitored the status of her patients for signs of hemorrhaging, shock, and other complications. One time, a patient suffering from a severe chest wound was having trouble breathing because of the lower amount of oxygen available in the plane's cabin. Jacquet asked the pilot to fly as low as he could. The pilot, the cream of the crop among the air forces, willingly obliged, telling her he would "skim the waters" if necessary.[28]

The pilot and medical crew were cognizant of battles erupting all around them. On another flight, Ensign Jacquet looked out one of the windows and saw the nose of a kamikaze airplane impaled in the ground. She landed on Okinawa ten times during her service as flight nurse. Every nurse had an Aviators Flight Log Book in which her flights, the name of the pilot and the corpsman, the hours flown, and the character of the mission were recorded. Nurses were limited to eighty hours of flight time a month.

On Guam, the wounded were removed from the airplane and examined. Some were moved to the base hospital; others were airlifted to Hawaii and the continental United States for further treatment. The flight nurse onboard was then off duty

FIGURE 2.5. Flight nurse Ensign Miriam R. Serrick fills a syringe with
penicillin prior to an injection during an air evacuation flight. *Courtesy*,
National Museum of the United States Navy, Washington, DC.

for a couple of days. However, off duty did not necessarily mean no duties. The
airfield's reception hut displayed a bulletin board for messages and posts of new
orders or regulations. The hut was also where new patients were checked in after
their flight from Okinawa. Litters were placed on poles. Once that was done, a call
went out to the nurses' quarters: "Any nurse that is off duty and can come and give
patients ice cream, please come."[29]

After two flights to and from Okinawa, a nurse earned a flight to Pearl Harbor.
Sometimes, Jacquet caught the hospital airplane taking wounded servicemen on
the next leg of their journey to the States; other times, she simply caught a cargo
plane that had space for her. At Pearl Harbor, nurses received manicures, got
their hair done, and rested. Jacquet went to the Sears Department Store, which

made her "feel human again."[30] Later, back on Okinawa, recreation between flights included swimming, sunning on the beach, writing letters home twice a week to her folks, and attending outdoor movies. Ensign Jacquet was friends with two marines who possessed a dark green Packard the Japanese troops had abandoned. They drove her to outdoor movies where they sat on wooden benches driven into the sand. The United Service Organizations (USO) flew in entertainers to regale the servicemen and women. Jacquet once caught sight of "the Polka-Dot Girl" in the nurses' quarters getting ready to shower.[31]

As the war raged in the Pacific, the air evacuation school trained new flight nurses. Omilo "Omi" Halder was initially a classmate of Jacquet's but was bumped to the third training class after contracting pneumonia. She and Jacquet were 2 of only 112 women who earned Flight Nurse Wings during the war. Her first evacuation flight was on March 31, 1945. Twenty-four years old and only 5 feet 2 inches tall, Halder knelt on the airplane's floor to help the soldiers in the lowest berths before pulling herself up to help the men in the top berths. In addition to her medical ministrations, Halder bolstered the men's spirits. "I talked to them, wanted to know where they were from, if they were married," she said. "I would go around to the amputees because I wanted to offer to make phone calls to their families because the loss (of a limb) would be a sudden shock to their loved ones."[32] Although they suffered from abdominal wounds, burns, and amputations, Halder insisted that the men never complained; they were simply interested in getting home. Of more help than the medicine she dispensed was food. The sheer logistics of battle, where men had little time to do anything but fight, left the wounded famished.[33]

Landing on a Pacific island was never a sure thing. Halder remembered one particular landing on Johnson Island. The landing gear initially would not come down. It did so right before the airplane hit the small air strip. Also a key component in the survival rate of those airlifted were the corpsmen assigned to the flying hospitals. Halder emphasized that those men deserve a lot of the credit and that nurses could not have done their job without them.[34]

Navy nurses trained corpsmen. Six hospitals were set up for that purpose. Sue S. Dauser, superintendent of the Navy Nurse Corps, carefully selected nurse-instructors from her ranks to teach classes in physiology, field hygiene, minor surgery, and first aid. The men and women of the Hospital Corps continued their training at naval hospitals under the direct supervision of navy nurses. Because the male members of the Hospital Corps provided most of the care in hospitals and on ships, the navy nurse-instructors understood the necessity of being the best instructors possible. As one nurse said, "Their failure would be her failure," and failure was not an option. The hospital corpsmen and the nurses' teaching acumen stood the test. Corpsmen were among the most highly decorated men of the war.[35]

Ann Harduk was one of those nurse-instructors. Born in New Jersey, Harduk attended nursing school at Cooper Hospital (New Jersey) before joining the corps. With several sons already in the service, Harduk's parents were supportive of their daughter's enlistment. Her first duty station was at Philadelphia Naval Hospital, where she learned how to instruct naval corpsmen. Harduk was next assigned to the US Naval Hospital in Sampson, New York, before being shipped to Livermore, California, near San Francisco. Navy nurses perfected their swimming skills and learned strict navy protocol as they awaited deployment to the Pacific Theater of Operations. Harduk and thirty other nurses finally boarded a ship bound for the Russell Islands, their duty station for the next two years. Traveling unescorted on the USS *Monticello*, the passengers were often confined to general quarters because of enemy submarines in the waters. More nurses joined them from Okinawa and Iwo Jima. Doctors helped build the nurses' Quonset huts, complete with real linen sheets on the cots, before patients began arriving from Guadalcanal and the Admiralty Islands.[36]

With the surrender of Japan in September 1945, navy nurses, like their counterparts in the army, had choices to make. Lieutenant Jacquet considered remaining in the navy but instead joined her nurse friends who could not "wait to get out." Her log book lists her last flight on February 8, 1946. By March, she was separated from the navy. Flight nurse Omi Halder had contracted dysentery and was in a Hawaiian hospital on V-J Day. From her bed, she watched Americans dancing around the flagpole.[37] Halder resigned her commission in late 1945 and returned to the United States.

At peak strength in June 1945, the Navy Nurse Corps numbered 11,086 active-duty members scattered across six continents.[38] In the United States, navy nurses served at 263 stations and instructed the Cadet Nurse Corps, the WAVES, and youth in the Hospital Corps. Throughout the war, the NNC played a significant role in the evolution of naval medicine. As trained professionals, its nurses cared for the sick and wounded men of the United States Navy, Marines, and Coast Guard. They faced enemy fire; some suffered wartime imprisonment.[39] From the eastern seaboard to the West Coast, navy nurses served at large naval hospital complexes, smaller convalescent hospitals, and training station facilities. Navy nurses served on hospital ships from the waters of Great Britain to the Mediterranean Sea and the Pacific Ocean. Some cared for the wounded aboard air evacuation flights.

Amphibious medicine, as it developed during World War II, started with corpsmen who tended to the wounded on the landing beaches and progressed to aid stations. The injured were transported to hospitals, ship hospitals, and fleet and advance hospitals. By 1945, the special augmented hospital linked field and fleet hospitals in combat areas. Under this system, 98 percent of wounded United States Navy and Marine personnel survived.[40]

No members of the Navy Nurse Corps lost their lives in combat; however, nine died while serving overseas. Thirty-one nurses died in the United States. Their valor and dedication earned them 303 military awards. Navy nurses richly deserved the praise of Admiral William F. Halsey, commander of the Third Fleet, who wrote, "Their untiring service, their professional skill, and their ability to sustain the unparalleled morale of the wounded in their care will always reflect the highest credit to the Nurse Corps, US Navy."[41]

The American public, servicemen, and military brass accepted, supported, and praised army and navy nurses. Their job—nursing—did not threaten a man's status or his masculinity. A female nurse did not take a man's job so he could be sent into combat. Instead, she saved him from his battlefield wounds. The same could not be said for American women who enlisted in the Women's Army Auxiliary Corps. Those women faced a much different and at times hostile reaction from servicemen and the American public.

3

The Women's Army Auxiliary Corps and the Women's Army Corps

Rising early, Oleta Lawanda Crain and two other Black women, Margaret Ellen Barnes and Lilla M. Walker, shrugged into their long overcoats, gathered their toiletry supplies, and quietly slipped out of their rooms. Braving the chilly air of central Iowa, they passed through the Fort Des Moines gates, entered the barracks, and showered. As women of color in Officer Candidate School with the Women's Army Auxiliary Corps, they were required to shower before the white officer candidates arose. It was perhaps the only advantage of the army's segregation policy—the three Negro women did not wait in long lines before bathing and enjoyed the luxury of their own rooms in private homes rather than being shoe-horned in army barracks with almost 300 other women. But more often than not, segregation's ugly head posed obstacles for African American women (and men) in the military. For Crain, the first occurred when she enrolled in September 1942. After seeing a recruiting poster that declared "Women can play in the Army band and help win the war," Crain immediately signed up. What could be better than getting paid to play her cornet or saxophone? But the band was only for whites. Undeterred, Crain completed basic training and worked as a mail clerk before being selected for Officer Candidate School. It would lead to a twenty-year military career.[1]

In 1941, Representative Edith Nourse Rogers (R-Massachusetts) introduced a bill providing for a women's army auxiliary corps. Although she was well aware of the inadequacies of an *auxiliary* corps, she knew even that would face stiff opposition in the US Congress and from the military establishment. Her bill languished

 DOI: 10.5876/9781646420339.c003

in the US House of Representatives until the Japanese attack on Pearl Harbor changed everything in the United States. General George C. Marshall, the army's chief of staff, fully supported Rogers's bill. Believing that America's impending two-front war would cause a serious manpower shortage, his testimony on the Hill was crucial. The general understood that the army could ill afford to spend time and money training men in typing, stenography, and switchboard operations when highly skilled women were available.[2] But hiring civilian women for army positions was less than ideal. Civilians were no substitute for subordinates who could be ordered to work long hours, be transferred as needed, and stay on the job as long as necessary.[3] In March 1942, hearings were held on House Resolution 6293 establishing the Women's Army Auxiliary Corps (WAAC). Following a 249–83 vote, the House sent the bill to the Senate, where it was ignored for two months. Nearly 30 percent of the senators chose not to go on record as either opposed to or in favor of the bill. It eventually passed by a mere 11 votes. On May 15, 1942, President Franklin Delano Roosevelt signed the bill. Oveta Culp Hobby, who headed the Department of War's Women's Interest Section, was selected as its first director.[4]

On July 20, 1942, the first WAAC officer candidates reported for basic training at Fort Des Moines, Iowa. Forty African American officer candidates formed a separate battalion. The next month, auxiliaries (enrolled or enlisted women) began training. WAAC requirements were as follows: a recruit had to be a US citizen between the ages of twenty-one and forty-five with no dependents, at least 5 feet tall, and weighing at least 100 pounds. There was also a maximum weight allowance. Emilia Duran of Trinidad was so intent on becoming a WAAC that she lost 26 pounds and, even more amazing, gained an inch in height to qualify after first being rejected.[5] Oleta Crain and Edmonia Lewis were among the first African American women from Colorado to enlist in the WAAC. Crain, a former teacher, inspected bullets at the Denver Ordnance Plant. Lewis, a divorced African American seamstress whose schooling ended after two years of high school, enrolled in October 1942, one month after Crain.[6]

After basic training, Crain served as platoon commander and recreational officer in one of the Negro WAC companies at Fort Des Moines. Segregation again posed a challenge. One of Crain's duties was to lead her troop to the swimming pool every Tuesday. White WAACs swam on Mondays. When the Black women reached the pool, they were told that the schedule had been changed. If they did swim, the pool was cleaned on Wednesday so the white WAACs would have "untainted" water the following week.[7]

Crain was discharged from the WAAC to enlist in the Women's Army Corps in September 1943 and to attend Officer Candidate School with Margaret Barnes and Lilla Walker. The problem of the segregated pool continued. Crain complained to the captain in charge, who refused to change the policy. Undeterred, she pleaded

FIGURE 3.1. Oleta Crain joined the Women's Army Auxiliary Corps in hopes of playing her cornet in the band. Instead, she served for twenty years, retiring as a major. *Courtesy*, Denver Public Library, Western History Collection, Oleta Lawanda Crain Papers, Blair-Caldwell African American Research Library, C MSS ARL 48, Denver, CO.

her case to the commandant, reminding him that they had hoped he would end segregation at Fort Des Moines. Following their meeting, the captain integrated the pool.[8] Later, Crain served at air bases in Lincoln (Nebraska), Amarillo (Texas), and Columbus (Ohio). She was a commanding officer at Camp Shanks (New York), the largest army embarkation center in the United States, and at Lemoore Army Air Field (California).[9]

Black officer candidates were spared life in the army barracks, but the vast majority of WAACs endured the new experience. Some women had a difficult time adjusting to its communal nature. The major issue was the large latrine and communal shower area where everybody went and cleaned up. Each recruit was issued a cot and a footlocker. Daily inspections were a "little nerve-racking" at first, but the recruits soon adapted to the routine and were no longer nervous about coming to attention and staring straight ahead.[10] WAACs also learned to circumvent clothing regulations. Anything that was not GI (government-issued) was banned from the barracks. However, women hid their "regular things" in laundry bags, which were never inspected, or at the bottom of the footlocker if no inspections were scheduled. Inspectors knew banned items were probably in laundry bags because they, too, had such articles.[11]

FIGURE 3.2. Interior of a WAAC/WAC barracks showing two rows of cots and trunks. *Courtesy,* Anne Elizabeth Heyer Collection, Martha Blakeney Hodges Special Collections and University Archives, WV0320.6.018, University of North Carolina at Greensboro.

Six days a week, the trainees rose at 6:00 a.m., marched to mess, carried out morning duties, and attended classes and close-order drills. Alice Starr clearly remembered her first morning. She was assigned to clean the latrines, but she did not know what a latrine was. She and the other girls assigned to the task decided they would "go clean the toilets."[12] After the noon mess, WAACs attended more classes, including physical education, before evening mess at 5:00 p.m. The rest of the evening was spent studying before lights out at 9:00 p.m. Eager to perform well for their own sakes and to prove women's army-worthiness, many women surreptitiously read under the red EXIT lights in the barracks. At night they covertly practiced marching by flashlight.[13]

A second WAAC training camp opened at Daytona Beach, Florida, and a third at Fort Oglethorpe, Georgia, in the spring of 1943. Thelma Detweiler, an early recruit who broke her parents' hearts when she enlisted—they had already "lost" their son to military service—surmised that with all the problems securing proper winter uniforms for WAACs in Iowa, the army thought new camps in a southern climate might be a solution. Detweiler's pair of army shoes was the only part of a uniform she wore for the entire six weeks of basic training. She complemented those with two of her own cotton dresses.[14] In contrast, recruit Betty Heyer was issued everything but shoes when she arrived at Daytona

Beach. The fact that she wore size 10½ shoes would plague her throughout her time in the WAAC.[15]

Recruiting efforts were initially successful. Women, anxious to help in the war effort, stormed recruiting centers. The women were married, single, divorced, or legally separated; they came from rural communities and urban centers. The reasons women joined were as diverse as the women themselves. When she enlisted in 1942, Adrienne Stratton, a receptionist and switchboard operator at the state capitol, told the *Denver Post*, "I am proud to say that I am leaving a fine job to enter the service. If I'd been a man I would have enlisted last December 8."[16] Alice Starr joined because she did not see a future as "a little country girl" at that time. College was out of the question for the daughter of a deceased sharecropper. Only seventeen years old, Starr lied about her age to the staff sergeant who signed her up.[17]

Some women left higher-paying jobs while others were lured by the prospect of a steady paycheck. Some were the only ones in their families to serve in the military during World War II. Bernice Moran was living in a boardinghouse and teaching in a rural school when Pearl Harbor was attacked. Her mother had died while she was a college student; then her father died in November 1941. After his death, her "world kind of just fell apart."[18] Feeling as if she had no anchor and no home, she enlisted. Betty Jo Melvin and Martha Gorder of Pueblo and Boulderites Alice Noxon and Louise Wolcott also left their classrooms. Noxon and Wolcott had been teaching since graduating from the University of Colorado in 1924. At the time of their enlistment, they were in their forties. Noxon lived with her mother, sister, and nephew prior to enlisting.[19]

Other WAACs followed brothers or other family members into the armed forces. Colorado native Betty Jo Span followed her father, a former World War I army sergeant, into the army.[20] Helen and Josephine Lakner of Pueblo joined five of their brothers in the military. Tony, Bill, Joe, Frank, and Louis were in the navy when the two sisters enlisted in the WAC in February 1944. Of Mrs. Mary Lakner's twelve children, only Dolores, a senior at Central High School, remained at home. She, too, hoped to enlist after graduation—in the United States Marine Corps.[21]

Women sometimes had an extra incentive to join the corps. Catherine Boland Oldham's husband, Captain Orville Oldham Jr., a member of the 355th Fighter Squadron, was killed in action in Europe. Four months later she quit her job at Higgins Aircraft in New Orleans and enlisted. Beverly Orton, from Alamosa and a member of the Signal Corps, also lost her husband in a plane crash. She had secretly married Corporal Vernon W. Clark in July 1944. They were married for only four months before he was killed in the Philippines.[22]

Women encouraged each other to enlist. The first Pueblo WAAC enlistee was Livona Vay La Montine, who boasted to her former co-workers at Colorado Fuel & Iron (CF&I) that "the life of a WAAC can't be beat, since they get the best of everything."[23] The company newspaper, *The Blast*, reported regularly on employees who enlisted in the armed forces and on their subsequent duty stations. Joining La Montine was Alice Dussart, a native of Trinidad and six-year employee of the Tabulating Department. Dussart later became the first former CF&I employee and WAC to be sent overseas. From Europe she encouraged her former co-workers to keep up the good work. Stationed mostly in North Africa and Italy, she reported, "We, in the heart of the war zone, know too well how badly steel and other CF&I products are needed."[24] The steel company reported that from 1941 to 1945, 18 female and 2,629 male employees left to join the military.[25] Pueblo stenographer Edna Greening joined her three brothers, John, Richard, and Victor, in the military.[26] Edith R. Williams was assigned specialist duty with the Army Air Corps at Hendricks Field in Sebring, Florida; her brother John was in the army, while their father, Edward, worked with the American Red Cross overseas.[27]

Like the fuel company, Colorado towns and cities were proud of their native sons and daughters. In 1946 Montrose County acknowledged WACs Ardith E. Beam (nee Gribbin), who served in California and Oregon; Alice Mae McNeer, a graduate of Colorado A&M College who trained at Fitzsimons General Hospital; Virginia E. Nichols, who served overseas in the Philippines, Australia, Hollandia, and Dutch New Guinea; Eva M. Wilkinson, who served in France and Germany; and Velma M. Woods, who was serving in Tennessee at the end of the war.[28] Many town newspapers, including the *Julesburg Grit-Advocate*, ran a column titled "Our Boys in Uniform." In May 1943 one of those "boys" was Emma Ebke. With only a grammar school education, Ebke worked as a nurse's aide in Alamosa prior to enlisting. After basic training, she was assigned to Fort Merced, California, where she rose to the rank of corporal. The *Julesburg Grit-Advocate* changed the headline to "News of Our Men and Women in Uniform" by the end of 1943. Similarly, the *Monte Vista Journal*'s early reports on the town's military women were listed under "With Monte Vista Boys in Service." By the end of 1944, the *Journal* had changed the title to "With Monte Vista Boys and Girls in Service."[29]

Whether is was "boys" or "girls" in uniform, it was the uniform that was crucial. Historically, uniforms have not only been required to be practical but have been highly symbolic. A uniform allows one's branch of service and one's rank to be easily and quickly identified. A uniform—whether for a civilian job or the military—emphasizes regularity, cohesion, group cooperation, and solidarity. Specifications are designed to maintain its functionality. The WAAC uniform, in the words of military historian and retired USAF major general Jeanne Holm, was "a disaster." Even though military brass had not designed the uniform, it "could not have been worse from any standpoint—cut, fit, color, tailoring, material, quality."[30] Jackets were heavily padded in the shoulders, skirts were too narrow for women's hips, and skirt and jacket colors rarely matched. Men's shirts and neckties and low-heeled, laced oxford shoes produced a distinctly unfeminine appearance. Worse, uniforms were not ready for training; when they did arrive, they were often the wrong size. It has been said that GI clothing came in two sizes: too large and too small. Betty Heyer's overcoat was four sizes too large. The uniform Thelma Detweiler was finally issued needed alterations. Of course, simply reducing the length of sleeves or skirts does not create a sharply tailored uniform: "It was the worst uniform you ever saw in your life. The pockets weren't in the right places and it was horrible."[31] Fortunately, as time went on, uniforms were improved, although they never brought the admiring looks WAVES uniforms did.

Training at military bases and not on college campuses combined with low pay hampered recruiting. But the WAAC's auxiliary status (no overseas pay, life insurance, or death benefits) was a more significant factor for women considering the armed forces. In July 1943, the Women's Army Corps (WAC) replaced the initial WAAC, giving its members full military status and benefits. WAACs were given a choice: join the Women's Army Corps or return to civilian life. The majority, especially in the officer ranks, opted to enlist, but about a quarter of WAACs chose to end their military service. Alice Starr liked what she was doing, felt it was important, and stayed in. She "felt like it was a big thing when I became a real soldier."[32] Emily Collinsworth, stationed at Camp Hale, was also pleased that she was now "really in the regular army."[33] Studies discovered that if a WAAC felt she was being utilized to the best of her ability, she continued with the WAC. Women in the Army Air Corps and those with General Dwight Eisenhower in North Africa—including Denverite Dorothy Schooley Amato—re-enlisted "in droves."[34]

Recruitment materials emphasized both the fun and the valuable war work done by WACs. An "Air-Wac Life" brochure was distributed to Colorado recruiting stations. The large piece of paper was folded into fourths. Inside the first fold were testimonies from Brigadier Generals L. A. Lawson and Albert L. Sneed, commanders at the AAF Technical School at Buckley Air Field and Lowry, respectively, lauding women's service. Inside, the second fold stressed first the fun and then the duty of being a WAC: "Air Wacs TRAVEL! Air Wacs PLAY! Air Wacs WORK!" in bold letters. Lowry WACs were shown swimming, taking free flights while on leave, and playing basketball. WACs at work were shown with a weather balloon, in the flight control tower, and in the supply room.[35] As with nearly every war publication, the brochure showed only Anglo WACs, although African American women served at Lowry beginning in November 1944 — as well as in the rest of the nation and overseas.

Newspapers regularly ran advertisements and articles encouraging women to enlist. A *Brush Tribune* article asked, "Most of Your Friends Away? If most of your friends are away now—in the service—doing war jobs—don't YOU feel left behind sometimes? Why not get in the midst of this war? JOIN THE WAC! You can see new places, make new friends, learn interesting things—while you are doing vital work to speed victory."[36] Six months later the paper ran a full-page ad encouraging women to enlist and become medical technicians at Denver's

Fitzsimons Hospital. Captain Irene Stanley, the Colorado and Wyoming District liaison officer, met with the mayor of Brush and Mrs. Bates, the American Legion Auxiliary representative. The army understood that part of the appeal to potential enlistees was the opportunity to remain in Colorado.[37] Of course, recruiting lures seldom reflect reality. Heyer wrote her sister, "When you mentioned the fact that the Wac's could choose their stations, I couldn't help but laugh. It's one of those old recruiting gags to get enlistments. I have never heard yet of one girl who has gotten where she was asked." As Heyer pointed out, once a woman was in, she was in. There was no turning back.[38]

Unfortunately, the next issue—a slander campaign against women in the army—threatened to erase all the hard work of Director Hobby, active WAACs/WACs, and supporters. Without a public relations staff to officially refute allegations and with many authorities mistakenly believing the issue would simply "blow over," the slander increased in volume and maliciousness. It began around training centers. Detractors claimed that army women engaged in prostitution, lesbianism, and public drunkenness. Part of the problem was that civilian Women Ordnance Workers (WOWS) wore uniforms similar to the WAC's. There were incidences around the country where WOWS drank in bars, took men to their hotel rooms, and engaged in barroom brawls.[39] Some soldiers forbade their wives and female relatives and friends from enlisting, saying they would disown them if they did. Other Americans hoped to discredit the Roosevelt administration by asserting that the real reason the WAAC was formed was to provide the United States Army with women to fulfill "morality" purposes. In other words, WACs were army-issued prostitutes for officers and enlisted men.[40] Mary Andrea Kelles, stationed at Camp Hale, recalled that her brother-in-law was one of those who believed that story.[41] At Lincoln Air Base (Nebraska), the last stop for 20,000 servicemen going overseas, a colonel asked First Lieutenant Crain to investigate the accusation that WACs on the base were prostitutes. She discovered that Black soldiers sometimes entered the women's quarters uninvited; others tried to take advantage of the women and became upset when they refused to date them. Crain found no evidence to support the allegation of prostitution.[42]

By the summer of 1943, the situation had grown so dire that the president and first lady tried to defuse the stories. Some suspected that Nazis had initiated the slander campaign. However, an army investigative report concluded that there was no evidence of that being true; rather, the rumors were widely circulated by American military personnel, businessmen, civilian women, factory workers, and others.[43] Evidence indicated that in most cases the heinous stories originated with servicemen about the time large numbers of WACs were releasing men for combat duty. The report surmised that servicemen were upset for a variety of reasons—WACs were of higher rank, servicemen could not get dates with them, military tradition was a male prerogative, and the men were fearful of replacement.

Vicious slander was not the sole outcome of the feelings of WAC detractors. In Denver, Bernice Moran and another WAC had a frightening incident. They were out walking when a soldier came up, pushed between them, took hold of their arms, and started calling them "everything but ladies and wanted to know why on earth" they were in uniform.[44] Townspeople, unhappy that WACs monopolized their restaurants, theaters, and streetcars, created or spread lies about army women. Officers' wives, jealous of WACs working alongside their husbands and receiving lots of favorable publicity, also fanned the flames. People who loved to pass on "dirt" about others, disgruntled and discharged WAACs, and Americans who could not fathom women in nontraditional wartime roles all had a part in the viciousness.[45]

"Unfavorable comments" prompted a WAC officer to write to the Camp Hale newsletter: "It is our conviction that a few serious thoughts about the Women's Army Corps are in order at this time." She pointed out that women willingly joined the WAAC and, after conversion, stayed with the WAC even though they had the option to return to civilian life. They stayed true to the corps even though they were "the objects of many jokes, jibes, and even jeers." Acknowledging that it was not easy to be a male soldier or officer, she asserted that it was likewise not easy to be a woman soldier. "It takes brains, courage, and an adaptability beyond the demands of ordinary civilian activities. It calls for courage and moral stamina that are the exception rather than the rule." As the army investigation had concluded, she also believed that "the sight of women in military uniform has apparently been a bit too much for some people." She reminded those people that "women wear the uniform of the Army of the United States . . . the counterpart of the uniform worn by our men in deadly combat the world over."[46]

The accusation that thousands of WAACs were lesbians was never substantiated. Interestingly, although the military wrote guidelines and procedures to deal with male homosexual soldiers and sailors, the female branches did not.[47] There were no policies or specific recruitment questions or methods to "discover" lesbians before they enlisted. Although admonishments to recruiters, officers, and WACs were made to downplay "manly" looks, characteristics, and traits, the WAC at first did not put a great deal of effort into ferreting out lesbians in its ranks. However, if a particular WAC was suspected of being a lesbian, she could be discharged under a different accusation, such as public drunkenness or insubordination. Wanting to present a public image of respectable womanhood for the corps, Director Hobby did not wish to publicly air its "dirty laundry" of lesbianism or of sexually active heterosexual women.[48]

Of course, lesbians did enlist. It is impossible to ascertain how many lesbians enlisted or tried to enlist in any of the service branches during World War II, a time when homosexuality was considered deviant and sufficient cause to deny a person housing, a job, and child custody in divorce proceedings.[49] A study conducted in late 1942 discovered that some lesbians enlisted because they "always wanted to be a boy and join [the] Army" or wanted the "opportunity to mix with other girls."[50] But the majority of gay women joined for the same reasons heterosexual women did—patriotism, adventure, family tradition, and a steady job. Jacquelyn Beyer was an undergraduate student at the University of Colorado when she decided to enlist. A WAC recruiter who had visited the Boulder campus made the army seem inviting. Although her mother raised her to be independent, she forbade Jacquelyn to join the army until she attained her degree. Beyer, a graduate of Evergreen High School in Jefferson County, took summer classes so she could finish her degree in three years. After basic training, Sergeant (T/4) Beyer worked on experimental photography processing techniques in Arlington, Virginia, that helped break Japanese codes.[51] In an interview over forty years later, Beyer admitted that she felt a little "fraudulent" being interviewed as a gay servicewoman because she had no experience as a lesbian while in the service. Her World War II social life had been "pretty dull." Although she had "passionate feelings" for other WACs, they were always already involved with other women, so she never acted on those feelings while in the army. Instead, she found the ban on fraternization between enlisted personnel and officers more difficult to deal with than her sexual orientation.[52]

A scandal at the training center at Fort Oglethorpe in the spring of 1944—in which a mother of a WAC wrote a letter stating that women were afraid to enlist because the corps was "full of homosexuals and sex maniacs"—prompted a secret investigation. Six investigators traveled to eleven sites to take depositions. They found only four couples that could be identified as active lesbians. The mother, when informed of the expensive investigation, dismissed her original letter, stating she would take it back and had written it while angry.[53] Nevertheless, Director Hobby and other military personnel persuaded the Department of War to institute more stringent screening of applicants. In October, General Marshall directed medical examiners to "be on guard against the homosexual who may see in the WAC an opportunity to indulge her sexual perversity." Although mandating the rejection of lesbian applicants, the policies failed to include guidelines for identifying them.[54] When Charity Adams asked for guidance from the next echelon of officers, she was told that she should be alert to any homosexual activities that negatively influenced the performance of the unit. It was suggested that she conduct surprise inspections during the hours when troops were in bed. Unwilling to do bed checks without a company commander or to wake an officer to accompany her, she did not conduct bed checks. Unable to confirm or deny the presence of homosexual activities among those under her command, she adamantly swore, though, that "the efficient performance of the unit was not impaired."[55]

In spite of the slander campaign and increased scrutiny of enlistees, WACs continued to enlist. In April 1943, Beula Tee Fant, active in the Denver-based Colorado Civic Organization and A.M.E. activities and secretary of the Phyllis Wheatley

YWCA, enlisted in the Women's Army Auxiliary Corps. She was three weeks shy of her forty-fourth birthday. After completing basic training, Fant was stationed at Walla Walla Air Field (Washington). Although one of the older enlistees, she remained in the army through the Korean and Vietnam Wars.[56] Soon after Fant joined the army, Margaret Mead, another Black woman from Denver, was one of a hundred Negro WAACs selected for the bakers and cooks school in Iowa.[57]

From an initial three specialties—switchboard operators, mechanics, and bakers—the positions WACs held grew to dozens. They included postal clerk, radio operator, driver, and armorers who repaired small arms and heavy weapons. A small group of Colorado women were trained in radio maintenance and repair at Trinidad Junior College before enlisting in the Women's Army Corps. Ordway resident Mrs. Inez Rooney joined Kiowa teacher Florence Pemberton, a stenographer from Karval; Myrtle Thurston; and Lily Mae Larsen, the registrar at the college; in joining the WAAC in 1943.[58]

At Lowry Field, the army air force set up WAAC/WAC classes at the Photolaboratory School. In January 1943, the first class of fifty WAACs began specialized training. This was the second group of women, after army nurses, to be stationed at the air field. First Lieutenant Elizabeth Johnston, commanding officer, and Second Lieutenant Dorothy L. Starbuck, squadron adjutant, arrived with three WACs to make final preparations for the debarkation of the bulk of the corps. For Starbuck, a native of Brighton and a 1940 graduate of Loretto Heights, it was a homecoming of sorts.[59] Officials in the photography department insisted that the women's course of study mirror that of the enlisted men. WAACs received instruction on using C-1 and C-3 air corps cameras. They learned to develop negatives, print pictures, mix their own developing solutions, and repair cameras. In April 1943, the first class of WAACs received their diplomas. Major Joe M. Cates, director of the school of photography, announced that the class completed the course "as satisfactory [sic] as . . . enlisted men."[60] By October 1943, WACs were a large part of the aerial photography program; by 1945, there were approximately 400 women in several all-WAC photography companies.[61]

Two Lowry photography graduates were Denver-born Betty Heyer and Bernice Moran. After graduation in 1943, Heyer was sent to MacDill Field (Florida) to be a photographic repair technician. She later served with a photographic mapping squadron. Moran served with the Second Squadron at Felts Field, Washington, while Heyer served with the Third Squadron in New Guinea and the Philippines. After nearly a year, Moran was transferred back to Lowry Field for twelve months before being sent to Wright-Patterson Field (Dayton, Ohio), where she analyzed photographs to identify German scientific and factory equipment. Moran's unit took negatives men shot from B-25 airplanes and developed photographs. The photographs were then sent to Washington, DC, to the group that had taken the pictures. The men identified checkpoints, overlapped the photographs, and made

FIGURE 3.3. Bernice Moran, in photography school at Lowry Field in 1943, wearing the WAC enlisted olive drab winter uniform and olive drab garrison cap. *Courtesy*, Bernice Moran Miller Collection, Martha Blakeney Hodges Special Collections and University Archives, WV0104.6.004, University of North Carolina at Greensboro.

maps. Moran's unit had so much work that at times they worked seven consecutive days before getting a day off.

As more women joined the WAC, they were assigned to a variety of billets. The top four fields occupied by WAC enlisted personnel of the army air force in 1945 were administrative, medical, vehicle operator, and supply.[62] Within the Army Medical Department, WACs were used as laboratory, surgical, X-ray, and dental technicians. Sunshine Cloud was the daughter of Edwin Cloud, a Southern Ute Indian Sun Dance chief and tribal sub-chief. The Southern Ute and Ute Mountain Utes, removed to reservations before 1900, made up less than 2 percent of Colorado's population in the twentieth century.[63] Forty-three Utes joined the US military during World War II, including four women. Sunshine Cloud Smith worked in an Indiana defense factory producing land mines before enlisting. She recalled that she did so because "all her friends" joined. As a WAC she served as a surgical technician in Utica, New York. Annie Bettine, Martha Mayor, and Dorothy Burch Box of the Southern Ute Tribe also enlisted.[64]

FIGURE 3.4. Sunshine Cloud
Smith of the Southern Ute
Tribe of Colorado served as a
surgical technician during the
war. *Courtesy*, Lorelei Cloud.

As one would expect, army women with the Transportation Corps worked in the motor pool, but they also issued guns and ammunition to soldiers before they were shipped overseas for combat duty. At Fort Des Moines, PFC Emily Nydigger attended six weeks of motor transport school. For training, WACs temporarily moved out of the barracks and into a hotel. They learned to change tires, check the oil, and perform other maintenance functions. Instructors would "sabotage" a vehicle, and the women had to ascertain the problem. On night bivouacs, WACs learned how to keep the right distance between vehicles while driving during blackouts. Nydigger found that exciting. The women learned to drive a jeep, a staff car, a 1½-ton truck, a carryall, and an ambulance. Nydigger was later assigned to the motor pool at Camp Hale, the training site for the Tenth Mountain Division. She drove officers to headquarters, to different parts of the camp, and to places in Leadville. After the Tenth Mountain Division shipped out, the WACs were also reassigned. Nydigger was sent to Camp Crowder, Missouri, where she enjoyed driving army jeeps.[65]

At ports of embarkation, WACs served as boat dispatchers, reporters, draftsmen, checkers of piers and ships, and classifiers of men and supplies. Technician fourth class Hester Deacon of Monte Vista, a member of the Transportation

Corps at Fort Slocum, New York, was named WAC of the Week for her clerical and stenographic expertise.[66] The camp was originally a port of embarkation for soldiers on their way to the European Theater of Operations. By 1944, with the decreased need for soldiers in Europe, Fort Slocum instead received soldiers returning to the United States.

Other WACs served with the Signal Corps. Helen Brecht was one of thirty-one Colorado and Wyoming women to enlist in the WAAC in Denver on November 23, 1942. Her father, Charles, and mother, Marian, owned a farm in Crook. On January 3, 1943, the twenty-seven-year-old became the first WAAC recruit from eastern Colorado. Although she had been a beautician prior to enlistment, she requested to be assigned office work for which she had some training. Barely over the required height minimum of 60 inches, Brecht definitely did not want to be assigned as a truck driver. Of course, that is exactly what her first duty was after basic training. Fortunately, she later attended Officer Candidate School (OCS). As a second lieutenant, she was sent to England where she served during the German V-bombing of London. Her small room and bath was on the third floor of the quarters. Upon arriving, Brecht had heard about a male American officer who had been blown out of his third-floor room while taking a bath. Terrified of having the same fate befall her, Brecht never undressed completely for her baths. She bathed one area, dressed it, and moved to the next. Every night the sound of buzz bombs sent her running to the basement air raid shelter. But each night she found herself the only occupant. Born on the eastern plains of Colorado and therefore a stranger to urban mass transportation, Brecht later learned that the "bombs" were merely subway trains rumbling beneath the building.[67]

Brecht rose up the ranks and was soon made commander of fifty women. She led them to Paris, where they became part of the first all-female Signal Corps Battalion.[68] Soldiers in the Signal Corps operated radios and keypunch and tabulating machines. They served as cryptographic and message center clerks as well as photographers. The journey to Paris was not one of ease. The trip across the mine-filled English Channel took several days in total blackout conditions. Then, the women were transported by truck to Paris. Because the area was not cleared of mines, the WACs were not allowed to leave the truck. As usual, the women adapted to their situation as best they could: "We had to use our helmets to go to the bathroom and then throw it out of the back of the trucks."[69]

Cryptography was another field in which WACs were heavily utilized. Shirley Sears wanted to enlist as soon as the WAAC was created, but her father, a Spanish-American War veteran, wanted her to wait because of its auxiliary status. Although he died in July 1942, she honored his wishes and did not enlist until the conversion to the Women's Army Corps was complete.[70] She attended basic training at Fort Oglethorpe, where she had more than her share of kitchen patrol (KP). Following graduation, Sears was sent to Fort Knox, Kentucky, for additional training as a tower operator. However, because the army desperately needed cryptographers, she was assigned to Presque Isle, Maine. After going through basic training in the Georgia mud, she and the other WACs now had to dig themselves out of snow-covered barracks.

Months later, yet another drastic change of scenery and climate ensued. Sears was transferred to Kindley Field, Bermuda, the midpoint for transmissions and flights to the Azores and Europe from the United States. Arriving in time for Christmas dinner in 1944, Sears lived in a converted stable adjacent to a runway. Her work was top secret. Inside a code room she received a coded message, de-coded it, re-coded it, and sent it on. The room had a window through which people inside communicated with people outside. One day an officer arrived and demanded to be let into the code room. When he was unable to supply the correct password, she refused to open the door. He left; she never heard anything about the incident and always wondered if it had been a test to see if she would follow protocol in keeping out unauthorized personnel, no matter their rank.[71]

One thousand WAACs were sent overseas prior to the WAC conversion. They served as typists, stenographers, and telephone operators. In January 1943, female drivers, cooks, and bakers joined them in North Africa. Initially, army commanders overseas wanted nothing to do with servicewomen because they assumed women could not handle the adverse conditions, feared they might distract male soldiers from their own work, and did not recognize the skills the women possessed. Commanders quickly changed their minds after observing army women at work. Commanders such as General Douglas MacArthur discovered that the women "worked harder, complained less, and were better disciplined than men."[72] Lieutenant General Mark Clark, commander of the Fifth Army, made sure "his" WACs were appropriately awarded medals and insisted on their inclusion in postwar occupation units. WAC Dorothy Hinson was under his command. Originally an inspector of tracer bullets in a North Carolina defense plant, Hinson had somehow managed to enlist at the young age of sixteen. Disappointed with her base post office assignment, she hounded her superiors for overseas duty until she was finally shipped off to join General Clark's group in Verona, Italy. She remained with the occupation unit until her discharge in March 1946.[73]

General Dwight D. Eisenhower, too, was initially reluctant to employ WACs. He quickly changed his mind after witnessing the work of British servicewomen. Captain Starbuck, who had begun her military career at Lowry Field as officer in charge of photography trainees, was later sent to Fort Devens, Massachusetts, for orientation and training before being shipped to England. There, she was assigned to Eisenhower's London headquarters. With top-secret clearance, she worked for Colonel Thurston Hughes. Her responsibilities included controlling every document from every military service that came into the European Theater of Operations USA. Those documents included every detail of Operation Overlord, the D-Day invasion of France. In July 1944, *Stars and Stripes* reported that Captain Starbuck, five other officers, and forty-nine enlisted WACs were in Normandy, not just on the heels of the troops but close enough to share stories and play a game of baseball.[74] Starbuck continued her top-secret work in Paris. Another WAC working in military intelligence was Boulderite Rosalie Kilzer, one of the first women to enlist in the WAAC at the Denver recruiting office. A 1940 graduate of Nebraska Wesleyan University, Lieutenant Kilzer was assigned an office in the Pentagon with the chief of staff. Later, Kilzer served with the European Command Headquarters in Germany and the Army Security Agency.

Other WACs in the European Theater of Operations served as clerks and typists. Maud "Totty" Sundvik joined the WAAC in March 1943. When the medical WAC measured her, she fell short of the required 5 feet. The officer told her to take a deep breath and stand as tall as she could. She qualified by a hair's breadth.[75] In August 1944, she arrived in England to serve with the Eighth Fighter Command Headquarters. Within a couple of months she was transferred to Belgium. The port at LeHavre, France, was so devastated by bombs that the gangways were rubble, forcing Sundvik and the other WACs to clamber down a landing net wearing full packs. Former Greeley resident Edna Heinecke served as a stenographer in North Africa and Europe. She was awarded the Bronze Star for Meritorious Service for coordinating communications for and serving as stenographer at the Yalta Conference involving President Roosevelt, Prime Minister Winston Churchill, and Premier Joseph Stalin.[76]

About 10 percent of WAACs/WACs served overseas.[77] While male soldiers were sometimes the instigators of gossip about the WACs stateside, overseas they seemed to respect the women's work: "Contrary to what had been feared, there was no indication that the men's efficiency was impaired by the presence of women. In fact, the men seemed glad to have American women along. The parity in living and working conditions may have put a damper on the normal male griping."[78] In a very short time, demand for servicewomen in the European Theater became "insatiable."[79] The Services of Supply recommended to the Department of War that legislation be sought to draft a sufficient number of women into the WAC to meet demand, but the matter was so controversial that nothing was done about it.[80]

In the Pacific Theater of Operations, Betty Heyer trained other WACs in photography, mapping, and physical training (PT). The latter elicited dares from male GIs who wanted to know just how strong she was. Stationed in the Netherlands East Indies and Dutch New Guinea, she coped with wood and water cockroaches, sand fleas, and mosquitoes. In the spring the pests were so thick in the Orderly Room that it was "misery." She sprinkled "Skat," a vile insect repellant, throughout the room and on herself, but it did little good. A "mild" hurricane sent the insects scurrying into their holes, but not for long. Other visitors to their living quarters were rats who ran across the top of mosquito

FIGURE 3.5. WACs Betty Heyer (*left*) and Goyette (*right*) consult maps and photographs on a table with Sandy, a soldier from the Nineteenth Photographic Group, at MacDill Field in Tampa, Florida, in 1944. All three wear men's flight suits. Courtesy, Anne Elizabeth Heyer Collection, Martha Blakeney Hodges Special Collections and University Archives, WV0320.6.009, University of North Carolina at Greensboro.

netting. Periodically, some managed to get under the netting and run directly across a woman's chest.[81]

Even more irritating to Heyer were the GIs who would not take "no" for an answer. She complained to her sister that she could not understand why men always wanted to neck. As the war wound down, she confided that she found most men boring: "I haven't seen but a couple of fellows I would bother wasting time with. It's much more fun to go out swimming or hiking or something with a bunch of girls. You can talk, if you want, or not say a word, it doesn't make any difference. I think I'll get a nice little dog and hibernate when I get home."[82]

In 1943 the War Relocation Authority, in charge of the ten internment camps, began allowing Japanese Americans to leave camps under three prerequisites: acquiring employment in either the midwestern or eastern US region, indicating on a loyalty questionnaire that he or she was loyal to the United States and supported the war effort, and agreeing not to affiliate with other Japanese Americans.[83] Nisei men (second-generation Japanese Americans) were concentrated in the army's 442nd Regimental Combat Team.[84] WAC director Hobby set a quota of

500 Nisei women—including sixty-five from Colorado, Iowa, Kansas, Maryland, Minnesota, Nebraska, North Dakota, South Dakota, and Wyoming—for the Seventh Service Command.[85] Aiding in the recruitment effort was Private Shizuko Shinagawa, an Arizona native who was visiting California at the time of the roundup of Japanese Americans. She was interned at the War Relocation Center in Poston, Arizona, for ten months before returning to her home in Phoenix. She was inducted into the Women's Army Corps in August 1943. After basic training, she was transferred to Denver to serve as a recruiter: "It's a wonderful opportunity for my people to participate actively in the greatest battle for democracy the world has ever known . . . Before I joined up, I felt useless and restless because I wanted to do something for my country. I wouldn't exchange for anything the experience I've gained in the WAC."[86] Frances Iritani did not need a recruiter to persuade her to join the Women's Army Corps. A Colorado native living with her family in Arapahoe County, Iritani enlisted on November 10, 1943, making her the first Nisei non-internee to join the army.[87]

A number of Nisei WACs were trained in linguistics at the Military Intelligence Service Language School at Fort Snelling, Minnesota. Kisa Noguchi followed her older sister, Yoshi, into the army. Both Noguchi daughters attended public schools in Iliff, Merino, and Sterling and earned college degrees from Colorado universities. Whereas Yoshi served as an occupational therapist at MacDill Field and later as a draftsman in Florida, Kisa served in military intelligence as a linguist. After schooling at Fort Snelling, Kisa was stationed in Maryland and Washington, DC, where she was assigned to the Allied Military Intelligence Research Section.[88]

Nisei WACs also filled clerical, medical, and supply positions. Margaret Uemura, one of eight children of the Reverend Seijiro and Hana Uemura, graduated from Colorado Women's College in 1938. Her first job was as an assistant laboratory technician at Colorado General Hospital in Denver. Inducted in January 1945, she continued her work as a laboratory technician at Tilton General Hospital in Fort Dix, New Jersey. Kumi Matsusaki earned a pharmaceutical degree from the University of Colorado before working at Beth-El Hospital in Colorado Springs and St. Luke's Hospital in Denver. Her father, disappointed that he did not have any sons to join the American armed forces, suggested that she enlist. After basic training, Matsusaki was stationed at Nichols General Hospital in Louisville, Kentucky. Instead of dispensing penicillin and sulfa derivatives by the prescription as she had done at St. Luke's, her military duties entailed dispensing them in bulk.[89]

Takako Kusunoki and Iris A. Watanabe had been interned at Colorado's Amache Relocation Camp in southeastern Colorado. Prior to enlisting, Kusunoki wrote for the camp newspaper, the *Granada Pioneer*. Originally from California, she was sent to Amache in September 1942 and released on October 18, 1943. A year later she enlisted in the WAC.[90] Watanabe was first interned at the Poston Relocation Camp and transferred to Amache in 1943, from where she was released

FIGURE 3.6. Iris A. Watanabe
and Sue Ogata at induction ceremonies where the two women,
along with seventeen others,
formally entered the Wom-
en's Army Corps. *Courtesy*,
Bancroft Library, University of
California, Los Angeles.

to take a job in Chicago. She was working there when she was accepted into the
Women's Army Corps. In Denver, Watanabe was sworn in with two other Nisei
women, Sue Ogata of La Salle and Bette Nishimura of Rocky Ford. Watanabe's
December 1943 enlistment date garnered her the notoriety of being the first
Colorado-based evacuee to join the WAC. Although presiding officer Lieutenant
S. O. Reed forbade reporter Harry Tarvin to interview Watanabe because he was
afraid the enlistment of a Japanese American woman might discourage white
women from enlisting, Tarvin circumvented the officer by convincing Governor
John C. Vivian to allow him to photograph the governor with Watanabe and two
other Nisei women enlistees.[91]

Watanabe was proud to serve her country. On the eve of her induction she
told a newspaper reporter, "I hope to make the land of my ancestors pay for its
unwarranted attack on my country."[92] Another WAC stationed with Watanabe at
Fort Snelling, Minnesota, was Traoda "Trudy" Oda Hirokawa. Born to Japanese
immigrants, she graduated from high school in Grand Junction and from the

University of Colorado. After nursing school, she enlisted in the Women's Army Corps at age twenty-five. Hirowaka was originally stationed at Fort Harrison, Indiana, before being selected for the Military Intelligence Division stationed at Fort Snelling.[93] The intelligence work of Nisei WACs helped defeat the land of their ancestors.

By the end of the war, almost 150,000 women had served in the Women's Army Corps. The WAC proved to be the most inclusive of all the military branches, recruiting Anglo, African American, and Nisei women. Ignoring the original ugly uniforms, the vicious slander campaign, the resentment of male soldiers, and the ingratitude or jealousy of some civilians, most WACs felt they had "meaningfully contributed to winning the war" and looked back on the experience "as one of the high points of their lives."[94] One WAC detachment, disbanding at Leyte, the Philippines, celebrated their experiences. They had lived in tents, worked by candlelight, dealt with the lack of supplies, stood and walked in mud, run to foxholes for safety during bombing attacks, and been drowned by persistent rain. They summed up their military experience thus: "We'll never have a detachment so ideal and so perfect again."[95]

The United States Army was not the only military branch that needed enlistees. The United States Navy had initiated a massive buildup during the 1930s. In 1940 President Franklin D. Roosevelt, a navy man himself, persuaded the US Congress to allocate $4 billion for a two-ocean navy.[96] The navy needed administrative and support personnel to handle this increase in force and manpower. After the Japanese attack on Pearl Harbor, it needed to reassign naval men from non-combat billets to combat billets for the war effort. In short, the United States Navy needed its own version of the Women's Army Corps.

4

The Women Accepted for Volunteer Emergency Service (WAVES)

On the evening of December 14, 1942, Martha Scott Trimble, an unhappy, restless English instructor at Colorado State College of Agriculture and Mechanics, wrote in her diary: "Up at 3:30, caught the 4:45 bus, blessed angel—Mother walking down with me at the early hour. The trip was propitious. Schedule was satisfactory. I passed physical, aptitude, and interview. Now I can scarcely believe that at 3:30 this afternoon I was sworn into the United States Navy, V-9, U.S.N.R. Oh I tell you the oath brought beads to my eyes, and I felt light hearted afterwards. Only one fear—that something might go wrong even yet!" She need not have worried. On January 29, 1943, Trimble was ordered to active duty at Smith College in Massachusetts to begin US Naval Reserve Midshipmen's School. She excitedly reported for duty on February 13, 1943.[1]

The Japanese attack on Pearl Harbor struck at the core of the United States Navy. Reeling, it scrambled to recover from the loss of 88 ships, 188 aircraft, and 2,403 Americans. Shipyards on both coasts ramped up production, and recruiters hastily enlisted men. Both efforts were successful. Between 1940 and 1945, the number of ships and ocean crafts increased from under 500 to more than 6,600. Concomitantly, the number of officers grew from 13,162 to 325,074; the number of enlisted men ballooned from 144,824 to 3,005,534.[2]

As the United States Navy expanded, its need for support and administrative personnel increased. However, it—and the other military branches—were reluctant to employ huge numbers of civilian workers. The military could not enforce

 DOI: 10.5876/9781646420339.c004

discipline, impose wartime security on them, or force them to remain on the job. Following the lead of Great Britain, which formed the Women's Royal Naval Service (WRNS), and the United States Army, the navy turned its attention to establishing a women's auxiliary. However, only the Chief of Naval Operations (CNO) and the Bureau of Aeronautics embraced the idea of female navy personnel. Despite this lack of enthusiasm, Secretary of the Navy Frank Knox recommended a women's branch as part of the Naval Reserve. The director of the Bureau of the Budget rejected the proposal unless the navy adopted an organization similar to the Women's Army Auxiliary Corps (WAAC). After much discussion, the Senate Naval Affairs Committee recommended a naval version of the WAAC. President Franklin D. Roosevelt approved it in May 1942. But Secretary Knox, aware of the problems the United States Army and the WAAC organization were experiencing, asked the president to reconsider.

As this scenario was unfolding, the navy asked female educators' advice on how to best organize and administer its upcoming women's program. A Women's Advisory Council was created. Professor Elizabeth Reynard (Barnard College) visited Canada to observe its female services, surveyed domestic naval establishments regarding potential employment of women, and evaluated various college campuses for training sites. The council unanimously selected Smith College for officer training. Most important, it recommended that Mildred Helen McAfee, president of Wellesley College in Massachusetts, be appointed director of the future women's naval organization.

Even though Roosevelt approved a WAAC-like organization, female educators continued to insist that women be *in*, not *with*, the navy. As others had done throughout the president's political career, women appealed to his wife, Eleanor. She forwarded their letters to naval leaders and to her husband.[3] The strategy proved successful. In June, Secretary Knox convinced Senator David I. Walsh, chair of the Senate Naval Affairs Committee, to revise the bill to create a Women's Reserve in the United States Navy. President Roosevelt signed the bill on July 30, 1942. Its role was to "expedite the war effort by releasing officers and men for duty at sea and their replacement by women in the shore establishment."[4] Volunteers would serve for the duration of the war plus six months, they would serve only in the continental United States, and they could not board naval vessels or combat aircraft.

In early August, Mildred McAfee was sworn in as a lieutenant commander in the United States Navy. Reynard was commissioned a lieutenant; she created the apropos acronym WAVES—Women Accepted for Volunteer Emergency Service. In the next two months, 108 additional women from education and business fields became officers, including Dorothy Stratton, the future director of the United States Coast Guard Women's Reserve, or SPAR.

The navy originally estimated a women's reserve of 1,000 officers and 10,000 enlisted personnel. Over the course of the next three years, those numbers increased dramatically as over 104,000 women served in the WAVES. As was the case with women joining other military branches, women reservists wanted to serve their country, were looking for adventure or professional advancement, or were following family traditions of military service.[5] Recruiting stations were opened in Colorado Springs, Denver, Grand Junction, Greeley, and Pueblo.[6] By the time of its second anniversary, the WAVES had enrolled 61 women from Pueblo and another 47 from other towns in southern Colorado. Doris June Rew wanted to follow in the footsteps of her mother, Oldham Rew, who served as a yeomanette during World War I.[7] Kathryn Chittenden, in tooling design at Boeing Aircraft Company, joined the last WAVES Officer Training Class, hoping to meet eligible bachelors in the military. She loved her Boeing job, but she also wanted to marry; the men she met at work were either not to her liking or already married. The opportunity to experience new adventures also played into her decision.[8]

Recruiting posters and advertisements emphasized WAVES' pay rate, which was equal to men's. An officer received $200 a month plus an additional allowance for uniforms and housing. However, her benefits were not commensurate with a navy man's. No WAVE received a death gratuity or retirement pay. Not until November 1943 were WAVES granted allowances for dependents—and then only for children, not husbands, and only if the child's father was deceased or the mother was their sole supporter.[9] Louise Nash, a Boulder native, pondered joining the army but felt it treated its women as second-class citizens. When the formation of the WAVES was announced, she immediately left her dead-end job with Carolina Power and Light. She liked the idea of equal pay for equal work, earning more money as an officer than she had with the power company.[10]

Professionally designed uniforms also lured women into enlistment centers. Eunice Birkett returned to her hometown of Steamboat Springs in uniform. A reporter for the *Steamboat Pilot* was so impressed that he thought she "might easily have been the model for the attractive WAVES and SPARS posters."[11] Yeoman Second Class Virginia Haynes, the daughter of Howard and Agnes Haynes of Julesburg, did pose for publicity purposes. A former bookkeeper and stenographer with a Denver wholesale supply company, Haynes was shown in a 1944 photograph with an unidentified navy man whom she released for active duty.[12]

Edna Guise, born in Missouri, studied for two years at St. Benedict's College before transferring to Drake University in Iowa, from which she graduated with a law degree in 1944. After a friend left for WASP training in Texas, Guise enrolled as a WAVE officer candidate at the navy recruiting office in Des Moines. She took the required tests, was accepted, and was soon bound for indoctrination at Smith College. Along the way she met another officer candidate, Mary Devlin, who would become her lifelong friend. Devlin had enlisted even though most of her family was apprehensive and some were even "ashamed and humiliated." Her father was her sole supporter. Her mother took her to the parish priest to ask his opinion. Both were surprised when he told them enlistment was a great idea: "If a girl wants to get into trouble, she can do so right here in Wichita."[13] On their first day, Guise and Devlin were fitted for their "very classy" uniforms.[14]

Because requirements for the WAVES were more stringent than those for navy men, navy women, on the whole, were better educated and had more work experience than their male counterparts. Officer candidates were required to be between the ages of twenty and forty-nine and to hold a college degree or have two years each of college and professional or business experience. Enlisted women had to be between the ages of twenty and thirty-five and hold a high school or business school diploma or equivalent experience. Women also had to meet minimum weight requirements. Pueblo native Elizabeth Weidenfeller reported to her enlistment examination underweight. Determined to qualify, she trained and increased the amount she ate. The day she made weight, her brother George convinced their aunt and guardian to give her consent for him to enlist in the navy.[15]

Marriage policy for WAVES changed as the war dragged on. At first, no WAVE could be married to a man in the armed forces. By August 1943, WAVES could marry, with permission, during specialized training. Ensign Neva Anderson, an Alamosa native, was a graduate of Adams State Teachers College (currently Adams State University). Before enlisting in the WAVES, she taught at schools in Manassa, Fort Garland, La Veta, and Wiley. In 1943 she married another former teacher, Lieutenant William Moyers, who was serving in the United States Navy. After a quick honeymoon she returned to her work with the Bureau of Ordnance in Washington, DC, and Lieutenant Moyers returned to his duty station in New Jersey.[16]

Smith College, located in western Massachusetts, quickly became known as "USS *Northampton*" after its namesake town. The first class, reporting on August 28, 1942, was taught naval history, organization, administration, correspondence, law, communications, protocol, and ship and aircraft identification. The women drilled and took physical education. Edna Guise recalled that the nine-week course was "quite intense." She was chosen platoon leader; her good friend Mary Devlin was selected assistant. Guise marched in front of the group, calling cadence and directions, while Devlin marched in back. Because the required heavy black oxfords made her feet sore, Guise was allowed to temporarily wear her civilian brown-and-white saddle shoes. Assistant Devlin, who "reveled in the marching, the singing, the camaraderie," was haunted by the fear of "washing out."[17] Every morning their rooms in Northrup Hall were thoroughly inspected. Years later Guise recalled: "I remember standing at attention with sweat dripping from my nose, I remember shots in my left shoulder every Wednesday morning, I remember eating muffins, cobblers, pies, anything made with blueberries which were in season in Massachusetts in August . . . I remember our graduation day when we 'passed in review' for our superior officers." She regretted that her parents were unable to see her receive her first commission as ensign and her first order for duty.[18]

FIGURE 4.1. WAVE Martha Scott Trimble had the pleasure of hearing First Lady Eleanor Roosevelt speak to her training class at Smith College. *Courtesy,* the Archive at Fort Collins Museum of Discovery, HH14449, Fort Collins, CO.

Martha Scott Trimble reveled in her new life as a WAVE. In her diary she wrote, "Up at 6:25, dressed, mustered, messed. School all day—our regular schedule and home exhausted in the evening. It is wonderful!" Four days later she reiterated, "How I like this new life! It is especially invigorating and lovely." Trimble also remembered one very special visitor to Smith College: "Today, Mrs. Roosevelt. Mother long ago saw Teddy in Northampton. Here in So. Hadley I see Mrs. F.D.R. . . . The party drove up outside, came into Skinner, came directly into our [class]room! She was gracious and polite, neat in black silk suit, blue moire, three strands of pearls, black felt hat and veil. . . . At 1530 she addressed the school, talking in general about women's work in the war. She caught me! I liked her quiet poise, the gleam of Teddy's fire in her eyes."[19]

The second class of officer candidates began in October. For the first month, trainees were apprentice seamen; the second month, midshipmen. Then they received their commissions as ensigns or lieutenants junior grade. Newly commissioned ensign Dorothy Sunderland spent her first six months as an instructor of new recruits at Smith College. A former student at Loretto Heights and the University of Denver, Sunderland was a secretary in the advertising department at the *Rocky Mountain News* prior to her enlistment.[20]

On February 1, 1943, the navy took over Hunter College in the Bronx to provide indoctrination for all enlisted WAVES. Instruction included naval traditions, customs and history, ships and aircraft, and ranks and ratings. Although—or perhaps because—Colorado is a landlocked state, a number of women from the Centennial State joined the WAVES. Mildred Doherty, a Denver native, joined in 1943. She enlisted to be patriotic and to "see the world." Her naval career—which spanned World War II, the Korean War, and the Vietnam War—took her from Hunter College to Washington, DC, to Hawaii, England, and Japan.[21] Enlisting at the recruiting station in Grand Junction were Lenetta J. Austin, Alice L. Champlin, Shirley I. Brady, Rosemary Buskirk, Patricia E. Chandler, Margaret E. Chase, Myrtle M. Jones, Lois W. Sisson Seago, Mabel Lujan, and Jean McCoid. Bustling New York City was quite a change of scenery from the landscape of the Western Slope. Recruits marched, drilled, and completed physical conditioning in the urban setting of the Bronx, New York.

After indoctrination, WAVES were sent out for specialized training. Although nearby Mount Holyoke College originally agreed to handle the overflow as enlistments surged, it soon became an officers' specialized communications school instead. Virginia Moore, born in Fort Collins, was sent to Mount Holyoke after indoctrination. Although she had hoped to be assigned to a base in the East, she was sent to San Diego where she lived in barracks on Coronado Island and learned to shoot a pistol. Every morning she and the other WAVE officers boarded a small boat and were taken to the San Diego Repair Base. After decoding messages, Moore hopped into a motorcycle sidecar with her "little pistol" around her waist. An enlisted man drove her to navy ships in the San Diego harbor to deliver the messages. She found it eerie decoding messages regarding battles and then reading about the events in the newspaper weeks later.[22]

Brooklyn-born Natalie O'Brien graduated from college with a mathematics degree and a teaching certificate in 1939. Because the United States was still suffering from the Great Depression, jobs were scarce. O'Brien took a secretarial job at a shipbuilding firm in Delaware. She momentarily considered joining the newly formed Women's Army Auxiliary Corps but decided not to because of its unflattering khaki uniforms. Once the WAVES were formed in July 1942, O'Brien immediately went to Philadelphia and took the required physical and psychological tests. After training at Smith College, she was sent to Miami in January 1943. The navy valued recruits with mathematical ability because of its value in code breaking. She became the first WAVE officer to take over for a male officer. At first, the code room was all male, but gradually the entire communications department was run by WAVES. O'Brien found her three-and-a-half years in the navy fascinating: "I loved doing code work. They used to tell us in training, 'Communications cannot win a war, but communications can lose a war.'" As meticulous as she was, O'Brien did make a significant error one day. She assigned the wrong day's code to a warning to merchant ships about a submarine. Fortunately, there was no submarine, but she felt guilty for making what could have been a critical mistake.[23]

So many WAVES were assigned to the Naval Communications Annex in Washington, DC, that finding housing was a problem. Kathryn Chittenden first stayed in a "miserable hovel of a dark, unfinished basement with a slovenly woman." Then she found a place that was accommodating nearly twenty other servicewomen, but she and several other WAVES moved out when the proprietor's boyfriend started dropping in on women when they were sleeping. Finally, Chittenden and another officer found a room in a V-shaped apartment building. The owner, an attorney for the US government, lived on one side of the first-floor apartment. The two WAVES lived on the second floor, complete with a view into the apartment occupied by Vice President Harry Truman and his family.[24] Ensign Louise Nash was fortunate to be able to room with a cousin who had been living in the capital since World War I. She knew many WAVES who moved from hotel to hotel every three days until they found a permanent place to live.[25]

The housing situation undoubtedly affected two Colorado-raised WAVES. Elizabeth Wright, granddaughter of architect Frank Lloyd Wright, received training in communications and served as a draftsman during the war.[26] Ina Elizabeth Renkel was born in 1917 at Rago, 24 miles northeast of Akron. Armed with a scholarship, she attended and graduated from Barnes Business School. She worked as a stenographer for a county agent before enlisting in the WAVES. She, too, spent two years with the Department of Communications in Washington, DC.[27]

Naval Air Stations throughout the United States trained WAVES. The Bureau of Ordnance held classes in aviation ordnance training in Jacksonville, while the Naval Aviation Training School in Hollywood, Florida, trained air navigation instructors. There, Ensign Martha Trimble trained for sixteen weeks before teaching celestial navigation, instrument-phase engineering, and long-range flight. In the process she earned her silver bars, designating her lieutenant junior grade. These specialized training courses were coeducational, a result of the work of Joy Bright Hancock. As the Women's Reserve liaison officer at the Bureau of Aeronautics, Hancock strongly believed that men and women who would later work together needed to train together. Her idea was adopted by other naval bureaus.[28]

The navy also established specialized training sites for WAVES on college campuses. In October 1942, the first enlisted trainees reported to Oklahoma A&M (now Oklahoma State University) for yeomen training and the University of Wisconsin for radiomen. Other WAVES reported to the Supply Corps School at Harvard University (boarding at Radcliffe College), meteorology classes at Massachusetts Institute of Technology and the University of California–Los Angeles, and serological engineering at the University of Chicago. Indiana University, the site for training for storekeepers, received a substantial number of WAVES. Virginia Hudson attended an IBM keypunch school in New York City in the late 1930s before being hired by a British purchasing commission. When the United States entered World War II, Hudson decided she should be working for the United

States instead of Great Britain, so she applied for army jobs as a civilian employee. With her skills and experience, she was immediately hired. Working for the army, Hudson was sent to wiring school, where she became an IBM operator. Later, an army scout recruited her for work in Stockton, California. However, her brother had joined the marines and Hudson had always told her mother that "she wanted to go into the same kind of service if they let women in." After the creation of the WAVES, Hudson applied and was accepted. She graduated from the Storekeepers School at the University of Indiana in January 1943 and was assigned to Corpus Christi, Texas. Although trained as a storekeeper, she worked as an IBM operator in the navy once the chief discovered her skills. After three years in Texas, she was deployed to Hawaii.[29]

While some women reported to their duty stations immediately after graduation, others had a few days' break. After receiving her commission, Ensign Guise and several of her friends spent five days in New York City before reporting to their duty stations. For three nights they stayed at a women's service club on Sixty-ninth Street and Park Avenue. The grand mansion had marble staircases, thick oriental rugs, and stained glass windows—a far cry from their dormitory rooms at Smith College, which the women heard had been condemned for use by Smith students. The WAVES attended an open house for officers at the Biltmore Hotel, rode the ferry to Staten Island, had cocktails at the top of Radio City, took in movie shows, spent "a small fortune" on a salad at the Stork Club, and window-shopped on Fifth Avenue. On their last day in the city, Guise and Devlin "subwayed and trolleyed" to the Navy Ship Yard. The array of fighting ships impressed the two WAVES: "I couldn't help but just stand there and gape at rows and rows of fightin' ships—actual ocean-going men-of-war." Those "fightin' ships" would house the seamen whose records Guise would later work with in her new assignment.[30]

One benefit of the WAVE policy requiring them to wear their uniforms is that civilians heaped favors on the uniformed women. Louise Nash remarked that "New York just turned itself upside-down" for women in uniform. She and her sister WAVES rode the train for about 60 percent of the regular fare.[31] Betty Johnson Hice wrote that it was "quite thrilling, not only to see New York, but to be free and have people actually see us in our uniforms." Despite the fact that thousands of WAVES had descended on the city over the past year, people still stopped them to ask questions and admire their service. Hice found it "even more fun" to salute officers. Calling her day in the city "the biggest thrill I've ever had," Hice and her sister WAVES spent most of their time in Manhattan. Dining at Longchamps, an upscale restaurant, was especially memorable—silverware, cutlery with handles, and a full-course meal. The next day they visited St. Patrick's Cathedral and the Statue of Liberty.[32]

After training, WAVES served stateside at 900 shore stations. Most women performed stereotypical jobs—clerical work, healthcare, or storekeeping. Rose

FIGURE 4.2. Lieutenant Edna
Guise, a law school graduate,
worked in Virginia for the Bureau
of Naval Personnel processing
benefit and casualty claims.
Courtesy, Diana Doyle.

Margaret Gerk, born in Iliff, Colorado, was a clerk in a coal sales office prior to enlisting. With her retail experience she was sent to the Storekeepers School before being stationed in Miami with the Naval Air Transport Squadron in aviation supply.[33] Pueblo native Adela "Dell" Chavez left nurses training at Colorado State Hospital to enlist in the WAVES. After completing training for storekeepers, she was sent to the Bureau of Supplies and Accounts in Cleveland, Ohio. Her nurses training proved invaluable when she had to set up a dispensary at the bureau.[34]

After her New York City foray, Lieutenant Guise was assigned to the Bureau of Naval Personnel located in the Navy Annex Building in Arlington, Virginia. She served with the Office of Dependent Benefits and later with Casualties. There were about 60 officers in the department—most of whom were law school graduates—and about 200 enlisted men and women and a few civilians. Guise's job was to determine the proper beneficiaries when a navy man lost his life or was missing in action. Although she worked six days a week, there was still plenty of time to enjoy all that Washington, DC, had to offer. Weekends were often spent visiting historic sites around the city, driving to Rehoboth Beach in Delaware,

FIGURE 4.3. WAVES Aviation Machinist's Mates (AMM) working on an SNJ training plane and its Pratt and Whitney R-1340 radial engine at the Naval Air Station, Jacksonville, Florida, 1943. They are (*left to right*) Seaman 1st Class (AMM) Inez Waits, Seaman First Class (AMM) Lucille H. Henderson, Seaman First Class (AMM) Mary Anne Gasser, AMM Third Class Helen Adams, and Seaman First Class (AMM) Leona Curry. *Courtesy*, Naval History and Heritage Command.

or seeing the beautiful Blue Ridge Mountains of Virginia. Many of the WAVES belonged to an officers' club and spent evenings there, primarily to meet and dance with young men who were stationed at the multitude of bases in and around Washington. Once a month, WAVES had three days off. On many of those three-day weekends they took a 4:00 p.m. train out of Washington for the four-hour ride to New York City. Because of the railroad's crowded conditions, they usually stood the entire way, arriving in time for a theater show. At first they stayed at the Commodore Hotel but later discovered an elegant mansion called the James Foundation, which rented rooms only to WAVE officers for two dollars a night.[35]

Ensign Nash, who also reveled in her time in New York City, spent her long workdays routing requests from ships for materials to the appropriate technical desk. For workers unfamiliar with naval terms, the job proved challenging at times. Her section of 50 or so people began their six-days-a-week work at 8:00 a.m. They closed only when they could. Sometimes, when the paperwork piled up, they worked until 9:00 p.m. After working thirteen days straight, they received a Saturday off.[36]

Although many WAVES served as clerks, typists, and stenographers, break-throughs did occur in the Bureau of Medicine and Surgery, which accepted female physicians and surgeons; in the Dental Corps; and in the Hospital Corps, which had 13,000 WAVES serving in naval hospitals, stations, and dispensaries. Juanita Joseph, born in Pueblo and raised in San Luis, first drove large military 6 × 6 trucks at Buckley Air Field before additional training qualified her as a pharma-cist's mate third class. She served at St. Albans Hospital (New York) before being transferred to the submarine base at New London, Connecticut.[37]

The Bureau of Aeronautics was by far the most progressive organization in the United States Navy, employing WAVES in a wide variety of billets. They were researchers in the Chief of Naval Operations office and weather forecasters at naval air stations. Chief Petty Officer Lillian Mae Bainbridge was supervisor of her unit in the Weather Division in Washington, DC.[38] WAVE officers were assigned to technical billets in engineering, gunnery instruction, navigation, Link train-ing, and radio and radar. In aviation, enlisted WAVES served as metalsmiths, machinist's mates, parachute riggers, and control tower operators. WAVES Mary H. Cyphers of southern Colorado was a parachute rigger. Chloe Matilda Nelson of Sedgwick was a teacher in Fort Collins before enlisting. As a WAVE, she held the rank of aviation machinist's mate second class. The model-like seaman second class Eunice Birkett entered AMM school following her brief leave in Steamboat Springs.[39] Florence Gahm was an AMM who served six months in Hawaii. She was one of four daughters of Charles and Eleanor Gahm of Westplains, Colorado, who enlisted in the armed forces.[40]

Elaine Watkins was a twenty-two-year-old teacher in Denver when she enlisted. She told her parents, "I am going to enlist because I do not want to sit around here and go to [United Service Organizations] parties. I want to do something for the war effort."[41] While her mother was not supportive of her enlistment, her father, who had three daughters and no sons, was positive because it allowed him to display a star in the window of the family home. Following graduation from boot camp at Hunter College, at which First Lady Eleanor Roosevelt spoke, Watkins was sent to flight instruction school at the Atlanta Naval Air Station for a ten-week training program. After completing training, Watkins and three other WAVES were selected to remain in Atlanta to teach pilots how to fly using the Link Flight Trainer. Housed in a dormitory, the four women were fed in a din-ing room separate from the rest of the base personnel. Eating "wonderful" food, Watkins gained thirty pounds in six weeks. The women alternated among work-ing with an individual pilot occupying the Link Flight Trainer, teaching a class-room of pilots, and working on the Link Flight Trainer, which they had learned to disassemble and reassemble.

The bill creating the WAVES specifically barred women from serving out-side the continental United States. However, at the urging of naval leaders,

FIGURE 4.4. Elaine Watkins (*fourth from left*) and other WAVES celebrate her transfer to Kansas City as a Link Flight Trainer instructor. *Courtesy*, Elaine Watkins Brennan.

an amendment to the Naval Reserve Act in late September 1944 allowed navy women to serve in Alaska, Hawaii, and the Caribbean. Eventually, 350 officers and 3,659 enlisted personnel served in Hawaii, but permanent assignments to the other areas never occurred. Katherine "Kay" Keating, a Pueblo native, enlisted in the WAVES as a pharmacy student at the University of Colorado. As a radio operator, she was one of the first to be assigned to Hawaii, where she sometimes worked underground in a pineapple field. Because the area was so infested with flies, her captain brought her a toad to take care of the issue naturally.[42] Natalie O'Brien, a code room watch officer, was transferred from Miami to Hawaii in 1945. Later, she left the navy to become a civilian code worker for General Douglas MacArthur in Japan.[43]

Translation work was invaluable to the armed forces, and WAVES played a key role. In 1922 the US Navy Japanese Language School, a three-year Japanese-language course, opened in Tokyo, Japan. Nearly twenty years later, with war on the horizon, the school was relocated to the United States. Commander Albert E. Hindmarsh was ordered to find Japanese linguists in and out of the navy to create a training course. Of the 600 men identified as possessing sufficient knowledge of Chinese or Japanese, 65 were selected. In August 1941, Hindmarsh submitted a plan to set up two training centers, one at Harvard University and the other at the University of California–Berkeley. The navy paid each student's tuition while the universities employed and paid the instructors.[44]

Florence Walne was recruited to design the program at Berkeley. Walne, the daughter of Christian missionaries, was born and spent her childhood in Japan. She received a BA from Georgetown College (Kentucky) and returned to Japan to work with her father before earning a master's degree from Radcliffe College. She then became a professor in the Department of Oriental Languages at the University of California. The Harvard program expired at the end of the initial contract in September 1942; the Berkeley program, with Walne as director, flourished. However, Executive Order 9066, authorizing the removal of Japanese Americans from the West Coast, posed a direct threat to the program. In June 1943 Walne, her elderly mother, instructors, and students relocated to the University of Colorado (CU) in Boulder. President Robert Stearns had assured Hindmarsh that Boulder would accept the program and its Japanese American staff. Male students were housed in dormitories while the instructors, most of whom were married, found accommodations in town. To avoid the draft, students were made yeomen second class, V-4, United States Navy Reserve and placed on active duty. Once they graduated, they were assigned to either Washington, DC, or the Pacific Theater.[45]

Walne's program was originally an intensive year-long immersion in the Japanese language. In the fall of 1943, the faculty recommended expanding it to fourteen months to provide time for naval indoctrination, an introduction to Japanese geography, and more specialized naval readings. Several of the instructors in Boulder were women. Elizabeth McKinnon was born in Tokyo to Shinko Mishima McKinnon of Chofu, Japan, and Daniel Brooke McKinnon of Massachusetts. She grew up in Japan where her father taught English. After graduating from Ochanomizu Women's University (Tokyo), she taught high school students in Sapporo. In 1941, as war between Japan and the United States loomed, McKinnon and her sister, both American citizens, were sent to live with an aunt in Massachusetts. McKinnon taught at both the Harvard and CU Japanese Language Schools.[46] Another female instructor was Kimiko Miyamoto. Living at the Tule Lake relocation center, she and her husband were recruited for the program—he as an instructor and she as a teaching assistant.[47]

Kaya Kitagawa, a California native, was a student at San Francisco State College when the Japanese attacked Pearl Harbor. The next day, the entire student body was requested to attend an emergency meeting in the auditorium where they heard the United States declare war on Japan. Years later she recalled her reaction: "The day before, Sunday, December 7, 1941, I had already shouldered the blame of Pearl Harbor onto myself and hardly had the courage to appear on campus the following day. Participating with the student body in hearing the audible declaration of the justified war on Japan, my feelings of humiliation and guilt became a weightier burden."[48]

Kitagawa's father, a physician born in Japan, was "furious" about the attack but became indignant when he learned that the US government was incarcerating people of Japanese descent. He immediately decided that Kaya and her brother, George, a student at Stanford University, would not become "pawns to the war hysteria." The only university west of Chicago to accept the two Kitagawas was CU. Although reluctant to leave their family, who were soon held at the Tanforan Race Track (California) pending removal to a relocation camp, Kaya and George boarded the Zephyr train for the eastbound journey. With stories of shootings and lynchings in Wyoming and other states on their minds, they imagined themselves being intercepted at every station. Fearing for their lives, they huddled together and did not go to the dining car during the entire trip. Fortunately, the trip passed without incident. Upon arriving in Boulder, the Kitagawa siblings were greeted by a welcoming committee. In time, they adjusted and began to feel comfortable at the university and in the city of Boulder.[49] The siblings later asked the Department of Navy to release their father and the rest of their family from Central Utah Relocation Center in Topaz, Utah, so he could teach at the school. The request was granted and the family was reunited.[50]

Just as it was necessary to recruit women for the army and navy, it was vital to employ female linguists who could help on the home front while their male counterparts served overseas in the Pacific Theater. Commander Hindmarsh persuaded his superiors and the newly appointed WAVE director, Captain Mildred Helen McAfee, that women reservists could be trained for linguistic duty in the continental United States. That would allow male graduates to be sent overseas. He issued a call for volunteers in the *Key Reporter*, the newsletter of Phi Beta Kappa, and made a quick national recruiting tour in July 1943. Like other women who joined the military, applicants wanted to help in the war effort. Massachusetts native Ruth Halverson graduated from Pomona College in 1943 but searched in vain for a job in Southern California. Industrial jobs were plentiful but unsuitable for her. Douglas Aircraft would have hired her to weld, but she was "all thumbs, mechanically." Union Oil Chemistry offered her a job doing chemical tests even though she had not even had high school chemistry. Frustrated, she read a bulletin board notice about Hindmarsh interviewing women to learn Japanese for the navy.[51] For most future linguistics, the chance to learn a new language was "irresistible."[52]

Female linguistic students came from a variety of occupations. Nancy Rebecca Pearce took Civil Service examinations in typing, shorthand, Spanish, and German after the United States entered the war. She was hired by the Federal Bureau of Investigations (FBI). After spending one particularly hot and humid summer working in San Antonio, the Texas native decided a change was in order. When she read in the *Key Reporter* that women were eligible for the US Navy Japanese Language School, she immediately applied. After her interview, she returned to Texas, resigned from her FBI job, and arrived back in Boulder in time for the July 19 opening.[53] Some women accepted into the program recalled that the commander asked them one question, accepted them, and moved on to his next stop. The one question Hindmarsh asked Marie Edwards was to verify that she had studied Latin (it was her college major). When she answered that she had, he simply replied, "You're in."[54] Kaya Kitagawa saw her chance to "give restitution to the war effort and perhaps shed the 'devastating guilt-feeling' that had plagued her since December 7."[55] She and her friend Mary Louise Hendricks applied, but only Hendricks was accepted. In desperation, Kitagawa applied to become an instructor at the school. The navy accepted her application because of her two years of study at the Soai College in Japan.

The women were housed in three former fraternities at 111 College Avenue, 1005 Broadway, and 1029 Broadway. In July 1943, Betty Knecht wrote to her mother: "We have meals at the Faculty Club, served cafeteria style. We use Navy time: 0800 for 8 a.m. and 2000 for 8 p.m. We have reveille at 0630, breakfast at 0715, rooms ready for inspection at 0800, classes or study until 1200, etc. Our rooms must be kept in prescribed order—beds made taut and with square corners; no loose gear floating around the room; clocks, radios and photographs on top of bureaus; neat bureau drawers; no dresser scarves, no pictures on walls."[56] Had the women first been trained as WAVES and then joined the Japanese-language program, none of this would have been new to them. Instead, the women were sent to Smith College for naval indoctrination only after graduating from the language school.

Unlike the men but similar to women in other American universities in the 1940s, WAVES were closely supervised. Lieutenant (jg) Rebecca Smith, the WAVE officer-in-charge, warned the new students not to be too active the first few days so they could acclimate to the high altitude. Knecht told her mother that some women got swollen feet while others got light-headed. She experienced a nose-bleed. As sympathetic as Lieutenant Smith was at the beginning, she ran a tight ship. She did, though, allow the women to keep photographs of Byron "Whizzer" White, a CU football star, on the walls of the former Phi Delta house. WAVE Abby Jane White had the additional privilege of being housed in the football star's old room.[57] Lieutenant Smith must have also had a soft spot in her heart for dogs because she allowed the WAVES to keep Heidi, a massive Saint Bernard that came with one of the houses. A collie named Nami (Japanese for "wave") was shuttled between the other two houses.

WAVES were enrolled in the same program as the men but were taught in sep-arate classes. Students spent three hours in the classroom and an additional nine hours of study every day, six days a week. They were required to learn 100 new vocabulary terms a day and 500 word usages a week. After the first two weeks of class, no English was spoken in the classroom. Every Saturday, students took a nerve-racking three-hour comprehensive examination on that week's material. Male and female linguistic students "dreaded" those Saturday exams.[58] At the end of each term, students took three more tests followed by a final comprehensive test at the end of fourteen months.[59]

FIGURE 4.5. WAVES Helen Craig, Ann Sheffer, Ruth Halverson, and Barbara Shuey (reading newspaper) were members of the Japanese Language School at the University of Colorado. *Courtesy*, Special Collections and Archives, Norlin Library, University of Colorado Boulder.

A male ensign led mandatory physical exercises for the WAVES. At later reunions, the women remembered the ensign requiring them to perform ship evacuation drills, something the women found ironic since they were restricted to serving in the continental United States and could not even board navy vessels.[60] They usually marched two days a week, four times a week if preparing for visits from naval superiors or for graduation exercises for one of the naval groups at the university (CU also hosted V-12, navy radio, radar, and marine students).

In addition to attending classes every day, studying, and drilling two to four times a week, other aspects of navy life were an adjustment for many of the women. In August, Knecht wrote her mother that the navy had finally come through with their first checks. Hers was for $48; however, they were also simultaneously handed their room and board bills of $75 from CU, payable in advance for both July and August. Later, before making the rank of ensign, the female naval agent's monthly pay was $130, with $53 going for room and board. Getting laundry done was also a problem: "We haven't found anyone to do our laundry, so most of us do our own. The kitchen and the basement are a madhouse on Saturdays. The line begins forming right after exams and continues all day. There aren't enough clotheslines either."[61]

The WAVES and the male linguistics in the Japanese Language School worked hard but also enjoyed hiking, horseback riding, and ice skating. Favorite hiking spots were Green Mountain, Flagstaff, the Flatirons, and Boulder Canyon. Heidi, the Saint Bernard, often joined them on their hikes. She returned so exhausted and stiff that the women had to carry her to her sleeping spot on the stairway landing. WAVES slid down Boulder Glacier and watched the sun rise sitting on a perch on the Flatirons. Irene Slaninka rode horses and toured "a marvelous iris farm."[62] A number of WAVES rode their bicycles out of town to watch newborn calves cavort in the fields. That must have been a novel experience for the women, most of whom were from cities. Mary Lou Siegfried could easily recall the names of many of the "watering holes" and area restaurants the WAVES and other students frequented—Canyon Park, Blanchard's (later the Red Lion), Louisville's Blue Parrot, Nederland's Silver Dollar, and Denver's Buckhorn Exchange.[63] Of course, dating also occurred among the male and female linguistic school students, resulting in several marriages.

In 1944, the name of the program at the University of Colorado was changed to the US Navy Oriental Language School to reflect the expanded curricula that now included Chinese, Malay, and Russian. Following graduation, male students were stationed in Washington, DC, or the Pacific. WAVES were stationed only in the nation's capital, where they worked with captured Japanese documents. Ensign Pearce's team, assigned to the Hydrographic Office, translated sailing directions for the Carolines and Marshall Islands and for Okinawa and Iwo Jima. They also translated captured documents that showed the location of mines and other up-to-date features of various harbors.[64] Ensign Kay Hoeriger, assigned to translate hydrographic records, helped assemble a list of non-naval Japanese shipping.[65]

Avis Pick's job at the Office of Naval Intelligence (ONI) consisted of translating captured aircraft operating manuals. Like other WAVES, she sometimes found the work boring and wondered if her job was truly important to the war effort. At times it seemed that their talents were underused in translating everything from the most prosaic to the most technical.[66] Boredom may have been the reason Barbara Shuey once had a few sheets of "uninteresting translations" fall out of the window at the Communications Annex. Fortunately, the war was already over and rather than imposing the court-martial she was threatened with, Commander Ernst Kroll solved the matter by having the window screen nailed shut.[67]

Boulder-trained WAVES in Washington, DC, consoled themselves with the thought that perhaps some of their work was necessary if only to keep their Japanese-language skills honed for the next stage of war in the Pacific, in which their skills might come into greater play. Many people in and out of the military anticipated that the United States would soon invade the islands of Japan. The dropping of atomic bombs on Hiroshima and Nagasaki ended that speculation. Instead, after concluding their stint in the Naval Reserve, some former

WAVES—including Blanche Belitz, Margaret Dilley, Betty Knecht, and Avis Pick—were hired by the United States Army as civilian translators with the US occupation forces in Japan.[68]

While the Japanese Language School was successful in training linguists, the most unique use of WAVES was as code breakers. In November 1941, cryptic letters were mailed to students at America's top women's colleges. The United States Navy, which had been recruiting male intelligence officers to be cryptographers or code breakers, now enlisted the help of women. Once chosen, the women were mailed manila envelopes with a brief history of codes and ciphers and problems to solve each week. In the late spring of 1942, women who had successfully completed the problems reported to Washington, DC, to begin work.

The military believed women were well suited for code breaking because it was often boring work that required slavish attention to detail. Navy female cryptographers were reluctantly given a leave from their code breaking to attend Officer Candidate School at Smith, Hunter, and Mount Holyoke Colleges before hurriedly being put back to work.

Sworn to secrecy (most women could not bring themselves to utter certain words or tell about their war work decades after that requirement had been lifted), the female code breakers were "instrumental at every stage of the war."[69] They ran complex code-breaking office machines. They compiled libraries of public speeches, shipping inventories, and lists of ship names and commanders to help break messages. As noted, WAVES worked as Japanese translators. A number of predominantly female teams broke major code systems.[70] Women also tested the security of American codes. For a female code breaker, it was gratifying to know that one's efforts were key in cracking codes, intercepting messages, and helping American and Allied forces defeat the enemy. Female intelligence workers developed and instituted fake messages that helped fool the Germans into thinking the Allies' D-Day invasion would occur at Pas-de-Calais rather than at Normandy.[71]

Some code breakers came from the ranks of the WAVES. Ida Mae Olson was a nurse's aide in Denver when her roommate joined the WAVES. Olson, a Colorado native whose family farmed north of Bethune, graduated from Burlington High School. When she decided to follow her college roommate into naval service her mother was upset, believing that only "bad women" joined the service. Olson ignored her mother's objections. When she later came home on leave, her mother proudly took photographs of her daughter in her WAVE uniform.[72] On one visit, Olson brought a friend, Mary Lou. Raised in the city, Mary Lou took off her shoes and ran in the dirt. She was frightened to encounter Native Americans and asked Olson if they were going to attack them.[73] Although some women continued in intelligence work after the war, Olson returned to Colorado where she met and married John E. Brueske.[74]

Like other women serving in the military, WAVES enjoyed their military service and were proud of the work they did for their country. Hazel Marie Hester, who enlisted in Denver in 1943 and experienced no harassment from men—"we were treated very well actually"—"wouldn't have traded that time for a million dollars."[75] WAVE Pauline (Polly) Parish explained, "We all felt, even though I wasn't out there on the firing line, I felt that I was doing something very worthwhile and we were all fighting, and in effect, we felt we were fighting for the world. We felt we were fighting for democracy and we were making our contribution. There was no question about that. I don't think I ran across anyone, man or woman, who didn't feel like they were making a contribution that way. They were fighting for their country and for the other people in this world to have a democratic way of life."[76] As Doris June Rew stated, "It was such an honor to serve."[77]

Service records of many WAVES were destroyed in 1973 when a fire broke out at a National Personnel Records Center. As important a loss as that is, it was an accidental and only a partial "erasure" of WAVES' service. Women who served in the United States Navy still received the GI Bill, veteran status, and recognition. The same cannot be said for the Women Airforce Service Pilots who, after their deactivation in December 1944, were forgotten and their wartime records deliberately sealed and hidden. The record was not rectified for nearly thirty years.

5

Women Airforce Service Pilots

Montrose native Peggy Moynihan, a 1944 graduate of the Women Airforce Service Pilots training program, sat in the cockpit and performed her pre-flight safety checks. Satisfied that she and the BT 13 Vultee trainer were ready to test its repairs, she taxied down the runway. On her climb over Bainbridge, Georgia, the plane flipped into a spin. Soon she was going down faster than she had gone up. Summoning the good Lord upstairs, she popped the stick. Nothing. She popped it a second time. Again, nothing. Still spinning toward the earth, she popped it a third time. Finally, she pulled out of the spin. Finding a safe place, Moynihan held the plane steady as she landed. Unbuckling her harness, she jumped out and began inspecting the basic trainer. Realizing that the air foils were not receiving the correct air flow, she ran her hand along the plane. Bubble gum! A huge wad was stuck on the wing. Removing her gloves, she pried it off. Refusing to dwell on how and why the gum had come to be on the aircraft, Moynihan lifted off and completed the test flight. Without its added "decoration," the Vultee flew fine.[1]

In the late 1930s, the US government sponsored the Civilian Pilot Training (CPT) Program in an effort to draw young college-age men and women into flying and to help struggling flight schools. The forty dollar registration fee paid for on-ground and in-air instruction. Beginning in 1941, as the storm clouds of the war in Europe drifted menacingly closer to the United States, women were no longer accepted into the program. Slots were reserved for men who could become military pilots should the need arise. In response to this exclusion, the Women

FIGURE 5.1. WASPs stationed at Bainbridge Army Air Field, Georgia, ferried AT-6s and BT-13s. Colorado natives Peggy Moynihan and Jane Dyde are standing fourth and fifth from the left, respectively. *Courtesy*, WASP Archive, Texas Woman's University, Denton.

Flyers of America (WFA) recruited women to their training program at the cost of $275 per woman. Its membership exploded by 900 percent in 1941.[2]

In 1940, Jacqueline Cochran, considered the best female pilot in the United States, suggested to First Lady Eleanor Roosevelt that the army air force establish a women's flying division.[3] She believed qualified female pilots could fly domestic, non-combat assignments to release more male pilots for combat duty. She also wrote a letter to Lieutenant Colonel Robert Olds, who was organizing the Air Corps Ferrying Command. Lieutenant General Henry H. "Hap" Arnold, chief of the Army Air Corps, suggested that Cochran take a group of American women pilots to England to see how their program of using female pilots was working. A quarter of the British Air Transport Auxiliary (ATA) pilots were women who ferried planes from manufacturers to the armed services. In 1942, Cochran took twenty-five American female pilots to join the ATA.

The first lady continued to advocate for the use of female pilots. In her September 1, 1942, column "My Day," Roosevelt, who had observed the work of women fliers in England, wrote: "It seems to me that in the Civil Air Patrol and in our own ferry command, women, if they can pass the tests imposed upon men, should have an equal opportunity for non-combat service . . . We are in a war and we need to fight it with all our ability and every weapon possible. Women pilots, in this particular case, are a weapon waiting to be used."[4] It was not long before others agreed with her.

While Cochran was in England, Lieutenant General Arnold authorized the formation of the Women's Auxiliary Ferrying Squadron (WAFS) under the direction of Nancy Harkness Love.[5] WAFS began training at New Castle Army Air Base (Delaware) in October 1942. To be eligible, a female pilot was required to have 500 pilot hours, be between the ages of twenty-one and thirty-five, be at least 5 feet 2 inches tall, be a high school graduate or equivalent, and hold a horsepower (HP) rating of 200. Thirty women passed the flight test and the army flight physical and were accepted into the program. As they began their thirty-day army indoctrination program, Love presented the WAFS uniform. Significantly, it mirrored that of military pilots. The jacket was short so as not to interfere with the wearing of a parachute. WAFs were required to wear their uniforms while on ferry duty or at their station. Khaki flight coveralls, a parachute, goggles, white silk AAF scarf, and leather jackets with the Air Transport Command (ATC) patch were worn when flying.[6]

The WAFS' objective was to ferry military airplanes. After flight checks, these highly qualified pilots immediately began repositioning military airplanes. Cornelia Fort earned her pilot's license after she graduated from Sarah Lawrence College. She worked as a flight instructor for Massey and Rawson Flying Service in Fort Collins before moving to Hawaii, where she taught flying at John Rodgers Airport outside Honolulu. On December 7, 1941, she was in the air over Pearl Harbor with a male student when they were suddenly in the midst of the Japanese attack. Grabbing the controls, she quickly landed the airplane. As she and her student ran away, the plane was riddled with bullets. Following the attack, all civilian flying was canceled; Fort returned to the mainland where she received a telegram from Love, inviting her to join the WAFS. In September 1942, she was the second woman to report.[7]

On March 21, 1943, Fort was one of seven pilots ferrying BT-13As to Dallas Love Field when her airplane and one piloted by Frank E. Stamme were involved in a midair collision. His landing gear apparently struck the left wing of Fort's airplane, causing part of it to break off. Fort did not attempt to right her airplane or open the hatch to parachute out, an indication that she was either knocked unconscious or killed instantly. She and her plane plummeted to the earth. With over 1,100 flying hours, the twenty-five-year-old pilot became America's first woman to die while on war duty.[8] Only one month earlier, Fort had written to her mother about the danger of flying: "If I die violently, who can say it was 'before my time'? I should have dearly loved to have had a husband and children. My talents in that line would have been pretty good, but if that is not to be, I want no one to grieve for me. I was happiest in the sky—at dawn when the quietness of the air was like a caress, when the noon sun beat down and at dusk when the sky was drenched with fading light."[9]

Once Cochran learned of the formation of the WAFS, she returned from England convinced that women could do more than ferry planes. She earnestly lobbied Arnold, who approved the formation of the Women's Ferrying Training Detachment (WFTD). Most requirements for the first class, Class 43-W-1, were similar to those for WAFS except that the number of pilot hours required was significantly lower.[10] The original 200 hours were progressively lowered until the number was only 35 hours by August 1943. Similarly, the minimum age requirement was lowered to eighteen years and six months.

By 1943, the two distinct women's divisions were deemed superfluous, and they merged into the Women Airforce Service Pilots (WASP), with Cochran as director. Love remained in command of ferrying pilots. Although the women received the same training as male cadets, there were a number of inequities. A man's transportation to flight school and his room and board were supplied at no expense; a woman paid all her own travel expenses and was charged $1.65 a day for room and board during training. After graduation, male lieutenants and captains received a base pay of $150 to $200 per month, a per diem of $7, $45 for quarters, and a uniform allowance of $200. Women received a base pay of $150 per month during training and $250 per month after graduation. But they were given no uniform allowance and no flight pay, and they had to pay between $15 and $20 a month for BOQ (Bachelor Officers Quarters) if it was available. Otherwise, they paid for civilian housing, which was scarce and expensive during the war.[11] Uniforms and $10,000 in insurance were provided to the men. Insurance companies cancelled personal policies held by women. Death benefits were perhaps the cruelest of the inequities. The body of a male cadet was escorted home and given a military funeral with a US flag on the coffin, and the family was authorized to display a Gold Star. For Cornelia Fort and the other thirty-seven women killed while serving as a WAF or a WASP, there was no military escort, death benefits, or American flag draped on the coffin. Usually, the woman's family paid to have her body shipped home. In a number of instances, other WASPs donated money for expenses. WASPs' survivors had no right to display the Gold Star. Elizabeth "Kit" MacKethan was stationed at Georgia's Cochran Field flying advanced trainers when she learned that her classmate Marie Mitchell Robinson died after her B-25 crashed. During training at Sweetwater, the two women had promised each other that if one of them died, the other would be with the deceased woman's mother. While waiting to fly to Robinson's memorial service in Michigan, MacKethan penned "Celestial Flight," a poem that was quoted at later WASP services and burials.[12]

Cochran actively recruited female pilots for her first class, sending telegrams to women asking if they were interested. She also relied on word-of-mouth recruitment and news articles. Women earned pilot's licenses at local airports or through the CPT. Some women took flying lessons secretly because their parents did not approve. Mary Elizabeth Trebing, 43-W-4, learned to fly and earned her ratings in Wilburn, Oklahoma. She had been flying for six months before her parents found out.[13] Betty Haas was a freshman at Bennington College when she attended an

FIGURE 5.2. Colorado native Anna Mae Petteys was a test pilot assigned to Garden City Army Air Base (Kansas). *Courtesy*, WASP Archive, Texas Woman's University, Denton.

aerial show during Parents' Weekend. For a dollar, one could take a ride, but her parents did not approve. Haas obligingly demurred. However, after her parents left, she and a friend squeezed into the plane's front seat for a ride. She was "smitten." She made a deal with her father that she would stay in school and earn good grades if he paid for flying lessons. In her senior year, she received a telegram from Cochran inviting her to apply to the WASP. Thrilled, she persuaded Bennington to allow her to graduate early with her marine biology degree. In the meantime, Haas's brother had joined the navy as a pilot. While Haas was in training, he was killed on a takeoff from an aircraft carrier. Undeterred, Betty Haas graduated with Class 43-W-5.[14]

Sadly, Colorado native Anna Mae Petteys had a similar experience. She learned to fly while a student at Stanford University. Her younger brother also attained a pilot's license. After earning a bachelor's degree, Petteys attended the University of Denver for a master's in social work. At Denver's Combs Field she earned her pilot's license and entered the WASP program. Her younger brother was a navy flying instructor in Phoenix when he was killed in an airplane crash. Like Haas, Petteys took some time off from training before graduating with the second class in 1944.[15]

Millicent (Millie) Peterson, like Betty Haas, circumvented her parents in her quest to fly. As a six-year-old, she fell in love with airplanes when a pilot flew in to see her neighbors. When she was old enough she began taking flying lessons, but the instructor would not let her fly solo. With money saved from farming wheat, she told her parents she was going to Denver to buy clothes for college. Instead, she boarded the bus and yelled out to her mother, "I'm going to learn to fly." When her mother arrived home, her father asked where Millie was because he had a chore for her. Her mother said, "Well, she's gone to learn to fly." Her dad replied, "Well, I'll be damned."[16] Nobody discussed it after that.

Lucile Doll, who had dropped out of college and gotten a job in Wichita, Kansas, had a friend who took her up in his Piper Cub and showed her how to operate the controls. She was hooked. Her first lesson was on December 6, 1941. Although she "never expected to do a thing with it" except fly for her own enjoyment, when the WASP lowered the requirement to thirty-five flying hours, she applied and was accepted.[17]

While some parents were hesitant to have their daughters take flying lessons before the war and apply to the WASP program, other parents suggested the program to them. Dori Marie Jugle, who had changed her surname to Marland (her father's middle name) for her acting career, wanted to donate blood for the war effort but was told she was too young. When her father told her about the WASP program, she thought, "This is perfect." She took flying lessons, built up her hours, applied, and, after an interview in Denver, was accepted.[18] For Jane Dyde, her mother was her motivation. Marguerite, the wife of University of Colorado (CU) professor W. Farrell Dyde, heard about the WASP program while her daughter was a student at CU: "I always say mother pushed me into the cockpit because she said that sounds like it would be kind of exciting, would you like that? And I said I'd love it."[19] Dyde took ground school and flying lessons at a nearby airport.

The first three classes of female pilots trained at the municipal airport in Houston, Texas. Bad weather and crowded skies forced Cochran to move future classes to Avenger Field in Sweetwater, Texas. More than 25,000 women applied to the program; 1,830 were selected. They came from all over the United States, from large cities, small towns, and farms; from all socioeconomic groups; and representing the full spectrum of religious and social values. But attired in men's baggy coveralls, covered in sweat in the Link Trainer, swathed in Urban's turbans (named after base commander Major Roger Urban), or freezing in open cockpits, the women all looked the same.[20] Despite their differences, they were united in their love of flying and their desire to help win the war.

During 1943 and 1944, WASP trainees lived at Avenger Field in wooden barracks in rooms called bays. Each bay contained six army cots, six lockers, two study tables, and six chairs. Adjacent to the bay was a latrine, with two showers, two sinks, two commodes, and a connecting door that opened into an identical bay. Because of the high temperatures in Sweetwater, women were given permission to sleep outside in the summers. As Gayle Snell wrote, "Never having been away from home, except for girl scout camp, living with five other women in a bay was certainly a new experience. It seems we all had to fight everything at Avenger, except each other. There were windstorms, dust storms, eternal heat,

FIGURE 5.3. WASP trainees pose in men's overalls, which they called "zoot suits." A number of WASPs experienced scary moments because of their immense sizes. Doris Bristol is third from the left. *Courtesy,* Julie Tracy Geiser.

snakes (yikes!), trying to live through our instructor's swearing and yelling, food that was never worth the march to the mess hall (except when VIPS were on the field). . . ."[21] The ubiquitous wind and sand are also evident in the WASP motto: "We live in the wind and the sand, and our eyes are on the stars."

The lack of a proper and functional training uniform nearly proved fatal. With no female flight suits available, trainees were issued used mechanics' coveralls sizes 42 to 48. These were gigantic on the women and caused some frightening moments in the air. One day Lucile Doll was practicing solo spins. Just before she put her airplane into its first spin, she glanced down and discovered that her belt buckle was undone. In an open cockpit plane, she would have been unceremoniously dumped out of the airplane. Not believing she would have omitted that number one pre-flight safety check, Doll figures that the sleeve on her large coverall may have caught the buckle and opened it.[22] Gerry Ashwell remembered pulling her aircraft out of a diving spin and realizing just in time that the stick was caught in her flight suit.[23]

Trainees received the same arduous twenty-three-week flight training instruction as male cadets training at other air fields. WASPs also drilled and performed calisthenics. Unlike the sometimes dubious reasoning behind requiring servicewomen to perform certain aspects of physical training, pushups and other exercises to increase a woman's upper body strength were necessary as women progressed to piloting larger aircraft. And they marched—everywhere. A typical training day began at 6:15 a.m. with bugles and bells followed by breakfast. Women flew between 2 and 2½ hours every morning. After lunch they attended ground school, taking classes in navigation, flight training, aerodynamics, electronics, mathematics, weather, communications, meteorology, Morse code, military law, and aircraft mechanics. By the time Mary Trebing was in Emergency Equipment class, she was nearly finished with ground school and ready to take an acceptance check ride, a necessary test before going on cross-country trips. Drill and calisthenics were held before supper, at 6:30 p.m. Trainees studied for 2 hours before "Taps" at 10:00 p.m.[24]

Women transitioned from flying primary trainers (PT-19s and PT-13s) to basic trainers (BTs) to advanced trainers (AT-6s). The primary phase concentrated on fundamental flying skills. Prior to flying basic trainers, a woman had to complete thirty hours of Link training work. The original Link Trainer was developed in 1929 by Edwin Albert Link as a safe way to teach new pilots how to fly by instrument flight rules. During World War II this Basic Instrument Trainer, known to 500,000 fledging US pilots as the Blue Box, was standard equipment at every air training school in the United States, including Avenger Field. Every WASP trainee was required to pass the Link Trainer course before she could move out of the instrument phase of flight training and into the advanced phase. The Link Trainer simulated cockpit conditions and flight patterns as it responded to a pilot's maneuvering. Seated inside the dark box, a student kept an eye on compasses, a clock, turn indicators, a gyro, an artificial horizon, and an altimeter. A student had to keep all the instruments in proper alignment to execute the required turns or movements. It was difficult to rely on instruments rather than on the student's own sense of balance. This was made even more arduous by suffocating temperatures inside the Blue Box. For that reason, Gerry Ashwell hated it.[25] The next step of instrument flying was to fly a plane "under the hood" with a flight instructor acting as the Link operator had on the ground. The trainee could not see out of the cockpit while under the hood. The instructor gave the student pilot commands to perform a particular move by following the indication on the cockpit instruments.

One-third of the women washed out for flying deficiencies, about the same percentage as male students. Doll believed some students failed not because they were poor pilots but because the course was so concentrated that they were forced to transition too quickly from one type of airplane to another. Check rides were stressful because they could mean the end of her training if a woman failed.[26] As was the case in industry for a "Rosie the Riveter," some male instructors made coursework and flying lessons even more punishing. One instructor was particularly beastly. He habitually shoved the control stick back and forth, bruising the knees of his female students. He swore, screamed, and yelled. He tried to convince Ann Craft and other trainees that they had no chance of graduating. However, either because of his strictness or because his students stubbornly refused to prove him right, all of his students graduated.[27]

WASP classes quickly adopted a mascot. Walt Disney had created a gremlin named Fifinella for a proposed film of Roald Dahl's book *The Gremlins*. The movie was never made. The WASP asked permission to use the image as its official mascot. Fifinella, or "Fifi," adorned WASP leather patches. The recruits also created traditions that eased the stress of flight school and celebrated student successes. When a woman was called for a check ride in primary, basic, or advanced training, she first tossed a coin into the fountain on base. The first trainee to solo in each of the three phases was ceremoniously dunked or voluntarily jumped into the wishing well.

Official WASP uniforms were not available for the first two classes. In the summer of 1943, an official uniform was revealed. After a woman graduated, ill-fitting "zoot suits" were replaced with the official WASP Santiago Blue flying uniform. Like the WAF uniform, it, too, included a short—or Eisenhower—jacket. Mindful of her pilots' image, Cochran had the uniform created by fashion designers at Bergdorf Goodman in New York, receiving Generals "Hap" Arnold's and George C. Marshall's approval. Graduates purchased tan slacks, known as "General's Pants," and a white blouse for graduation exercises at which they were expected to "pass in review" before visiting generals and other dignitaries. When Director Cochran attended graduation ceremonies, she pinned silver wings on the graduates.

Graduation Day was a proud moment for the women. Cornelia Fort perhaps best described the pride and sense of achievement a WAF or a WASP felt:

> For all the girls in the WAFS, I think the most concrete moment of happiness came at our first review. Suddenly and for the first time we felt a part of something larger. Because of our uniforms, which we had earned, we were marching with the men, marching with all the freedom loving people in the world . . . I, for one, am profoundly grateful that my one talent, my only knowledge, flying, happens to be of use to my country when it is needed. That's all the luck I ever hope to have.[28]

From Avenger Field, women were assigned to one of 120 bases at the behest of the Army Air Corps. Three of the bases—La Junta Army Air Field, Pueblo Army

Air Base, and Peterson Army Air Base—were in Colorado. Three WASPs served in La Junta, nine in Pueblo, and twenty-one in Colorado Springs. One of the women's jobs was to ferry aircraft from one place in the United States to another. Colorado native Marion Carlstrom was the state's first WASP. While an exchange student at the University of San Marcos (Lima, Peru), she became only the second woman in the country to earn a pilot's license. When she heard about the formation of the Women Airforce Service Pilots, she returned to the United States to apply.[29] Carlstrom had the pleasure of ferrying a P-51 Mustang from Texas to Newark, New Jersey, where it was scheduled to be sent on to England. Betty Haas enjoyed the opportunity to fly all kinds of planes: "One day it would be a little one, the next day it would be a big one. I was able to fly a B-17 and that was really exciting for a 21-year-old."[30] Coloradans Jane Dyde and Peggy Moynihan were stationed at Bainbridge Army Air Field in Georgia. Pilots received notices from headquarters to ferry several AT-6s and BT-13s from their home field to some other site. Once the pilots delivered their aircraft, a C-47 flew them back to Bainbridge. On one ferrying assignment, Dyde got lost while flying over Norfolk, Virginia, home to several navy bases. Without a number to call in, she simply landed at one of them: "A guy came running out and jumped up on the wing and, you know, looked at me. I took off my helmet and that's when he said, 'Jesus Christ, it's a broad.'"[31]

Ferrying could be a dangerous job. In November 1943, Mary Elizabeth Trebing was sent to Oklahoma City to ferry a PT-19 back to Love Field. Her plane ran into difficulties near Blanchard, Oklahoma. Heavily forested, there were few open fields to land her plane. To get to a clearing, she had to fly over a farmhouse and then immediately under high-tension electric lines. She cleared the house, but the vertical stabilizer of the plane caught on the high wires and nosed her PT-19 into the ground, killing her instantly. That same day her brother Bill Trebing, also a pilot, was in Utah awaiting his assignment to a crew. A friend called him to report the happy news that his wife had given birth to their first child, a daughter. He then plunged Bill into despair with the news that Mary had been killed. Accompanied by a WASP escort, Trebing's body was carried by train to Louisville, Colorado, where she had attended elementary school.[32]

Towing targets for gunnery training was one of the more unique assignments. WASPs—Kathryn Stark, Millicent Peterson, Dori Marland, Betty Clark, and others—flew a B-25 or an AT-6 with a target attached to its tail. Lois Lancaster Nash, 43-W-8, towed targets at the Pueblo Army Air Base during World War II. A target was towed approximately 150 feet away from the tail of the plane. On the ground, gunnery students fired as the plane and target passed by. Bullets were coated different colors—red, blue, green, and so on. In this manner, instructors could tell from the color of the bullet hole which gunner had struck which part of the target. Sometimes the aircraft itself was hit. In fact, two WASPs were killed flying target planes.[33]

FIGURE 5.4. Stationed at Pueblo Army Air Base were front (*left to right*): Esther Mueller (443-W-8), Lois Nash (43-W-8), and Moya Mitchell (43-W-6). In the back (*left to right*) are Elvira Griggs (43-W-7), Mary Gresham (43-W-7), and Florence Niemiec (43-W-6). *Courtesy*, WASP Archive, Texas Woman's University, Denton.

Many WASPs were assigned to several bases and performed several different duties. Anna Hopkins and Ruth Humphreys towed targets for live gunnery practice but also trained bombardiers. This entailed flying an AT-11 or similar aircraft to a fixed altitude and then turning it over to bombardier cadets for simulated bomb runs. Having WASPs fly the "practice" airplane allowed more male combat pilots to be deployed overseas on bombing runs.

Female pilots tested aircraft that were new, that pilots complained about, or that had been damaged and then repaired. Because male instructors and students at army air bases were forbidden to fly airplanes that came out of the maintenance hangar until they were flight tested and approved, WASP pilots flew the test flights. As Betty Haas explained, "We were expendable and the men were not."[34] Anna

Mae Petteys's family thought her assignment as a test pilot was funny "because they thought I couldn't be that practical." When a squadron at Garden City turned in a plane that had something wrong, it was Petteys's job to fly the plane and determine what was required to get it right. Then she flew the plane again before it was returned to the squadron.[35] Gerry Ashwell, assigned to Minter Field (California), flew a number of planes, but the Cessna UC-78 Bobcat made quite an impression on her: "That was a terrible plane. It was made out of tissue paper and toilet paper." Actually constructed of lightweight wood in the fuselage and wings, the plane was dubbed the "Bamboo Bomber." This "no-good plane" was a twin-engine light personnel transport and advanced trainer. Ashwell was also not fond of the Lockheed UT-76 that she dubbed "no good." But the WASPs "were pretty smart." As Ashwell explained, a WASP "would ask the mechanic who repaired it to fly with us and if he said he was too busy, we'd say, 'Well, you know, we'll just wait until you have time to go up with us.' Because we figured he wasn't about to fly in any plane that he didn't think was safe for him."[36]

In this way, most WASPs were able to avoid some of the scary experiences that jolted pilots. However, not all WASPs were able to command such obedience from mechanics. Haas noted that a few mechanics sabotaged aircraft by putting sugar in the tanks, which would plug up the engine. While she admitted that the sabotage did not occur on a grand scale, it "was enough to scare the heck out of you."[37] In the case of Betty Taylor Wood, it was more than scary; it resulted in her death. Author Marianne Verges reported that Cochran found enough sugar in Wood's airplane to stop an engine in no time. Not wanting to jeopardize her program, Cochran did not go public with her discovery.[38]

Other pilots experienced fatal or near-death flights. Peggy Moynihan's "bubble gum incident" nearly cost her her life, but she also had a close call ferrying a DC-3 from Florida to a northern base. She ran out of fuel—the gauge was broken—and had to make a forced landing.[39] Gayle Snell experienced a similar problem. On a flight from Independence Army Air Base (Kansas), her BT-14 engine quit over the mountainous terrain near Tucson, Arizona. Snell successfully crash-landed and hiked to a nearby ranch, where she waited until someone from the Army Air Corps could send a staff car to pick her up.[40]

Misogynistic instructors, sabotaging mechanics, and flight mishaps did nothing to lessen WASPs' love of flying. Jane Dunbar, Class 44-W-4, described the beauty to be found among the clouds: "The sun was shining on the tops of the clouds and the sky was so blue up there it took my breath away. Now and then our wingtips would disappear in whiteness but the sky was smooth and even the engine seemed quite quiet. I guess it's times like this the angels sing." But not all flights were so angelic. On one particular flight, Dunbar was piloting an AT-6 aircraft to Craig Army Air Field in Selma, Alabama, when she flew into a horrendous thunderstorm upon her approach. She asked for permission to land but heard no reply on her radio. Those in the control tower did not see her through the driving rain until she was nearly on the ground. They told her proceed to another airstrip 10 miles away. Knowing that the storm was even worse ahead of her, she landed at Craig Field without permission. It turned out to be the right decision.[41]

Fortunately, most flights were uneventful. Doris Bristol flew engineering test flights out of Columbus Army Air Base (Mississippi) before her transfer to Casper, Wyoming, as the only WASP assigned to the base. She co-piloted B-24s and flew administrative flights in the C-45. She flew to Cheyenne several times to pick up United Service Organizations (USO) shows.[42] Because of her skills, Pueblo native Ann Brothers was a test pilot for prototype aircraft out of Garden City Army Air Base (Kansas). In 1941, Brothers started flying with the Civilian Pilot Training Program and served as first lieutenant of the Pueblo Civil Air Patrol. A graduate of Colorado State College of Education, she taught in her hometown for many years before joining the WASP.[43]

The last kind of assignment was personnel flying. WASPs flew officers to different duty stations to check out bases, facilities, programs, and personnel. Patricia Seares, 43-W-7, was one of the first seven WASPs assigned to Hamilton Field (California). Their primary job was to fly Headquarters Fourth Air Force personnel to various locations around the West Coast. As was often the case, there were no barracks for the female pilots, so they were housed with WAC officers. Like Bristol in Casper, Ann Craft was the only WASP sent to Randolph Field (Texas). "Randolph was a very difficult assignment. They didn't want any girls there. I think I was sent there because I was a very easygoing person. I was a smooth pilot and had never had an accident." She could not live in the barracks because WASPs were civilians, so she roomed with two women who worked at the base.[44]

Lucile Doll loved flying for the Weather Bureau. After spending her first six weeks with the army air force Weather Service in Asheville, North Carolina, she was transferred to the regional office in Kansas City. She flew weather officers to inspection sites and meetings. In essence, she was a corporate pilot. The seven-state area included plenty of weather stations that needed be inspected. Doll replaced a male pilot in Kansas City who made a big deal out of assessing her flying skills before he left. At first, the Weather Bureau officers were skeptical since they had never flown with a woman pilot. They soon realized that Doll and the others were serious and not just seeking glamour. In fact, like all the other assignments, it was not a glamorous job. It was hard work. Doll originally flew Cessna UC-78s and later the larger Beechcraft C-45, which held about ten passengers.[45]

In Kansas City, the bureau's office was in town, so Doll lived in an apartment. Although she would have preferred living on the base, she did not complain because she received plenty of flying time. The weather officers "couldn't have been nicer." Flights usually left on Monday and returned on Friday, leaving Doll the weekend to do as she pleased. She often spent it recovering from the trip.

FIGURE 5.5. Lucile Doll (43-W-7) in front of the Cessna UC-78 she flew to Sioux Falls Army Air Base (South Dakota) in September 1944. With her are two weather officers she transported. *Courtesy*, WASP Archive, Texas Woman's University, Denton.

While she was traveling Doll was usually given a room in the nurses' quarters on a base, but once in awhile she stayed in a hotel in town. In those circumstances, she had to pay for her room. WASPs were only paid six dollars a day for travel expenses, and rooms often cost that much a night. On one trip there were only male nurses on base and no hotel in town. The Weather Bureau put her in a hospital room for the night.[46]

Female pilots, unlike women in the United States Nurse Corps, Army, Navy, Coast Guard, and Marines, were not military personnel but rather civilian employees. The original plan had been to militarize the WASP, but that took an act of Congress. With the overwhelming demand for pilots in 1942, the Army Air Corps could not wait for that to happen. By the time a bill to militarize the WASP was introduced into the US Congress in June 1944, the need for pilots had decreased. After a long and bitter fight, the measure failed. For women in the Classes 44-W-9 and 44-W-10, deactivation was a tremendous blow. Jean Harman, 44-W-9, had only been flying on active duty for two months when the ax fell: "We were all broken-hearted."[47] General "Hap" Arnold spoke at the final graduation on December 7, 1944:

You and more than 900 of your sisters have shown that you can fly wingtip
to wingtip with your brothers. If there ever was any doubt in anyone's
mind that women can become skillful pilots, the WASP have dispelled that
doubt. I want to stress how valuable I believe the whole WASP program
has been for our country. We . . . know that you can handle our latest
fighters, our heaviest bombers; . . . that you are capable of ferrying, target
towing, flying training, test flying, and the countless other activities which
you have proved you can do. So, on this last graduation day, I salute you
and all WASP. We of the Army Air Force are proud of you, we will never
forget our debt to you.[48]

In a letter to WASPs, he acknowledged their accomplishments. However, "The
war situation has changed and the time has come when your volunteered services
are no longer needed. The situation is that if you continue in service, you will be
replacing instead of releasing our young men. I know that the WASP wouldn't
want that. So I have directed that the WASP program be inactivated and all WASP
be released on 20 December 1944."[49]

Ultimately, 1,102 women flew 60 million miles for the paramilitary WASP and
the United States Army Air Force (USAAF). They delivered 12,650 aircraft representing 78 different types. They flew every aircraft in the USAAF inventory including the P-51 Mustang and the B-17 and B-29 bombers. They towed targets for cadet
fighter training, transported military personnel and cargo, and flew engineering
test flights. They flight-tested repaired aircraft; they worked as flight instructors
in aircraft or Link Trainers/simulators. Accident and fatality rates for female and
male pilots were the same. Thirty-eight women were killed in the course of duty.[50]

After deactivation on December 20, 1944, women pilots scattered like so many
birds rustled out of the trees. Some WASPs joined other activities to support
the war effort while others tried to find other aviation work. Many faded into
the background with their service untold, even to family members. While other
female servicewomen were remembered and extolled, the WASP "experiment"
was shoved aside, records were sealed, and their story was buried and forgotten
by the US government and public. Then in the 1970s, the navy and the air force
announced that they were going to start training women to fly military aircraft.
The United States Air Force Academy (USAFA) in Colorado Springs announced
that the incoming class of 1976 would include the *first women ever* to be trained
to fly military aircraft.

One could have heard the WASPs' outrage over the noise of a supersonic
jet. Former WASPs organized and lobbied for their rightful recognition. Lucile
Doll Wise, living in Washington, DC, at the time, volunteered to work at WASP
headquarters. Bruce Arnold, son of General "Hap" Arnold, and Senator Barry
Goldwater, a former ferry pilot himself, helped tremendously in this battle.

Initially, most committee members were opposed to the measure, but favorable testimonies eventually swayed enough members of congress. As is sometimes the case, the bill was attached to another and was passed in the fall of 1977 with the pound of a gavel. There was no recorded vote, which meant that members of Congress could avoid culpability—as well as praise—for the measure's passage.[51] President Jimmy Carter signed the bill into law "Officially declaring the Women Airforce Service Pilots as having served on active duty in the Armed Forces of the United States for purposes of laws administered by the Veterans Administration." In 1979, the Department of the Air Force authorized and began issuing honorable discharges to WASPs who served during World War II. On March 10, 2010, WASPs were awarded the Congressional Gold Medal. At the White House ceremony, ten Colorado WASPs were presented with their medals: Betty Ashwell Lotowycz (who was known as Gerry Ashwell when she was a WASP), Doris Bristol Tracy, Ann Craft Moss, Lucile Doll Wise, Elizabeth Haas Pfister, Ruth Humphreys Brown, Josephine Kater Robinson, Peggy Moynihan McCaffrey, Millicent Peterson Young, and Kathryn Stark Gunderson.[52] Having experienced the heights of flying, the depths of deactivation, and the abyss of being ignored and forgotten by the country for which they so bravely served, WAFs and WASPs finally received their due recognition.

Nurses, soldiers, naval reservists, and pilots. Serving on land, on sea, and in the air, over 300,000 women proved themselves to be invaluable partners in America's fight to win the war. Joining them in the war effort were smaller but equally important numbers of women—those in the United States Coast Guard, Merchant Marines, and Marine Corps.

6

Women of the Coast Guard, the Merchant Marine Corps, and the Marine Corps Women's Reserve

WOMEN OF THE COAST GUARD

A self-described "dry-land westerner," United States Coast Guard Women's Reserve (SPAR) Ensign Jane Silverstein rose from her desk to take a much-needed break. She walked over to the bay of windows and marveled—as she did every day—at the view below her. Glinting in the sun were Governor's Island, the Statue of Liberty, Ellis Island, and the Hudson and East Rivers. After a few moments of reflection, Silverstein returned to the mounds of paper on her desk. Picking up the list of vessels and escorts containing the in-bound convoys sailing to New York City, she created a schedule of their arrivals. She assigned each vessel a secret identification signal that had to be flashed or hoisted when carrying out recognition procedure. Completing her chart, she added berthing and anchoring instructions for each vessel. Her last task was to send all the information to the pilot boat stationed at the seaward end of the entrance to New York Harbor. Her task done for the day, she thought how very "shippey" the work was compared to her earlier assignment as a SPAR. It was also decidedly different from her pre-war job as a landscape architect.[1]

The United States Coast Guard (USCG) had the fewest women enlisted of any branch of the US military during World War II—10,000 volunteers and 1,000 officers—but it was also the only branch that trained its female officers at its own military academy. Missouri native Dorothy C. Stratton took a leave of absence from her position as full professor and dean of women at Purdue University to

DOI: 10.5876/9781646420339.c006

enter the armed forces as a senior lieutenant in the WAVES. After completing her training at Smith College, she was assigned as assistant to the commanding officer at the radio school for enlisted WAVES in Madison, Wisconsin. On November 23, 1942, the US Congress passed legislation creating the Coast Guard Women's Reserve. Stratton was tapped as its new leader. With the transfer to the USCG, she was promoted to the rank of lieutenant commander and then captain. One of her first contributions to the USCG was creating the name SPAR for the Women's Reserve from the guard's motto "Semper Paratus" ("Always Ready"). In her memo to the commandant, Vice Admiral Russell Waesche, she explained, "As I understand it, a spar is . . . a supporting beam and that is what we hope each member of the Women's Reserve will be."[2] Lieutenant Commander Stratton brought along a number of WAVE officers to form the nucleus of the newly created SPAR.

To build a cadre of officers, letters were sent to thirteen civilians. Elizabeth Barmes had attended Purdue University. Her telegram informed her that if she qualified, she would receive a commission in the United States Coast Guard. Out of college for two years, she was working as a Girl Scout field agent when she accepted the invitation. In Detroit, she was sworn in and sent to the Coast Guard Academy in New London, Connecticut, for three weeks of officer training. There, they were "giving it to us as fast as they could, trying to make military people out of us." Marching practice was "pretty funny" because there were "an awful lot of people who had two left feet."[3] Officers received the same specialized training as would future recruits but also took leadership courses to prepare them for their supervisory roles. After training, the newly commissioned SPAR officers were sent back to the general geographic area of the United States from which they came to enlist women.

In the Detroit area, Barmes spoke to Rotary Clubs, women's groups, and schools. Male and female coast guard recruiters often spoke to the same groups and attended events together. Once when Barmes and a male recruiter were driving to a ship launching, the car's clutch suddenly stopped working. He looked under the car and saw that a cotter pin had worn out. They looked around for it on the ground or for a nail to use in its place. Unable to find either, he asked her if she had a bobby pin. Of course she did. After all, female Coast Guard members were "Always Ready." He replaced the cotter pin with her bobby pin and bent in the ends. With the problem fixed, they drove off, arriving in time for the ship launching.[4]

The basic general requirements for all candidates for SPAR were the same as those for WAVES and the United States Marine Corps. The SPAR application was fairly standard. It asked the usual biographical information—birth date and place, address, marital status, arrest record, education, leadership and extra-curricular activities, and special qualifications. Under "Vocational Record," an applicant listed her jobs, titles, earnings, and employers. The last page asked the applicant to check the civilian fields in which she had experience. A sampling of the listed fields included typist, radio repair, clerk, accounting, dental technician, photographic developer, hand welding, baker, messenger, telegraph operator, and IBM machine operator. Barbara Kipper of Ordway was accepted into SPAR as an accountant, in part because of her two years of college and experience working in an abstract office.[5]

An applicant took an aptitude test consisting of questions on antonyms, word definitions, mathematics, and coding. She underwent a physical examination of her vision, hearing, teeth, and general build and appearance. Pulse and blood pressure were taken. The back of the one-page physical questionnaire asked the applicant to indicate if she had ever had any of thirty symptoms or medical issues. These included asthma or hay fever, headaches, lung trouble, venereal disease, broken bones, or needing to wear glasses. Originally, a woman was disqualified if she needed eyeglasses.[6]

Women from all over Colorado enlisted in the coast guard. Effie Irene Graham, Marjorie Davis, Bernice Irene Graham, and Ruth Alene Sheppard of Fort Morgan all joined SPAR in its first twelve months. Later, Yeomen third class June Scheckler and Harriet Miller from the Denver recruiting station were sent to Sedgwick County in the far northeastern corner of the state. They met with and administered aptitude tests to potential enlistees at the Julesburg Post Office. To complete the application process, enlistees reported to Room 20 in the Denver office at 625 18th Street.[7] The following month, Yeoman Miller was sent to Alamosa to recruit.[8] Recruiters also crossed the Continental Divide into Routt County. In February 1943, Lieutenant (jg) Dorothy M. Davis, Ensign Grace M. Reineman, and Yeoman third class Bessie Mai Allen attended women's club meetings and an assembly of female students at Mesa Junior College.[9] Aiding in the recruitment process was a modification in WAVES and SPAR vision requirements. Women with less than 20-20 vision were eligible as long as their deficiency was not the result of a disease. The services realized that "wearing glasses does not seriously impair a woman's efficiency in releasing a man to fight at sea."[10]

Recruiters also reached large audiences at war bond rallies and civic activities. Elizabeth "Betty" Jane Marr, born in Craig, enlisted in the USCG in 1943. After basic training, she was sent to Stillwater, Oklahoma, for additional schooling before being assigned to a recruiting station in Long Beach, California. While on the West Coast, she participated in a radio broadcast "Furlough Fun" with singer Rudy Vallee and the Coast Guard Band. She also appeared at the Pasadena Civic Auditorium on behalf of SPAR.[11] That was followed by six weeks of officers' training at the Coast Guard Academy, where she received her commission as ensign. Continuing to move up the ranks, she was promoted to lieutenant (jg) and served as officer in charge in Omaha, Nebraska.[12]

Recruiting was given a huge boost when Victor Mature—movie actor, chief petty officer, and SPAR recruiter—visited Denver. Dolores Plested, a member of the Denver Woman's Press Club and copywriter for radio station KMYR, noted that a casual radio announcement caused a mob scene. KMYR invited its listeners to come to the studio to see the actor. An overflow crowd jammed into the studio and an estimated 2,000 listeners, mostly women, filled the street, blocking off bank customers on the building's lower floor. The riot squad helped police control the crowd. Lieutenant Catherine W. Cockburn, the officer in charge of the movie actor's visit, told station owners, "I hope never to be caught in a mob again such as was assembled outside your station."[13] Mature participated in a series of war bond tours in 1944 as a featured player in the musical revue *Tars and Spars*. It was probably while touring the United States with the revue that he visited Denver and KMYR radio station.

Tars and Spars was inspired by the SPAR band. The band was so popular that women rejected Officer Candidate School to become members.[14] They took special pride in their marching ability—done while playing an instrument and wearing the SPAR uniform. The uniform was so similar to the one worn by the WAVES that many civilians confused the two. The fact that most people were unaware of the male coast guard, never mind the existence of female coast guard units, only aided the misconception. The SPAR band performed a weekly live radio show, *SPARs on Parade*, every Saturday for a national audience. They also recorded music onto VB-discs that were sent to servicemen on ships to hear at a later date.[15] It was exciting and musically affirming to band members to be broadcast across the nation like the famous Glenn Miller Band or the Andrew Sisters.[16] Unlike the army and navy female bands, the SPAR band was the only one in which its members were given special musicians' ratings and wore distinctive insignia on their uniforms, signifying that it was their primary SPAR duty.[17]

Basic training consisted of classes, physical training and exams, and drilling. Classroom instruction included basic military indoctrination, USCG history, nautical terms, and customs and courtesies. During physical training a recruit crawled on her belly under barbed wire, ran on logs across water, and zigzagged through automobile tires. The most terrifying test for one recruit was climbing up a cargo net strung between trees and descending down the other side.[18] Because SPARs did not serve on ships or overseas, one can only surmise that physical training was designed to build esprit de corps and not to prepare women for their duty stations.

Following graduation, enlisted SPARs specialized in thirty different USCG ratings. These included yeomen, storekeeper, parachute rigger, air control tower operator, boatswain's mate, coxswain, radiomen, and pharmacist mate. Caroline Kerr, the daughter of William and Wilma Kerr of Cameo, graduated from basic training at the University of Indiana–Bloomington. As a petty officer grade of storekeeper third class, she was stationed in St. Louis, Missouri. Two years later she was promoted to second class in charge of all coast guard recruiting in Kansas City, Kansas.[19]

Other enlistees received their indoctrination training at the Coast Guard Training Station in Palm Beach, Florida. Coloradans Corinne Cramer, Grace Pinson, Shirley Vincent, Doris Spinner, and Ruie A. Spannier were in one of the last classes, graduating as seaman second class in 1945. The daughter of a professor at the School of Mines in Golden, Cramer was an office secretary for an airline prior to enlisting.[20] On her twentieth birthday, Harriet Butler reported to the Navy Recruiting Station to enlist in the WAVES. However, when she was informed that a new and elite group of women was being formed—the women of the USCG—she chose SPAR instead. During training, she lived in a hotel with three other recruits. Hotel furniture had been replaced with bunk beds. With their own bathroom, the accommodations were far more glamorous than WAC barracks at Fort Des Moines in Iowa and other army bases. A native of Minnesota who did not like snow, Butler loved Florida's tropical climate. Hoping to replicate that, she put in for a California duty station and was assigned to an intelligence unit at Long Beach.[21] Military agents filed reports on Japanese Americans and other possible subversives. Yeoman first class Butler typed up the reports. Because of the nature of her work, the Federal Bureau of Investigation interviewed her neighbors before giving her a high security clearance. Everyone in the office got along well. In an interview over sixty years later, Butler recalled no discrimination or hassles from her male co-workers. SPARs dated and had parties with male intelligence agents and other military personnel.

Just as families had more than one son join or be drafted into the armed services, sisters also followed each other into the service. Both Rosalin Baker and her younger sister, Jessie, served as SPARs during World War II. Rosalin was a radio technician in New York while Jessie, born in Deer Trail, enlisted following high school in Wheat Ridge and Edgewater. She was assigned to the Norfolk, Virginia, station.[22]

Although most recruits were in their twenties, Jane Silverstein was thirty-four years old at the time of her enlistment. Born to Harry S. and Eva W. (Sickman) Silverstein, Jane attended East High School in Denver and the University of Colorado for one year. One day her parents asked if she would like to be a landscape architect. The following autumn she enrolled at the Lowthorpe School of Landscape Architecture in Groton, Massachusetts. She and the other thirty or so women had little idea what they were going to learn. Soon, they were mesmerized with landscapes and gardens. The long hours of study every night were not a hardship because of the "fascinating and exciting" subject. Students studied architecture, painting, sketching, construction details, surveying, grading, plant materials, horticulture, botany, and "design-design-design."[23] Following her graduation in 1932, Silverstein began her professional career working with Denver landscape architect Irvin J. McCrary before opening her own office in 1935. In the early 1940s she designed war housing projects in Cheyenne, Wyoming; La Junta, Colorado; and Sidney, Nebraska.[24]

After joining SPAR, Silverstein completed six weeks of training at the Coast Guard Academy. Her first duty station was with the headquarters of the district coast guard officer of the Third Naval District in New York City. She was assigned to the civil engineers and spent her first two weeks bent over a drafting board drawing barracks and lookout towers.

Her next orders made her the shore establishment property survey officer. Her task was to submit the entire inventory of the Third Naval District properties in New York, New Jersey, Connecticut, and part of Vermont to headquarters within five weeks. Equipped with thousands of forms and supervising two SPAR yeomen and two SPAR storekeepers, "the task of listing all land, buildings, docks, structures, utility systems, vehicles, boats, machinery, tools, equipment, apparatus and ordnance; to give the history of its establishment, date purchased, the costs and sizes of each thing was all a bit staggering." An enormous amount of research was required because some coast guard properties such as lighthouses had been built as early as 1721. The task had no chance of being completed by the original deadline. Given an extension and more staff, Silverstein's group submitted the report in six months.[25]

Following her stint as shore establishment property survey officer, Silverstein was assigned to the C. G. Pilot Command at the navy port director's office. In addition to creating a schedule of convoys arriving in New York City's harbor, she attended the masters convoy conferences as a representative of the Sandy Hook pilots and tracked all last-minute changes in sailing orders. Over the course of three years, the New York port director routed 75,000 ships in 1,500 convoys. Obviously, war is not just about production and machines; it is also a war of logistics. It was imperative that the right materials were in the right places at the right time in the right quantities. Silverstein facilitated this phenomenon on a daily basis.[26]

The most unique assignment for SPARs was with the then–top-secret LORAN (Long Range Navigation) system. The system used radio signals to help ships and aircraft obtain an accurate position. Early systems had a range of 1,200 miles. The LORAN station in Chatham, Massachusetts, was completely run by SPARs—the only female-run unit during the war.[27]

The majority of SPARs served in the continental United States, but once the navy allowed women to serve overseas, the coast guard followed suit and SPARs served in Alaska and Hawaii. Elizabeth Barmes, one of the first officers, was transferred to Hawaii in 1945. Her troop ship went "blacked out" because they did not know where the submarines were. She lived in a Quonset village across from Hickam Field. As the only SPAR officer on base, she was the liaison between the USCG and the United States Navy. There she met her husband, Otis Lipstreu, a coast guard officer, prompting her to remark, "I could hardly have any regrets about my service of three and a half years. I met an awful[ly] nice husband and we were married after the war."[28]

FIGURE 6.1. Denver landscape architect Jane Silverstein joined SPAR after designing war housing in several states. Stationed in New York City, she oversaw the compilation of naval properties in a four-state area. *Courtesy*, Jane Silverstein Ries Papers, WH 1785, Western History Collection, Denver Public Library, Denver, CO.

THE MERCHANT MARINE CORPS

Between 1874 and 1936, a variety of federal legislation supported maritime training through school ships, internships at sea, and other methods. After a tragic accident aboard a passenger ship in 1934, the US Congress decided that direct federal involvement was needed to assure efficient and standardized training. In 1936 it passed the Merchant Marine Act. Two years later the US Merchant Marine Cadet Corps was established. A permanent site at King's Point, New York, was dedicated by President Franklin Roosevelt in September 1943. World War II required the academy to devote all of its resources to meet the increased need for Merchant Marine officers. Enrollment rose to 2,700 men, and the planned course of instruction was reduced from four years to eighteen months. Although women had served on ships as hostesses and in other capacities prior to the war and some had been

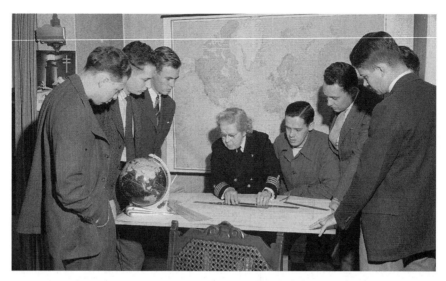

FIGURE 6.2. Captain Mary Converse instructing V-7 students (candidates for United States Navy ensign commissions) on use of sextant, compass, and gyroscope in the dining room of her Denver home. *Courtesy*, Prints and Photographs Division, FSA/OWI Collection, LC-USW3-055474-C, Library of Congress, Washington, DC.

captured in the first year of America's involvement, women were not accepted into the academy.[29] However, one landlocked, sea-experienced woman taught navigation to navy officer candidates. In 1872, Mary Caroline Parker was born in Malden, Massachusetts. After high school she married Harry Elisha Converse, a yachtsman and capitalist. They had five children before his death in 1920. Shortly afterward, she and her daughter Mary moved to Denver. In 1938, during a visit to Boston, Converse decided to renew her sea pilot's license. The Merchant Marines insisted that she meet certain requirements. Between 1938 and 1940, she made four voyages and logged over 33,000 miles while practicing navigation. In September 1940, the sixty-six-year-old became the only woman sworn in as a United States Merchant Marine captain. The commission verified her as a "Master of Steam and Motor vessels of any gross tons, upon the waters of oceans, yachts only."[30]

A month later, the commanding officer of Denver's navy recruiting office asked Converse to teach navigation and seamanship to young men who had enlisted in the V-7 officers' training program for college graduates. The purpose of the course was to provide men, many of whom had never even been in a rowboat, with a head start on their future midshipman's schooling. For Converse, the timing was fortuitous—her daughter had recently been killed in a horse-riding accident, and the teaching would occupy her time.

For three years "Captain Mary" taught ten to fifteen men on Tuesday and Thursday evenings. Three-and-a-half-hour classes were held in her dining room at 195 High Street in Denver. Students were from the United States Coast Guard, Navy, Merchant Marine, and Maritime Commission. Classes were divided into groups. Some studied signaling and international code, some solved assigned problems, and others worked with a sextant on her back porch using the bird bath as an artificial horizon. Captain Mary had no use for excuses or whining from her students. One asked, "Captain Mary, do I have to do all this work before the next class?" She simply replied, "No, you don't even have to come again if you don't want to." Another student complained that there was so much to learn that he did not think he could master navigation. She effectively dismissed his concern with "if I could do it at sixty-eight, you surely can get it with a little concentration."[31]

Her classroom became known as "Annapolis Annex at the Port of Denver." A sign with "Capt. Mary P. Converse V-7 USNR Instructor" in 5-inch-high letters greeted students as they crossed the threshold into her dining room. A navy officer periodically gave talks to the men on a variety of sea-related topics. Captain Mary also acted as hostess, distributing cigarettes and candy during class. After each session, she offered students sandwiches and other refreshments. Sometimes a songfest or a billiards game was held after class.

Captain Mary became quite a legendary figure in Denver. She had endeared herself to its citizens in the 1920s and 1930s with her presence in a number of social circles and as a supporter of the Denver Symphony Orchestra. Appearing in her captain's uniform in public and when she was teaching cemented her reputation. An article called her a "society matron" who "has gained a wide reputation through her obtaining a certificate in navigation at a time in life when the average woman sits down and admits she is only waiting for the end."[32]

THE MARINE CORPS WOMEN'S RESERVE

Although the United States Marines Corps (USMC) employed 300 "marinettes" during World War I to release male marines from desk duty, it was the most reluctant of the US military branches to enlist women during World War II. But like the other branches, the USMC had little choice. It desperately needed personnel and had already lowered recruiting standards and raised the age ceiling to thirty-six. Bowing to pressure from the secretary of the navy, the public, and the US Congress, the Plans and Policies Section proposed that a women's reserve be placed in the Division of Reserve. On November 7, 1942, President Roosevelt approved the move. Major General Commandant Thomas Holcomb requested from marine post commanders their best estimates of the number of women reservists needed to replace officers and men as office clerks, drivers, radiomen, mechanics, and so on. Ruth Cheney Streeter was selected as the first director of the Marine Corps Women's Reserve (MCWR). The public, accustomed to the acronyms of other female branches, anticipated a catchy nickname for these women. Dainty Devil-Dogs, Glamarines, and Sub-Marines were suggested. General Holcomb ruled out all nicknames, insisting: "They are Marines. They don't have a nickname and they don't need one."[33]

Being the last of the armed services to enlist women had its benefits. The marines not only avoided mistakes made by other services but also received valuable advice and resources. From the beginning, the navy was an important partner in getting the fledging MCWR off to a solid start. Marine procurement sections used navy procurement offices. Women interested in either branch went to one office to enlist and undergo physical examinations. Soon, the USMC developed its own network of recruiting offices. Eligibility requirements included a minimum weight of 95 pounds. Potential recruits were known to stuff themselves with food prior to their weigh-in. Corpsmen looked the other way when a woman stood on the scale clutching her handbag and coat to meet the requirement. Officer candidates had the same requirements as those for WAVES and SPARS. Geraldine Bower, a Keenesburg native, was eligible because she had attended Colorado A&M for two years. She steadily rose up the ranks from PFC to corporal to sergeant, serving in the supply division in San Francisco and San Diego.[34] African American women were not officially barred, but they were not knowingly enlisted.[35]

Women Reservists (WRs) joined for a variety of reasons: (1) there was a marine corps heritage in their families, (2) they were conscious of the corps' elite reputation, (3) they had brothers or male friends in the corps, (4) they believed someone in their family should be serving in the military, and (5) the uniforms were striking.[36] For many women the marines' reputation as an elite fighting force was such a draw that they wanted to enlist before turning twenty. Dorothy Griffin, who was attending secretarial school at Mary Washington College near Quantico, "never met a Marine that wasn't proud to be a Marine and didn't think it was the best." Her sister, who had enlisted as soon as the USMC accepted women, encouraged her even though her parents were initially unhappy and she had to convince them to sign her enlistment papers.[37] For Fort Collins native Shirley Gunston, all it took was one look at a WR at a sorority meeting at Colorado A&M. The hard part was persuading her father to sign for her. But he did. He put a service flag in the window of his train. Fellow workers commented, "Gordy, you've got a son in the military." "No," he boasted, "I've got a daughter in the Marine Corps."[38] Another Colorado native, Betty Lee "Bea" Megenity, explained, "I always wanted to be a boy because I wanted to be a Marine. There was just something about the tradition that appealed to me." She, too, required a parental signature.[39]

Other recruits left good-paying jobs or college studies to join. Velma Comstock worked as a stenographer with a railroad in Minneapolis but was unhappy. Her biggest excitement was bowling on Thursday nights. So one day she left the office for lunch and signed up for the marines. Her boss was "rather horrified" that she would join the corps.[40] When a recruiting poster with the slogan "Free a Marine to Fight" arrived at the ration board office where LaVerne Marie Novak worked, she instantly decided to enlist.[41] After graduating from Montrose High School in 1940, Lula Mae Tyler dreamed of becoming a teacher. However, her father's illness steered her to Central Commercial Business School. She graduated in August 1941 with a business degree. While working at the Montrose Bank, she helped her mother take care of her father until his death in 1943. The following year, Tyler joined the USMC.[42] Mary Morgan, born in Steamboat Springs and raised in Central City, was attending the University of Colorado on a scholarship from the Colorado Federation of Women's Clubs. When she enlisted in January 1944, she informed the organization that she would be foregoing her final year to be a marine.[43]

Recruiting efforts were so successful that the MCWR put a hold on new recruits for a period of time. Unfortunately for Jeanne Barrenche, it was then that she applied to the marine corps. A friend in the navy convinced her to apply to the WAVES. Barrenche passed the required tests and physical. At the last moment she decided against joining: "It was the Marine Corps or nothing." Luckily for Barrenche, the WR began accepting new applicants.[44] Another enlistee who had to wait before reporting to Camp Lejeune in North Carolina was Julia Jane Johnson, whose older sister was serving in the WAVES. A graduate of Dickinson Secretarial School, Johnson was working in Denver when she enlisted. Within months she was a PBX (post exchange box) operator for the furlough transportation division in San Francisco.[45] The corps goal of 18,000 enlistees was reached by June 1, 1944.

The first group of marine officer candidates arrived at the Midshipmen School (Women's Reserve) at Mount Holyoke College on March 13, 1943. They had been given precise instructions before leaving home—bring a raincoat and rain hat, lightweight dresses or suits, a plain bathrobe, soft-soled bathroom slippers, easily laundered underwear, and play suit or shorts for physical education (no slacks). Because drilling enlarged one's feet, comfortable dark brown laced oxfords were also listed. Recruits were warned not to leave home without orders, not to arrive before the listed time and date stamped, and not to forget their ration cards.[46]

Officer candidates joined as privates and after four weeks were promoted to officer cadets. Women who failed to meet officers' standards were given two options: transfer to Hunter College to complete basic enlisted training or be discharged. The first group of seventy-one marine officer candidates was formed into companies under the command of a male officer, Major E. Hunter Hurst. During the first four weeks, the MCWR curriculum was identical to that of the WAVES except for drill, which was taught by male drill instructors. Recruit Bea Leist was disappointed in boot camp. She did not think it was tough enough.[47] Phyllis Marie Ilgen, a farmer's daughter from Byers and Basalt, joined the marines because she wanted to be different from her friend who had joined the Women's Army Corps. Ilgen found Camp Lejeune "pretty scary." As soon as she got off the bus, sergeants yelled at her to straighten up and shape up. She thought, "I want to go back home."[48] The first few weeks of training at Hunter College was definitely an eye-opener for Marie Jansen: "I was a city girl from New York and just dumb to the ways of life . . . one of the first things I learned was how to live with them [women from different backgrounds] and get along with them. The first night in the barracks, we talked all night . . . It was scary away from home for the first time. I don't think we got any sleep."[49]

Officer candidates studied naval organization and administration, personnel, history and strategy, law and justice, and ships and aircraft. Part of their challenge was "Corpspeak"—learning terms such as boondocks, boots, topside, galley, and GI Party. The latter sounded like fun until a recruit discovered it entailed decontaminating the barracks in preparation for inspection.[50] The second phase of training was initially administered by male marines but later by themselves as WR officers. This portion was separate from the WAVES. It included USMC administration and courtesies, map reading, interior guard, safeguarding military information, and physical conditioning. Many WRs were hard pressed in later years to remember much about those classes; however, they easily recalled marching under the watchful—and resentful—eyes of male drill instructors. On May 4, 1943, the first women ever were commissioned as officers in the United States Marine Corps.

By late March 1943, enlisted women arrived at the US Training School (Women's Reserve) at Hunter College. Between March and July 10, 1943, six classes of recruits, approximately 525 each, arrived every two weeks. A recruit was assigned to Barrack A, B, or C, located on a hill several blocks from the college. Bea Leist recalled that after another physical, they lined up and went through a gauntlet of navy doctors and corpsmen who simultaneously "shot" them in both arms.[51]

Marine companies were formed into a battalion under the command of Major William W. Buchanan. Captain Katharine A. Towle served as Buchanan's senior female staff officer. Towle, formerly a dean at the University of California–Berkeley, had no marine training. She was the only female marine officer at Hunter until the first officers' candidate class was commissioned. Thirty-three male instructors (ten officers and twenty-three enlisted men) formed the rest of the marine corps staff. They taught classroom sessions. Fifteen to twenty male drill instructors supervised the close-order drill of both WAVE and WR recruits.[52]

Training sessions lasted between three-and-a-half weeks and six weeks. Although Marie Jansen felt guilty about leaving her widowed father alone, she was determined to help in the war effort. After high school she worked for Metropolitan Life Insurance Company, lived at home, and took college classes. When a girlfriend joined the navy she told her, "You take over the Navy; I'll take over the Marines."[53] She enlisted on March 3, 1943, and by April was training at Hunter College. There was no room for them on campus, so recruits lived in apartment houses.

With Mount Holyoke and Hunter Colleges swamped with WAVES and MCWR trainees, the corps moved its schools to Camp Lejeune, the largest marine training base on the East Coast. The move facilitated the famed marine esprit de corps. Housed in barracks previously outfitted for male marines, some young female recruits were confused when they checked out the "heads," or bathrooms. Never having seen urinals, some concluded that they were some sort of special military footbath or perhaps a place for one to brush her teeth. The accompanying non-commissioned officer (NCO) quickly cleared up the confusion.[54]

Dorothy Griffin enlisted in June 1943 but had to wait until August to report to Camp Lejeune. As she noted, "It was an awful time to go to Camp Lejeune to boot camp"—in the middle of summer in a humid, hot climate. Her class was rushed through their six weeks of camp because they had people backed up and waiting to begin their service. Her older sister, who recruited her, was there attending Quartermaster School. Griffin, who found boot camp "tough," credits her sister for her making it through by periodically bringing her a candy bar or a Coke.

With the move to Camp Lejeune, female marines received combat training, the only military women to do so during boot camp. Director Streeter was assured that recruits would receive instruction and exercises similar to those given to men. They were shown all phases of marine combat training. Streeter saw her marines fire anti-aircraft guns and drop from parachute towers.[55] Two "lady marines" were photographed practicing the "womanly art of self-defense, or how to disarm an opponent, be he man or mouse."[56]

Recruits arose early every morning with the grass still wet with dew. Mosquitoes swarmed all over them while they exercised and drilled. Reservists had two male drill instructors (DIs). One of the men would say "double time," and they were required to run until they fell out. Two or three of the women, including Griffin, never fell out. They kept up with the DI until he was forced to stop. Because Griffin had been a drum major in high school, she was made student platoon leader at camp.

As other service branches discovered, women improved the quality of military barracks. Reservists painted stark squad bays in pastel colors. They adorned crisply made bunks with stuffed animals. Reservists arranged dressers to provide a modicum of privacy and added doors to toilet stalls. Women uncomfortable with communal shower areas showered after lights out. In time, they hung shower curtains. They outfitted their day rooms in which they entertained dates with board games, pianos, and record players. Women hung clothing facing in one direction, sparkled mirrors, and polished floors to a sheen with Kotex sanitary pads. While commanding officers did not officially endorse these amendments, they proudly paraded visitors and dignitaries through the squeaky-clean barracks and mess halls.[57]

Per his insistence that the women were first and foremost marines, Commandant Holcomb wanted uniforms similar to the men's—traditional forest green with red chevrons. One distinction from other women's uniforms was the unique, visored bell-crowned hat, trimmed with lipstick-red cord. Patricia Jane Irvine could not wait for her first leave so she could show off her uniform in her hometown.[58] Wearing lipstick and nail polish was encouraged, but they had to match the red cord of the winter cap. WRs adopted "Montezuma Red," created in their honor.

In addition to the heat, humidity, and mosquitoes at Camp Lejeune, women reservists found themselves facing a barrage of male harassment and resentment. Being called "BAMs"—"broad-assed Marines"—tried the fortitude and perseverance of many a Woman Reservist. The BAM acronym did not faze Private First Class Marie Jansen. When a male marine hurled that epithet at her, she faced the offender and replied, "Yes, Beautiful American Marine," and walked away.[59] For other women, it was hard to ignore some of the stunts pulled by unhappy Seabees. A particularly mean-spirited stunt was when a group of Seabees captured every stray dog in the area, shaved them like poodles, and painted "BAM" on their sides. Then they released them in the middle of a platoon of graduating Women Reservists. Finally, in August 1943, Commandant Holcomb sternly warned unit commanding officers that they were personally responsible for any further disrespectful treatment of WRs by fellow Marines. By mid-1944, open hostility was reduced to a truce of sorts. Soon, the competence of WRs won over most of their critics.

After graduation, women were assigned temporary jobs such as kitchen patrol (KP) while commanders decided where to station them. Griffin's two weeks of KP was one of the least onerous duties. She waited on tables at the officers' end of the mess hall, which was definitely better than peeling carrots or cleaning large pots.[60] After her KP stint, she was assigned recruiting duty. The marines wanted to station her in Cleveland, but she told them she "joined to go somewhere else." Denver was the farthest available assignment from Chicago, so she was sent there. The Mile High City turned out to be one of her most favorite places to live. Because "every cab driver in Denver was an ex-Marine," she never paid cab fare. The recruiting office was so busy that she "typed her fingers to the bone" processing not only new male and female recruits but also the paperwork for draftees. The office was open ten hours a day Monday through Saturday. Recruiters usually went home by 6:00 p.m.; if there was a big rush of people going through, they stayed later.[61]

Selected officers and enlisted women were given specialist training at schools run by civilians as well as the United States Army, Navy, and Marine Corps. Aviation machinist's mate, Link Training instructor, and aviation storekeeper were three of the earliest specialties. Corps schools opened for cooks and bakers, motor transport, and quartermaster. After graduation from Officer Candidate School, many officers were sent to the navy's Communication School in South Hadley, Massachusetts. By the end of the war, thirty schools were operating for

FIGURE 6.3. Group photograph of Denver Marine Recruiting Office staff, 1944. Dorothy Griffin is second from the left (front row). *Courtesy,* Dorothy Mae Griffin Rice Collection, WV0112.6.002, Hodges Special Collections and University Archives, UNCG University Libraries, University of North Carolina at Greensboro.

women. Reservists held positions as first sergeant, paymaster, parachute rigger, control tower operator, aerial gunnery instructor, celestial navigation, aircraft instruments technician, radio operator, automotive mechanic, aviation supply, and photographer. Barbara L. Kees was sent to Omaha, Nebraska, for radio materiel school and was then stationed at Quantico, Virginia. She and the other reservists rotated through twenty-four-hour shifts.[62]

The USMC took several factors into account in assigning reservists to a military post. Of course, the needs of the particular base and the training of individual marines were considered. But so was the culture of the 1940s in which "nice girls" seldom lived away from home in an un-chaperoned environment. To prevent loneliness and avoid unfavorable comments (such as the scandal that racked the Women's Army Corps, pages 53-55), no fewer than two female marines were assigned to a station or sub-station. Enlisted women could not be assigned to a post unless there was a woman officer in the vicinity. On most posts, a female commanding officer reported to the post commander. However, the women, as an autonomous entity, handled general administration, barracks-area maintenance, and mess halls. The few reservists stationed in large cities were given subsistence, a monetary allowance for housing and meals. Recruiter Dorothy Griffin and the male marines working with her in the Denver office were made sergeants, effectively raising their pay so they could afford to live in the city.[63]

Although not always the case for servicemen and women, some reservists were actually placed in jobs that utilized their civilian work experience or skills. Prior to enlisting, Jeanne Barrenche had worked at a major steel mill in its War Bond/Accounting Department. At Camp LeJeune, she convinced her bunk mates to use their clothing allowance money to buy war bonds. After boot camp, she was transferred to the War Bond Sales and Promotion Office at Camp Pendleton in California. There she worked with actors and actresses and helped with a swimming pool exhibition featuring Johnny Weissmuller (aka Tarzan).[64]

Other women purposely hid their expertise in a certain civilian field. Shirley Gunston made sure she kept her college home economics major a secret because she did not want to be assigned a mess job. She attended transport school for six weeks to become a truck driver. She hoped to be assigned to "someplace glamorous." Much to her dismay, she was assigned to Parris Island, "an ugly saw."[65]

Marie Jansen, another transportation school graduate, was luckier in her first assignment at Cherry Point, North Carolina. She drove people around the base in buses and jeeps. During her off-duty hours, PFC Jansen studied for her corporal test. After passing the exam, she was transferred to El Centro, California, in December 1943. She ferried ten-wheelers and drove jeeps back and forth from San Diego. She also drove a semi-truck that pulled long, partially enclosed trailers. The trailers had wooden benches lining their sides on which military passengers sat as Jansen ferried them around the base and into town.[66] At one point, there were so many WRs assigned to transportation that she was given PX (post exchange) duty. That experience turned out to be one of her military highlights when she sold cigarettes to movie star Tyrone Power, a marine pilot, and got his signature on the required paperwork.[67]

As in the navy, aviation and aircraft squadrons more readily accepted female personnel. Dorothy A. Gahm, one of four Boulder, Colorado, sisters to enlist, served at the USMC Air Station at Cherry Point, with the aircraft engineering squadron.[68] Marjorie "Marge" Arlene Alexander was a corporal in the Aviation Women's Reserve Squadron 4 at the Marine Corps Air Depot at Miramar (San Diego). Sergeant Leist was in charge of aviation supplies at El Centro (California) after attending Storekeeper School. Pilots reported to her office to receive necessary parts before they went overseas.[69]

The 2,400 WRs stationed in Washington, DC, necessitated the building of a new and independent post. Henderson Hall, named after the first commandant, General Archibald Henderson, quickly acquired the moniker "Hen Hall." Coming from small towns and cities to serve in the nation's capital was a bit of culture shock for some Colorado women. One of the first to be stationed there was Mary Lou Gillan, whose first assignment was at Mare Island (California). By July 1943, PFC Gillan was at Henderson Hall. When she was discharged in October 1945, the Julesburg native had risen to the rank of staff sergeant with Company G.[70]

FIGURE 6.4. Marie Jansen drove large trucks, buses, and jeeps as a transportation school graduate. *Courtesy*, Marie Jansen Rugg.

Corporal Patricia Irvine also lived at "Hen Hall." Six days a week she walked across the street to the Navy Annex where she filed marine allotments. As the war wound down, she was granted one weekend off a month. She took trains to Boston, New York City, and Philadelphia. In New York City, she stayed at a large mansion on Madison Avenue that had been ceded to servicewomen.[71] The nightly rate was fifty cents. A fourth Coloradan was Victoria Norman, the daughter of a sheep shearer and his wife, a farmer in Brush. Norman rose through the ranks at Quantico, finally mustering out as a sergeant.

Marine Reservists took advantage of the amenities offered in towns and cities in which they were stationed. In Denver, recruiter Griffin went to movies and on dates. She did not go to a USO (United Service Organizations) center in Denver, however. One time, on a date, Griffin tried to enter the USO but was told, "We don't allow servicewomen." Her date could go in but not her. It was the one time as a marine that she felt discriminated against.[72] Other women met their future husbands in the service. After Corporal Marie Jansen met her future husband, Clarence "Larry" Rugg, they often spent their evenings at the home of friends. Rugg, a navy man attached to the marine corps, was later sent to Guam and the Marshall Islands. During that time, Jansen regularly wrote him letters. She also spent much of the war years writing to and receiving letters from her father, who addressed his letters to her with "Dearest Little Corporal." Sadly, her father died while she was stationed at El Centro. The marines arranged for military planes to fly her to and from New York to handle her father's affairs and funeral.[73]

Other female marines enjoyed the company of servicemen. Coloradan sergeant Marguerite Moore took full advantage of the night life at Parris Island. Town buses were regularly sent to the base to pick up servicewomen. During one month,

Moore attended twenty dances in twenty-one nights.[74] Sergeant Novak—stationed at San Diego—enjoyed dances on the base, swam in the Pacific Ocean, and visited the San Diego Zoo. Reservists loved shopping at the PX because it carried nylon stockings.[75] Corporal Jansen had the unique pleasure of riding in a two-seater navy advanced trainer aircraft. She and several friends were at the air field one day talking to pilots when she confessed that she had never been in an airplane. One pilot immediately offered to take her up. He flew her in an open cockpit airplane to a town 90 miles away. They circled a baseball game being played down on the ground.[76] Private Phyllis Ilgen, promoted to corporal before her discharge in 1946, spent most of her off-duty hours with a group of other women marines. They learned to ride horses English style in their free time in San Diego, although the Colorado native preferred western style.[77]

In 1944, new legislation allowed Women Reservists to serve in Hawaii and Alaska. Director Streeter asked Colonel Hobby, the Women's Army Corps director who had overseen thousands of WACs serving overseas, for suggestions on choosing volunteers for Hawaii. The criteria announced were a satisfactory record for six months of military duty, motivation, desire to do a good job (versus the desire to be in beautiful Hawaii), stable personality, sufficient skill to fill one of the billets that had been requested, and age. Age was a factor because the minimum tour was two years, with little chance for leave. Thus the health and status of dependents and family members were considered.

In October, Colonel Streeter flew to Hawaii to prepare for the women's arrival and inspect housing. On December 2, more officers flew in to make preliminary arrangements. A staging area was established at the Marine Corps Base, San Diego, where women marines underwent a short but intense physical conditioning course. They ascended and descended cargo nets with a 10-pound pack strapped to their backs and jumped into the water from shipboard. Reservists took classes in recognizing Allied insignia, shipboard procedures, and the importance of safeguarding military information.[78]

On January 25, 1945, Captain Marna V. Brady led the first contingent of 5 WR officers and 160 enlisted women up the gangplank of the SS *Matsonia*. Three days later, female marines disembarked in Honolulu as the Pearl Harbor Marine Barracks Band played "The Marines' Hymn," the "March of the Women Marines," and "Aloha Oe." Curious male marines welcomed them warmly as they disembarked dressed in dungarees, boondockers, and overseas caps. The durable and comfortable boondockers with high ankle support were the official boots of the armed forces because they were reliable on all types of terrain. Commanding Officer Major Marion Wing "bribed" a group of Seabees with Cokes to modify the women's quarters.[79]

On the island, nearly two-thirds of the women performed clerical jobs. More than a third came from Cherry Point and immediately went to work on airplanes. At Pearl Harbor the WRs ran the motor transport section, serving nearly 16,000 persons a month. They expertly navigated mountainous roads in liberty buses, jeeps, and all kinds of trucks. They carried mail, people, ammunition, and garbage. Grease-covered female mechanics worked under the hoods or chassis of 2½-ton trucks.[80]

After Germany surrendered in May 1945, the Denver recruiting office was informed that the staff would be halved. Griffin and a girlfriend transferred to El Toro, California. She spent the rest of her time in the military clerking in the flight clearance office, which handled all the flight plans for pilots who went through the base. Because she felt it was "real Marine Corps duty," Griffin enjoyed this work more than she had her recruiting job.[81]

When the war ended, Women Reservists were working in 225 specialties in sixteen of twenty-one functional fields. They filled 85 percent of the enlisted jobs at Headquarters Marine Corps. They comprised between 50 percent and 67 percent of the permanent personnel at all large marine corps posts and stations. Now came the demobilization process. Demobilization, instead of requiring fewer marines, actually resulted in the need for more female marines to process discharged servicemen and women. Procedures called for the mandatory resignation or discharge of all Women Reservists by September 1, 1946.[82]

A point system similar to the men's was developed to control the flow of separations. A woman with twenty-five points on September 1, 1945, was eligible for immediate discharge unless she was declared "essential." Corporal Jansen, one of the first female marines, had the required points but because she was the "lead" in the transportation unit, she was considered essential. However, Jansen had married Larry Rugg and soon became pregnant. That allowed her to be discharged.[83] The required number of points was progressively reduced until it reached zero the following July. Exceptions were made for women at least thirty-eight or older and for married women whose husbands had been discharged. Shirley Gunston had met her future husband, Max Brown, in their freshman year of college. After he went off to war, she received "beautiful letters" from him. Once their points "came up," they were discharged and got married.[84]

As the September deadline approached, General Holcomb authorized keeping 200 WRs on active duty until June 30, 1947, ten months beyond the original deadline. The USMC desperately needed clerk-typists, payroll clerks, and auditors as the corps demobilized. Monte Vista sisters Leona M. Fox and Twila Fox Richardson processed discharged marines at the San Diego staging area.[85] As Women Reservists and male marines were discharged, General Holcomb, one of many who had originally fervently opposed allowing women in the corps, admitted his mistake: "Like most Marines. . . . I didn't believe women could serve any useful purpose in the Marine Corps. . . . Since then I've changed my mind."[86]

As two of the three military branches with the fewest women, SPAR and the Merchant Marine Corps are often forgotten. Women marine corps veterans highlight their lack of numbers in the unofficial motto of the Colorado Women Marine Association: "The Fewer, the Prouder, the Women Marines."[87] Women in the armed forces found great satisfaction in a job well done for the war effort. Some servicewomen (and servicemen) who served only in the United States felt almost guilty for having had such a good time doing their jobs when those in Europe and the Pacific were fighting for—and losing—their lives in the struggle against the Axis Powers.

To support those in the armed forces, a legion of women removed their aprons, found someone to care for their children, and worked in thousands of defense plants across the nation. In Colorado, existing plants and newly constructed factories rushed to produce war materiel. Under the auspices of the federal government, the military, and private industry, they churned out ammunition, chemical weapons, and parts for ships.

Part II

Women and Defense Work

Across the nation, women were heavily recruited for jobs in war-related factories. Posters, radio spots, and newspaper advertisements all extolled women's duty. By the war's end, 19 million American women had filled jobs on the home front.

In Colorado, women were a force for the Arsenal of Democracy. Large plants—the Denver Ordnance Plant and Colorado Fuel & Iron Company in Pueblo—were joined by smaller plants to produce and store ammunition, weapons, and chemicals for the war effort.

Aircraft plants and shipyards employed the largest numbers of women during World War II. Although they were thousands of miles from the nearest ocean, Denver companies produced parts for battleships.

Defense plants—like the military—initiated, reviewed, filed, and compiled reports and orders and ran on food produced and processed by American farmers, ranchers, and gardeners.

7

WOW!—Women Ordnance Workers

As the buses pulled up to the gate at Colorado Fuel & Iron, occupants began gathering their belongings. Unlike other war plants, there was a substantial number of men of all ages. Their lengthy experience at the steel mill was a recognized asset; one could not realistically claim that they could be readily replaced if they were drafted into the armed forces. Women, ranging from their late teens to their sixties, wore overalls, their hair covered in snoods or brightly colored bandanas. Others wore one-piece navy jumpsuits, while a few sported skirts and crisp white blouses. They carried purses and, like the men, lunch boxes or bags. As they exited the bus, voices that had been still and quiet from sleepiness suddenly came alive and called out to friends disgorging from buses and individual cars. Queuing up at the gate, workers exchanged greetings and small talk. Guards checked identification badges clipped to shoulders and pulled from purses. Surnames on the tags testified to the diversity of Pueblo's population. Once through the gate, Rose Abbate and Anna B. Stark headed to the Forge Shop; janitresses Rachel Blazich and Anna Butkovich jostled past graveyard shift workers hurrying to catch a ride home; Dora Baca, Anne Nicasio, and Mary Garcia split from a large group to wend their way to the Brick Shed; Bolt and Spike Mill Department workers Veda Novak and Faye Weaver kidded each other about the article in *The Blast* calling them and their co-workers "a host of charming girls." Charming or not, they took their jobs seriously. After all, producing 15 mm projectiles was serious work.[1]

DOI: 10.5876/9781646420339.c007   123

FIGURE 7.1. Sparkplug Club, ca. 1940s. Women workers at Colorado Fuel & Iron were a diverse group in ethnicity, race, and age. *Courtesy*, Steelworks Center of the West, Pueblo, Colorado, mm22_sparkplugs.

Historically—in comparison to Pennsylvania, Illinois, and Michigan—Colorado has not been a heavily industrialized state. When it was time to establish factories for war materiel, Colorado was given strong consideration. Denver, its largest city, had a relatively low population density and could handle an influx of new workers. Fearing German and Japanese attacks, the US government and military complex searched for sites that would be less vulnerable than the East or West Coasts. Colorado fit the bill. Manufacturing companies already located in Colorado expanded during the war years, and new plants opened. For most women, it was their first experience with production-line work.

To fully staff defense plants, vast numbers of male and female workers were needed. At first, industries hoped they could minimize the numbers of female war workers. But just as the eligible ages for draftees were stretched over the course of the war, so was the net cast to capture female war workers. Originally, married women with young children at home were discouraged from applying for war jobs. But soon, recruiters targeted even those women. If a woman could not work in a factory, perhaps she could do a less war-related job, thus freeing a single woman or a woman with older children to take a defense job. Numbers tell the tale: over the course of the war, the US female labor force grew by 6.5 million, an increase of 50 percent.[2] By 1945, 37 percent of all adult women were employed and comprised over 36 percent of the civilian labor force.[3] From 1940 to 1944, the percentage of women workers employed in factories increased from 20 to 30 percent, while the percentage of female workers employed as domestic servants declined from nearly 18 percent to less than 10 percent. Female employment in defense industries grew by 460 percent from 1940 to 1944.[4] In Colorado, 22 percent of females age fourteen and older were in the labor force in 1940. By 1950, that figure had grown to 28 percent.[5] During World War II, the number of manufacturing establishments in Colorado increased from 1,298 in 1939 to 1,602 in 1947.[6] The Denver Ordnance Plant, Bluhill Foods, Cobusco Steel Products Co., Gates Rubber Company, Groswold Ski Company, and the Rocky Mountain Arsenal all employed women in their respective plants. In Pueblo, Colorado Fuel & Iron Company and the Ordnance Depot hired women for practically every department, while Littleton's Heckethorn Manufacturing Company utilized women in making projectiles and mortar fuses.

THE DENVER ORDNANCE PLANT

In 1940, when the federal government announced plans to build an ordnance factory, Denver officials lobbied earnestly for the plant. Through the efforts of US representative Lawrence Lewis and Denver manager of parks and improvements George Cramner, Denver was selected. Occupying over 2,000 acres, the plant was bounded by Sixth Avenue, Alameda, Kipling (formerly Howell Avenue), and Green Mountain.

On January 4, 1941, a contract for $122.2 million was awarded for an ordnance plant to be run by Remington Arms. Construction began in the summer of 1941. Alice Claudine Trott Baker started working at the site during this phase. Her parents "farmed" her out to Kansas neighbors when she was only twelve years old. She milked cows, scrubbed floors, and helped deliver babies. By the time she was eighteen, she "had had enough of it," so she boarded a Greyhound bus bound for Denver. She worked as a housekeeper and later at a café. When construction began, she and several other women made box lunches for the workers in assembly-line fashion.[7] Four general manufacturing buildings (a fifth production facility was opened in May 1942), a guard house, storage facilities, and a railroad depot filled the site. The administration building housed a hospital staffed by eleven physicians, six technicians, and forty-eight nurses.[8]

On October 25, 1941, the Denver Ordnance Plant (DOP) was dedicated. Under the watchful eyes of 200 police officers, 3,000 Denverites followed the prescribed automobile route through the grounds. A separate tour through building interiors was given for 400 official guests. At the dedication ceremony, Governor Ralph Carr and the plant commander lauded the speed with which the massive construction project was completed—almost six months ahead of schedule.[9]

Of the initial 10,000 workers, 40 percent were women. Thousands were hired as secretaries, clerks, and inspectors. Authorities anticipated an output of 4 million cartridges a day. The Japanese attack on Pearl Harbor less than two months later altered those goals. Because plant processes were almost entirely automated, the DOP became capable of producing 10 million rounds of ammunition daily.[10] Under the Remington Arms contract, the plant produced ball cartridges, tracer and incendiary bullets, and armor-piercing shells.

Between 1942 and 1945, production and employee numbers ebbed and flowed at the DOP, a result of its efficiency and of changing war needs. During the summer of 1943, at its height of production, workers produced 6 million bullets a day. Of the 19,500 employees, 50 percent were women. Layoffs commenced until by February 1944, only 3,500 employers were working one shift. To fill the void, the Kaiser Company produced 8 inch and 15 mm shells, M-52 point detonating fuses, M-184 boosters, and 90 mm shells, Remington produced artillery shell fuses, and General Foods packed C rations.[11] As the war ended, layoffs continued until only 1,805 men, 2,639 women, and 305 African Americans, who were not distinguished by gender, were working.[12]

ROCKY MOUNTAIN ARSENAL

After the attack on Pearl Harbor, the United States Army wanted a location to produce chemical weapons that was far from both coasts; close to transportation corridors, airports, and rail lines; but not too close to a large metropolitan area. By May 1942, the War Board had selected nearly 20,000 acres of land east of Denver. Construction of the $50 million weapons complex began in June. Crews laid railroad spurs. They built production plants, an administration building, a large logistics and warehouse complex, and munitions storage bunkers. The army and navy awarded construction companies an "E" pennant for efficient coordination among the military, management, and employees in readying the plant. For the ceremony, workers chose representatives to receive official pins. The assembled crowd cheered loudly for Mary Jo Negel of C. G. Kershaw Contracting Co., Dorothy Guida of Ferguson Co., Harriet Bolin of E. I. duPont de Nemours and Co., and Mabel K. Mock, Area Engineers, Civilian Employees.[13]

On January 1, 1943, the Rocky Mountain Arsenal began producing mustard gas, lewisite, and chlorine gas. Within a year, production of mustard gas and lewisite were stopped. Storage areas were filled to capacity, and the demand for poison gas had decreased because neither the Germans nor the Japanese used gas on Americans. President Franklin Roosevelt's strategy of "stockpile poison gas so they don't try" worked (the only major use of gas during the war was by the Japanese against the Chinese). In 1943, the arsenal shifted to producing napalm and a pyrotechnic fuel to fill bomb casings.[14]

COLORADO FUEL & IRON COMPANY

By 1903, Colorado Fuel & Iron Company (CF&I) in Pueblo was the largest coal producer in the Rocky Mountain region, with mines in six counties. During the Great Depression, the company reorganized as the Colorado Fuel & Iron Company. By 1940, CF&I company towns were Tercio, Frederick, Morley, Pictou, Farr, Tioga, Nonac, Crested Butte, and Wagon Wheel Gap. Colorado Supply Company stores existed in Crested Butte, South Cañon City, Morley, Farr, Valdez, Tioga, and Weston.[15] CF&I holdings in Pueblo were Minnequa Works, Corwin Hospital and Minnequa School of Nursing (established in 1903), and the Steel Works YMCA.

In January 1941, CF&I began producing forgings for 155 mm shells. By the end of the war, the plant had manufactured 3.5 million projectiles and earned four "E" awards—a rare accomplishment as only 5 percent of the nation's war production plants earned that many citations. Through the war years, the plant expanded from a production level of 43 percent in 1939 to 72 percent in 1940, nearly 98 percent in 1942, over 100 percent in 1943, and by 1944 to 104 percent capacity.[16] While women worked in nearly every department at CF&I, many men were exempt from the draft because their expertise was needed at the company.

OTHER COLORADO COMPANIES

The Pueblo Ordnance Depot (POD) opened east of the city in July 1942. From the beginning, it was planned to be a permanent facility. Over the course of three years, the depot handled more than 1.6 million tons of war materiel. It received, stored, and shipped ammunition ranging from .22 caliber bullets to 16 inch armor-piercing shells; artillery; medical and quartermaster supplies; and weapons and parts for weapons such as arming wires, to name a few.[17] Men and women were promised equal opportunities for advancement.[18]

Other smaller Colorado companies employed women. Colorado Builders Supply Company originally fabricated accessories and building contractors' equipment and materials. During the war it organized a subsidiary, Cobusco Steel Products Co., located at West Evans and Mariposa Streets in Denver in what had been the Cotton Mill. It manufactured 75 mm fragmentation bombs and 90 mm armor-piercing shells. Approximately 900 men and women worked three shifts in alternating six- and seven-day weeks. A slightly smaller plant was Heckethorn Manufacturing Company, or "Heco," which manufactured pulleys and hardware before the war. In 1941, owner William Heckethorn signed United States Navy contracts to manufacture photographic products, 200 mm projectiles, and 4.2 chemical mortar fuses. In 1942, 160 people worked three shifts at the South Prince Street shop in Littleton. At the height of production in 1945, 700 women and 400 men produced approximately 50 million 20 mm anti-aircraft projectiles for war use. Heckethorn had many workers in their sixties and seventies. Laura Ukena, a grandmother of six, had a daughter in the Army Nurse Corps (ANC) and sons in the air corps, army, and coast guard—good reasons to "do her part" for victory.[19]

As war-related plants across the country opened and expanded, women applied for defense jobs. Their reasons for doing so—economic necessity, adventure, patriotism, boredom—were as diverse as the women themselves. One result was that women experienced upward job mobility during the war.[20] With factory work paying substantially higher wages than traditional female occupations, women quit those jobs in favor of defense jobs. Women, who earned an average of less than $25 a week as service workers, applied for defense jobs that paid over $40 a week. Longmont resident Cecelia Borrego was the fifth of ten children of Frank and Julia Borrego. Her father, a former sugar beet laborer, was a Denver city street worker. In 1939 he earned $140 for the entire year. His twenty-two-year-old daughter was the oldest offspring still living at home with five younger siblings who ranged in age from sixteen to four. Working forty-eight hours a week as a hospital cook, her total salary in 1939 was $780. Her salary sustained the family. By 1943 she was at the Denver Ordnance Plant, earning significantly more money.[21]

Laundry workers, maids, nurse's aides, and other service workers jumped at the chance to leave their physically hard, low-paying jobs. Nationwide, over 600 laundries were forced to shut down for lack of workers.[22] Mary Bradish and Theresa Santos quit their laundry jobs to work at CF&I. Bradish became a steam operator in the 25" (inch) mill plant, while Santos became a lathe operator in the Forge Shop. Santos was joined by Elizabeth Pritchard and Anna B. Stark, both of whom had been employed by Corwin Hospital. Pritchard had been a nurse's aid, and Stark had been a cook.[23] A crane "man" in the Forge Shop was Rose Abbate. She had been a clerk in her family's grocery store.[24] Rachel N. Blazich changed one job—maid at the Steel Works YMCA—for a similar one as plant janitor. Another former maid, Susie Montoya, became a wharf "man" in the coke plant.[25]

Female students abandoned their schooling at the University of Colorado, University of Denver, and Colorado Woman's College; and teachers left their classrooms to work at the Denver Ordnance Plant. Throughout the war years, town newspapers listed the names of local teachers who resigned to take factory jobs. Dorothy England, a grade school teacher in Craig, quit to take a job at the DOP at a "substantial increase in salary," as did Antoinette Ash, a teacher in Steamboat Springs. Mary Margaret Robichaud followed her husband, joining him at the plant.[26] Colorado teachers who chose to remain in the classroom and not take a defense job for higher pay struggled with overcrowded classrooms, anxious students, and higher absenteeism and student mobility.

Some women prepared for defense work by taking classes at local schools or plants. At Boulder High School, Wilma Garwood, Beulah Beayer, Barbara Lilly, and Ann Tavelli took classes to learn basic sheet metal skills. They made eave troughs, elbow and T-joints, and various types of connections from flat sheets of metal.[27] They also learned to weld and to handle equipment used in aircraft factories. They did not find the classes or the work difficult.[28]

The federal government and industries urged women to take defense jobs as production goals rose concomitantly as more men were needed in the armed forces. One estimate was that fourteen war production workers were needed to support one man in combat. A questionnaire by *Modern Industry* noted that, *exclusive of office employees*, 1 percent of aviation workers were women in 1941, 15 percent in 1942, and an expected 65 percent in 1943. In the electrical industry, corresponding percentages rose from 6 percent to 9 percent to an anticipated 35 percent during those same years. By 1943, the instrument industry would be composed of 60 percent women, and employees in the pharmaceutical industry would increase from 45 percent in 1941 to 75 percent in 1943. Similarly, the machinery industry would increase from no women employed outside of offices to an anticipated 50 percent in 1943.[29]

A key component was convincing women to apply for jobs that had been historically closed to them. Equating certain aspects of defense work with women's skills in sewing, cooking, and using kitchen appliances was a common recruiting tool. One advertisement from the American War Manpower Campaign told women, "If you've sewed on buttons, or made buttonholes on a machine, you can learn to do spot welding on airplane parts. If you've done fine embroidery, or made jewelry, you can learn to do assembly on time fuses, radio tubes. If you've used an electric mixer in your kitchen, you can learn to run a drill press. If you've ironed your sheets in an electrical mangle, you can learn to run a blueprint machine."[30] The US Department of War suggested that industries compare cutting sheet metal to cutting a dress pattern.[31] Regardless of whether that was a legitimate comparison, women applied for defense jobs in droves and, once hired, agreed with the assessment. Garwood, training at Boulder High School, believed that some knowledge of mathematics helped in drawing patterns for sheet metal work but echoed the industry in saying that knowledge of dress patterns was helpful, too.[32]

Among those first hired at defense plants were secretaries, office clerks, stenographers, and typists. It was imperative to fill these positions at the very beginning of plant work to process job applications, handle payroll, take dictation at meetings, and file reports. Women left office jobs for a war plant office or the production line because those positions paid better. Women also wanted to more directly help the war effort. Luella D. Clark, who had been a stenographer before the war, did similar work in the CF&I Accounting Department.[33] Edith Daugherty, a stenographer with the US Employment Office in Routt County, resigned to take a similar job at the Rocky Mountain Arsenal.[34] Dorothy Y. Bates quit her job as a bookkeeper at the White Feed Store to join the finishing crew at Minnequa Works, while Ada M. Bowers moved from being an assistant bookkeeper at a motor accessory and parts store to a de-scaler in the 40" (inch) mill division. Ruby D. Lucas used her experience as an advertising company worker to secure a job in the CF&I print shop.[35] Fadonna Carr had a number of jobs before becoming a defense plant employee. She graduated from high school in Bayfield and then worked as a secretary, a nanny, a switchboard operator, and a drug store clerk. Wanting to help the war effort, she went to work at Chemurgic Corporation in California.[36] After December 7, 1941, the company—which had been making chemical products and insecticides—expanded to produce railroad torpedoes, aircraft parachute flares, red parachute flares, orange smoke signals, and hand grenade fuses.

In particular, African Americans experienced upward job mobility as a result of working at defense plants.[37] Tens of thousands of Blacks who had been toiling in fields fled the South for defense plants in St. Louis, Chicago, Detroit, Los Angeles, and Richmond; in doing so, they bypassed Colorado. Black residents in Colorado—unlike those in the South—generally did not move out of state for defense jobs. Equally desperate, though, to leave dead-end laundry and domestic service jobs, Black women in Colorado applied for jobs in the state's defense plants.

Although Remington Arms Company publicly claimed that it did not discriminate on the basis of race, it initially hired African American women in only three areas—restrooms, cafeterias, and the Lead Shop. Restroom and cafeteria work, although little different from what many Black women had been doing before the war, still paid more at the ordnance plant. The Lead Shop paid even better. Working there was dangerous, however. A worker in the Lead Shop was tested for lead poisoning every three weeks. If the level of lead in her blood was too high, she was removed from the shop and temporarily assigned to cafeteria or restroom work. Although this was done for the worker's protection, it also meant a decrease in pay.

One of the first Black women hired at the DOP was Oleta Crain. Prior to enlisting in the Women's Army Auxiliary Corps, she got a job cleaning and mopping floors at the DOP.[38] Crain criticized the plant's hiring policies: "The colored girls work only with men and not with any white girls. We have to walk two blocks to the cafeteria and a rest room. We did not have a couch or chair or table and if we got tired had to walk two blocks to another building. Two or three times the forewoman found girls lying on the floor to rest, so after closing a rest room in another building they gave us one couch from there."[39]

Denver's Black press also criticized discriminatory practices. The *Denver Star* reported, "We have learned that the Negro women have not one job in the industry plant, only maid and janitresses. That there has never been a 'white' maid or janitress. Such jobs have been reserved to Negro women." It encouraged its DOP workers and African American community leaders to take their concerns to the

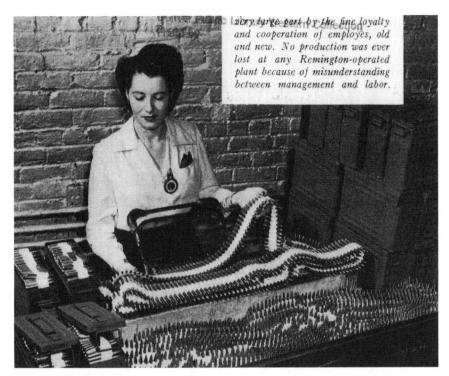

very large part by the fine loyalty and cooperation of employes, old and new. No production was ever lost at any Remington-operated plant because of misunderstanding between management and labor.

FIGURE 7.2. A woman at the Denver Ordnance Plant packs ammunition cartridge belts into metal storage containers. While the caption reads that there was never any lost production as a result of management-labor issues, the plant did face criticism for its discriminatory hiring of African American women. *Courtesy*, Western History Collection, Z-123, Denver Public Library, Denver, CO.

proper authorities at the plant.[40] The Phyllis Wheatley YWCA branch (where Crain and other Black female employees lived), the Black media, and civic and religious organizations eventually brought about minor changes. Crain replaced a white female high school dropout in the Lead Shop. Plant managers thought it was safe to transfer Crain, a college graduate, because "colored girls who have gone to college are honest."[41]

Crain was one of twelve Black women who worked outside the restrooms and kitchens. Another was Marguerite Grant Baker. Baker's mother, a domestic servant for the William Gray Evans family, wanted a better life for her daughter. When she was unable to find a job as a trained dietitian, she became a domestic servant, following in her mother's footsteps. After the plant opened, she got a cafeteria job before moving on to the production line. For the first time in her life, she received wages comparable to a white woman's.[42] In 1943, the percentage of African American workers at the plant rose from 3.29 percent on January 1 to 3.7 percent in September, slightly more than Denver's per capita percentage of African

Americans (3.26 percent). By 1945, the number of female African American workers in the Inspection Department had risen from 0.0 to 2.5 percent.[43]

Women made up the majority of janitors in Colorado defense plants. Lila Dilworth, supervisor of janitors at the Pueblo Ordnance Depot, created a family environment that resulted in nearly zero absenteeism. Although they worked in one of the lower-paying jobs, janitors overwhelmingly enrolled in the 10 percent payroll deduction plan for war bonds. Olla Wensell devoted 50 percent of her paycheck to purchase war bonds, and others periodically bought bonds beyond their paycheck deduction amounts.[44] Colorado Fuel & Iron also employed large numbers of female janitors—or janitresses in company parlance. Janitress Anna P. Butkovich was born in Yugoslavia in 1896. She was joined on the CF&I payroll by her twenty-four-year-old son, a welder; her twenty-three-year-old daughter, a kitchen staff member at Corwin Hospital; and her nineteen-year-old daughter, a stenographer at the Steel Mill YMCA.[45]

Female workers also dominated inspection jobs. Defense plants quickly realized that women made excellent inspectors, or inspectresses, as they were classified on DOP documents. At first, the plant hired many young women for whom this was their first position. New hires were enrolled in a two-week class in gauges, micrometers, and dividers to give them broader knowledge of the work. Marriage and the subsequent induction of their husbands created a large turnover. When the supply of young women was exhausted, the plant extended the age limit and employed middle-aged women. It was reported that "these women have proved to be steady and to take their work very seriously. The younger girls appear to be more adept in the gaging of cartridges and have keener eyesight for visual inspection."[46]

At the DOP, nearly every inspector was a woman. Four of the five female inspectors in the Ballistics Department were Maxine V. Williamson, Mildred A. Swink, Jacquin Ashworth, and Betty Vinske.[47] In the Packing Department, all twenty-three inspectors were women, including Magdalen Fiest Lampman. After marrying in Bismarck, North Dakota, she and her husband, Dean, moved to Denver, where Dean got a job with Remington. When war was declared, he enlisted in the United States Air Corps and she took a job at the plant. Her duties included using a micrometer to measure production-line samples of machine gun bullets before they were loaded. She noted that her job was not physically hard, but it did require concentration because everything had to be very precise.[48] The diligence with which all production workers and inspectresses did their work was rewarded in 1942 and 1943 when the United States Army and Navy awarded the plant "E" pennants. The navy even "complained" that the cartridges were too good—they did not have enough defective ones for machine gun training.[49]

CF&I hired Ada Sullivan, Agnes Fitzpatrick, and Vivian Aileen Henley as its first three female inspectors (not inspectresses). Their job was to ensure that quality products entered their departments and to maintain that quality when the

FIGURE 7.3. Ada Sullivan, Agnes Fitzpatrick, and Vivian Aileen Henley (*left to right*), the first three female inspectors at CF&I, interviewed by a *Pueblo Chieftain* reporter, 1942. *Courtesy*, Steelworks Center of the West, Pueblo, CO, cfi_pla_0287.

products left their work space to move to other departments. Henley, a Pueblo native, widowed and working as a hotel kitchen maid in 1940, had four children living with her. Two years later she was the housekeeper at Corwin Hospital. By 1943 she was working as an inspector at CF&I, a position she held until the mid-1960s when she retired from the company.[50]

At the Pueblo Ordnance Depot, checkers reviewed incoming shipments. Because they worked outdoors, they were required to have excellent stamina in addition to a passion for accuracy. Checkers were eligible to become inspectors after a training period as long as they had completed one year of high school chemistry.[51] Women made up 75 percent of the depot's Inspection Department. Pay for inspectresses/inspectors ranged between seventy-two cents an hour at the ordnance plant to ninety-one cents an hour at the fuel company. Employees received accident and health insurance, wage disability and group life insurance, and two weeks' annual paid vacation.

Cobusco also relied on female inspectors. Roy R. Waugh, general superintendent of the plant, reported, "We have to use men on the bomb production line because the work is heavy. Women [45 percent of the labor force] work as inspectors and on automatic machine operations." No powder was used at the plant. The fragmentation bombs were loaded in Nebraska and sent to the Pacific and European Theaters of Operation. The 90 mm shells, with the exception of the fuze, powder, and windshield, were complete when they rolled off the conveyor belt at the Mariposa plant. They weighed almost 17 pounds at that point.[52]

As the war progressed into its third and fourth years, women were hired in greater numbers and in more jobs. The Denver Ordnance Plant's female bullet makers proved to be "most satisfactory" in handling lapping and polishing work in machine shops.[53] In mid-1942, supervisors stepped into a new frontier when they trained female employees to handle testing, including the firing of four types of caliber .30 machine guns, velocity tests, and accuracy tests.[54] After training a cadre of women, supervisors reported that there were enough to take over all proof firing, assembling, inspecting, and reporting done at the inspection station. In early 1944, the Ballistic Department employed five female gunners—Casita M. Thompson, Anna K. Dudley, Mary Ridgway, Loretta M. Quinn, and Minnie E. Stander—who earned between $1,440 and $1,800 a year.[55]

CF&I, insisting that women would not be barred from any job simply because of their sex, hired women for jobs ranging from operating cranes to handling molds. The Bolt and Spike Mill Department employed women, such as Florence Slaten, to crush large pieces of ore from company mines. At forty-three, Slaten was one of the older workers; her job was to check grinding balls. The next year she changed jobs, becoming a sorter in the packing room and earning over seventy-five cents an hour.[56]

In 1944, Colorado Fuel & Iron Company was lauded for setting a world record for the production of 155 mm shell forgings. Five hundred employees working in three shifts turned out 27,844 projectiles in six days. Three months later, the plant manufactured its 3 millionth shell forging. Helen Aasterud, an inspector at the plant, was prominently shown in *The Blast* photograph noting the occasion.[57] On April 20, 1945, *The Blast* honored the company's record-making Forge Shop workers. A two-page spread featuring twenty workers showed mostly women employees. The majority were clad in work clothes while a few wore skirts or dresses, indicating that they were clerks or secretaries.[58]

Other women worked in the Brick Shed, loading and unloading bricks for furnaces. Mary Horvat was a foreman and Irene Smith a timekeeper. Horvat's parents, the Poders, immigrated to the United States from Slovakia and were naturalized in 1919. Born in Colorado, their daughter married Anthony Horvat in 1933. Other shed workers were Jennie Lucero, Lillie Acuna, Caeilda Sanchez, Ramono Soto, Dora Baca, Jean Perko, Anne Nicasio, Mary Garcia, and Mabel Smith.[59]

Defense plants, whose products were most directly tied to helping a woman's husband or son or other male relative return home from the war as quickly and safely as possible, were particular draws for female workers.[60] Producing bombs was one of those jobs. Marge Brandau was one of twenty-six female workers on an assembly line at the Rocky Mountain Arsenal. In Building 741, the women filled bomb casings with napalm. The plant ran twenty-four hours a day. Each of the three shifts filled between 250 and 300 bombs. Because the work was tedious, women passed the time singing and chatting. Brandau was typical of the workforce at the arsenal. About 70 percent of the 3,500 workers were women, many of whom had never worked outside the home. Although inexperienced, the women set production records.[61]

Gates Rubber Company employed 4,000 workers to make rubber buckets, containers, ladles, and jugs to hold TNT and other explosives while chemicals were mixed. One of the bucket workers was Betty McAfee. Others, such as forty-eight-year-old Christina Coan, who sewed gas masks at the Broadway plant, had not been employed outside the home before the war. Other women trimmed parts, checked pieces, and tested, packed, rolled, labeled, and finished a variety of products, including fan belts, tubes, hoses, and tires. Margaret Casias worked in the Tire Department, while Katharina Fraser put finishing touches on a "vital rubber part of the bombing apparatus" for one of "Uncle Sam's big bombers."[62] Male workers did the heavier work of loading, mixing, and curing tires. As was typical in all plants, men were department supervisors. Male and female technicians produced a synthetic rubber known as Buna. To observe its reactions to a wide range of conditions, they cooked, burned, froze, soaked, pounded, stretched, vibrated, and chafed the product.

Newspapers teemed with articles about the types of work women did at the Pueblo Ordnance Depot. As the war wore on and more men left for the armed forces, women were increasingly hired in less traditional jobs as carpenters, auto mechanics, and fork lift operators.[63] Carpenters' pay ranged from $3.65 to $6.56 a day for a 48-hour work week (hours over 40 paid time-and-a-half for overtime). Women made up the majority of workers in the Crate Shop, where they sawed and hammered crates and warehouse pallets for other departments. When her son joined the service, Mary E. Jones closed her home, rented an apartment, and joined the depot. It was her first paying job. The widow was praised as the "ideal example of the housewife type" who worked in the shop.[64] Carpenters were aided

FIGURE 7.4. Women truck drivers for the Colorado Supply Company, 1944. *Courtesy*, Steelworks Center of the West, Archives, Pueblo, CO, cfi_sub_csc_0001.

in their work by Virginia Smith, the only female saw filer in the nation. She and her husband handled saw service at the POD. She also invented a guard for power saws that was used in the Crate and Carpenter Shops.[65]

Less than a year after its opening, the depot began training women to be auto mechanics. Their $0.70 hourly wage was slightly more than that of female fork lift operators in the warehouses. Bored with housework after working as a beautician and a stenographer, Harriet Keller applied for a depot job. She was initially hired in the Crate Shop. After her transfer to the combat equipment warehouse, she vowed that her supervisor's only way of getting her to dismount her fork lift and leave would be by brutal force or an unconditional termination.[66]

While some plants or departments emphasized the femininity of their female workers, others praised their strength. Women like Byrde Girsky painted, stenciled, and packed crates at the depot. Girsky's "huskily built" physique was wasted doing stenciling, so she and Lila Smith practiced using strapping machines during their rest periods to be eligible for that job. It took physical strength to operate the machines strappers used to crate ammunition shipments.[67]

Another department that required a "husky build" was the lumberyard. Because she did not like to sew, Rosie L. Jackson quit her job at an awning factory. In the late 1930s, she cooked for the hot lunch program that provided meals for school-children before being hired at the depot. Clad in overalls, a work shirt, and a straw hat, she supervised and worked alongside seventeen other women who lifted and neatly stacked huge pieces of lumber for the Crate Shop.[68]

In addition to those in the mill and other manufacturing areas of CF&I, females were hired for non-production-line jobs. Some women—like Mattie C. Rolen—drove pickup trucks for the Colorado Supply Company Store Division of CF&I. Located in nearly every CF&I mining community, the stores sold goods for home and work from a warehouse located just west of Minnequa Steelworks in Pueblo.[69] Other women worked white-collar jobs. Reta Copeland was the first woman chemist at the plant since World War I. Following in the footsteps of her father, Jay D. Thomas, a chemical engineer, the Pueblo native majored in chemistry at Pueblo Junior College. She worked the swing shift in the Main Chemistry Laboratory while her husband, Bob, worked the graveyard shift. Each week, they switched shifts.[70] Another woman hired to do an unusual job was Margie Thornberry. A high school graduate from Huerfano County who had completed two years of college engineering classes, Thornberry was hired to work in the Mining Engineering Department.[71]

Guard duty was another less traditional job for women. Women guarded at the Pueblo Ordnance Depot and at the Climax Mine. The depot's guard force of 183 employees included 18 women. Typical of the depot's female workforce, Maude E. Moser was a housewife and mother. She was also a schoolteacher. Moser was trained as the first female radio operator but returned to the guard force when other operators were trained and placed at the radio controls.[72] Although there is a long-held superstition among miners that it is unlucky for a woman to enter a mine, it did not apply to other jobs at the mine. During the 1940s, the US Department of War designated Climax Mine, the nation's largest producer of molybdenum, the highest-priority mine in the country. Immediate emergency production was ordered.[73] Wooden guard towers equipped with searchlights and a 3,000-foot-long chain-link fence topped with barbed wire encircled the mine and mill. Mattie Cora Custus Lee Simpson was one of at least two women employed at the Climax Mine as an armed guard. In her early thirties during the war and with a stepdaughter living at home, the Colorado native stood guard at the entrance gate. She wore a uniform and carried a long-barreled .38 special revolver.[74]

Approximately 40 million Americans, including Charlotte Billows, were on the move during World War II, either to join the armed forces or to relocate for work.[75] In March 1943 Billows packed up her belongings and moved from Minturn to Climax for her job in the mine's lamp room. There she charged, serviced, and issued all cap, hand, and flame safety lamps to workers. Myrtle E. Staup Borah, who lost her husband in 1945, was the hostess at the mine's club.[76] Although women were sprinkled throughout the mine complex, no woman worked as a miner at Climax during World War II.[77]

In addition to the satisfaction they received from helping the war effort and receiving a good salary and benefits, employees at defense plants joined athletic teams that competed in city leagues, enjoyed reduced rates at the YMCA, and participated in seasonal "Frolics" at amusement parks. There were also USO units for women war workers at 1772 Grant Street and 1545 Tremont Place in Denver. In 1943, the DOP created the Ordnance Employees Association for recreation. Nearly 100 percent of the plant's employees joined.[78] Likewise, the Pueblo Ordnance Depot organized an employee recreation group that planned dances and offered sports activities. The first event was a benefit show for the local USO.[79] During the last two years of the war, the POD staged a rodeo in which employees participated. No rodeo is complete without a rodeo queen; in 1945, nine young women vied for the honor. Three were checkers; five were clerks, secretaries, or typists; and one was the supervisor in Reports. Depot employees chose Katherine Hall, a warehouse checker, rodeo queen. Her attendants were Jeanne Blevins (clerk) and Betty Hall (an auditor).[80]

Whether they worked in the company office, on the production line, or in a shed, female—and male—workers struggled with housing and transportation issues. As early as October 1942, the *Chieftain* urged Puebloans to open their homes to depot workers. Even after a great response from the community, an additional 650 houses and 350 sleeping rooms were still needed.[81] Denver newspapers were filled with want ads from people seeking housing. Women and families with young children had a particularly difficult time finding a place to stay.

As the rubber shortage grew critical, employees at the Pueblo Ordnance Depot were first encouraged and then practically mandated to ride buses to work. In July 1943, the depot started planning to bus as many workers as possible from city hall to the depot. The workers protested at the idea of piling into two sixty-four-passenger buses for their shifts. The following month, employees with B or C rations received a "suggestion" from the Office of Price Administration to start carrying four to five passengers if they wished to continue to receive gasoline rations. Depot commander Lieutenant Colonel L. S. Barr announced that only in rare circumstances would cars with fewer passengers merit the continued use of gas rations. While Barr acknowledged that some cars arrived full of passengers, he pointed out that more workers could carpool.[82]

Workers struggled with changes in work shifts. DOP worker Helen Osborn recounted that her commute by streetcar took two hours one way. When plant managers changed her schedule from a day shift to a night or graveyard shift, she was able to sleep only a few hours before returning to work.[83] While both men and women experienced shift changes, it was especially difficult for women who had to shop for the family and find alternative childcare arrangements.

Childcare became a significant problem when women with young children began working in the factories. The Denver Ordnance Plant was the largest civilian employee of women in Colorado. But the number of its female workers paled in comparison to those employed in America's heavily industrialized regions. At the height of production, the DOP employed just under 10,000 women. In contrast, two Kaiser shipyards in Portland, Oregon, employed 25,000 female workers during World War II. Edgar F. Kaiser, the son of Henry J. Kaiser, consulted child development experts about constructing two large childcare centers. The buildings were built at the entrance to the shipyards, convenient for mothers on their way to and from work. Each of the large centers accommodated over 1,100 children. In a similar way, the Douglas Aircraft plant in Santa Monica opened a nursery within 4 miles of its plant.[84]

Nationwide, there were 3,000 on-site daycare centers located at defense plants.[85] But no daycare center existed at the Denver plant, forcing its working mothers to cobble together their own childcare solutions. Neither the Denver Council of Defense nor the Council of Social Agencies planned for childcare for working mothers. Finally, to aid its female employees, the DOP published a list of low-cost childcare centers and licensed private homes. Under the direction of Grace Penfold, the plant's Welfare Division established a service that helped working mothers find childcare for their children.[86] Seventy-two licensed, twenty-four-hour-a-day private homes were available at a cost ranging from one dollar a day to ten dollars per week per child. Nine publicly operated nursery centers and seven pre-school centers run by the Denver Public Schools (DPS) and the Denver Bureau of Public Welfare were also available. DPS daycare centers were located at Cole Junior High School, Dora Moore School, and Lincoln School. They were open twelve hours a day, beginning at 7:00 a.m. Each accepted forty children between the ages of two and five. Only the children of full-time working mothers were accepted. Three teachers, a cook, and a helper were employed at each school. The fee of forty cents a day included breakfast and lunch.[87] Care in private twenty-four-hour nurseries cost between seven and ten dollars a week, including all meals.[88] Fortunately for her, Alice Baker was able to rely on her parents to tend to her children when she worked day shifts at the ordnance plant.[89] Pueblo depot worker Dolores Killion, a widow with two children, solved her childcare problem by sending her children to live with her father in Nebraska.[90]

In addition to housing, transportation, and work hour difficulties, wartime work could be dangerous. Munitions factories were particularly dangerous. Ill-fitting work clothes, the lack of safety devices, and the presence of explosive materials could quickly produce a dangerous situation. Amounts of explosives and alignment had to be exact. The monotonous work made it difficult for workers to stay awake, compounded by the use of solvents containing sleep-inducing ether.[91] At the Rocky Mountain Arsenal, a foreman was severely burned about his face and throat during a plant accident. In June 1945, "despite all safety precautions," two M74 bombs exploded on the assembly line. Four women were badly burned. One later died at the hospital. The cause of the explosion was never determined. Because damage to the production facility was slight, work quickly resumed.[92]

Chemical plants were equally dangerous. After a year's work, Chemurgic employees in California could take a two-week vacation. The first time Fadonna Carr visited her parents in Colorado, her department had an explosion and several people were killed. A similar accident happened in a different department the second time she took a vacation. The third year, as she was preparing to take a vacation, several female employees vowed to quit until she returned. The plant manager handled the situation by shutting down the plant and giving every employee simultaneous vacations.[93]

As noted, the Lead Shop at the Denver Ordnance Plant was inherently dangerous. Workers there—mostly African American women—were exposed to toxic levels of lead every day. Other parts of the plant, with the exception of the gunpowder storage areas, were relatively safe. The plant recorded no serious injuries to workers, unlike other ordnance plants that experienced explosions.[94]

CF&I solicited suggestions for improvements in safety from its employees. In 1944, the company newspaper noted that the most recent suggestions from female employees were "particularly appreciated."[95] Martha Jones, a Black woman with the "girls' labor gang" in the Open Hearth Department, was the first female employee to receive a coveted safety button. Supervisors recognized her for submitting fifty green slip suggestions. She was also selected "Woman of the Week" for her individual safety record. She had lost no time to injuries since she started working at the plant two years earlier.[96] A Colorado native and the wife of librarian Theodore Jones, she held a four-year college degree. Jones was nearly thirty-seven years old when she started working at CF&I. Both her son and daughter were under the age of five.

Stories of racial discrimination, unequal job opportunities, pay inequities, and sexual harassment abound in the literature of defense plants during World War II. As noted, the Denver Ordnance Plant did not initially honor its anti-discrimination clause with the federal government when it hired Black women only for restroom, cafeteria, and lead shop work. Even after the plant was forced to hire African Americans on the production line and as inspectors, Blacks always constituted a small percentage of those workers.

Women were seldom hired in supervisory or managerial positions at any of the plants. Although they made up 100 percent of the Inspection Department, women were not supervisors. Inspectresses at the Denver Ordnance Plant were supervised by three males—a supervisor, assistant supervisor, and foreman. One exception occurred at the Pueblo Ordnance Depot. Leta Bowyer supervised an all-female staff in the fiscal section. The only female executive at the depot, Bowyer graduated from Northwestern University with a major in economics. She worked for a large insurance company before joining the POD.[97]

While women made big gains in employment during World War II, little changed in regard to equal pay for equal work.[98] CF&I claimed that male and female employees were paid the same wages as long as their job codes were identical. The question is, who determined the job code and subsequent pay scale? Domenic Chiaro, Florence Silvio, and Dorothea Menger were all "finishing helpers" at the Minnequa Works. Chiaro and Silvio, with job code 50091, were paid $0.785 an hour. Menger, code 50092, was paid $0.755. Janitors were given a numerical code of 01001. The code for janitresses was 01002 while the head janitress in 1944, Amelia J. Vidic, had the code 01003. Janitor Herman Rowe was paid an hourly wage of $0.755. Perhaps he was responsible for more physical labor than a janitress who was paid only $0.635. However, Vidic was a supervisor, and yet she still earned less than Rowe.[99] Without access to job descriptions at CF&I, it is hard to discern if the jobs were truly different or if this was an underhanded way to pay female workers less than men. It would not have been the first plant to do so. Across the nation, companies got away with pay discrimination by calling female workers "helper trainees" instead of "mechanic learners" or by substituting pre-war job categories of "male" and "female" with "heavy" and "light."[100]

The experience of Olga Peters and Helen Youngman illustrates this point. In 1943, they filed a grievance with CF&I's Industrial Relations Department. The two truckers demanded that management pay them the same rate male truckers were paid—an additional seven cents an hour. Peters and Youngman argued that their three months on the job qualified them as experienced. They claimed they were able to perform all of their required work. After months of research, the trucking supervisor, D. E. Mayhugh, and employee representative J. R. Irwin determined that "these female truck drivers are used almost exclusively in the driving of dump trucks at one specific location. The work required of them does not require considerable physical effort, as they are neither required to load or unload the equipment. They have been instructed also that they are not expected to assist in the removal of the tire[s] or repair them." The men concluded that the two women were not "performing the same duties as male employees, and therefore, are not entitled to the same rate of pay."[101]

As irritating and wrong as pay inequities and fewer opportunities for supervisory roles were, unwanted sexual advances, harassment, and pressure were more ignominious, although not universal.[102] Diaries, interviews, and recollections of female defense workers contain incidences of male supervisors who demanded sexual favors in exchange for preferred working shifts, male co-workers who glued a woman's lunchbox to a bench or hid her tools, men who whistled and verbally harassed or embarrassed female workers, and others who sexually groped, assaulted, and attacked female employees.[103] In Colorado, company bulletins and newsletters, however, are free of any such happenings. That, of course, is not to say they did not occur. To maintain a sense of cohesiveness and teamwork, such things would not have been printed. Second, many victims did not report transgressions. Just fifteen months after the plant opened, the Denver Ordnance Plant bulletin interviewed women workers about their bosses. Most said they were fair and approachable.[104] Again, fears of losing one's job or receiving lousy shift assignments have often kept employees from being less than candid when interviewed about their jobs. Third, unlike the huge aircraft factories and shipyards that employed tens of thousands of female workers, the plants in Colorado employed relatively fewer women, most of whom worked in traditional jobs. Alice Baker, who made sandwiches for construction workers at the Denver Ordnance Plant and then went into the factory once it opened, said she was not treated differently because she was a woman.[105] Magdalen Lampman believed "the men very definitely respected all the women . . . there were no problems at all."[106] It is safe to assume that there were in fact problems, but they were alternatively unreported, ignored, not believed, or swept under the company rug.

In spite of discrimination, harassment, and the exhaustion of doing double duty as homemakers and employees, women were successful defense workers. They earned praise from employers, supervisors, and co-workers alike. The ease with which women adapted to their new responsibilities surprised many. The Office of War Information noted that war production work had disproved the old saw that women have no mechanical ability.[107] One of the most definitive examples of how women were accepted on an equal basis—as far as their ability to do the work, not to be paid the same wage—was observed by members of the Women's Bureau. After a lengthy tour of a shipyard, the bureau noted that men did not show the typical deference to women workers associated with traditional male-female relationships, such as picking up their dropped tools.[108] Colorado newspapers noted regularly that women were fulfilling their duties and doing so, notably, without whining about the weather or factory conditions. Managers praised women's "greater patience and greater enthusiasm" compared with male employees.[109] Supervisors at the Pueblo Ordnance Depot found that the women were conscientious checkers and inspectors, safe and courteous truck drivers (no swearing!), strong workers in the lumberyard, and competent stencilers, packers, and painters.[110]

Women's supposedly innate talent for being organized, tidy, detail-oriented, and well-suited for tedious, monotonous work was a significant asset in defense plants.[111] A 1943 government publication, "You're Going to Hire Women," listed several positive attributes of females. They were dexterous, accurate precision workers who were good at repetitive tasks and adept at distinguishing fine color and material differences. The author compared women to plastics: "A woman is a substitute—like plastic instead of metal. She has special characteristics that lend themselves to new and sometimes to such superior uses."[112] Supervisors at the Pueblo depot claimed their warehouses were neater and in better order when a larger percentage of "housewife type" women worked in them. Elsie Oreskovich, with twenty years experience in a meatpacking plant, led an all-female crew in one warehouse.[113] One of her workers was Virginia Andrews, who had never been in a warehouse before. Andrews had been a maid in a private home before the war.[114] Managers at the DOP noted that "girls have been very satisfactory in performing the visual inspection duties. They are *adapted temperamentally* to do this tedious, confining work" (emphasis added).[115] That sort of damning praise from managers and supervisors was not unusual. More than one supervisor and efficiency expert commented on women's "natural" talent for tasks that were repetitive in nature and required a high degree of dexterity, patience, attention to detail, and manipulative skill.[116]

Throughout the war years, there was also a distinct sexist emphasis on a woman worker's "comeliness" and an assumption that she needed to always be attractive.[117] *Transportation* magazine advised male plant supervisors to "give every girl an adequate number of rest periods" so she could keep her hair tidy, apply fresh lipstick, and wash her hands several times a day.[118] CF& I's *The Blast* published a story of "a host of charming girls" doing "every conceivable job." Helen Magan, "our favorite drill press operator," was shown in *The Blast* oiling up before starting her work at the Machine Shop in the Bolt and Spike Mill Department. The "comely" Margaret Hedstrom added "charm to a bolt mill machine and does a good job too." Veda Novak weighed kegs while Faye Weaver took over a "man's job" as heater on a bolt mill furnace. Rose Garcia Arellano, Elsie May Pechek, and Margaret Selby added a "new twist on plow bolts on CF&I grader blades."[119] Similarly, the caption accompanying a photograph of two female employees noted the physical benefits—for *women* employees—of working at the Rocky Mountain Arsenal: "Calisthenics aren't half as good for the figure or as much fun as stacking 90 mm armor-piercing shells, according to Miss Esther Garcia . . . and Miss Esther Smith . . . who do their daily dozen with these tough little 17-pounders."[120] Garcia and Smith would soon be looking for other ways to stay in shape.

But not until total victory was secure. After the surrender of Germany, President Harry Truman's exclamation "Our Victory Is But Half Won" reminded Americans that the war was not over. Remington Arms, Heckethorn, and the Rocky Mountain Arsenal advertised for skilled and unskilled men and women in the windows of department stores. Cobusco's broadside in Joslin's announced its need for female machine operators and inspectors.[121]

Within months, though, female employees punched their last time card. Germany surrendered in May and Japan in September 1945. There was no longer a need for millions of defense workers. Factories reverted to their original products or closed shop. General Foods, which produced 10-in-1 combat rations at the DOP, cut 200 workers in August. Although manager James R. Thomas did not believe that more than 5 percent to 10 percent of the workers had jobs waiting for them in the postwar economy, he appeared unconcerned: "Most of them were women, a considerable number of whom will go back to housekeeping."[122] Scores were servicemen's wives who expected that their husbands would be home soon. He assumed that with their husbands home, women would not need or, more significantly, desire to work outside the home. The *Denver Post* presumed that 10,000 Remington and Kaiser employees could be absorbed by home and industrial construction companies. Of course, those companies hired women only for lower-paying office jobs.

It is not what women wanted. Between 1943 and 1945, polls indicated that 47 percent to 68 percent of married women workers wanted to keep their jobs.[123] Helen Hankins, past president of the Colorado and Denver Business and Professional Women's Clubs, stated that women had found their wartime jobs to be profitable and had no intention of relinquishing them come V-J Day. Speaking on behalf of women workers, Hankins insisted, "We don't want to be legislated into our homes. We can be lured there by the right men, but we want the right to work."[124]

It was not to be. Production at the Denver Ordnance Plant ceased immediately; a week after hostilities ended, 2,000 workers were discharged. In October 1945, with a workforce of only 600, the plant was declared surplus property.[125] The Pueblo Ordnance Depot remained in operation after the war, hiring male veterans to replace workers who quit or were terminated.[126] A similar situation existed at Colorado Fuel & Iron. On August 10, 1945, *The Blast* announced on three different pages that veterans (read: males) were welcomed back to the plant.[127]

Although unemployed after 1945, WOWs had shown that they could handle men's work. Women proved to be equally capable and adaptable in the aircraft and shipbuilding industries, both in Colorado and in other parts of the United States.

8

Colorado Women in the Aircraft and Shipbuilding Industries

Barbara Mae Byron, welding rod in hand, could hardly believe her string of good luck. When her sister had written that she was making fifty-four dollars a week at Marinship in California, Byron immediately quit her job as principal of a consolidated school in northwest Colorado and caught the next train. She found an apartment in San Francisco and attended welding school in Sausalito. After two weeks, she "graduated" to sub-assembly work in which massive sections of ships were welded and preassembled. Huge cranes moved the pieces to be incorporated onto the ships themselves. Her luck in finding a place to live, succeeding at welding school, and getting a job continued when she was placed on a crew with Marie Mason. Mason, a Black woman and a top-notch welder, taught her skills to Byron and other female welders. When they had time, they practiced on small pieces of metal. Now Byron was welding alongside Mason on the swing shift. In the hours between 4:00 p.m. and midnight, the shipyard took on a beauty all its own. Fog—a rare sight in Byron's home state of Colorado—rolled in over the Marin County hills. Dazzling showers of sparks from their welding rods twinkled in the night sky as they welded a thousand feet of ship metal. In Byron's mind, the sight only slightly surpassed that of a completed battleship sliding into the bay.[1]

As previously noted, landlocked Colorado was invaluable to ammunition and chemical plants because it was far from the vulnerable coasts. For that reason, it was also critical to the aircraft and shipbuilding industries, the largest employers of women during World War II. By 1943, 65 percent of aviation workers were

DOI: 10.5876/9781646420339.c008   145

women.[2] During the war, Denver companies modified military aircraft and manufactured parts for warships. Recruited by both industries, Colorado women worked both in and out of state.

THE AIRCRAFT INDUSTRY

For industrial jobs that required skills, schools provided training. In 1943, the University of Denver announced a new program. The posting emphasized, "Classes are open to *both* men and women. Two or more friends who want to join the same class may do so."[3] Perhaps it was felt that potential students would be more apt to join if they could do so with their buddies. The classes trained men and women in drafting to combat the serious shortages in aircraft production. Vultee engineers taught the twelve-week tuition-free classes. Trainees were paid a salary; after completing the classes, they were hired by the Engineering Department in San Diego at higher wages. The Emily Griffith Opportunity School in Denver, which had trained workers and volunteers during World War I, played an even larger role in World War II. The school added an airframe shop, new auto mechanic and machine shops, a foundry, and a heat treatment plant. The Trades and Industry Department added metal casting and shipbuilding courses.[4] The school operated on a twenty-four-hour, seven-days-a-week schedule for much of the war. More than fifty Denver companies participated in the school's various war program courses. When twenty-six Denver metal and iron companies won "E" awards, the Opportunity School was also recognized for its work in training employees.[5] One graduate was Virginia Gordon who learned the proper method of extracting carbonized steel from a gas furnace roaring at 1,700 degrees.[6]

Another aviation training school was Frye Aircraft Company. Recognizing the need for skilled aircraft workers, Donald Frye, a former employee and manager of the Douglas and Consolidated Aircraft Companies, established his first school in Kansas City prior to opening schools in five other cities, the last in Denver. The six-week program included fifty-eight separate basic projects, each of which students mastered before moving on to the next one. Male and female students attended sheet metal training classes nine hours a day, six days a week. After training, they were placed in aircraft plants such as Continental's Denver Modification Center.

While huge aircraft factories in Michigan and on the coasts churned out thousands of military aircraft, the Army Air Force (AAF) Materiel Command selected Continental Airlines and its Denver headquarters to handle bomber retrofits. The Denver Modification Center was "devoted to altering, equipping and fitting bombers with whatever additional equipment" was needed for any specific flying task at any particular moment.[7] The facility at the Municipal Airport was given two 600 foot × 400 foot hangars erected at a cost of $5 million. Work began in

FIGURE 8.1. Men and women at Frye Aircraft Company in Denver work at tables with vises and metal brakes. *Courtesy*, Denver Public Library, Western History Collection, X-23869.

July 1942. By September, 250 skilled workmen had been hired. Between April and October 1943, Continental expanded the center to accommodate the increasing flow of aircraft.[8]

One of the first hired was Denver native Helen Louise Warren. In July 1942, she decided to apply for a defense job. Only sixteen years old, she lied about her age and became a riveter at the center. During training she learned to operate drill motors, rivet guns, and bucking bars. She became proficient in "every aspect of plane modifications right down to the last nut, bolt, rivet, and screw."[9] She and her bucker partner Annie reported to the Tool Crib, showed their security badges, picked up their tools, and reported for work.[10] B-17s, B-29s, and North America Mustangs (P-51B) were flown from factory production lines to Denver. Warren and her partner fitted B-17s with long-range fuel tanks, after which the planes were test-flown and then turned over to the army ferrying command on their way to active service. In large hangars, Warren modified B-29s. Because she was so small—only 90 pounds and 5 feet tall—she was often called on to work in the wing areas. Fumes limited the amount of time she could rivet there, though. Workers stripped the aircraft of all confidential instrumentation, installed gun listers and turrets, and placed guns in the nose area. Warren also converted many Superfortresses for photo reconnaissance operations. Other teams extended the flight range of the P-51B and increased its capacity for weather flying by adding more navigational equipment.[11]

Other women at the center ensured that airplanes were properly serviced and maintained from the time they landed until they were released to the military. Lois Ann Coan, Inez Howard, Margaret Tucker, Leona Mahoney, Dorothy Rees,

FIGURE 8.2. Riveter Helen Warren modified B-17 and B-29 aircraft at the Denver Modification Center. *Courtesy*, National Park Service Museum Collections, Helen Louise Warren Tucker Collection, RORI 2679, Rosie the Riveter WWII Home Front National Historical Park, Richmond, CA.

Helene Watts, and Jeanne Pylman called themselves "gun-molls."[12] Every third day, they inspected and oiled .50 caliber machine guns on B-17s. Aircraft sat outside the hangars, which meant that the women worked in snowstorms, windy conditions, and summer heat. One of the crew sat on the concrete and rammed oil-soaked cloths down the throats of the machine guns in the lower gun turret. Then she wrapped the barrels carefully with moisture-proof tape. Other "gun-molls" climbed the backbone of the ship to reach guns in the top turret. Standing on swaying ladders, they oiled waist guns and tail guns. After all the machine guns had been serviced, the crew moved on to the next B-17.[13]

Mothers with sons in the armed forces worked at the plant: Edythe Berry and Jennie Melius, dismantling crew; guards Pearl Hayward, Dazarene Owens, and Mrs. Roy Brown; Gladys Dean, Mildred Kennavy, and Sara Spears, Sub-Assembly Division; Rose Grill, Nina Olsen, Stella Wilt, and Beulah Jones on the production line; Gladys Freelove, Sheet Metal Department; Fern Sweeney and Geneva Kettrey, Upholstery Shop; Bertha Rosenberger, mechanic and inspector; and Barbara Lynch, Edna Henry, and Ursula Holly, janitresses. Among them, the women had thirty-five sons, sons-in-law, and grandsons serving in the armed forces. One mother displayed a Gold Star for her deceased son while another worried about her son, a prisoner of war.[14]

Like most defense plants, the Denver Modification Center did not offer childcare. However, it did employ Lottie E. More, the first women's counselor at a defense plant in the Rocky Mountain region. More helped the center's 1,500 women remain on the job. New female employees started their first day by having lunch with More. They talked informally about the problems a new hire might face as a defense plant worker. They discussed the best kind of clothing for safety and convenience. If a woman needed a nursery for her children, More found one so the worker could concentrate on her job and not fret about her children. If she was concerned about her husband in the service, More took those concerns to the local Red Cross chapter. As the war wound down, female workers worried about future job prospects. More organized and stocked a library with literature on topics ranging from "how to increase skill as a secretary" to "short cuts in homemaking." Insisting that she was "just an assistant" to the foremen, More explained that as a women's counselor, she was "to try to alleviate all sources of worry for the individual worker so that that person will not be worried while working, be absent from work because of outside causes, or have to terminate employment because of outside responsibilities." Statistics proved she was successful, as there was a "decided decrease" in terminations at the center after she was hired.[15]

In March 1945, Continental started equipping B-17s and B-29s with "Mickey," a secret radar device that allowed bombardiers to release their bombs accurately through cloud cover. The device detected submarines at night and also located downed Allied flyers in the ocean.[16]

In mid-1945, Seattle factories took over modification of B-29s. The new task for Denver crews was to turn standard Superfortresses into super-reconnaissance planes. Because the war in Europe was over, US armed forces turned their attention to the war in the Pacific. The B-29 fuselage was cut almost in two to produce the F-13-A, a long-range photo reconnaissance plane. It took aerial photographs in preparation for an Allied invasion of Japan.[17]

The US bombings of Hiroshima and Nagasaki eliminated the need for an invasion. As the war ended, Robert F. Six, president of Continental Airlines, was free to report on his company's war work. Over the span of three years, 8,000 men and women made nearly 1,500 different kinds of modifications on 2,155 Flying Fortress bombers, 25 P-51 Mustang fighters, 6 British heavy bombers, and 402 B-29 Superfortresses. Workers had modified bomb bays, installed cooling baffles and defrosting systems, and made wiring changes.[18] Women workers were proud of their contribution. Riveter Helen Warren declared, "I feel we were an important component of the war effort, since the airplane assembly lines could not keep up with the rapidly changing modification requirements. We stepped up to the plate and kept them flying . . . We showed the enemy that the women of America were a force to be reckoned with."[19]

In addition to modifications of aircraft fresh off the assembly line, repairs were also made in Denver. At Lowry Field, civilian employee Virginia Wilson, a Colorado Springs native, welded and riveted B-24s and B-17s. Wearing coveralls purchased at JC Penney's, Wilson worked twelve hour days, five days a week. She welded necessary parts at worktables and riveted inside the airplane. Her pay of $125 a month was a substantial raise over her salary doing telephone work for an ophthalmologist in Grand Junction. Her stint on the Western Slope also did not provide her with a perk she received at Lowry. After one B-24 was patched up, she was invited along on the test flight. She quickly accepted the offer and flew over Pikes Peak.[20]

Smaller-scale aircraft modifications and repairs were done in Colorado Springs. Charlotte Clark was born on a farm in Phillips County in the far northeastern corner of the state. As any farmer can attest, one either repaired his or her farm equipment or did without. Having "messed around on the farm and learned more or less the basics" of being a mechanic, she went to school to formally learn the necessary skills. With training in hand, she was hired at Peterson Army Air Base. Planes arrived at the airfield with "big ol' nicks" in their propellers. Clark smoothed out the nicks and sanded them down so the planes could fly again. She never complained about doing this tedious job eight hours a day every day. If there were no airplane propellers to repair, she basically worked as a "handyman" doing whatever needed to be done.[21]

Other Colorado women joined the masses that swarmed to the West Coast for defense jobs. The summer between her junior and senior years in high school, Viola "Vonny" Strutzel visited her sister and brother-in-law in San Diego. After graduating from Rocky Ford High School in 1943, she returned to San Diego and got a job as a riveter at the Naval Air Station. Every afternoon she caught a ferry over to Coronado Island. Working the swing shift, she riveted the wings of airplanes, placing rivets inches apart in horizontal and vertical rows.[22]

Leeta Crook, who grew up in Del Norte, was one of many teachers who could not resist the allure of a job in a California defense plant. In the early 1940s, Crook was teaching elementary students in Fort Collins. She enrolled in a shop training course designed to prepare people for wartime jobs. For two summers, Crook stayed with relatives in Menlo Park, California, and worked at an airplane parts factory in nearby Redwood City. She was designated machinist's grade but worked wherever the plant needed help. She started out making leather washers with a diamond cutter and also sorted parts into proper bins. She did not mind this repetitive, mind-numbing work because she knew it was only, at the most, for the summer. Crook also filled in for the company nurse when she went on vacation.[23]

In April 1943, Boeing Aircraft Company based in Seattle, Washington, placed advertisements for war workers in western papers.[24] That spring Turza Briscoe, a Pueblo native, graduated from Colorado Springs High School. Immediately upon

FIGURE 8.3. Vonny Strutzel, a graduate of Rocky Ford High School, riveted airplane wings on Coronado Island. She married her high school sweetheart, Bill O'Leary, in 1944. *Courtesy*, Viola "Vonny" Strutzel O'Leary.

turning eighteen, she boarded a train bound for Seattle. As the train approached the city and passed by huge Boeing hangars, she was astounded to find "little towns" on top of the hangars. To camouflage war factories and keep them safe from bombing raids, Lockheed and Boeing installed netting to hide their factories from Japanese air attacks. Boeing also added fake houses and trees. John Steward Detlie, a Hollywood set designer, helped hide the Seattle plant. Boeing's fake housing development covered nearly 26 acres with netting, plywood, and other materials.[25]

Briscoe started work at once. As a draftsman, she sat alone at a long drawing table about 10 feet long by 4 feet wide. She drew on vellum, a very fine linen with a covering. At the end of each shift, employees were checked to make sure they were not leaving with any vellum. Soon, Briscoe had an opportunity to apply for a scholarship at the University of Washington. The calculus course was only for Boeing employees. Selected for the program, she spent half a day at the university and half a day at work. After completing the course, she was moved to the main plant to analyze flight test data. She worked on a monometer board that showed pressures on different parts of the plane after a test flight. Because Boeing, like other war factories, was desperately trying to maximize output, Briscoe worked nine or nine-and-a-half hours a day for five days each week. On Saturday, she "only" worked eight hours. Sunday was her lone day off, making her work "terribly wearing and terribly tiring."[26]

In late 1944, after nearly a year at Boeing, Briscoe went home to Colorado Springs for a vacation. Because her father was concerned that she would not finish college, she returned her badge and other employee materials to Boeing by special mail and "retired" from war work. She enrolled in Colorado College in November 1944, earning a degree in math and physics in 1948.[27]

Dolores Divine also moved for a defense job. When her husband joined the army, she returned to her family's farm in Lenexa, Kansas, about 70 miles from Kansas City. Like many wives of servicemen, Divine felt the need to keep busy and help out in the war effort. She moved to Kansas City and got a job at Pratt and Whitney working the second shift (3:30 p.m. to midnight). The company built almost half of all plane engines used during World War II. The demand for airpower was so great that the company expanded from manufacturing 5,000 airplane engines a year to 50,000 at the height of the war. Employment skyrocketed from 3,000 workers to 40,000. Divine was one of those 40,000 employees. She first used a turret lathe to create tools that were used in making airplane engines. After a short time, she was trained as a teacher of precision inspection. However, when no opening was available in that area, she shifted to magnetic inspection, a process called magne-flux. Parts were magnetized and then dipped in a solution of iron and oil to detect flaws in the metal. Motors were assembled and run for seventy-two hours. Then they were taken apart and re-inspected. Divine meticulously inspected knuckle pins and push-rods: "I felt that if I missed a flaw in one of these parts, a plane crashed and people were killed, I might just as well have taken a gun and shot them."[28]

The aircraft industry also provided a better job for Jewel vanBuskirk Mosher. After high school graduation, she worked odd jobs before getting hired at a wool factory in Pascagoula, Mississippi. After the United States declared war on Japan, she enrolled in a class on engineering drawing and drafting. In class, she drew the parts; assemblies and blueprints were made from her drawings and sent to the shop where "Rosies" took over the process. After her training, she was hired at Consolidated Vultee, where she made drawings for PBY airplanes. One of the most widely used seaplanes during the war, the PBY Catalina was used in anti-submarine warfare, patrol bombing, convoy escorts, search and rescue missions, and cargo transport.[29]

Another woman hired at Consolidated Vultee (also called Convair after the merger of Consolidated Aircraft and Vultee Aircraft) was Ruth Wall. The company's workforce was 90 percent women during the war.[30] When the war broke out, Ruth's future husband, Ted Johnson, joined the navy. She reasoned that if he was going to fight in the war, she would work in a defense plant. She applied at Consolidated Vultee but was told that since she had no experience in riveting or assembly-line work, they could not hire her. Instead, they hired her for the cafeteria front counter. One of her customers suggested that she enroll at Lindsey Hopkins Vocational School (Miami, Florida) if she wanted production-line work. She failed three classes in riveting, much to the amusement of her classmates. One evening the instructor took her aside, gave her a book, and asked her to draw a three-dimensional figure of an object. When he returned at the end of class, she had several drawings to show him. He was visibly relieved to discover a job she could do.[31]

Wall was assigned to the Template Department, where she drew parts for the PBY aircraft. From a blueprint, workers made a template to fit that part of the plane. Wall was only allowed a margin of error of three-thousandths of an inch in filing everything down. Then the template went across the aisle to the Tool Department, where it was given a filling from which the part was made. Magnifiers and small files similar to emery boards were used to make the piece according to specifications. If there was no work to do on templates, Wall worked with the counter-sink machine in the Assembly Department. It was there that she made her most satisfying contribution to the war effort. She noticed that the girls on the drumming jigs often drilled holes that were crooked or off-center. The counter-sink machine pin was shaped like a dowel. Wall figured that if the pin was tapered, it would automatically center itself in the hole, eliminating the problem. She took her idea to her boss, who created an experimental one. It worked perfectly. She next submitted her idea to the suggestion box. When it was accepted, she received a monetary award and was interviewed by *Wings* magazine.[32]

After working at Consolidated Vultee, Ruth Wall Johnson (she married Ted Johnson when he was stateside) got a job at the army air depot, where she did sheet metal work. Her last job was at the naval station at Opa-Locka (Florida), working on damaged fighter planes. The damaged part was found on a blueprint; a piece of metal was then cut and made to specification. If necessary, Johnson bent, cut, or drilled the piece before she installed it on the airplane. Installation could be dangerous work. One day she was installing a piece and the tail fell off. Because she was small in stature, Johnson was chosen to squeeze into the airplane to fix the problem. Unknown to her, someone was in the cockpit. All of a sudden the tail wheel started closing in on her. She "screamed bloody murder." Others started yelling, which caught the attention of the worker who had been fiddling with the instruments.[33]

Over the course of the war, the aircraft industry faced a shortage of engineers. In 1942, C. Wilson Cole, supervisor of Curtiss-Wright's Engineering Personnel Bureau, suggested that women be trained to replace male engineers. The following year, the company established the Engineering Cadette Training Program. Curtiss-Wright directly contacted college deans of women to help identify potential participants; 4,000 women from forty-four states replied with applications.[34]

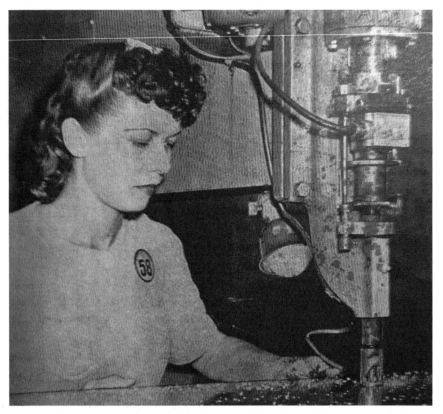

FIGURE 8.4. Ruth Wall Johnson at the counter-sink machine for which she invented a design modification that earned her and her boss a prize of $100 from Consolidated Vultee. Courtesy, Ruth Wall Johnson Mullis.

The company tendered offers to 1,000 women. Louise Fayram, a mathematics major at the University of Denver, was one of 918 women who accepted an offer from Curtiss-Wright. She was sent to the University of Minnesota for training. The other six colleges that offered training were Cornell University, Iowa State College, Ohio State, Pennsylvania State College, Purdue, and Rensselaer Polytechnic Institute.[35]

Curtiss-Wright provided tuition, room and board, and pocket money of ten dollars a week.[36] One hundred students were subdivided into four cadres based on their college transcripts. A core group of engineering faculty was assigned to teach the cadette classes. At first, college professors were a bit intimidated by the thought of teaching women in what had been a male-dominated major. Although he was single, one professor wore a wedding ring, thinking he might have to fight off advances from his female students. When the women heard about this, they found it particularly amusing, stating that no one they knew would have been interested in him, married or single.[37] While that professor may not have made an impact on his students, the female students made an impact on the Engineering Departments. A report made midway through the first training program reported that "there is unanimity of opinion to the effect that the girls were outstanding. In one college, after they had been gone six months, they were still acclaimed the 'best group of students that had ever been on the campus, men or women' while another college professor proclaimed that in twenty-two years of teaching mathematics, he had never had a class like his women."[38]

On the University of Minnesota campus, Shevlin Hall was converted from barracks into a dormitory. Urinals were replaced, bunk beds were painted pale green, and walls were lined with pink wooden lockers. Smaller rooms housed fourteen cadettes, while larger ballrooms accommodated almost forty each. In the evenings, the basement cafeteria doubled as a study area. The main lounge had a vaulted ceiling, leaded windows, a fireplace, and a small "date lounge." Women who lived upstairs had a two-flight walk to meals and shower facilities but were compensated with a balcony from which they could check out frequent male visitors in the lounge.[39] Some of the visitors may have been navy students the cadettes encountered while marching to and from classes. Blind dates were often arranged between the two groups of students.

One hundred new women on a campus as large as the University of Minnesota were not noticeable; however, male professors were shocked to see a roomful of female engineering students. A slide rule was the "badge of honor" for engineering students. It went wherever they went. Traditionally, male students hung their slide rules from the belts of their pants. At first, cadettes dangled theirs from their notebooks, but after tiring of changing from dresses or skirts for classes to pants for the Machine Shop, most wore slacks all day. At that point they adopted the male custom of hooking their slide rules to their belts. It was reported that one professor broke out in laughter upon entering his classroom and being confronted with twenty-five cadettes dangling slide rules.[40]

After completing training, Louise Fayram worked in the Engineering Department of Curtiss-Wright in Columbus, Ohio. Of the 766 cadettes who graduated from the training program, 365 were sent to Columbus. The plant produced the SB2C Helldiver, a dive-bombing airplane. In a room of nearly a hundred engineers, Fayram worked on hydraulic systems. Others worked on landing gear, bomb equipment, bomb bay, and electrical systems. As airplanes were tested, modifications were brought to the drafting room. Each engineer had his or her own long drafting table.

Curtiss-Wright engineers were assigned to work five-and-a-half days a week; however, when there was a particular problem that needed to be solved, Fayram worked overtime to the tune of forty-eight to sixty hours a week. She rather enjoyed it because it made her feel "kind of superior" to be the one needed. In a

FIGURE 8.5. Curtiss-Wright cadettes examining metal model airplanes in a classroom on the campus of Iowa State College, 1943. *Courtesy*, Iowa State University Library, Special Collections and University Archives, Ames.

2011 interview, she could not recall her wage or overtime pay scale, only that she and her two roommates, also Curtiss-Wright employees, were happy with it.[41]

Sara V. Johnson, from northeastern Colorado and a student at the University of Colorado, trained at Iowa State College in Ames.[42] In April 1945, T. R. Agg, chairman of the Faculty Committee on Naval Training Schools, submitted a report to the president of Iowa State College. Classes in mathematics, sciences, drawing, and design, as well as special courses and applied courses, began on February 15, 1943. Special courses included aerodynamics, thermodynamics, electrical currents, and engine laboratory.[43] The daily schedule was daunting. During the first term, students took classes Monday through Wednesday from 8:00 a.m. to 6:00 p.m., with an hour for lunch at 1:00 p.m. Students had Thursday morning "off," with supervised study for three hours in the afternoon. On Friday mornings the women attended three morning classes and four hours of supervised study in the afternoon. On Saturday there was "only" one two-hour class. The schedule for the second six months was similar.[44] Cadettes took no other courses, such as English or social sciences, which enabled them to absorb two-and-a-half years of a standard aero-engineering curriculum in ten months. Of course, being very intelligent was an even greater factor in their success.

Although students were not told their grades while they were at the universities, a 1945 Iowa State report included individuals' grades, plant ratings, and remarks.[45] Sara Johnson received 4 As in Engineering Problems, Properties and Processing of

Aircraft Materials, Aircraft Problems, and Aircraft Materials and Assembly; 5 Bs in Airplane Design and Construction, Aircraft Drafting, Elementary Engineering Mechanics, Theory of Flight, and Strength of Materials Structural Analysis; and 1 C in Aircraft Drafting and Design. After graduation, Johnson worked for Curtiss-Wright in St. Louis, Missouri, for six months before dropping out of the program. No reason was given in "Remarks." However, one can surmise that it was not because she was unable to do the work—her plant rating was "Excellent."[46]

THE SHIPBUILDING INDUSTRY

During World War II, shipbuilding boomed in the San Francisco Bay area. Over thirty shipyards and scores of machine shops created the largest combined shipbuilding complex in the world. Four factors were crucial in producing the huge output of ships in Northern California. Local experienced yards, a ready labor supply and building sites, proximity to the war in the Pacific, and established railroads keyed the expansion, as did the "can-do" spirit of men such as Joseph Moore, Warren Bechtel, and Henry J. Kaiser. Major yards received raw materials and preassembled components from Bay-area shops as well as from distant places such as Colorado and the Midwest. Other American companies supplied nuts, bolts, and other parts.

Prior to the attack on Pearl Harbor, the US Navy selected Mare Island Naval Yard to build twenty-four destroyer escorts to be leased to Great Britain. Because the yard was already at full production, it was impossible to complete the ships by the target date of summer 1943. Denver manufacturers joined with the navy yard to fabricate ship hull sections, bulkheads, and decks. The consortium consisted of Ajax Iron Works, E. Burkhardt and Sons Steel and Iron Works, Denver Steel and Iron Works, Midwest Steel and Iron Works, Silver Engineering Works, Thompson Pipe and Steel, R. Hardesty Manufacturing, and Eaton Metal Products. Construction was scheduled to begin January 1942. Many crews worked twenty-four-hour days to meet the deadline.[47]

On February 27, railcars bearing the slogan "Pike's Peak to Tokyo—or Bust!" and laden with prefabricated parts made the 1,300-mile trip to Mare Island for assembly. Governor Ralph Carr and Denver mayor Benjamin Stapleton were joined by company officials and Jean Alley, a secretary in the War Production Board office in Denver. After Carr's remarks, Alley smashed a champagne bottle filled with Pikes Peak snow water over the railcar, christening it the USS *Mountain Maid*. On August 22, a delegation from Denver went to Vallejo to officially launch the first destroyer escort built in Colorado. Eighteen-year-old Cynthia Carr christened the ship the HMS *Bentinck* as her father, Governor Carr, looked on.[48]

As Denver crews worked around the clock supplying Mare Island with ship components, shipyards on both coasts ramped up production. In California, the

San Francisco Bay area experienced unprecedented growth in both industrial plants and population. Thousands of unemployed Americans left their homes, moved hundreds of miles, and were hired at the shipyards. However, as demand for ships increased, the yards on the West Coast could not meet production goals. The huge influx of workers since 1942 was taxing local communities. Medical facilities and schools were overburdened. Workers could not find housing.

Marinship in Sausalito was built to supply fuel oil tankers for the US Merchant Marine Corps, but a dozen Liberty Ships were its first products as tankers were still in the design phase. The yard was built in only three months while Marin City, built to house shipyard workers just outside Sausalito's city limits, was planned in three days and built in three weeks. For a time, the city was the second largest town in Marin County. One of the new resident workers was Barbara Mae Byron, a schoolteacher from rural Colorado. When she received a letter from her sister bragging about her pay, Byron jumped on the next train. Her teacher's salary of $95 a month paled in comparison to her sister's pay of over $200 a month.[49]

In welding school, Harry Freeze taught Byron as much as he could in the short time allotted. After two weeks she was sent to sub-assembly, where huge sections of ships were welded and preassembled. While aircraft and automobile manufacturers used assembly lines, this process did not work for building ships because of their immense size. Instead, huge cranes brought component parts—preassemblies—to the hull and lifted them onto it. While preassemblies and cranes were useful, the real key to speed in ship production was welding. Riveting had been used previously, but it had several disadvantages. It took time to align steel plates and drill holes for rivets and to set and drive them home. A "driller" had to position each hole in the proper place and drill through the 1-inch-thick hull plate. After the plates were aligned on frames, they seldom matched the pre-drilled holes precisely, so a "reamer" had to enlarge the holes to eliminate overlap and allow the rivet to fit. Rivets and drill plates could add as much as 300 tons to a ship's hull. That added weight lessened the payload. It took two workers—a riveter and a bucker—to place each rivet, one on either side of the plates. A typical hull required 150,000 rivets. In all, four workers were needed for riveting.[50]

Arc welding meant fewer costs and quicker production time. Welding eliminated drilling and reaming. One welder could replace the riveter and bucker. The problem with welding was the skill necessary to make a good solid seam anywhere—horizontal, vertical, overhead, and angled. Wartime shipyards had neither a sufficient number of skilled welders nor the time to train new workers to perform welding in every possible position. One solution was to position the seams so the welder could work in a "down-hand" position. The electrodes were held at waist level or below to reduce fatigue. The work piece was often brought to the worker. Large vertical pieces were turned horizontal.[51] Experienced welders, like Marie Mason, mentored new workers.

For weeks, Byron and Mason wielded welding rods that looked like very long cigars. Each rod produced so much heat that one had to "move like hell" or it cut a hole through 1-inch-thick metal. Each woman was able to weld about a thousand feet every shift. Byron, like a multitude of women welders, loved welding and its attendant "perks." She found the launching of a ship an exciting "bonus" in her line of work. During production the keel, pinned down in front by a heavy steel plate, was covered with what looked like 2 or more inches of yellow grease. Wood timbers staunched the ship in place on the sides. When a ship was launched, the timbers were knocked down and someone cut the chain holding the steel plate to the ship. That released the ship to slide into the water on its grease. After working an average of forty-three days to construct a tanker, it thrilled Byron to watch its launching, knowing she had a hand—and a welding tool—in the process.[52]

After six months on sub-assembly, a foreman asked Byron to take a crew of women onto the ships themselves. Although "every sort of person imaginable" worked at Marinship, Byron did not perceive much in the way of discrimination except in this one instance. Marie Mason, an African American, was the most skilled female welder. But Byron, an Anglo, was asked to head the first crew of women to weld on the ship. Byron was afraid of heights, but her compulsion to defeat Hitler was stronger than her phobia. The first night, when she and her "motley crew" of five women boarded the ship, some male workers crossed themselves in hopes of warding off evil spirits that might be accompanying the female welders. By the end of the night, the men were willingly cooperating with their new co-workers. Working as tackers, women stood by with a welding rod to make one piece of metal stick lightly to another. This was done at different places on the ship. Some of the female crew members also welded steel that had already been placed. During one stretch, the women worked for ship fitters who were laying the bottom section of the tanker. Within weeks, the ship fitters were asking management to assign the female crew to help lay bottom sections of the tankers. In the meantime, Byron's crew had grown from five to twenty-three, six of whom were male welders.[53]

The insatiable need for more battleships forced the navy to continue to "farm out" contracts to companies in the US interior. This decision enabled other Denver companies to acquire naval contracts for steel parts.[54] Between July 1942 and December 1944, Midwest Steel and Iron Works of Denver received navy contracts to manufacture parts for escort vessels, crosstrees for Victory ships, and prefabricated hull sections for aircraft carriers.[55] In January 1944, the army and navy bestowed upon the company an "E" award in an impressive weekend of activity. Officials from Mare Island, former governor Carr, Governor John C. Vivian, and Mayor Benjamin Stapleton attended the festivities at the West High School auditorium. Also on hand were WAVES, a contingent of members of the American Women's Voluntary Services led by Major Thelma Cox, and a United

States Marine Corps color guard. WAVES pinned "E" awards on four male work-ers selected by their co-workers to represent all employees. Commander William E. Howard from the naval yard presented the "E" pennant to company officials, including Vice President Mabel Bower. Officials announced that 1,000 railroad cars had been sent from Colorado to Mare Island filled with Denver steel work. Later that afternoon all employees were invited to a party at the Coronado Club to receive their "E" pins.[56]

Denver Steel and Iron, Eaton Metal Products, and Thompson Pipe and Steel were also awarded contracts to manufacture prefabricated parts for LSTs (land-ing crafts) for Mare Island. This allowed the naval yard to increase its production by 46 percent.[57] In April 1943, the companies were presented with an "E" award. Among the companies' presidents was Herbert H. Wolleson of the Denver Steel and Iron Company. He was flanked by Minnie Crook, vice president, and Constance Crook Stauffer, secretary. Crook and her daughter may have been the only female owners of fabricating plants making navy destroyer hulls in the United States. The widow of John Anthony Crook, Minnie Crook was no disinterested official of the company. She arose early every morning and reported to the office by mid-morning to complete payroll, write checks, and perform other financial duties. In an interview with the *Rocky Mountain News*, Crook pointed out the changes the war had brought to her life: "It's all quite different from housekeeping. I could take time out to sit and relax—or chat over the telephone. But not now—it's push and go until the closing whistle blows." The "E" award pinned to her business suit was a constant reminder that she was "right in there fighting with our men."[58]

Eaton Metal Products received numerous "E" pennants over the course of the war. The company employed 450 workers at its plant at 4800 York Street in Denver. As early as December 1941, the company began filling military contracts. By 1942, 90 percent of its products were war-related, a percentage that remained constant through the war years. Eaton had contracts for navy pontoons and hot water stor-age tanks and generators. It also constructed hull sections for destroyer escorts and LCT-6s. The plant expanded four times, adding warehouses, additions to the Steel Shop, and a new Drafting Department. The plant ran three eight-hour shifts a day, six days a week. With the expansion came an additional 150 workers. The company's first female welder was Leona Seeley, hired in August 1943. On her first day on the job, she fainted. But it had nothing to do with the nature of her work. According to the company newsletter, she had donated blood to the Red Cross Blood Bank five times in the previous six months—about twice as much as was prudent. After two days in Presbyterian Hospital, she was strong enough to return to work.[59]

Another female welder was Bonnie Young who partnered with Ulysses Sherman Sellers, the oldest welder at age seventy-eight, in a multigenerational effort to win the war. Because the plant utilized precision welding, beginning welders were employed. As the company added to its list of products, more workers—including women—were needed.[60] Aldor Olson, Eaton's foreman, recalled that the women "all worked hard, and endured a lot of abuse in the beginning. There were no special changes made for the women, they just came in and worked right beside us." Lieutenant John H. McQuilkin described the Denver women as "really tough females!"[61]

Pay for workers in the aircraft and shipbuilding industries varied according to job, plant location, company, and—in most cases—a worker's gender. As a template maker, Ruth Wall earned $1.35 an hour at Consolidated Vultee, more than the amount earned by women on the assembly line—the same women who had laughed at her inability to succeed in vocational school. Helen Warren at the Denver Modification Center earned more than a dollar an hour, substantially more than the $8 a week she earned at her first job as a sales clerk at S. H. Kress & Co., a local five and dime store, or as an elevator operator at the May Company Department Store. With wages double a teacher's salary, it was no wonder that teachers like Barbara Mae Byron left their classrooms, moved to the West Coast, and took defense jobs. Overtime work with overtime pay was always available. Dolores Divine's overtime rate was more than $2 an hour as an inspector at Pratt and Whitney.[62]

Yet pay inequities persisted. During World War II, Arthur J. Hurt and Company manufactured airplane parts for a number of aviation companies. In 1943, sixteen-year-old Margaret Bradley, a graduate of South High School, was hired to work in the Machine Shop. During high school she had taken welding classes at the Emily Griffith Opportunity School, but because she was under age eighteen, she could not be hired to weld; instead, she ran lathes and drill presses and did spot welding on B-17 parts. She worked six days a week and up to ten hours a day. She recalled that the company had a majority of women working at the South Navajo Street shop. However, they were paid less than men holding the same job and performing the same work.[63]

With their high-paying defense jobs, many women workers agreed with Leeta Crook that they were "rich." Between her teacher's pay and her factory earnings—a machinist's pay was one of the highest—she had more money and fewer things to spend it on.[64] Dolores Divine bought expensive train tickets every weekend to visit her family in Kansas. She also bought herself a fur coat and collected $100 bills for the fun of it. She purchased gifts for her family and for her home in anticipation of her husband returning from the service.[65] Ruth Wall Johnson wanted a home for herself and her husband so much that she worked nights as a cocktail waitress after her shift at Consolidated Vultee.[66]

Aircraft plants and the shipyards employed women in a variety of jobs. They worked on assembly lines, on the decks of ships, and on the wings of airplanes. They supplied the weapons and vessels for the United States to successfully wage a two-front war. And yet they still faced criticism for taking war jobs and skepticism that they could drop their "girly" ways and become productive factory workers. A reporter for the *Rocky Mountain News* seemed astounded that female employees at the Denver Modification Center were successful: "Women who used to handle nothing more complicated than a waffle iron or a washing machine now gossip about things like baffle plates, lorenz brackets, and flex-feeds. Women who used to hate to miss an hour's sleep now work through the night in strenuous jobs."[67] Unfortunately, the reporter was not the only one who doubted or resented the women. Mosher reported that she and the other women working at Consolidated Vultee "took a lot of guff" from male co-workers.[68] Fayram at Curtiss-Wright recalled that some of the male engineers resented the women's arrival and were a "little nasty" to them.[69]

The next phalanx of war workers faced fewer criticisms and problems. Pink- and white-collar women worked diligently for the red, white, and blue. Office workers were a significant number of female war workers in Colorado, as they were throughout the country. If "an army marches on its stomach," surely it runs on paperwork.[70]

9

Office Workers and Other Non-Industrial Workers

Frances Hale sat at her desk surrounded by dozens of identical desks. One of the thousands of young Black women who had qualified for a federal Civil Service job in Washington, DC, she diligently typed a letter from her steno pad. Concentrating on her task, she barely noticed the return of the typist who regularly worked next to her. Without warning, the white girl poured her bottle of soda pop on Frances. Then, laughing, she sat down. Hale calmly rose from her chair, took one determined step toward the desk, and shook the liquid back onto her offender. Angry, the white girl declared, "You should be in Oklahoma picking cotton." Hale picked up her pocketbook and hit her. No one in the office said a word. No one.[1]

Clerks, stenographers, typists, and other office workers were actively recruited for personnel positions in defense plants, government offices, laboratories, and schools. The number of female office workers grew by 2 million from 1940 to 1944. The federal government played a significant part in this increase, as the number of female Civil Service workers grew from fewer than 200,000 in 1939 to more than 1 million in 1944.[2] In April 1942 the Alamosa newspaper reported that the US Civil Service Commission's efforts were hampered by the "refusal of a sufficient number of young women to accept jobs as stenographers and typists" in Washington, DC. The problem of transportation to the nation's capital and reports of its high cost of living were cited as two reasons large numbers of women had not applied. To remedy the situation, several agencies assisted newcomers in making living arrangements, and job requirements were cut to a

DOI: 10.5876/9781646420339.c009   163

minimum. The article cited a salary of $130 a month, with "unlimited" opportunities for advancement.[3]

One young woman who was only too happy to apply for an office job was Jennie Walker. Walker started her war work at the Denver Ordnance Plant (DOP). Her father cleaned coaches for the Union Pacific Railroad. Walker's mother was a live-in cook for an Anglo family, so Jennie only saw her mother on Thursdays and Sundays. Because her mother wanted her to pursue a college education, Walker signed up for shorthand and typing classes in high school. The school counselor said she would never find a job as a secretary and refused to approve the classes. Instead, she registered Walker for a cooking class. When Walker told her mother, she replied, "You tell the teacher to teach you shorthand and typing. I'll teach you how to cook and sew!"[4]

Following her freshman year at the University of Colorado, Walker took a job in the Remington cafeteria but did not work there for long. Through the efforts of Mary McLeod Bethune, the National Association of Colored Women, the National Association for the Advancement of Colored People (NAACP), and President Franklin Roosevelt, photographs of applicants were no longer required on federal Civil Service tests.[5] Black leaders in Colorado encouraged young women to take federal Civil Service shorthand and typing examinations. Walker's score of 97 earned her a call to Washington, DC. She was one of 600 African American women hired. However, because of blatant racial discrimination, none of them were assigned jobs, so they sat there idly for five months drawing the equivalent of a $1,440-a-year salary. Walker was finally assigned to work with the US Corps of Engineers. She worked for seven years in the nation's capital before being called to the corps' Omaha office to fill a stenography vacancy. When Walker reported, she was told that no charwoman's work was available. After she announced that she was there for the stenographer's job, she was told that they "didn't hire coloreds for office jobs."[6]

Joining Walker in Washington, DC, was Frances Hale, a Denver native. Hale had always wanted to work in an office, unlike her two sisters who were planning on becoming teachers. While she was a senior at Manual High School, Hale won a contest in which she took dictation and transcribed information. Her prize was a job with the American Woman's Insurance Company, a Black insurance company. She started work after graduating in 1941.

That year, the federal government was one of the few entities that hired Black clerks and secretaries. Between 1938 and 1944, the number of Blacks in the employ of the federal government grew from 90,000 to 274,000, 60 percent of whom held clerical or administrative positions.[7] Welcoming Blacks did not necessarily mean the federal agencies purposely sought them out, as is evident in a recruiting poster depicting a saluting white woman in front of a typewriter with the caption "Victory Waits on Your Fingers—Keep 'Em Flying, Miss U.S.A." As soon as Hale turned eighteen in November 1941, she took the qualifying tests without telling her parents. Her secret lasted only until a letter arrived informing her that she had passed the tests and was to report to Washington, DC. Later, she found out that her mother had asked her former teachers at Manual High School if her daughter was mature or capable enough to do the job. Everyone told her to allow Frances to leave Denver. The problem was housing. Hale's sister had a boyfriend, George Walker, the brother of Jennie Walker. George told the Hale family that his sister would take care of Frances, which she did. She secured a place for her with her landlady.[8]

In March 1942, Hale rode a train to the nation's capital. She naively thought the other girls in the apartment would help her get to her job the first day. She was dismayed to find that she was on her own, as they all had their own jobs to go to. With her office "way across town," she learned to stand on her own two feet right from the beginning. Her first "office" was in a temporary building hastily erected for the war effort. Her initial assignment was in a typing pool. Women were not assigned to any particular person. When someone from the War Production Board wanted dictation taken, he selected a member of the typing pool.[9]

Early on, Hale's roommates told her to save her money in case she ever needed to go home. It was wise advice. After working for only three months, Hale was called home when her younger sister was killed in an automobile accident. She stayed in Denver for quite a while before her parents relented and she returned to Washington.[10]

The last year Hale worked in Washington, DC, she was assigned to the Liaison Office between the War Production Board and the US House of Representatives. Working in the basement of the US Capitol, she took a walk to see where the representatives worked. Encountering a group of Native Americans in traditional dress, she first felt fear before admonishing herself with the thought that her fear "is stupid." She continued on her way and peeked into the office of Clayton Powell, the only African American representative. In the basement of the US Capitol that day, she saw the only other people of color—two male barbers.

In earlier assignments, Hale and the other office workers had eaten in a cafeteria in their building. The food was good, and the workers could sit wherever they wished. However, she was not told about any cafeteria in the US Capitol Building. Each day Hale took a bus or walked to the nearest federal building. One day she overheard a visitor say she was going down the hall to have lunch. Not knowing where the woman went, Hale wandered the tunnels that connect the House to the Senate. She found a "Cafeteria" sign at the entrance to a small, crowded room. Hale went in, proceeded through the line, and paid for her food. She spied an empty chair at a table with a number of men, two of whom she recognized as having been in her office. They said she could join them. Soon she heard the talk around her—"Oh! I didn't know today was *maid's* day." Ignoring the comments, she finished her lunch and vowed to return. Her parents had taught their children not to be timid. She "marched back the next day to eat even though it was uncomfortable." She was met by two guards at the door who asked for her pass. She replied, "What pass? I never heard of a pass." They informed her that she had to work in the building to eat there. They did not believe her when she told them that she did work for the War Production Board in the House of Representatives. They then sent her on a wild goose chase to secure a pass that did not exist. Reporting to one office, she overheard the secretary on the phone say, "There's a *charwoman* here who wants a pass." She ignored Hale's assertion that she worked in the building and sent her to yet another office. Knowing she was never going to get the nonexistent pass, Hale ate lunch that day in the Social Security Building. It was one of the final straws. Hale decided that she did want to attend college. She requested a transfer to work in the Social Security Building where she had worked earlier. In June 1945 she submitted her resignation letter.[11]

On the whole, Hale enjoyed her years working in spite of the poured bottle of soda pop and the lunchroom experiences. On Sundays, she and her friends played tourist. They visited the Lincoln Memorial, the National Gallery, the amphitheater at Arlington National Cemetery, the Supreme Court Building, and Mount Vernon and went across the Potomac River into Maryland. The United Service Organizations (USO) took Hale and her friends to dances at the army camps in Virginia. At one of them she met a handsome GI who was in Officer Candidate School. They dated for several months. Because he could not leave the base, he paid her bus fare when she visited him on Sundays for a movie and dinner. On those visits she rode a segregated bus. Denver buses were not racially segregated, so Hale had not previously been in such a situation. She boarded the bus and sat down. The bus driver stood up and tried to stare her into moving to the back of the bus. Hale gazed out the window. He finally said something and she realized that she'd better move. She had heard that she could be jailed for not sitting in the back of the bus, which was the law for African Americans in Virginia; if she could not pay the fine, she would be in more trouble. From then on, she immediately sat in the back of the bus. One Sunday evening she boarded and all the rear seats were taken. Angry, she walked to the back of the bus and said, "Get up and go sit where you belong" to the white people sitting there. A number of them jumped up "like they were frightened" of her and moved to seats closer to the front.[12]

In addition to office stenographers, typists, and clerks, the government needed code breakers or cryptanalysts in Washington, DC. In 1942, the United States Army sought qualified women to be code breakers. Like the WAVES who broke code for the United States Navy, civilian employees with the army were smart, educated, adept at math or science or languages (or all three), dutiful, patriotic, and willing to take on a mission about which they knew very little. Perhaps most important, they did not expect any public recognition or glory for their service.

FIGURE 9.1. Eugenia Simms (*left*) and Frances Hale were two of thousands of young African American women who were hired by federal agencies to process millions of pieces of paperwork and documents on the home front. *Courtesy*, Frances Hale Currin.

Many of the women were schoolteachers who had proven to have those character traits. Another schoolteacher asset is that they were unmarried—as was required in practically every school district in the United States—and therefore not tied to the status of their husbands.[13] During the war, 10,500 people worked for the United States Army in code breaking, an astronomical jump from 181 in 1941. In 1945, 70 percent of the members of the army intelligence force were women.

In 1944, Nancy Thompson was recruited by the United States Army Signal Corps to become a code breaker in Washington, DC.[14] After graduating from the University of Missouri with a degree in journalism, she initially wanted to join the Red Cross; however, her mother—with a husband stationed in Italy with the Judge Advocate General's office (JAG), her first husband (Nancy's father) serving as the psychiatrist on General Dwight Eisenhower's staff in London, and a son in the Army Air Corps—asked her daughter to find war work in the states. After passing FBI clearance Thompson boarded a train for the nation's capital. She initially lived at Arlington Farms, barracks hastily erected to house civilian workers. There were thirty rooms on each floor. Thompson's small room was at the opposite end of the single bathroom on her floor. Every time someone walked down the hall, the whole building shook. After nine months, Thompson and three other female civilians found better accommodations—complete with a doorman who doubled as the elevator operator—at 1616 Sixteenth Street in downtown Washington, DC.[15] Their place was a furnished one-bedroom, one-bathroom apartment on the seventh floor of the building. The bedroom had two double beds; depending on their respective work shifts, one of them slept on the sofa. Thompson and other code breakers worked eight-hour shifts at Arlington Hall, a former girls' school in Arlington, Virginia. She rode an unmarked bus to work. Although the entire campus was utilized for the war effort, her color-coded badge allowed her entry only to her building and the cafeteria for which she had a timed meal ticket. Given slips of paper on which numbers and letters were written, the code breakers, or cryptanalysts, deciphered Japanese code. When she got a "hit," Thompson turned in her papers to the captain. Working on messages from Fukuoka and Kumamoto on Kyusu, Thompson did not know the messages' meanings because the codes were in Japanese. She worked twelve days before receiving two days off.[16]

The top-secret nature of her work permeated her living situation. The roommates never mentioned what they did at work or even the building in which they worked. Decades after the war's end, one of them visited her in Denver. Seeing a government document stating that Thompson was a cryptographer, her roommate asked what that was. She herself had worked in the library—and Thompson never knew there was a library there! One of their other roommates had worked in the main building as a receptionist, a fact Thompson did not know at the time.[17]

Like other women working in Washington, DC, Thompson and her friends enjoyed going to the theater, attending USO events, taking the train to New York, and enjoying each other's company out on the town. A group of them were in the Willard Hotel Bar when they heard the news of President Roosevelt's death. Given the day off for his funeral, they watched the solemn funeral procession down Pennsylvania Avenue.[18]

Over the course of the war, Thompson moved from being a cryptanalytic aide at a salary of $1,800 a year to a research analyst at $3,200 a year in 1945. She worked for the Department of War's Military Intelligence Division after V-J Day, deciphering South American codes as the United States tracked the flight and settlement of former Nazis in Brazil, Argentina, and Chile. Because the codes were written in Spanish, Thompson was able to understand some of them.[19]

Denver, with its numerous bases and defense plants, also needed hundreds of women to type, file, and take dictation. In October 1942, newspapers reported that the need for typists and clerks had grown so great at the ordnance plant and at Lowry and Buckley Fields that Mary Pollard was recruiting girls interested in

FIGURE 9.2. Nancy Thompson (*back row, second from right*), shown with her work group, spent the war years as a cryptanalyst for the United States Army Signal Corps in Washington, DC. *Courtesy*, Nancy Thompson Tipton.

being typists. Girls between the ages of sixteen and twenty-five could enroll in a training program. The girls would be housed in a National Youth Administration residence center in Denver. During training, they would receive nearly eleven dollars in cash in addition to room, board, and transportation. At the conclusion of training, they would take a Civil Service examination and replace male typists at one of the air fields or the defense plant.[20]

Sisters Enid and Kathleen Clay moved from Steamboat Springs to Denver. In October 1943, Enid was a clerk at Lowry Field while Kathleen worked at the DOP. Their five siblings were also busy in the war effort. Sister Lillian served with the Army Nurse Corps, Vivian was a nurse's aide, Phyllis attended nursing school, and brother Jack served in the Army Air Corps. Henry, the oldest sibling, worked in Alaska.[21] Dorothy Angle, an Oak Creek resident, was hired at Remington Arms after Pollard's visit.[22] It may have been because of that visit or it may have been that the Clay sisters and Angle simply followed the lead of women who had earlier crossed the mountains west to east for a defense job.

Unlike women employed in production areas, office employees worked a regular 8:00 a.m.–4:00 p.m., Monday through Friday shift. Leota Broman, born in Burlington and raised in Lakewood, was a secretary when Pearl Harbor was attacked. Having been trained in typing, bookkeeping, and general business at Lakewood High School and in her one year at the University of Denver, she was readily hired by the Denver Ordnance Plant. Her previous job paid twenty dollars a month. At Remington, her take-home pay was seventy dollars a month. Unfortunately, she often had no work to do because her supervisor worked "very slowly." It was not an unusual complaint. Hale, while working in Washington, DC, also commented that there was often little work to do. She spent a great deal of time writing letters to her family and her serviceman beau.[23] It has been suggested that unaccustomed to the speed and accuracy with which women took dictation, typed, filed, and performed other office tasks, offices hired too many women.

Throughout the plant, an employee could get another family member a job. Shirley Grainger, originally from Victor, attended Barnes School of Business before World War II, after which she worked as a secretary before being hired at the DOP. Her younger sister, Roberta, married Frank Vinyard before he enlisted in the army. When he was sent to New York City for specialized training, she went with him. While he trained, she worked in retail. After he was shipped overseas, she returned to Colorado. Not wanting to return to her family's home in Victor, she moved in with her sister, who told her supervisors that Roberta would be a great stenographer. Roberta was hired, but she was not the secretary her sister was. She could type but did not know shorthand. For several months she "faked it." She wrote as much as she could from her supervisor's dictation and then took her notes home. Shirley typed the letters for her on a portable typewriter. The next morning Roberta placed the letters on her boss's desk. Every day she was a nervous wreck, fearing her supervisor would find out she was "a fraud." To her relief, a job opened up in the production area. She immediately applied and was accepted. Now she did not have to pretend to be something she was not, and she did not have to wear the nice clothes required in the office. To top it off, she made more money on the production line than she had earned as an ersatz secretary.[24]

Secretaries and clerk-stenographers received a base pay between $1,440 and $2,300 a year. Bertha Beaton [no known relation to the author] started her stint at the DOP as secretary-clerk to Major Willis T. Moran, the executive officer. Her CAF-4 classified job paid $1,800 a year. Within twelve months she was promoted to senior clerk-stenographer. By March 1943, she was head principal clerk, supervising a female secretarial assistant clerk-stenographer and a male assistant clerk. Her pay increased to $2,300. In May 1944, she was placed on the newly created Records Administration Board for the DOP. She and the other two members, Kathleen C. Hayes and Steward A. Shafer, were charged with supervising and coordinating the review and consolidation of records.[25]

While women were employed as inspectors, machine operators, and truck drivers at Colorado Fuel & Iron Company (CF&I), the Pueblo company also hired women for office positions. Wages for those working in personnel ranged from 62 cents to 88 cents an hour. Chief Clerk Vivian M. Kelly earned over $1.10 an hour. Single and the daughter of an Irish-born realtor, Kelly was in her fifties during World War II. *The Blast* reported that many of the male employees reacted calmly to the "invasion" of female workers in CF&I's various departments. In May 1942, the newspaper quoted one man as saying "it's war," while others "merely slicked down stray locks of hair and adjusted non-existent neckties."[26] Of course, the first "invaders"—Helen Huber and Josephine Spitzer—were clerks, not extraterrestrial visitors. The year before, Spitzer had been a cashier at Continental Baking Company. Presumably, a clerking job at the steel company paid more than a civilian cashiering job.

As men throughout the nation enlisted or were drafted, American cities became "female worlds." In Colorado, one "instant city" became the state's tenth largest city in 1942. After the attack on Pearl Harbor, citizens on the Pacific Coast, home to the largest number of mainland residents of Japanese descent, demanded their removal. Beginning on February 19, 1942, Japanese Americans could voluntarily evacuate and move elsewhere. But the government had frozen their assets, making a move difficult. Second, they had to consider what welcome they would receive if they voluntarily relocated. Wyoming governor Nels Smith warned that if Japanese Americans were given permission to move to his state, "There would be a Jap hanging from every pine tree."[27] Colorado governor Ralph Carr was one of the few statesmen of the hour. Risking political suicide, he welcomed Japanese Americans.

A small percentage of Japanese Americans voluntarily left their homes in California and resettled in other Nisei and Sansei communities. Nancy Sawada Miyagishima and an aunt moved to Colorado to work on the farm of another aunt, Doris Nakata, in Fort Lupton. Yoshimi Watada's family decided to return to Colorado where he had once worked. They first relocated to Oklahoma until their place in Colorado was ready. In July 1942, the family moved to Rocky Ford and began work as farm laborers.[28] Other Japanese Americans moved to the San Luis Valley and settled in Blanca, Fort Garland, and Alamosa. Once in the state, the US District Attorney's office required them to register and to obtain permission to make trips outside their home vicinity.[29]

When voluntary relocation did not quell fears of Japanese sabotage, President Roosevelt issued Executive Order 9066 authorizing the secretary of war to establish military zones and remove "any and all persons" from those zones. The War Relocation Authority subsequently moved 110,000 Japanese Americans—citizens and non-citizens alike—to ten internment camps in remote areas across the country. Southeastern Colorado was chosen for one site. Officially known as the

Granada Relocation Camp, it was situated on 10,500 acres of desolate prairie. It soon had a population of more than 7,300 people.[30] To distinguish the camp from the town of Granada, it was called Amache in honor of Amache Ochinee Prowers, the daughter of Ochinee, a Cheyenne Peace Chief who was killed in the Sand Creek Massacre in 1864. Amache was a Native American activist, advocate, and landowner.[31] Most of the Japanese Americans at Amache came from the Merced and Santa Anita holding centers.

Amache was laid out in twenty-nine blocks. Each block consisted of twelve barracks, divided into twelve one-room units each. A typical unit—housing a family of seven or fewer—included a closet, a coal stove, folding cots, mattresses, and quilts. When the camp opened in August 1942, it was only partially completed. Hot and cold water was available in only a few blocks. Evacuees assisted with completing the camp. When finished, each block consisted of a central mess hall and a utility room in addition to the barracks. The lack of privacy was particularly distressing. Rooms had little or no furniture and no dividers until internees scrounged the camp for lumber and other materials to construct their own. The common shower room had no stalls. The bathroom was a large room with fifty pots, twenty-five on each side facing each other.[32] Residents were supplied with food, fuel, and a small monthly allowance for clothing.

Monthly wages for workers inside Amache were twelve dollars for unskilled labor, sixteen dollars for skilled labor, and nineteen dollars for professional work. Chiyoko Sakamoto, a Los Angeles attorney and the first Japanese American woman to practice law in the United States, lived at Amache. She, two other Japanese Americans, and one Caucasian offered legal advice to camp residents.[33] Doctors and nurses also earned a professional wage in the camp's 150-bed hospital. Matilda Honda, a former public health nurse with the Los Angeles County Health Department, was on the staff. Although Honda was a voluntary evacuee, most of the rest of the nursing staff members were Anglo residents of the surrounding counties. Mildred L. Finley served as head nurse, and Wanda Oliver was the chief nurse. The hospital was staffed by an additional seven registered nurses, another evacuee nurse, thirty nurse's aides, and a War Relocation Authority dietician.[34]

Other women at Amache were stenographers, clerks, and telephone operators. The 1943 Amache Directory listed twelve clerks or clerk-stenographers, including True Shibata and Ruth Noda; three telephone operators, and one social case worker.[35] Hatsuye Sato, a twenty-seven-year-old American-born evacuee, was a stenographer in the public relations office. In an interview with Ross Thompson, the city editor for the *Lamar Daily News*, she said that "naturally the Japanese evacuees would have liked to have stayed home but . . . evacuees intended to prove that they were loyal Americans by working for, and cooperating with America's war effort."[36] One place in which camp residents did that was the silk-screening department. Taye Namura created colorful propaganda posters imploring American citizens to enlist, recycle metal, buy war bonds, and plant victory gardens.[37]

Because some women found office jobs less attractive than defense jobs, newspapers attempted to glorify the former. The headline "Masculine Traditions Totter—Denver Woman Gets He-Man Job" captured readers' attention. After fifty-four years as an all-male enclave, the Denver office of the US Secret Service welcomed new employee Ruth June Boyer McLearan. Only 5 feet tall and the mother of two-year-old Don, McLearan moved to Denver from Greeley, where she had been a US postal inspector. Her husband, Howard, was in the army. Reading that Mrs. McLearan "claimed to be an expert rifle shot," one could be excused for assuming that she had a novel job with the Secret Service. Alas, the reader was finally informed that McLearan would be "principally employed as a stenographer," replacing Earl J. McCarneny who had been called into active duty. Presumably, her marksmanship was not needed in the office.[38]

Also competing for female workers, Mountain States Telephone and Telegraph Company placed large notices in local papers. Although the company originally hired only male operators, by 1930, all but 3 of the state's 1,925 telephone operators were native- or foreign-born white women.[39] Posters extolled the war value of the company's employees. One showed a woman telephone operator at the control board and a male pilot in an airplane cockpit with the headline "Both Are at Battle Stations." It stated that battles were being fought on every continent and in every sea, aided by the nation's communication lines. It was the task and privilege of more than 10,500 Mountain States workers to see that Uncle Sam had "swift, reliable communication."[40]

Betty Lou Dale of Lafayette was one of those thousands of employees. She was born in Broadhead, 3 miles west of Aquilar. Her father was a coal miner in Las Animas County and in Lafayette. In October 1943, she began working at the telephone company office, which was short on help. She worked five days a week, earning thirteen dollars a week. She and two other operators who worked with no sick leave benefits "were really glued to that job."[41] Because very few people in Lafayette had telephones, a messenger system was employed. Her father was her messenger "boy." For twenty-five cents he drove his Oldsmobile to a person's home and took them to the telephone office to receive their phone call. Although there were public phones in the Highway Drugstore and city hall, most people felt more comfortable taking a call in the office.

Dale and other telephone operators were privy to the emotional costs of the war. Servicemen and women, such as navy nurse Margie Hackman, made one last heartrending call to their parents before being sent overseas. Sons and daughters could not tell their parents where they were being sent. Most of the time, they themselves did not know. When a member of the armed forces was injured, killed, or missing in action, a telegram was sent to the railroad depot.

The depot called the telephone company, which contacted the family. Dale was on duty when a telegram arrived stating that one of her male schoolmates had been killed in the Pacific.[42]

Also working in communications were women who worked for the railroads as telegraph operators. Elizabeth Gilbert of Castle Rock married in 1941. Her husband was drafted, discharged from the army because of hearing problems, and then walked away from his marriage. She divorced him. With no job and no education beyond high school, she applied to the Women's Army Corps. She was rejected because of her asthma. A Santa Fe Railroad employee told her that railroads were looking for young female telegraph operators. She applied to and was accepted by the Denver and Rio Grande Railroad. Her training period was brief—only long enough, in Gilbert's words, "to learn the engine from the caboose and take the train orders properly." She learned to stand along the railroad track and hand up the train orders. Gilbert worked seven days a week, eight hours a day, earning twenty-five cents an hour.[43]

She was transferred to Houston and then to Texas Creek, west of Cañon City, and to Fountain, south of Colorado Springs. In Colorado, she observed many troop trains passing through. When the trains stopped, she went out to the cars to visit with the soldiers. The GIs asked if she knew where they were headed. She told them she had a sneaking suspicion they were going to Camp Carson. The night the Eighth Army moved into the camp, she never sat down during her shift as troop train after troop train rolled in.[44]

In addition to modifying aircraft, women were hired for other jobs at Stapleton Airport in Denver. One unique job was assistant air traffic controller. Dorothy Wise had been a hostess for Continental Airlines before taking a three-month class to qualify for traffic control. The course included instruction in meteorology, navigation, weather code, and air regulations. When she was hired in September 1943, she was the first woman to work in the Denver control tower. From her glassed-in tower she calmly peered through field glasses at circling planes, manipulated the airport traffic signal, answered five telegraphs, and listened to four radios. Wise admitted that she was initially a little nervous but had to get over it because they would not retain jittery employees. Feeling like "a traffic cop at Colfax and Broadway," she directed airplanes landing and taking off at the airfield. To do so, she had to judge wind velocity, read weather code, and know what to do in an emergency. The biggest stress was trying to listen to four radios simultaneously: "When four planes are radioing at once, it's a regular hodge-podge of sound." During the day's five or six busiest hours, planes landed every fifty seconds. After that experience, she felt as though she had been "digging ditches." Emergencies—such as one-wheel landings—were rare. When they occurred, she directed other airplanes to another site, notified the crash department, secured the services of fire engines and ambulances, and guided the plane to a safe landing.[45]

Female employees of the US Weather Bureau also worked at Stapleton. In 1941, only two women were observers or forecasters. After America entered the war, the staffing ratio changed dramatically. In the Denver office, Dorothy Hurd and G. Fay Dickerson were two of several women workers. Hurd had completed a year-and-a-half at a teachers' college art school prior to the attack on Pearl Harbor. That schooling qualified her for a drawing job at the Curtiss-Wright Aircraft factory in St. Louis. Within a year, work had slowed down so much that she spent a lot of time in the library. Books on meteorology fascinated her, so she took tests for Weather Bureau jobs. When she passed, she was sent to Kansas City for a six-week training course.[46]

After training, Hurd was assigned to Denver's airport. She took observations every half-hour, sent up ceiling balloons every six hours, and put coded messages on teletype. She worked eight hours a day, forty hours a week. There were no lunch hours; the observers and forecasters brought their lunches and ate at their desks. She was paid about forty-five dollars a week the first two years. Hurd especially enjoyed doing a RAOB, or radiosonde observation (test). A radiosonde is a battery-powered telemetry instrument package carried into the atmosphere by a weather balloon. After measuring temperature, pressure, and humidity, it transmitted the data to a ground receiver. If conditions were adverse for flying, observers told the airport tower to send planes elsewhere or go to instrument landing when the ceiling or visibility was low. Tower men did not appreciate "young girls" telling them what to do. While it was difficult to resist the cajoling of "handsome, glamorous pilots" who wanted the women to change their reports, they "stuck by the rules."[47]

G. Fay Dickerson worked for the Weather Bureau from November 1942 until December 31, 1949. After teaching in rural schools for two years and attending summer classes at Colorado State College of Education and one year at the University of Denver, the Illinois native was looking for a job that would allow her to continue her studies. A part-time job did not pay enough, so when a friend told her about the Weather Bureau, she thought that would be an "attractive alternative." She was accepted and attended training in Kansas City, Missouri. She felt uncomfortable with her meteorological inexperience in comparison to other students. Their instructor, a Finnish American meteorologist, was an excellent teacher, though. They spent most of their time in the classroom but also took advantage of winter fog for practice observations.[48]

Although Dickerson hoped to be assigned to Denver, she was sent to North Platte, Nebraska. On-the-job training continued. There was enough routine work to keep each person in the office busy. Special weather conditions required constant attention. Dickerson was received well by her colleagues. The chief observer, however, made it a point to only order women to climb a pole above one of the hangars to remove the anemometer, carry it down for checking, and then replace it. Although the climb intimidated her, she tried not to show it, knowing that the male chief observer was testing the stamina and nerve of his female observers.[49]

The office regularly rotated its staff of four men and five or six women through day, evening, and night shifts. Routine duties included hourly and more detailed six-hourly weather reports, which were entered by teletype. As information was received, they plotted the six-hourly map with considerable detail on frontal activity and changeable weather conditions: low ceilings, reduced visibility, precipitation, thunderstorm activity, and strong winds. Whenever conditions changed, a special weather report was sent to the Civilian Aviation Authority for immediate transmission. After eighteen months in Nebraska, Dickerson was transferred to Denver's office, where she completed her wartime service.[50]

Some college students worked at defense plants during the summer. Helen Morgan was only four years old when her mother died, leaving her father with two sons, ages six and ten, and two daughters, Helen and her twenty-three-month-old sister. Walter Morgan kept his two boys. An aunt raised one daughter while Helen was raised by an aunt and uncle. In 1940, she enrolled at Kansas State Teachers College at the behest of her guardians, who insisted even though she had no desire to teach. Between her junior and senior years, she took a war job at North American Aviation in Kansas City. When the woman in charge of blueprints became pregnant, Morgan replaced her. As a blueprinter, her job was to make duplicates of aviation parts. The plant produced the B-25 bomber. Although it was a difficult decision, at the end of the summer Morgan chose to finish her college education rather than continue in the high-paying job.[51]

In 1944, Morgan graduated from college. Her desire had always been to return to California, her native state. She and a friend rode a train from Topeka to Los Angeles. Her friend became a riveter at Lockheed, while Morgan went to the Job Service Bureau to inquire about an office position, figuring that she would still have a job after the war ended. She was hired at Western Crown, Cork, and Seal Company. The company produced bottle caps for soda pop and lids for peanut butter and Max Factor cosmetics. Running the office also meant wrapping gifts for the company president when he made purchases for his wife. In her six years at the plant, Morgan worked her way up to the position of office manager.[52]

Like Helen Morgan, Elsie Virginia Mann lost her mother at a young age. In 1930 in Berthoud, Lottie Mann, the wife of Ralph Vincent Mann and the mother of seven children, died. Two of the children—twins—were sent to live with two different sets of relatives. Elsie, only five years old at the time of her mother's death, was immediately enrolled in first grade so she would be taken care of most of the day. During her fifth-grade year, the family moved to a farm in Weld County 9 miles east of Longmont. On the family farm she hoed corn, fed calves, and pulled weeds in the family garden.[53]

After graduating from high school, Mann moved in with her grandparents to attend the University of Colorado. She earned a degree in home economics with the hope of getting a job as a home extension agent. However, the job required a car, an asset Mann did not have. The head of the home economics department told her that a recruiter from the US Department of Agriculture needed women to examine cannery food for military consumption. Mann borrowed $100 from her grandparents and boarded a train for San Jose. At the cannery, she gathered samples and examined them in her office.[54]

Later, she was transferred across the bay to Centerville. Attired in a white uniform, she inspected tomatoes during her twelve-hour shift. Another tester worked the other twelve hours of the day. When one of them had a day off, the other was forced to work a twenty-four hour shift. Mann took samples off the production line. In the laboratory, she put them on a container that had a grid-like screw top. She poured a petroleum-like substance over it and then drained it off. In this way, she could count the number of hairs and bugs in each square. If there were more than a certain number, she failed that run of tomatoes. Later, Mann was transferred back to the San Jose side of the bay to a factory that canned fruit. Grading fruit cocktail was an onerous job, sorting out pineapple, cherries, peaches, and pears. She used a slide rule for the first time in her life. Prior to this job, she had only seen them in boys' pockets. She confessed that she did not do "too well" at that canning factory.[55]

Other women were employed at defense plants in different capacities. Mary Ann Gallegos, a native of now-defunct Tiffany, lived in several Colorado towns before graduating from high school in Silverton. Her father was often absent because he had a job with the Denver and Rio Grande Railroad. Her mother, Josephine, kept the large family together. Born in New Mexico, her mother spoke only Spanish while her father was bilingual. After graduation in 1941, Gallegos attended Benedictine College. She earned a teaching certificate and taught for one year. In the summer of 1944, Gallegos and her younger sister, Mabel, moved to Richmond, California, to join their two older sisters, one of whom welded in the Kaiser shipyards. Fifteen-year-old Mabel got a job at a movie house. Gallegos was hired as a secretary in the front office at Shipyard Number Three, which produced troop transports. In the office, Gallegos gave potential workers applications and helped them fill them out if necessary. Some people were illiterate and could only put an "X" for their name. Nevertheless, most applicants were hired since the plant needed production-line employees, janitors, cafeteria workers, clerks, and secretaries. Following a successful interview, the person was hired. Gallegos then drove the hires on a motor scooter with a side car to their new job. She worked there for three months before teaching at a school shipyard workers' children attended, and she then worked in the Ferry Building in San Francisco. There, she ensured that the necessary equipment was ready and orders were filled when ships sailed into port for repairs. She always knew how far out to sea the ships were and when they were due in port. For that reason, the Federal Bureau of Investigation interviewed her father and teachers prior to her hiring.[56]

Americans moving from one part of the United States to another during the war produced a housing crisis. Cities and industrial areas rushed to provide accommodations for thousands of new residents, but the issue was never completely resolved. Many boardinghouses and private homes were hesitant to rent to female boarders, afraid of unknowingly accepting "immoral" women. Landlords and landladies found that in comparison to males, female renters demanded better accommodations and complained when those expectations went unfulfilled. Their biggest concerns were women taking long baths and hanging their laundry everywhere.[57]

Frances Hale was one of thousands of women who descended on Washington, DC, worsening an already bad situation. She first lived with Jennie Walker, whom she knew from Denver. They soon wanted to move to another place. Her Denver minister's wife knew of a woman who was willing to rent to Walker, Hale, and a friend of theirs, Lorraine Hobbes. That living situation turned out poorly. The landlady was "the most difficult woman." When Walker's two sisters moved to the city, the three family members found another place to live.[58]

With so many women office workers in the city and surrounding area, dormitories were built for Caucasian women. First Lady Eleanor Roosevelt asked the head of the YWCA, "Where do the colored girls live?" When she was told that they rented rooms in people's homes, Mrs. Roosevelt insisted that Congress build dormitories for African American office workers.[59] Lucy Diggs Slowe Hall on the campus of Howard University was one of two built. Women lived in private rooms and took their meals in the dormitory cafeteria. After a vacation in Denver, Hale wrote to her employers saying that if she could not get into the university dormitory, she would not return to her job. They found her a room for the last year of her employment. She also attended classes at Howard University, as did many of the other residents.[60]

Women who found war work in their hometowns continued to live with their families. Leota Broman, who worked at the Denver Ordnance Plant and at Higley Aviation, lived in her parents' home with her two sisters, who were also secretaries during the war. Until her brother joined the Army Air Corps, six family members shared one bathroom, not an uncommon situation during the 1940s.[61] Other women lived with married siblings or in-laws. Roberta Grainger, who started as a "fraudulent" secretary at the ordnance plant, first lived with her sister. Later, she moved in with her mother-in-law and sister-in-law. Among other benefits, they pooled their money to buy gasoline for their Sunday drives.[62]

Other workers boarded with families. In Los Angeles, Helen Morgan and her college friend lived with one family while another family occupied the upstairs apartment.[63] When she first reported to San Jose for her job, Lottie Mann was met by a company representative who found her a room in a woman's house. The woman was separated from her husband and had a young boy. She needed Mann to watch him while she worked evenings. When her landlady reunited with her husband, she quit her night job, and Mann was no longer needed as a live-in babysitter. At Sunnyvale, she boarded in another private home. Although the room had only one bed, it was rented out to three women. The arrangement was sufficient because they worked different shifts and slept at different times of the day.[64] On submarines and in other military situations, this is called "hot-racking." Civilian terminology includes "hot-bunking" or "hot-bedding." Mary Ann Gallegos and her sister slept in sleeping bags on the floor of a cousin's place in Richmond, California. Later, they lived in government housing built for plant workers.[65]

In whatever capacity they worked—in war plants and government offices as secretaries and clerks, as civilian code breakers employed by the United States Army, at airfields as traffic controllers or Weather Bureau observers, in telephone offices as operators, in laboratories as inspectors, or at railroad offices as telegraph operators—women were important war workers. They processed millions of forms and developed crucial reports and data. While they did not have the notoriety of women ordnance workers, they, too, kept the home front fires burning.

Also contributing on the home front were women on Colorado farms, ranches, and fruit orchards and in canneries and beet sugar factories. Victory gardens, of which Colorado had an estimated 138,000, were important components of the "Food for Victory."

10

"Food for Victory"

Colorado Farms, Ranches, and Victory Gardens

Ann Enstrom and other honor students from Grand Junction High School who had been bussed to Palisade stood waiting for the conveyor belt to start moving. It was September 1. Although the peach season was over, there were still hundreds of bushels of peaches on the trees and on the ground that needed to be saved. The boys had been let off the bus in the orchards while the girls reported to a cannery in Palisade. The heat in the old cannery was unbearable, and the girls itched from the peach fuzz of the recently picked fruit. But they were there to help. As the girls waited for the belt to start, they watched their classmates cut the peaches in half and remove the pits. They put the halves on the belt skin-side up. The peaches traveled through a steamer to make them ready for Enstrom and the other girls to pinch off the skins. The peaches were then ready to be canned and sent to American GIs. To make the heat and constant standing tolerable and to break the monotony, the girls sang popular jazzy songs like "I've Got a Gal in Kalamazoo" and "Chattanooga Choo Choo." At the end of the day, students were bussed back to Grand Junction, only to return the next day for more peach picking, peach cutting, and pinching of peach skins until all of the peaches were canned. Were Ann and the other students paid? No. They didn't expect it, and they would not have accepted any pay. America, after all, was at war, and they wanted to do their part to help.[1]

World War II presented a difficult dilemma for Colorado farmers, ranchers, and city dwellers. Agriculturists increased their output to feed American soldiers at the same time they faced a labor shortage. Between 1940 and 1943, more than

 DOI: 10.5876/9781646420339.c010

3.5 million men and women left agricultural jobs.[2] Some were "lost" to military enlistment or draft, others to defense plants. While the labor force on farms in southern states was decimated as African Americans left the region in droves to work in defense jobs, Colorado's Black population was largely non-agricultural and urban-based. In addition, during the war, farms in Texas, Southern California, and Arizona no longer shipped harvests to Colorado because of gasoline rationing and rail cutbacks.[3] Farm and ranch women added more chores to their lists while thousands of urban women grew their own vegetables in victory gardens, canned produce, and kept a wary eye on kitchen pantry supplies.

FARMS AND RANCHES

In October 1941, county supervisors from the Agricultural Adjustment Administration visited Colorado farmers. They announced that a national plan required American farmers to supply food for (1) more than 10 million persons in Great Britain, (2) the increased demand in the United States, and (3) a sufficient surplus to export to other countries. Substantial increases in dairy products and supplies of eggs, pork, beef, lamb, and mutton were mandated. Eliminated were the previous limits on the amount of acreage used for sugar beets and larger truck crops. Cattlemen were encouraged to increase the slaughter of cattle and calves by 19 percent and of sheep and lambs by 9 percent. Potato acreage was increased by 13 percent, oats and barley by 6 percent, and corn by 2 percent. Wheat was the only major Colorado crop that was reduced in 1942.[4] In 1943, Colorado wheat farmers experienced record crops. They reaped 30 bushels per acre, twice the usual amount, and sold the wheat for $1.20 a bushel—an income of $10,000 for 320 acres. In July of that year, Howard Lindfors, owner of the Farmers' Elevator in Strasburg, reported that farmers were selling 8,000 to 10,000 bushels of wheat a day.[5]

The problem with the demand for increased production was the labor shortage. The induction of one-eighth of the state's labor force left farming communities short-handed. Although the federal government recognized the farm labor shortage, it did not marshal its efforts to solve the problem. In May 1942, the federal government announced a shortage of 10,000 workers in Colorado, Wyoming, Montana, and Idaho. Each community was responsible for finding its own laborers. Farmers were told to use women and children in the fields. Businesses were told to close part-time so their workers could help out. The employment service anticipated that "even bank clerks may become cherry pickers."[6]

To counter these difficulties, federal and state governments formulated a three-pronged plan. First, farmers could hire prisoners of war (POWs), Japanese American internees, and Mexican Nationals to work in Colorado's fields. Thirty-two POW camps were spread from Adams County to Yuma County. In Weld County six towns—Ault, Eaton, Galeton, Keenesburg, Kersey, and Pierce—housed a total of

1,461 POWs. Fort Collins, Loveland, and Johnstown in Larimer County imprisoned 1,310 POWs, while Morgan County (Brush, Fort Morgan, and Wiggins) housed 902 prisoners of war. Tiny Yuma had 160 prisoners.[7] Because the nation's sugar supply was greatly reduced after the Japanese took over the Philippines, the government turned to domestic production. Since 1909, Colorado had been the leading sugar beet–producing state in the country. For decades, Chicanos and Chicanas had provided the physical labor in the fields. They continued to do so during the war, but male workers also enlisted or were drafted into the armed forces, eliminating their availability to work in the fields. The resulting shortage of workers greatly diminished farmers' ability to grow and harvest the labor-intensive crop. Anglos were reluctant to work in the fields because of the grueling stooping and bending involved in thinning, topping, and harvesting sugar beets. In November 1943 the *Brush Tribune* reported that 250 German POWs at Fort Morgan and 250 Italian POWs in Brush had harvested the sugar beet crop.[8] Ultimately, 3,000 Italian and German prisoners of war gathered sugar beets, onions, cabbage, and potatoes in Larimer, Morgan, and Weld Counties.

Sugar beet growers in Colorado's southeast corner also faced a labor shortage. Beginning in 1942, the War Relocation Authority allowed Japanese American internees at Amache to work in the sugar beet fields. An early frost threatened the year's harvest before Amacheans joined high school students in the harvest. Of the 1,260 Japanese American workers in Colorado fields during World War II, all but 180 toiled in beet fields. They were paid $52.75 a month with board or $81.00 without board. Daily rates were $3.55 with board and $4.30 without board. Those were the highest farm wages paid in Colorado since 1920.[9]

In 1943, farmers were required to give a minimum of thirty days' notice for laborers to the US Employment Service in Fort Morgan.[10] Farmers in Prowers County faced the loss of 60,000 tons of sugar beets if more laborers were not found. Their first volunteers were twenty high school students and twenty women from Amache who helped save their crops.[11] Amacheans also worked in Denver, Adams, Jefferson, and Arapahoe Counties, harvesting the equivalent of 18 million pounds of sugar. In addition, they harvested root vegetables, head lettuce, tomatoes, celery, and potatoes. Harold S. Choate, relocation supervisor, reported that without exception, the "evacuees have been willing and intelligent workers" who were proud to be contributing to the end of the war.[12]

Internees planted and grew food within the confines of the camps. The War Relocation Authority had established agricultural programs so the internment camps could be self-sufficient. At Amache, Japanese Americans grew mung bean sprouts, *daikon* (Japanese radish), celery, lettuce, tomatoes, and tea. They produced beef, pork, and dairy products. Surplus alfalfa, corn, milo, and sorghum were shipped to other camps or sold to the public. In the first year, Amache workers sent truckloads of crops to other relocation camps.[13]

FIGURE 10.1. Chicanas, who had toiled in Colorado's sugar beet fields for decades, continued to provide important stoop labor for farmers on the eastern plains during World War II. *Courtesy*, Prints and Photographs Division, FSA/OWI Collection, LC-USF34-028754-D, Library of Congress, Washington, DC.

Despite the use of POWs and Japanese American internees, farmers throughout the country needed more workers. On August 4, 1942, Mexico and the United States signed an agreement—the Mexican Emergency Farm Labor Program—allowing Mexican Nationals to enter the United States as farm laborers. Both countries hoped this bracero program would keep track of and control the numbers of workers crossing the border. The Mexican government agreed to recruit laborers while the US government facilitated employment, wages, working conditions, and transportation. The United States gave Mexican workers transportation to and from the farms they were working, a minimum wage equal to that of American domestic farm laborers, and decent housing to live in while working. Mexican workers had to provide their own food and health insurance, which were usually deducted from their pay. The two nations agreed that only male laborers over age eighteen were eligible.[14] At the end of the harvest, braceros were required to return to Mexico or face deportation. Of course, what was agreed upon and expected to happen did not align with reality. Farmers took advantage of Mexican Nationals and did not always provide adequate housing, wages, and working conditions. Mexican wives, not wanting to be separated from their husbands, illegally crossed the border with their children, as did Mexicans who were not selected for the program. Farmers turned a blind eye and hired them at cheaper wages.[15] It was estimated that there were 70,000 undocumented workers in the United States in the late 1940s.[16] Lastly, rather than ending up being a plan designed to only address wartime labor shortages, the bracero program continued until 1964 because it was advantageous for farmers who wanted cheap, compliant laborers and for Mexicans seeking work.[17]

The vast majority of braceros worked in Texas and California—states abutting Mexico. However, in 1944 the Union Pacific Railroad brought in 181 braceros to help with the harvest in Fort Morgan and Brush. Later, an additional 124 braceros joined 540 German prisoners. The influx of these workers was particularly necessary because 180 formerly farm-deferred Morgan County youths were ordered to report for pre-induction examinations at the beginning of 1944.[18]

Colorado requested 10,000 Mexican Nationals to help plant and harvest important wartime crops. Farmers, ranchers, and other rural residents supplied 80 percent of all agricultural work in Colorado but needed Mexican Nationals to get the job done. Helping with the harvest was bracero Abundio Duran, who worked for Frank Mares in 1943 and was planning on returning in 1944.[19] Duran's statement that he wanted to return to work in Colorado was echoed by the *Eagle Valley Enterprise*, which reported that "nearly all of the Mexicans who worked on farms in the United States last year want to return" in 1944.[20]

Colorado crop growers fared well during the war years. In 1942, 1943, and 1944, potato growers in the San Luis Valley reported record yields. In 1942, nearly 11,000 carloads of produce were shipped out of the valley by rail. Over 7,600 of them were loads of potatoes. In November 1944, sugar beet growers received the highest prices for their crop in the history of the industry.[21] In 1944, Morgan County potato growers enjoyed their best season in history with the help of German POWs.[22] On the Western Slope, the 1942 tomato yield was 30 percent more than the previous year. That same year, growers in the San Luis Valley reported bumper crops of spinach, head lettuce, cauliflower, cabbage, carrots, and other vegetables.[23] Between September 1942 and August 1943, alfalfa hay, mixed dairy feed, corn, oat, and linseed meal prices increased.[24] In 1943 the Colorado State Extension Service, which had taken over the emergency farm-labor program, placed more than 8,000 workers on Colorado farms and ranches. In July that was sufficient, but shortages loomed for the next month when Western Slope peaches would be ripe for harvesting.[25] That year's peach harvest set a record, with 239 car loadings a day in September. Some of the labor in Mesa County was supplied by Japanese Americans from Amache and German POWs.[26]

Using prisoners of war, Japanese American internees, and braceros was a boon for farmers. The second prong developed by the government was to use unemployed persons and high school students to work in the fields. In Mesa County,

FIGURE 10.2. Ann Enstrom, a high
school student in Grand Junction,
pinched the skins off peaches at a
cannery in Palisades as her contribution to the food line of defense.
Courtesy, Ann Enstrom Scott.

the peach harvest determined the date the school year began. In 1942, elementary
and junior high schools planned to begin on September 8, but the high school
schedule had not been set by mid-August. In 1944, school opening dates were not
set until September 3 because there had been "much difficulty in securing teachers."[27] No reason was given, but one can surmise that the lure of higher-paying
defense jobs might have been one reason there was a teacher shortage.

The National Farm Youth Foundation also used young men—and later
women—as part of the "food line" of defense. The foundation was Henry Ford's
idea and was sponsored nationally by the Ferguson-Sherman Manufacturing
Corporation of Dearborn, Michigan. The home-study course taught young men
modern, scientific farming techniques. In the second year, students, including
"lady-farmers," studied mechanics and care of farm equipment. The program officially ended in the fall of 1942, possibly because with America's full involvement
in the war, the sponsoring company had more pressing concerns than tractor pull
competitions and plowing demonstrations. However, the name National Farm
Youth Foundation remained and was used in connection with other farming ini-
tiatives and programs. In 1945 Littleton's Lois Rose, the first woman to enroll in
the program, operated a tractor; and a group of Denver girls learned tractor repair

under the supervision of the foundation.[28] With mechanics in high demand in the military, there was a shortage of repairmen for civilian equipment. Thirty shops spread throughout Colorado taught farmers how to repair equipment. The largest was at Waverly, near Alamosa.[29]

In 1917, the United States had established the Women's Land Army of America to meet the food needs of its Allies and itself during World War I. Although the situation was even more dire in the early years of World War II, the government showed no interest in reviving the program despite the support of the first lady. By early 1943, US Department of Agriculture officials changed their minds. In April the Women's Land Army (WLA) was established, with Florence Hall appointed as its head. The organization was part of the US Crop Corps.[30] The WLA worked closely with home demonstration agents in the Extension Service, state agricultural colleges, and women's organizations (such as the American Women's Voluntary Services, the General Federation of Women's Clubs, and the YWCA) to recruit workers. To be eligible, women simply needed to be physically fit and eighteen years of age or older. Media coverage resulted in five times more women recruited than the WLA's goal of 60,000. The initial plan was to bring in three different classes of workers: those who would work year-round and live on-site; seasonal workers, such as teachers, who could not or did not want to spend all of their time on a farm; and emergency laborers to work short-time assignments, such as harvesting for a day or two, or on weeklong projects.[31] One group on short-time assignments were Lakota women from the Rosebud Reservation (South Dakota), who were brought to Colorado to labor in sugar beet fields.[32]

The Women's Land Army initially encountered resistance from farmers and farmers' wives, who doubted that urban women could measure up and handle farm machinery.[33] Others predicted that female workers would distract the remaining male workers from their agricultural tasks. Some farm wives were mollified when young women offered to do housework and cooking as well as farm chores.[34] The participating farmer and woman agreed on her wages, which generally ranged from twenty-five dollars to fifty dollars a month, with room and board furnished for long-term workers. Other workers were paid twenty-five to fifty cents an hour.[35] Although a uniform of dark blue overalls, long- and short-sleeved shirts, and a hat was designed, most women did not purchase it, figuring there was little point in buying new work clothes before their own had worn out.

Despite initial skepticism, the WLA ably contributed to America's "food line of defense." By 1945, a half million non-farm women had come to the rescue by driving tractors, combines, and trucks; plowing; raking hay; shaking and stalking peanuts; picking cotton; harvesting and curing tobacco; riding the range; picking potatoes; pruning fruit trees; taking care of poultry; and harvesting fruits and vegetables.[36] The WLA reported that it had sent "hundreds" of women to Colorado and Nebraska to de-tassel hybrid corn.[37] The report filed by Mary

Sutherland, assistant state supervisor of the Extension Service of Colorado A&M, highlighted the contribution of the WLA. Several women had hauled grain to a Julesburg elevator, saving their husbands and fathers $1,000. Frances Hodges of Julesburg and her Denver friend Thelma Anderson hauled grain for three years. Also hauling grain was Ferne Dollison, a Sedgwick County high school student. Julesburg students Shirley and Helda Smyth drove tractors in eight-hour shifts alongside their brothers. Alma Sowder ran a rod weeder during harvest season in Sedgwick County.[38] W. S. Brown of Springfield was pleased with the work of the nineteen-year-old Oklahoma girl on his farm: "I have never had a hired man who was as efficient in farm work, milking cows, driving a tractor, etc. She was married this fall, and I would like to find another like her."[39]

Ranchers were also skeptical of hiring women to do cowhands' work. The Colorado War Manpower Committee told them to not be "so choosy" and that they must be prepared to take city youths and women. Dr. B. F. Davis of the Colorado Stock Growers and Feeders Association countered that industrial plants could use women workers, but punching cows was hardly lady's work: "Women are all right, but they're not cowpokes."[40] Ranch women in Nederland jumped to the challenge. At the expansive Lazy V Ranch, they asked their boss for a chance to prove themselves. Lynn William Van Vleet had 500 head of cattle and calves to round up and drive into branding corrals. The calves had to be separated from their mammas, and 300 of them had to be vaccinated and branded and have their ears notched. It added up to "12 hours of good, old-fashioned perspiration." Because a number of his cowhands were in the armed forces, Van Vleet gave the women a chance. The cowboys were "a bit skittish" with the women at first, but the new ranch hands "did a good job." Van Vleet considered it a successful day.[41]

Naturally, thousands of Colorado women continued to contribute to their own family farms and ranches. Traditionally, women on ranches and farms are responsible for poultry and milk cows. During World War II, farm women were encouraged to increase egg production. Uncle Sam urged farmers to increase their dairy herds and total milk production by 2 percent in 1944. Farm wives were essential in meeting those goals because they kept the records, fed the livestock, milked the cows, and took care of the milk.[42] In 1909, the five Beers Sisters started their dairy near South Wadsworth and Belleview Avenues in Littleton. Initially, the older sisters—Mattie, Edna, and Bessie—did most of the difficult work while the two youngest sisters, Marguerite and Ollie, attended school and became teachers. Later, all five sisters were involved in the growing dairy operation. By the mid-1920s, the sisters eliminated the middleman and sold their milk under the Beers Sisters Farm Dairy moniker. They continued in that manner through the war years.[43] To encourage more production, Yuma County extolled the profitability of chickens and eggs.[44] Colorado farm women made up 23 percent of the farm labor force, helping with every job except "heavier field work."[45]

The growing of peaches and tomatoes kept a large agricultural workforce busy in Mesa County. A National Youth Administration (NYA) project was run out of an old county farm. It canned 80,000 cans of fruit and vegetables for use in NYA centers. Four canning facilities operated in Palisade, Grand Junction, and Appleton. Each plant predicted a need for many more workers as the season progressed. A large number of Orchard Mesa women, taking a two-week break from making surgical dressings for the Red Cross, worked in the orchards just as their sons and daughters had during harvest season. Braceros were also brought in to help with the harvest. They were quartered in the Civilian Conservation Camp barracks for two weeks during harvest.[46]

In addition to work in the orchards, women were encouraged to apply for jobs in canneries in western Colorado. Although canneries in California employed thousands of Latinas, that was not the case in Colorado. The state's Spanish-speaking population lived mostly in the southern, southeastern, and northeastern parts of the state in the 1940s. Displaying a drawing of women processing fruit in the factory, a Grand Junction Canners Association's advertisement reminded area residents that when crops were ripe, they needed to be harvested fast and packed quickly. It was not just a job, it was "a duty." Norish Fine Foods reminded residents that seven of ten peaches went to America's fighting men—"if you don't bring 'em, we don't can 'em, and the boys don't get 'em."[47] A year later, the Kuner-Empson Company placed a full-page ad in the Grand Junction newspaper strongly urging women to fill out the attached job application. It promised that its war work was "pleasant and well paid, carried on under pleasant conditions," and that it was easier than putting up fruits and vegetables at home—although harder than playing bridge or typing a letter.[48] The peak of tomato canning season brought renewed pleas for help from area women, especially on the canning line where peelers were needed.

Farther north, Emily (Elaine) Becker Gay, married only a few years before the war, was a certified teacher, but she spent the war years helping her husband on their ranch in Pleasant Valley outside Steamboat Springs. She fed their ranch hands while raising three children. Like thousands of other farm and ranch women, she cured ham and bacon, fried fresh chickens, baked her own bread, churned butter, and canned fruit. The hard work was gratifying: "When you get through the day, you have really done something. You have helped put up the hay. You have made some clothes for your kids and you cooked a dinner for a bunch of men. It's what I would say is a sense of accomplishment."[49]

Harriet Kemry, the youngest of three children of George and Alta Kemry, found that ranch chores fell to her after her brother Lewis joined the army. There was no one else to do the work, so it was assumed that she would. In an April 1944 letter from Camp Walters (Texas), Lewis called on her to help and, as older siblings often do, added some brotherly advice: "Are you helping dad a lot? You are

FIGURE 10.3. Harriet Kemry raking hay on the family ranch, the Mesa Ranch, near Pleasant Valley. *Courtesy*, Tread of Pioneers Museum, Steamboat Springs, CO.

going to have to try to take my place helping him this summer so do the best you can. You might sometimes wish you could do something else, but when you do, just stop and think of the many thousands of people in this world that are doing things, and cheerfully too, that they don't want to. Even I am doing things every day all day that I don't like in the least, especially when I stop to think of the things I might be doing. I had much rather be home."[50] Fortunately, Harriet loved doing the chores. Her happiest days were spent raking hay.[51] Seven months later, Lewis closed a letter with "keep things going there."[52] His sister did not disappoint her older brother.

Rural women were also encouraged to meet wartime shortages with their "traditional ingenuity." The Farm Security Administration reported that women used flour and feed sacks to make dish and hand towels, shirts, slips, aprons, pillowcases, and layettes. Women made mattresses from oat straw or shredded corn shucks and fashioned orange crates into small tables and cupboards. They used hickory bark and walnut shells to make homemade dye. Farm women made their own syrup or sorghum, cheese, and soap.[53] All this in addition to cooking, washing clothes, raising children, and feeding and boarding hired hands.

This multitasking prompted one farm wife to write a tongue-in-cheek article. Hazel Hansen concluded that the "alphabet boys in Washington" thought a farm woman was different from the rest of her sex when it came to needing a morale boost. She did admit that there were times in the past when women fed chickens while dressed in cast-off Sunday clothes and pigs were slopped by a farmer's wife attired in a pair of her husband's pants. She wryly lamented the lack of a "snappy suit with a few bars and stripes tacked on the sleeves" for the noncommissioned farmer's wife. She theorized that some sort of calisthenics class for the female tractor crews would stimulate the spring work. And if there was a mauve cubbyhole to dash into for a bit of makeup when the husband decided to ask the truckers to stay for dinner, the graveyard shift would come off in a better humor. But Hansen realized that the closest thing to a factory whistle for a farm wife was the pressure cooker wheeze. She consoled herself with the knowledge that farm women are "supposed to be smart instead of good-looking." None of her suggestions would see the light of day.[54]

Another model farm woman was Della M. Henry of Brush. She was a gardener, painter, shepherdess, carpenter, poultry raiser, paperhanger, and homemaker. She also served as president of the Morgan County Home Demonstration Council. In 1944, Henry set out 300 strawberry plants and 14 fruit trees. The Colorado native had 200 chickens, assorted ducks and geese, and a garden large enough to supply vegetables for both the table and canning. Her husband, Charles, spent the war years raising registered Herefords and farming in two places. With him so busy, she did many tasks herself. With some help from her husband and uncle, she shingled the house and garage, painted their house and the hog house, built a back porch, cemented the dirt walls and the floor of their cellar, added new steps to the front entrance, and dug a new concrete well.[55]

While Coloradans toiled in the fields, Denver meatpacking plants processed food for the troops. During the war, the Armour, Swift, and Cudahy Packing Companies advertised for more workers. The Armour plant produced twice as much during the war as it had during peacetime. Thirty percent of its workers were women who did all types of jobs except those requiring heavy lifting. Mary Rickley's job was to "telescope" a lamb inside another lamb to conserve vital space when it was shipped overseas.[56] The Armour plant ran three shifts a day, six days a week. Swift and Company urgently needed 150 men and 25 women. Of the 1,061 workers in January 1945, 238 were women. Most departments at Swift ran three shifts. Time-and-a-half was paid after forty hours. The meatpacking company offered vacation with pay, sick benefits, and retirement plans. The Cudahy Packing Company slaughtered 10,000 head of livestock a week. It had the supplies and the facilities to add a night shift, but without additional workers it could not do so. Of the 100 more positions to be filled, one-third were for women.[57]

In addition to the three meatpacking plants described in the previous paragraph, other Colorado companies produced food for the armed forces. Denver's Bluhill Foods packaged over 400,000 peanuts for US troops. Bluhill Cheese Company, operating out of Market Street, provided cheese and cheese products.

In Greeley, Criselda "Kate" Espinosa Cassel and her sister, Eloysa Espinosa Tellez, worked at the Spud Chips factory making potato chips for soldiers. She had one child; Tellez had three. Cassel worked the day shift while her sister watched her son. When she came home from work, Tellez left for the plant and Cassel looked after all four children.[58]

VICTORY GARDENS

The Department of Agriculture promoted a third government plan to solve the food supply issue. The extensive "victory garden" program was established to teach citizens how to convert empty lots and backyards into produce gardens. Factories, businesses, and schools started "community gardens" on larger plots. Ann Enstrom's family grew carrots, strawberries, and other crops. Her high school in Grand Junction had a garden that provided fresh vegetables for school lunches.[59] Erstwhile gardeners were inundated with promotional posters. Slogans such as "Eat what you can, can what you can't" and "Grow your living. It may not be available for you to buy" encouraged citizens to start plants in window boxes, transplant them into gardens, use table scraps for fertilizer, and "can" leftovers in Mason jars sealed with molten paraffin and lids. Between 1942 and 1943, the number of victory gardens in the United States grew from 15 million to 20 million. It was estimated that the gardens produced 120 billion pounds of food in 1943.[60] That same year, 40 percent of all the vegetables consumed in the United States were grown in victory gardens. Eleanor Roosevelt planted a victory garden of the front lawn of the White House to show that it was the "patriotic duty of every person, from the First Lady to the lady next door, to plant and cultivate for victory."[61]

There were bushels of help for novice gardeners. The Emily Griffith Opportunity School offered classes in victory gardening.[62] The Alamosa Garden Club started a victory garden school to help gardeners prepare the soil, choose the proper variety of seed, and control insects. Classes were held on dehydrating, freezing, and storing produce.[63] Also in the San Luis Valley, a "Vegetables for Victory" circular was distributed.[64] In a school in Fruita, a canning center opened to the public. Frances Lister taught residents while Margery Monfort, Mesa County home demonstration agent, provided information on the methods of canning food. Out-of-town people—most of whom were in the area to help with the harvest—also used the facility.[65]

Colorado companies and factories urged their workers to plant victory gardens. Every issue of *The Blast*, the newspaper of Colorado Fuel & Iron (CF&I), had a column titled "Your Victory Garden." Subjects included canning, crop selection, and insect control.[66] Fuel company employees, including Patricia Twombly and Margaret Gramley, formed the Hoe and Grow Society, fondly called "HAGS." Hardware stores and authorities with the Colorado victory garden program encouraged citizens to share rakes, hoes, and other gardening implements with their neighbors, stating that it was just as unpatriotic to hoard a shovel as it was to hoard sugar or coffee.[67]

With men fighting the war, laboring in the fields, or working a job in town, it was women's responsibility to plant, weed, reap, and, later, cook or can the produce. Lula R. Moore harvested thirty-two varieties of vegetables in her 1,400-square-foot plot, earning her the title of the state's best adult victory gardener. Barbara Ann Bocovich of Colorado Springs, the elementary school winner of the state's Green Thumb contest, planted 2,100 square feet in her grandmother's vacant lot. A partial list included 27 dozen ears of corn, 350 pounds of cabbage, 7 bushels of root crops, 47 squash, 6 pumpkins, and "an abundance" of leafy crops. Eighty-eight pints were canned for winter use.[68] Elbert County women set the record for victory gardens. All but 34 of the county's 989 rural families planted gardens, and 275 of the 315 town families did the same. Gardening efforts in tiny Laird, near the Nebraska border, were also impressive. Twelve members of the Liberty Club tended thirteen gardens (one woman boasted having one garden in town and one in the country).[69]

By the end of the war, Colorado farmers, ranchers, food-processing plants, and victory gardeners had successfully provided "food for victory." Mexican braceros, Japanese American internees, Lakota women, farm women, the Woman's Land Army, and schoolchildren toiled on Colorado farms and ranches and in orchards to produce record yields during the war. In addition, urban and rural Coloradans planted row after row of victory gardens and canned thousands of fruits and vegetables. In 1942, there were 50,000 victory gardens. By 1944, that number had grown to 138,000, including 68,000 larger-sized "rural gardens." Denverites alone planted 42,000 small gardens, producing enough vegetables and tomatoes to "feed an army of 100,000 soldiers for six months."[70] Together, Americans across the country fed war-torn Europeans and evacuees, US and Allied troops, and American citizens. Although perhaps not as glamorous as building multi-ton warships, the "food battalions" helped set the table for victory.

While Japanese American —those who had lived in Colorado for years as well as the residents of Amache—helped provide food for victory, other Japanese Americans benefited from the actions of Coloradans who were unafraid to stand up for the rights of all Americans, even if the country of their ancestors was at war with America. The Cadet Nurse Corps, established to provide nursing care in the United States, proved to be as fair and just as Governor Ralph Carr.

Part III

The Home Front

On the home front, American women participated in and often led a variety of activities in support of the war effort. The federal government established the Cadet Nurse Corps program to train and utilize young women to alleviate the nursing shortage in civilian hospitals, clinics, and other medical facilities. Thousands of women worked with the American Red Cross as either paid employees or volunteers. Across the state and across the nation Americans recycled metal, rubber, and kitchen fats; bought and sold war bonds; donated blood; visited wounded servicemen in hospitals; managed USO centers; and hosted servicemen in their homes. Their actions were key factors in the United States winning the war.

11

The Cadet Nurse Corps

In early 1945, while perusing a women's magazine, Pauline Apodaca found her ticket out of an unhappy home life. Apodaca, the sixth child of Isidore and Antonia Apodaca, was the oldest of their surviving children. Two brothers and three sisters had died between 1913 and 1935. The youngest had been seven days old; the oldest, thirteen years old. After her mother's death in 1938 at age forty-eight, Pauline's father placed his three surviving daughters—Pauline, Theodora, and Anita, ages eleven, ten, and eight, respectively—in the Queen of Heaven Orphanage. Located at 4825 Federal Boulevard in Denver, it was regimentally run by the Missionary Sisters of the Sacred Heart of Jesus. Bells were rung for meals, class time, and bedtime. The Apodaca girls lived at the orphanage for four years until their father remarried. His daughters never warmed up to their new stepmother. After graduating from Cathedral High School in 1944, Pauline was left adrift. There were no funds for further education coming from her father with her "miserly" stepmother in control of the purse strings. A magazine advertisement caught her eye: "Be a Cadet Nurse—the Girl with a Future." It promised "A Lifetime Education FREE." Apodaca also learned that a monthly stipend was paid to students while they were in the program. Completing the break from her home life, Pauline enrolled in the Seton School of Nursing at Glockner Hospital in Colorado Springs rather than one of the schools in Denver. A lifetime of service to others was just beginning.[1]

As previously stated, World War II created a tremendous need for nurses. As the government and Red Cross authorities recruited graduate nurses into the

DOI: 10.5876/9781646420339.c011

Army Nurse Corps and the Navy Nurse Corps, additional nurses were needed to fill the void in stateside hospitals. In 1942, the US Congress passed the Labor-Security Agency Appropriation Act, which appropriated funds to nursing schools and assigned responsibility for allocating those funds to the Public Health Service. Funding for scholarships and courses was insufficient, however, and there were no centralized recruiting efforts. As the war progressed, demand for nurses intensified.

In 1943, Representative Frances Payne Bolton (R-Ohio) proposed the establishment of a government program to provide grants to nursing schools to facilitate the training of nurses to serve in the armed forces, government and civilian hospitals, health agencies, and war-related industries. After the House and the Senate unanimously passed the Nurse Training Act (the Bolton Act), President Franklin Roosevelt signed it into law on July 1, 1943. The Public Health Service (PHS), led by Surgeon General Thomas Parran, was responsible for the administration of the Cadet Nurse Corps (CNC) and accompanying graduate programs. Earlier that summer the PHS had established the Division of Nurse Education to allocate aid to participating nursing schools. Parran appointed Lucile Petry director of the division, making her the first female to head a major PHS division.[2]

Nursing schools received telegrams that announced the formation of the CNC and invited them to join. To qualify, a school was required to be accredited, to be affiliated with a hospital approved by the American College of Surgeons, and to have adequate staff and facilities. The Cadet Nurse Corps did not mandate a centralized curriculum; rather, individual schools of nursing developed their own curriculum, policies, and regulations. In Colorado, the director for the State Nursing Council for War Service, Irene Murchison, coordinated nursing services throughout the state. Colorado schools that were accepted included Children's Hospital School of Nursing, Denver General Hospital, Mercy Hospital, Presbyterian Hospital School of Nursing, St. Anthony's Hospital, St. Joseph's Hospital School of Nursing, and St. Luke's Hospital in Denver; the University of Colorado School of Nursing in Boulder; Beth El School of Medicine and Seton Hospital School of Nursing in Colorado Springs; and Parkview Hospital and Minnequa School of Nursing at Corwin Hospital (part of the medical department at Colorado Fuel & Iron Company) in Pueblo.[3]

A cadet nurse applicant was required to be between the ages of seventeen and thirty-five, a high school graduate who earned good grades, and in good health. After being accepted to a participating nursing school, qualified applicants were given scholarships to cover tuition and fees. They were also paid a small monthly stipend. The CNC also paid a stipend for room and board during the first nine months of training. The usual thirty-six-month nursing program was truncated to thirty months, although no instruction or classes were eliminated.[4]

After graduation, nurses were expected to provide essential nursing services for the duration of the war, either in the military or in civilian facilities. Most graduates remained in the United States. Postgraduate scholarships and refresher courses for nurse graduates were also offered by the CNC to remedy the shortage of nursing school instructors, public health nurses, industrial nurses, and psychiatric nurses. The Bolton Act stated that the corps would not discriminate. Nationwide, 40 Native Americans, 3,000 African Americans, and about 400 Japanese Americans joined the corps. The Cadet Nurse Corps allowed married women to apply; however, because the law allowed schools of nursing to make their own policies, certain schools did not accept married women.[5]

Having learned from the ineffectiveness of the 1942 Labor-Security Agency Appropriation Act, the CNC launched an aggressive publicity and recruitment campaign to meet its yearly quota of 65,000 nurses. Popular magazines—*Mademoiselle*, *Cosmopolitan*, *Harper's Bazaar*, and *Ladies Home Journal*—ran articles and advertisements. Eastman Kodak, Pond's Cold Cream, Pepsi-Cola, Sanka Coffee, and the National Biscuit Company ran advertisements featuring cadet nurses. To convince parents that nursing was a respectable and worthwhile profession, advertisements emphasized that nurses' training was invaluable for any young woman, whether she aspired to become a nurse or a housewife. Cadet nurses were featured in movie newsreels, radio soap operas, and variety shows and on numerous posters. Vanguard Films' ten-minute film, *Reward Unlimited*, starring Dorothy McGuire as Cadet Nurse Peggy Adams, was distributed to 16,000 theaters and viewed by an estimated 90 million Americans. The Office of War Information distributed several million leaflets with slogans such as "War Work Now" and "Scholarships for Complete Education." Almost 3 million car cards were distributed in towns and cities. Members of the Kiwanis, Elks, Lions, Rotary, parent-teacher associations, Daughters of the American Revolution, and the General Federation of Women's Clubs delivered recruitment materials.[6] Thousands of department stores, post offices, pharmacies, hospitals, and schools prominently displayed CNC posters. Donnen's Pharmacy sponsored a large advertisement titled "Wanted: 125,000 Student Nurses" in the *Del Norte Prospector*.[7] The publicity blitz was highly successful. The CNC met and even exceeded yearly quotas. Young women routinely noted on their application forms that they had heard about the program through radio spots, posters, and magazines.

Sister Damian Mary Simmons chose the CNC over a music scholarship at Drake University because of the movie *So Proudly We Hail*, starring Claudette Colbert, Paulette Goddard, and Veronica Lake as American nurses stationed in the Philippines. In one scene Veronica Lake put a hand grenade under each arm and walked into a group of attacking Japanese and blew them to bits. Simmons thought, "Any nurse that can do that—I wanted to be like her."[8]

Once accepted, women spent their first nine months as "pre-cadets" or "probies." They took academic classes and worked twenty-four hours a week in clinical situations. Their pay was fifteen dollars a month. Thelma Morey, who had considered a journalism career but decided that she could best serve her country as a nurse, enrolled in the CNC program at Lincoln General Hospital (Nebraska) right after high school. She took classes in anatomy and physiology, chemistry, microbiology, drugs and solutions, nursing arts, personal hygiene, history of nursing, professional adjustments, and physical education. Her favorite class was nursing arts. She recalled, "I loved caring for patients with nursing skills I was qualified to give at the time." Her nursing arts instructor, Mrs. Sorrel, became her role model and inspiration. Sorrell emphasized that the first step of every procedure was to "allay the patient's fear through patient education," a point Morey remembered through her entire nursing career.[9] Cadet nurses squeezed in hours of studying among class attendance, sleep, and work in the hospital. When pre-cadet Janet Cruickshank of the Colorado Training School in Denver received an "F" on a microbiology quiz on antitoxins and antibodies, her instructor remarked that she had obviously studied hard because her answers were consistently wrong.[10]

After successful completion of the first phase, junior cadets "served while they learned." They attended classes during their daytime "off" hours. At night they applied their book learning in medical, surgical, obstetric, and pediatric wards. Monthly pay was increased to twenty dollars. Cadets considered those twenty-one months the hardest part of the program. They often worked over forty-eight hours a week. At Thelma Morey's 250-bed hospital, there was only one registered nurse on the floors. The rest were student nurses who worked a strange combination of hours: 7:00–11:00 a.m. and 1:00–7:00 p.m.; 7:00–11:00 a.m. and 7:00–11:00 p.m.; 7:00–11:00 a.m. and 3:00–7:00 a.m.; and 7:00 p.m.–1:00 a.m. and 5:00–7:00 p.m. Cadet nurses worked a shift, returned to the nurses' home, perhaps caught a few hours of sleep, dressed in their school's uniform, and reported back to the hospital for classes. Usually, one of the "lowest" (in seniority) physicians taught classes on medical, surgical, and psychological issues. Doctors who were at the hospital for rounds did not want to leave the building only to return for later classes, so academic classes were scheduled to accommodate them. After working some night shifts, nurses were known to doze off in class, prompting one irritated physician to throw chalk at a sleeping nurse.[11] A distinct hierarchy of doctors and nurses existed in both schools of nursing and hospitals. Whenever a doctor entered the chart room, a nurse was required to stand as long as he remained in the room.[12] Morey found that younger doctors who had worked in field hospitals alongside army and navy nurses were more respectful of nurses and treated them as colleagues.[13]

At some institutions, the nursing school followed the model established by Florence Nightingale. Instructors were professional nurses, not doctors. St. Luke's Hospital in Chicago, to which Dorothy Bowen applied, was the nation's thirty-fifth nursing school. Bowen was already aiding in the war effort by working for the local rationing board. Although she had had no earlier desire to become a nurse,

FIGURE 11.1. Thelma Morey in the uniform of the Cadet Nurse Corps. *Courtesy*, Thelma Morey Robinson.

her excellent grades in high school qualified her for the CNC program. For the first six weeks, students performed menial duties such as giving baths, cleaning rooms, and learning to make perfect square corners on hospital beds. Then they were issued their probie hats, bib-less aprons, and long-sleeved blue uniforms with under-cuffs of starched white linen and starched white collars. White shoes and stockings (rayon because of rationing) completed the ensemble. Clad in this manner, women spent the rest of the year on floor duty, rotating between medical and surgical floors.[14]

A well-endowed school of nursing, St. Luke's provided private rooms for student nurses. Each room was furnished with a twin bed, lounge chair, desk and chair, chest of drawers, mirror, closet, and a sink set in an alcove. Afternoon tea served by hospital volunteers promoted camaraderie among the student nurses. When nurses completed the six-month probationary period, they earned bibs to attach to the aprons and the organdy cap of St. Luke's. In the past, nursing schools had held a "capping ceremony" for students in which they received a distinctive cap indicating their school. While nurses wore these caps proudly, the practice has been discontinued, in part because of sanitary concerns. In their junior year, cadet nurses at St. Luke's embroidered a blue cross on the upper-left-hand sleeve of their blue uniform, indicating that they were now members of the Blue Cross Guild.[15]

Senior cadets entered their final period of training having survived academic classes, floor work, and practical nursing in hospital wards. They were paid thirty dollars a month. Donning the official uniform of the Cadet Nurse Corps, a woman served wherever she was most needed and completed the last of her coursework. Her professionally designed uniform consisted of a two-piece gray-and-white-striped cotton suit. The jacket suit was adorned with red epaulets and large pockets; sleeves were marked with a silver eight-point Maltese cross—an early symbol of nursing dating to the Knights Hospitalers of the First Crusade—on an oval of scarlet. During the winter months, cadet nurses wore gray wool suits. An overcoat of gray velour and a gray Montgomery beret completed the ensemble. There was even an official lipstick—"Rocket Red" by Lentheric, Inc. Cadets furnished their own blouses, shoes, scarves, and stockings. Leg makeup, which some American women wore because of the scarcity of nylons during the war, was strictly taboo.[16] In July 1944, CNC director Petry announced the availability of watches with second-hands, manufactured especially for nurses. The War Production Board allowed local jewelers to sell the watches for five dollars if a woman showed proper identification indicating that she was a nurse or a nurse's aide.[17]

While most women applied to the Cadet Nurse Corps in their hometowns shortly after they graduated from high school, others came from a rather unlikely place. Executive Order 9066, authorizing the relocation of Japanese residents and citizens from the West Coast, removed 3,500 Japanese American nursing students from Pacific Coast universities and schools of nursing. In March 1942 Margaret Tracy, director of the University of California School of Nursing, expressed her concern for those student nurses whose education had been halted to Claribel Wheeler of the National League of Nursing Education. National nurse leaders assumed that no school of nursing in the United States would admit those students. Undaunted, Tracy contacted Henrietta Adams Loughran, director of the University of Colorado (CU) School of Nursing. Loughran, with support from Governor Ralph Carr, collaborated with directors of the university schools of nursing in California and Washington and arranged for the direct transfer of students to CU.[18]

On May 29, 1942, the National Japanese American Student Relocation was organized in Chicago. College presidents and deans, church leaders, and the student YMCA and YWCA were members. By the end of 1942, government procedures allowed the transfer of students from relocation camps to colleges. For a number of reasons, there was initially only a small trickle of transfers. Some parents were reluctant to see their families separated, especially after the disruptive move into the camps. Affordability was a significant obstacle, since families had been stripped of their financial resources during the move. Finding schools to take students was also a problem. Finally, Walter Godfrey, an advisory committee officer of the Student Relocation Council, queried Dr. Thomas Parran, surgeon general of the US Department of Public Health, about the Cadet Nurse Corps. He asked whether "Negroes and Americans of Japanese ancestry" were eligible for CNC scholarships. Parran directed the matter to Lucile Petry, director of the Cadet Nurse Corps, who responded with a copy of Public Law 74, which read, "There shall be no discrimination in the administration of the benefits and appropriations."[19]

Sumiko Kumabe Tanouye, a second-semester student in the University of Colorado School of Nursing, thereby enrolled in the CNC. Born in Hawaii in 1919, the oldest of seven children of Japanese immigrant parents, Tanouye worked in the fields after high school graduation to earn enough money to attend college on the mainland. After earning an associate's degree from Sacramento Junior College, she was accepted to the School of Nursing at Children's Hospital in San Francisco. After President Roosevelt issued Executive Order 9066, Tanouye was allowed to move to Denver with her invalid uncle. There she found a job as a live-in housekeeper for an Anglo family. Although she had also been accepted at the University of Chicago School of Nursing in 1941 at the same time she was accepted to the school in San Francisco, Chicago refused to admit her after the attack on Pearl Harbor. Instead, Tanouye enrolled at CU in 1943.[20]

Suzu Shimizu Kunitani also enrolled at CU. Kunitani had completed eight months of training at the University of California School of Nursing before she and her family were sent to the Tanforan Assembly Center (California). For Kunitani, it was a "traumatic and bewildering" experience. Several months later, they were sent to the Manzanar Relocation Center in California. Because she had some nursing experience, she was assigned to be a floor nurse at the camp. When she learned that she could leave Manzanar if she had a relocation plan, Kunitani applied to nursing schools. Admitted to CU, she, too, benefited from the actions of CU's director, Henrietta Adams Loughran.[21]

Loughran, from the University of Washington, was the University of Colorado School of Nursing's acting director in 1941. She stayed for nearly forty years—as dean for sixteen years and as a professor for another twenty-three years. Not only did Loughran directly admit Japanese American students who had been forced to leave nursing schools on the West Coast, but she also admitted Zipporah Parks Hammond to the program. A classmate of Kunitani's, Hammond was the first Black student admitted to the nursing program. The two women maintained a close friendship throughout their lives. Later in life Kunitani remarked, "The Cadet Nurse Corps restored some of my faith and trust in the United States government. I suppose if the war had continued and the government had wanted me to serve in the armed forces, I would have been willing to do so."[22]

Pauline Apodaca's future school, Colorado's Seton School of Nursing, accepted many Japanese American students. Margaret Baba Yasuda took the opportunity to leave the Minidoka Relocation Camp in Idaho. She was accepted to the CNC program at the Seton School of Nursing in March 1943. Fortunately for her, Yasuda's savings at Washington Mutual Bank in Seattle were available when she wrote for a withdrawal. Using the money she had saved as a youngster, she paid her train fare from Idaho to Colorado. After graduating from Seton in 1946, Yasuda returned to Seattle to earn a bachelor's degree from the University of Washington.[23]

Ruth Tanaka was removed from her home in Stockton, California, and sent to the Manzanar (California) camp for fifteen months. After leaving Manzanar, she was a student nurse at Denver's Children's Hospital before enrolling in the cadet nursing program. Part of her training at Seton was in the laboratory at Glockner Hospital, a tuberculosis sanitarium.[24]

Another Nisei graduate of Seton was Miyeko "Mickey" Hayano Hara, who grew up in the Platte River Valley of Nebraska. The third child of a "picture bride," Hara earned a scholarship to the University of Nebraska, but the family could not afford the other necessary college expenses, so Hara worked for a year as a farm laborer and planned on enlisting in the Women's Army Corps. However, after she found out about the Cadet Nurse Corps and Seton's willingness to enroll Japanese American women, Hara applied and was accepted.[25]

Some Cadet Nurse Corps graduates enlisted in the Army or Navy Nurse Corps during World War II. "Sue" Kumagai was born in McClave, Colorado, in 1920. Her mother died shortly after giving birth to Sue, and her father died when she was four years old. Her older sister, who had married at age seventeen, took over parenting duties. When Kumagai was nineteen, she worked in California citrus groves alongside other Japanese Americans. A slow packer of oranges and lemons, Kumagai received very little money for her efforts. She then worked as a domestic servant in California and in Cheyenne, Wyoming, where she moved to be closer to her sister. Her employers asked her to move with them when they relocated to Denver. She lived in their basement apartment, earning eight dollars a week with Sundays and Thursdays off, a fairly typical schedule for live-in domestic servants. A neighbor who was a nurse at Denver General Hospital suggested that Kumagai enroll in the Colorado Training School (CTS) for nurses. She completed a chemistry course at the Emily Griffith Opportunity School to fulfill the school's entrance requirements. Soon after she was accepted, Pearl Harbor was attacked. She and the other Japanese American students were called into the director's office, where they were told they could continue in the program but had to prove themselves. In her senior year at CTS, the Cadet Nurse Corps was established. While a CNC student, Kumagai visited her sister and her sister's six children who were interned at Amache, Colorado's War Relocation Center. In May 1944, she received her diploma from CTS and took the state boards for a registered nurse's license. After hearing that graduate nurses might be drafted, Kumagai enlisted in the Army Nurse Corps. Following basic training at Fort Devens (Massachusetts), the second lieutenant was sent to Camp Edwards (Maine), a receiving center for war casualties. She volunteered for overseas duty, but her commanding officer refused to release her. She served thirteen months and was discharged, but she remained on active reserve status. She later served during the Korean and Vietnam Wars before retiring with twenty-eight years of military service.[26]

About 73 percent of the senior cadets served in their home hospital. Others served in civilian, federal, or military hospitals as well as with the Indian, Public Health, or Rural Home Services. Claribel Carlson spent six weeks in the communicable disease ward at Children's Hospital in Denver; Pauline Morey, Thelma's younger sister and a member of the last CNC class, spent two weeks working at White Hall (a state orphanage), six weeks in public health, and her last six weeks as Carlson had, at Denver's Children's Hospital. She cared for patients with meningitis, encephalitis, whooping cough, and complications from mumps and measles.[27]

Cadet nurses also served in veterans' hospitals. Mable Evelyn "Lynn" Kitsmiller graduated from Montrose High School before enrolling in St. Luke's School of Nursing. She served in a veterans' hospital in San Francisco. Bonnie June Smith, a Minnequa School of Nursing graduate, served her last six months at the Veterans Memorial Hospital in Boise, Idaho.[28] Other nurses were sent to Indian reservations, rural communities, veterans' psychiatric hospitals, and military hospitals where their patients were returning soldiers, sailors, and prisoners of war. Margaret Kathryn Featherstone, a graduate of Seton School of Nursing, served with the corps at Fitzsimons Army Medical Center where she met her future husband, Sergeant John McDuff. Another Seton graduate, Dorothy A. "Dot" Zabrusky of Cañon City, served her time in Montana. After her discharge, she returned to Colorado to work at St. Mary Corwin Hospital in Pueblo as an operating-room nurse. Colorado native Mabel Alvina "Peggy" Meyer attended Beth El School of Nursing after graduating from Bethune High School. Her senior placement was in Sheridan, Wyoming.[29]

The end of World War II ultimately led to the end of the CNC, but not until the fall 1945 class graduated from the three-year program. That September, on the recommendations of Surgeon General Parran and Senator Elbert D. Thomas (D-Utah), President Harry Truman announced that all new enrollments in the CNC would end on October 15, 1945, thus saving the last class. One of the last women to graduate from the Cadet Nurse Corps program was Evelyn Sue Gahm, the youngest of four daughters of Charles and Eleanor Gahm of Boulder. Admitted into the program just two months before V-E Day, she graduated in March 1948.[30] Gahm and other members of the last class received full benefits of the corps minus a uniform. Corps director Petry encouraged CNC graduates to find new uses for their uniforms: "Rather than assign your cadet nurse uniforms to mothballs—and oblivion—you can make them over into attractive civilian suits. Remove the epaulets and pocket tabs; change the buttons. If you want a more complete variation, remove the collar and lapels—you will have a good

FIGURE 11.2. Pauline Apodaca enrolled in the Cadet Nurse Corps in 1945, withdrew a year later to join the Sisters of Charity, and then returned to the Seton School of Nursing, her original school, to complete her nursing degree. *Courtesy*, http://digital.auraria.edu/AA00001168/00001.Auraria Library Digital Collections, Auraria Library, Denver, CO.

looking cardigan suit. Remove the epaulets from your reefer, add a fur collar; consider dyeing all three pieces an exciting new color."[31]

The Cadet Nurse Corps provided a lasting legacy for nursing. The program significantly improved nursing education. It fostered a more academic approach to nursing rather than the previous apprentice-type training and encouraged the expansion of course offerings and faculty size. Federal money allocated through the Bolton Act improved and enlarged classrooms, housing quarters, and libraries of nursing schools throughout the United States. Cadet Nurse Corps scholarships enabled more women to attend university nursing schools than ever before as well as integrating nursing schools and programs. In February 1945, Parran stated, "The US Cadet Nurse Corps has been highly successful. . . . Our best estimates are that students are giving 80% of the nursing in their associated hospitals. By replacing graduate nurses who have already gone into the military, the US Nurse Corps has prevented a collapse of the nursing care in hospitals."[32]

Equally important, the Cadet Nurse Corps program trained approximately 124,000 women in the field of nursing. In Colorado, twelve schools of nursing graduated 2,382 nurses.[33] Many of them provided nursing care long after World War II was relegated to the history books. Those who enrolled in the last year or so of the war—like Estelle "Stella" Dracon—worked as nurses postwar in civilian hospitals. Dracon, born in Julesburg, graduated from the CNC program at St. Anthony's Hospital in 1947. For the next two decades she was a nurse at Rose Memorial Hospital.[34] Pauline Apodaca, who enrolled in the program in 1945, withdrew to join the Sisters of Charity. She was undoubtedly influenced by the work of Sister Cyril Mahrt, the nun who organized and administered the Seton School of Nursing from 1933 to 1950. Sister Apodaca later earned a nursing degree from Seton and served and taught in hospitals in Colorado, Ohio, and New Mexico. In Ohio in 1969, she became acquainted with the struggles of migrant workers. Five years later she moved to California to work with Cesar Chavez and the United Farm Workers in a clinic in Salinas. Ever on the move to help others, Sister Pauline worked in the village of Tierra Amarillo, New Mexico, at a mountain facility called La Clinica del Pueblo. Along the way, she earned two bachelor's degrees.[35]

American women joined the Army Nurse Corps and the Navy Nurse Corps to aid servicemen and servicewomen. Stateside, women enrolled in and completed the Cadet Nurse Corps program to provide nursing services to the American public and to be trained for a career. Other women wanted to help alleviate the nursing situation and desired to gain nursing and first aid skills and knowledge. Unable or unwilling to become full-time nurses, they enrolled in American Red Cross programs.

12

The American Red Cross

Eva Christensen woke up as usual at 5:30 a.m., feeling more tired than she had when she went to sleep. She swung her legs over the edge of the cot and stepped onto the linoleum-covered floor of "Ohio," her Red Cross clubmobile. As she dressed, she reminded herself, "Let's see, today we've got to make 2500 doughnuts instead of 2000 and an extra 100 cups of coffee." Only partially clad, she gave up and crawled back into bed. She berated herself: "What's the use: June 10, 1939, I got my degree from college; May 31, 1914, I was born; and what have I done about it? Absolutely nothing. I worked in my father's beet field because I had to. I scrubbed floors to work my way through college because I thought or hoped that I had a thinking mind, and now I'm making 2500 doughnuts a day and serving them because . . ." But then she remembered that there was an early-morning mission and a bunch of air corps fellows would be wanting coffee and doughnuts by 8:00. The bed was no longer comfortable. She got up and finished dressing.[1]

On the home front, American women joined and supported innumerable activities. One of the most important organizations was the American Red Cross (ARC), whose involvement in World War II preceded December 7, 1941. When war broke out in Europe in 1939, the ARC became the main supplier of relief efforts for civilian victims. Throughout the United States, Americans sponsored benefits for "Bundles for Britain," knitted items for displaced persons in Europe, and sent clothing and food to civilians across the Atlantic Ocean whose lives had been uprooted by the war in Europe.[2] In December 1941, Conejos County

 DOI: 10.5876/9781646420339.c012

reported an impressive list of articles made by members of its Red Cross chapter under the supervision of Maggie Christensen of Sanford. Her group completed layettes of diapers, sleepers, night caps, shirts, and washcloths and toddler packs of snowsuits, sleepers, rompers, diapers, sweaters, beanies, and mittens. A total of 1,092 items were sewn, 184 were knitted, and 9 were crocheted. The chapter also bought 65 items to donate.[3] Ten months before Pearl Harbor, the US government asked the ARC to begin a blood donor service to provide plasma for the armed forces. After the Japanese attack, the Red Cross quickly mobilized to fulfill its responsibilities "to furnish volunteer aid to the sick and the wounded of armies in time of war" and to "act in matters of voluntary relief and in accord with the military and naval authorities as a medium of communication between the people of the United States of America and their Army and Navy."[4] Services were provided in four categories: Services to the Armed Forces, Volunteer Special Services, Specialized War-Time Services, and war-related aspects of ongoing Red Cross services.

One part of the Services to the Armed Forces was Club Service. In the United States and overseas, the Red Cross staffed and supplied permanent service clubs, traveling clubmobiles, and other recreational facilities that stretched around the world. As they did in defense plants, teachers comprised an important part of the Red Cross volunteer force. Lois Barbour, born in Sedgwick, worked as a Red Cross recreation worker at the Station Hospital at Fort Ord, California. Dorothy G. Emery, a former teacher in Climax, Oak Creek, and Sedgwick, was sent to Hawaii in 1945 to await further assignment in the Pacific Theater. Lisette M. Anderson, who taught in Limon and Julesburg, was an American Red Cross assistant field director in Manila.[5]

Another recreation worker was Marjorie Carol Jarrett who was born in Denver in 1908, graduated from the University of Denver, and studied at the Bishop Tuttle Training School for Social Service in North Carolina. Beginning in 1930, Jarrett worked for twelve years as a social worker in St. Louis before joining the ARC. She was among the first contingent of five African American women to go to England to run the first Red Cross club for Black American troops. All five women were university graduates. Jarrett's father had been a waiter and porter prior to his death in 1939. Her mother, Hattie, had been in charge of the eatery at the O. P. Baur Confectionary Company for thirty-five years before she died in 1940. In letters home to her aunt and uncle in Denver, she told them about her activities but was forbidden to identify the war-torn town in which she worked. In England, Jarrett worked twelve hours days taking care of the injured in an Episcopal school building. After that, she reported to the Red Cross recreation center.[6]

ARC recreation centers in Europe were not always stationary; some followed the troops across the continent. Red Cross worker Jeannette McGrath endured primitive lodging, long hours, and the threat of enemy attacks. McGrath, born in

1919 in Lamar, earned two college degrees. She worked for the Federal Security Agency (which became the US Department of Health, Education, and Welfare in 1953 and the US Department of Health and Human Services in 1979) before landing a job planning wartime housing. As McGrath's friends joined the WAVES or the WAC, she "felt terrible" because she was not doing anything patriotic. She considered joining the navy until she discovered that she would be stationed in Washington, DC. Hearing that the Red Cross needed volunteers, she enrolled. American University in Washington, DC, hosted the training in which top recreation professors in the nation taught the classes. McGrath was given the option of working with recreation clubs, running a clubmobile at the war front, or providing recreation for hospital patients overseas. She chose the latter.[7]

In 1944, after training, she was assigned to the Ninety-fifth General Hospital. Aboard the *Aquitania*, she sailed for England. The Red Cross team consisted of a social worker, a secretary, a head recreation worker, and another recreation worker. There were 115 nurses assigned to the Ninety-fifth. After a short stay in London, the hospital moved to Ringworth 12 miles north of Bournemouth. When none of the Red Cross recreation and office furniture and supplies arrived, the team asked family and friends in the States to send personal items, playing cards, and poker chips. After supplies arrived, the Red Cross volunteers established a recreation hall for 500 or so ambulatory patients. They set up a craft shop, card tables, a record player, and ping pong tables. The team took books and crafts to patients who could not walk to the recreation hall.[8]

Team members worked twelve hours days for two weeks before getting two days off. There was so much to do and so many wounded to visit that McGrath often felt frustrated that she could not do more. To rejuvenate from her long work hours, McGrath bicycled through the countryside. She also took the bus to Salisbury and stayed in a boardinghouse on her days off. After stumbling upon Stonehenge on one of her trips, she frequently left the bus and strolled through the ancient site.[9]

One morning, McGrath slept in. When she awoke, there was no one else in the barracks. Startled, she rushed to the door to find the sky darkened by thousands of airplanes heading toward France. The D-Day invasion had begun. When the airplanes returned later that day, it was "hard to look at because you could see where the missing fighters were . . . You could see there'd been huge losses."[10] Ordinarily, their hospital did not receive wounded soldiers straight from the battlefield, but this time they were the closest to the coast. As men were carried in on stretchers, Red Cross workers placed a bar of soap, a washcloth, toothbrush, toothpaste, and a razor near the head of each wounded soldier.

In September 1944, the Ninety-fifth General Hospital received orders to cross the English Channel to France. Everyone dressed warmly, packed a ditty bag, and boarded a cruise ship that had been converted into a transport ship. Out in the channel, small groups were ushered into a few LSTs (Landing Ship, Tank). Two at a time, the Red Cross workers and nurses sat down, dangled their legs over the ship, held their ditty bags over their heads, and slid into the water. To McGrath's great relief, the water, which reached just under her chin, was not cold. As she carefully picked her way through the water and to the beach, she could not ignore the imagined noise and screams that resonated in her head.[11] Ashore, the group was loaded onto open-air trucks. A cold drizzle soaked everyone from head to toe and through their clothing. Shivering and with teeth chattering, they saw dead animals, shattered pieces of buildings, and craters in the road. One milk cow, still apparently alive, was precariously perched two stories high in a tree, her belly resting comfortably on a large branch and her legs dangling on either side. They camped in apple orchards for nearly two weeks, awaiting orders to board a train. As they made their way to Paris, the train mostly sat on the tracks as German troops continued to blow up rail lines in front of them. Finally, they arrived outside the city. No rail lines were in operation, so they disembarked, grabbed their ditty bags, and walked until a farmer gave some of them a ride in his wagon. As the horse-drawn conveyance drew closer to the city, Parisians flooded the streets to welcome them.[12]

For two days, the Red Cross workers were free to wander the streets of the liberated city. Then they were needed at a large American hospital outside Paris. Wards were full of severely injured GIs awaiting evacuation to the United States. One day, a GI in a wheelchair touched McGrath's arm. When she turned to greet him, she saw that his entire face below his eyes was missing. Remembering the training advice she received at American University, she looked straight into his eyes, grabbed his hand, and chatted with him.[13]

As the Allies continued their move toward Berlin, hospitals and Red Cross workers followed close behind. For McGrath and the Ninety-fifth General Hospital it was on to Verdun, where they spent a miserable time separated from the wounded. They were housed in huge tents with dirt floors. They had no candles or batteries and nothing to do except lie on their cots in the dark. The "latrine"— such as it was—was across a wheat field. It was merely a trench with slippery mud walkways and was shielded with khaki army canvas. For two weeks, it rained. Finally, they moved on to Alsace, but conditions did not improve much. Initially, their stuccoed one-story building looked heavenly even if it had no chairs, tables, or shelves. But soon the rats dashing in and out of the trash behind their building and the limited number of toilets and washbowls available to 100 women made the place less endearing. The recreation hall was not much better. It was a rectangular shack with an entrance at one end. There was no proper ceiling, just cross boards and roof-supporting beams that were completely visible. No insulation. The women appropriately nicknamed it "the Shanty." Less than 50 yards away, the Ninety-fifth General Hospital was housed in a two-story concrete building.[14]

Boxes of cigarettes, smoking and chewing tobacco, personal supplies, paperback books, and records arrived for "the Shanty." A GI drove the Red Cross workers to abandoned German military supply depots and dumps to gather pieces of aluminum, artificial German leather, and Plexiglas for the craft shop. GIs made skull caps from the yards of felt found lying around. The caps had a long tail in the back to keep their heads warm and comfortable underneath their steel helmets. Volunteers hosted bingo games in which winners received bottles of Hennessy cognac and French champagne. For Christmas, workers filled hundreds of ditty bags with personal care items. The wounded at the hospital decorated trees for a contest.[15]

The lull did not last long. Soon, the hospital received wounded from the Battle of the Bulge. Many had frozen feet. At one point the hospital had 1,500 patients and only 1,000 beds. On May 8, 1945, those at the Ninety-fifth were halfway through supper when they heard the distant ringing of church bells. Germany had surrendered. They jumped up, ran into town, and danced through the night. The celebration, though, was tempered by the possibility of being sent to the Pacific.[16]

The summer of 1945 was almost boring for McGrath. She was sent to a variety of places before ending up in LeHavre, France, awaiting a US troop ship home. She was the only one of the original five Red Cross volunteers on her team who remained. The others had been reassigned or replaced over the course of the year. Passage to the United States was uneventful. After arriving in New York, she and the others who had been on the ship were taken to a hotel near midtown. After the sparse and drafty accommodations in Europe, they found the hotel room crowded with furniture and hot. They cleaned up and went downstairs to enjoy dinner at the bar. The doorman stopped them because no men accompanied them. McGrath found that after months of working together toward a common goal, the women "had become misfits." Adjustment to civilian life came slowly.[17]

Other Red Cross volunteers served in Europe. Serving doughnuts and coffee to soldiers from Red Cross clubmobiles may sound like an easy and safe job, but it was not. Most of the twenty-nine Red Cross women who died overseas were killed while staffing clubmobiles.[18] In all, there were fifty-two female and thirty-four male ARC casualties.[19] American Red Cross clubmobiles followed fighting men to the front. Each vehicle was staffed by three women. The General Motors trucks were named for an American city or state or were given other names that had a patriotic or symbolic meaning for Americans. As mentioned, Eva Christensen's truck was named "Ohio." Christensen was from Brush, Colorado. While in England as a clubmobile worker, she wrote about her experiences. The *Ladies Home Journal* paid her $500 to publish the account.[20] Christensen likened the "Ohio" to an American cross-country bus. In the front were a compact little kitchen sink, a water heater, a serving counter, and a "very complicated" doughnut machine. The back third of the bus had a cozy little sitting room, phonographs, records, shelves filled with books, and settees that unfolded into three beds. Curtains, pillowslips, a linoleum-covered floor, and varnished woodwork made it a "very cheerful spot."[21] The diesel truck was driven by Ray, a Cockney whose pronunciation of his name as "Rye" had mischievous American GIs calling him "Bourbon" and "Scotch."[22]

When Christensen first started out as a clubmobile worker, she and her two co-workers were trained by Camilla. After three or four days, they—Eva, Mitzi, and Elma—were on their own.[23] Mitzi turned out to be a natural. One day Elma and Eva went to lunch, leaving Mitzi to watch the doughnut machine. When they came back, they realized that the machine had run out of dough. Mitzi was mixing dough with her right hand and adjusting the pressure with her left hand: "With her left foot she was stacking doughnuts, and since there was nothing else to do with the right foot she stood on it."[24]

Part of the job of Red Cross workers was to visit convalescing patients. In the wards, men compared their wounds and reveled in swapping tall tales. One fellow with a broken neck claimed his injury happened this way: "Our ship had been torpedoed and we were getting off the boat fast. I could see I wasn't going to make the lifeboat so I dived off, and you know, I hit that submarine and sank it. But it broke my neck."[25] Equally satisfying was hearing stories about American GIs from local Brits. At the cinema one night, an auction was held to raise funds for the prisoners-of-war relief. Although the bottles of Scotch and packs of cigarettes were offered at high prices because of their scarcity in war-torn England, whenever a GI bought one of these items, he would give it back to be sold over and over again.[26]

As Eva, Elma, and Mitzi spent more time around the patients, they lost their initial self-consciousness, although it was never easy to look at a man missing a foot, a hand, or half his face. They looked at pictures of wives and girlfriends left behind, signed their names on hundreds of plaster casts, and told jokes. Doctors and nurses asked them to visit as often as possible. The patients always asked, "When are those doughnut gals coming again?"[27] When serving at a psychopathic hospital, the men waited in line for an hour in driving rain to get their coffee and doughnuts—and for the opportunity to meet and chat with the doughnut girls.[28]

At one point, Christensen added up her efforts. She had made somewhere between 160,000 and 175,000 doughnuts and 3,000 cups of coffee. She estimated that she had washed around 60,000 cups, lifted 1,500 coffee urns, carried 2,000 pails of water, wiped the counter 1,360 times, and sifted flour for 580 batches of doughnuts. "Rye" had driven the team in the "Ohio" approximately 8,000 miles.[29]

After "setting an excellent record" in England and Scotland, Christensen became one of the first Red Cross clubmobile women to arrive in France after the D-Day invasion.[30] Similar to the schedule they followed in England, three staff members worked in shifts beginning at 5:00 a.m. They made doughnuts until 11:00 a.m. Because it took about 15 pounds of flour to make 275 doughnuts, they used almost 100 pounds of flour a day. They brewed gallons of coffee in 15-gallon urns. While the Red Cross was responsible for keeping clubmobiles supplied with

FIGURE 12.1. Mary Haynsworth Mathew (*first woman on left*) and a fellow Red Cross worker, both in Red Cross service uniforms, in front of a clubmobile while troops line up for coffee and doughnuts, 1945. Brush (Colorado) native Eva Christensen served GIs from a similar vehicle in Europe. *Courtesy*, Mary Haynsworth Mathew Collection, Hodges Special Collections and University Archives, UNCG University Libraries, University of North Carolina at Greensboro, WV0119.6.009.

flour and coffee, it was the army's job to keep the trucks, which averaged 7 miles to the gallon, fueled. Generally, a Red Cross team tried to visit four or five battalions a day. Before going to bed each night, the women cleaned out the greasy ranges. Without bath or toilet facilities, they had to make do with boiling water in the large tank to sponge themselves off. If there was extra water, they tried to clean their greasy blouses.[31]

Former pilot Peggy Moynihan joined the Red Cross Clubmobile Division after the WASP was disbanded in December 1944. She was initially assigned to England, but she wanted more action and requested duty in France. In Marseilles, she worked with a departure unit, where she met John McCaffrey.[32] They became such good friends that McCaffrey, who was supposed to be going home, extended his military service. He was stationed at Dachau, where he expatriated Polish prisoners of war. Moynihan was sent to work in Pforzheim about 90 miles from Dachau. A romance flourished; they decided to marry as soon as they both were free.

In the United States the Camp and Hospital Division was another part of the Services to the Armed Forces. It was responsible for supplying and furnishing recreation and battalion day rooms at military bases and hospitals. Red Cross volunteers served at Colorado bases and hospitals. Camp Hale near Leadville, the training site for the Tenth Mountain Division, was regularly supported by its neighboring communities. In April 1943, chairmen from Delta, Chaffee, Gunnison, Montrose, Saguache, and Rio Grande Counties met in Glenwood Springs to learn about the camp's needs. Each county was asked to furnish one of the twenty-three battalion day rooms. Because the recreation center was not large enough to accommodate all of the men, day rooms were scattered throughout the camp so each man would have access to a recreational facility. Recommended items included davenports, folding chairs, and ping-pong tables. Seven months later, fourteen counties had donated 1,250 books, 20 radios, 85 card tables, 15 rugs, 71 chairs, 35 lounge chairs, 114 lamps, 230 pairs of curtains, 7 ping-pong tables, 32 phonographs with records, 6 desks, 150 ash stands, and many puzzles and games.[33]

On the east side of the Continental Divide, Colorado communities provided items for Fitzsimons Hospital and the camps and hospitals at Lowry and Buckley Fields. Between March and April 1944, Morgan County residents contributed bingo prizes, decks of cards, jigsaw puzzles, magazines and magazine subscriptions, phonographs and records, radios, musical instruments, sheet music, a ping-pong table, writing desks, chairs, wastepaper baskets, lamps, magazine rack, a bookcase, library tables, and draperies. The northeastern county also furnished ash trays, a sewing machine, and boxes of gift wrapping and party materials.[34] Denver's Junior League donated equipment and hosted a Christmas party to christen the renovated Red Cross recreation room at Fort Logan.[35]

Red Cross blood drives were essential during the war. The first war-related blood collection by the ARC was the "Plasma for Britain" project held from August 1940 to January 1941. The project collected about 15,000 pints of blood and shipped 5,500 liters of plasma to Great Britain. In January 1941, US military authorities asked the ARC to organize a Blood Donor Service to meet anticipated future needs of the American armed forces. By the time of the attack on Pearl Harbor, the ARC was operating ten centers in the eastern United States. That number eventually grew to thirty-five centers located across the United States. Sixty-three mobile units supplemented the centers.[36]

Communities across the nation participated daily. By the end of the war, 6.6 million Americans had given 13.4 million pints of blood. While Americans living in urban areas had easy access to hospitals and blood-gathering facilities, rural residents had to drive to a city to donate. Gasoline rationing made it impractical for members of the Livermore Woman's Club to go to Denver to donate blood. Instead, the Red Cross asked that citizens have their blood typed at a doctor's office and be ready for local transfusions should the need arise.[37] Lydia Beery, in charge of the Red Cross Blood Donor Service, drove women from Brush to Denver to donate blood. Every day, the blood gathered was sent to Fitzsimons General Hospital, where it was processed into frozen plasma.[38] As the *Eagle Valley Enterprise* explained, processing laboratories had to receive blood within twenty-four hours after it had been taken from the donor. That time limit prohibited mobile units from traveling very far. For that reason, area newspapers urged their readers to visit the Denver Blood Donor Center on Fifteenth Street whenever they were in the capital city.[39] The Eagle Valley paper informed its readers of the requirements to donate blood.[40] When rural residents did donate, their efforts were duly noted by local papers. In July 1943 the *Louisville Times* reported that the community had forty-four regular donors who had given sixty-seven donations. Of that number, seventeen men and women had given twice; six had given three times.[41]

Communities close to Denver, such as Golden and Pueblo, were serviced by Red Cross mobile units. By August 1944, the Denver unit had visited Golden five times. In Pueblo, Blanche Bragg was the first to register to donate at one of the mobile units. The mother of three marines, Bragg promised to donate as often as possible. While two of her three sons served overseas and her husband was recovering from a broken back, Bragg operated a crane in the shipping department at Colorado Fuel & Iron Company.[42] The company's Corwin Hospital staff also held three day-long blood drives in concert with the ARC. The company's goal to collect 25,000 pints of blood was easily met by employees and hospital staff.[43]

In addition to blood, troops needed books. The American Red Cross participated in the Victory Book Campaigns in 1942 and 1943 in collaboration with the United Service Organizations (USO) and the American Library Association. Book drives were part of the Red Cross's Specialized War-Time Services. The first campaign started on January 12, 1942, when readers throughout the nation began sharing favorite books with American soldiers, sailors, and marines. The drive's initial goal was 10 million books for USO centers, army and naval bases, and ships. Town newspapers encouraged readers to participate. The *Craig Empire Courier* reminded readers to donate books of any genre that they loved because service members had equally diverse reading interests. The *Courier* also suggested that the donor put his or her name and address in the book so the soldiers would know "who gave what." A month later, the newspaper reported on the book donation efforts of the Maybell Woman's Club.[44] The Scribblers Club of the Junior League of Denver collected over 1,500 books, even though the club had lost a third of its members between 1942 and 1943 because they left to be with their husbands or for other war-related reasons.[45] Collectively, the book campaigns amassed 16 million books, magazines, and newspapers for American servicemen and women.

Local chapters were the linchpin in the Red Cross organization. Most activities were organized into eleven Volunteer Corps. The average American was most familiar and involved with the Canteen Corps, Hospital and Recreation Corps, Motor Corps, Production Corps, and Volunteer Nurse's Aide Corps. The Canteen Corps, which numbered 105,571 volunteers in 1942–1943, served snacks and meals at docks, airports, railroad stations, military posts, Red Cross blood donation facilities, childcare centers, and schools. Over the course of the war, the Canteen Corps served 163 million cups of coffee, 254 million doughnuts, and 121 million meals.[46] In Colorado Springs, the Pikes Peak Chapter of the Red Cross organized its Canteen Corps into six units. When the chapter recognized the needs of African American GIs at Camp Carson, a seventh unit composed of

Black women was established, with Mae Hammond as its chairwoman. Female volunteers served at dances for Black troops at Douglass Hall and assisted with parties at the post. Workers hosted picnics for service members and insisted on taking their proper turn serving canteen lunches at the chapter house. The 1942 annual report by Canteen Corps chair Anne Chenery Merrill praised the seventh unit, saying it had "shown itself [to be] faithful, capable and willing always."[47] The willingness of the African American women who insisted on equal participation in Red Cross activities at the base was not simply a case of proving their patriotism; they were also resisting efforts to segregate them and deny them the opportunity to prove themselves full citizens of the United States, with all the rights and responsibilities that entails.

Female drivers dominated the Red Cross Motor Corps. They drove over 61 million miles answering 9 million calls to transport the sick and wounded, deliver supplies, and take volunteers and nurses to and from their posts. Most members drove their own automobiles. Many completed training in auto mechanics so they could fix their own vehicles. In Boulder, Forrest Heath, a Red Cross instructor, taught motor mechanics to Rose Garbarino, Alice Noxon, Florence Burton, and Helen Duggan. Once they completed the course, they were available as ambulance drivers and messengers.[48] Several months later, Noxon, a forty-year-old schoolteacher, joined the WAAC, where her mechanics training was a valuable asset.

Josephine Tutt taught classes for the Motor Corp of the Pikes Peak Chapter. The Civilian Defense Council of Colorado Springs announced that to register for the thirty-hour class, a woman had to be between the ages of twenty and fifty. She furnished her own car and gasoline and paid a fee of forty dollars. In the 1942 annual report, Captain Tutt reported that the first class had graduated fifteen drivers on March 18. By the end of the year, there were eighty-five graduates serving the Motor Corps. In October, the corps started its work by operating Camp Carson trucks for the salvage drive. Volunteers drove trucks, jeeps, ambulances, and staff cars at Peterson Field. By the end of the year, it was the largest Motor Corps assignment, with twelve volunteers seven days a week. During 1942, volunteers drove for 760 Red Cross activities trips, including 182 for Home Service, 201 for General Office, 126 for Canteen, and 78 for Production. The year's total was 16,993 hours.[49]

The Production Corps was by far the largest of the Volunteer Services of the American Red Cross. During World War I, Americans spent countless hours rolling bandages, preparing surgical dressings, and knitting articles of clothing for military personnel and civilians disrupted by the war. Beginning as early as 1939, Americans again took up their knitting needles and plied their sewing machines. Nationwide, 3.5 million volunteers made and repaired 64 million pieces of clothing, prepared over 2.5 billion surgical dressings, and assembled over 30 million comfort kits and other articles for the US military, Allies, and civilian victims of the war.[50]

The Red Cross furnished yarn and other materials to people to knit and sew articles for the armed forces. In 1942, production work at the Pikes Peak Chapter began slowly because materials arrived late. In the meantime, the corps made dressings for the hospital at Camp Carson. In November, the group began a mending program at the army base. Three nights a week, the Motor Corps transported women to the base's Service Men's Clubs. They mended, did minor alterations, and sewed insignia on uniforms. By the end of the year, over 1,200 workers had sewn nearly 11,000 articles of clothing. More than 400 volunteers knitted 2,312 articles over the course of 42,810 hours. Of the 67,480 surgical dressings completed, 54,836 were part of the Red Cross quota; the remainder were for Camp Carson.[51]

The United States Navy needed large sweaters and watch caps, while the Army Air Corps needed sleeveless sweaters, helmet caps, and wristlets. The United States had scarcely officially entered World War II when the Craig newspaper reported that Mollie Davis's group had knitted 256 items. Davis gave the group instructions and distributed the yarn. Amanda Gregg, Red Cross production chairwoman of war relief, displayed the pieces as part of a Moffat County exhibit.[52]

Women's clubs and organizations in Colorado put aside their usual meeting agendas and spent hours knitting and sewing. The North Side Woman's Club (Denver) made garments, afghans, lap robes, slippers, and turtleneck sweaters for the Red Cross during club meetings.[53] Members of the nearby Twenty-second Avenue Study Club met twice a month to sew for the ARC. They arrived around 10:00 a.m., sewed until breaking for a lunch of sandwiches, had a meeting at 2:00 p.m., and adjourned by 4:00 p.m. to avoid the crowd of war workers on trolley cars. During informal meetings between the spring and October 1943, they made buddy bags, slumber robes, nightshirts, and diapers for a total of 784 hours of labor. In October 1943, members arrived at the home of Esther Gifford with portable sewing machines and boxes of Red Cross material to make aprons for marines. The following month, they filled little pillows to support the arms and legs of recuperating soldiers.[54] The large Woman's Club of Denver opened its clubhouse to the Red Cross. In one of the larger studio rooms, members made bandages.[55] Elsewhere, the American Legion Auxiliary in Moffat County sewed 17 hospital operating gowns while Seventh Day Adventists sewed 15 hospital bed shirts. The Baptist Auxiliary, LDS Relief Society, and Maybell Woman's Club made girls' dresses. A total of 580 layettes were made by eighteen different women. All the buttonholes were made by Jennie Starr. The Order of the Eastern Star was in charge of cutting the garments.[56]

When Kiwanians in the San Luis Valley were presented with a display of the work being done by production groups in Center, they were so impressed that they pledged their support. Although the United States had been in the war just over fifteen months, the newspaper's abbreviated list of items produced by volunteers was impressive: 2,401 garments sewed, 462 garments knitted for refugees, and 200 kit bags assembled for the army.[57] In Mesa County, workers sewed pads for splints under the direction of Mrs. Clarence Richey. The Red Cross also held evening sessions in its gauze room to accommodate women who worked during the day.[58]

Defense plants encouraged their employees to participate in Red Cross activities. Women employed at the Colorado Fuel & Iron Company produced kits and fatigue shirts and sewed operating gowns and hospital bed shirts for service members. The "steel women" met every Thursday morning to complete their work under the direction of Lena Bullington.[59]

Red Cross fund drives were also well-supported throughout the state. In anticipation of future funding needs, in 1941 the Perry-Mansfield Camp in Steamboat Springs made plans to put on a play to benefit the ARC. Less than a year later, the Maybell Better Homes Extension Club and the Maybell Woman's Club hosted a benefit dance at the town hall on Valentine's Day. Businesses and residents donated food and musical entertainment. The entire proceeds from the dance and supper were donated to the ARC. The two clubs asked each member to bring a cake. Leftover cakes were sold and the proceeds given to the Red Cross. In 1943, the communities of Saguache, La Garita, and Elkhorn in Saguache County oversubscribed by 60 percent, bringing in $1,651.[60]

When the federal government recruited women into the Army Nurse Corps and the Navy Nurse Corps, it left civilian hospitals and health centers short of nursing care. The establishment of the Cadet Nurse Corps somewhat eased the shortage, but the first graduates of the thirty-month program were not available until 1944, so hospitals were desperate for help. The Volunteer Nurse's Aide Corps of the Red Cross lent vital assistance to overburdened nurses. Across the nation, more than 212,000 volunteers donated 42 million hours of service in the Volunteer Nurse's Aide Corps.[61] Requirements for students were that they were between the ages of eighteen and fifty, physically fit, and able to serve without pay. Ellen Jensen, a graduate of St. Anthony's School of Nurses, was appointed instructor for the program at Eben-Ezer Hospital in Brush. Over the course of the ninety-five-hour class, she taught students the necessary skills for duty in hospitals, clinics, and other health agencies.[62] Trainees were regularly given course examinations. Short-answer questions included "how would you make a patient feel at home" and "list five things to observe while undressing and bathing a patient."[63] Once they satisfactorily completed the course, nurse's aides wore the blue Red Cross uniforms with a nurse's cap and white shoes.[64] The Red Cross served as the placement agency for the newly capped nurse's aides.[65]

Nurse's aides were heavily utilized. By early January 1945, Denver's Hazel Satterfield had served thirty months and given over 1,700 hours to the Red Cross Nurse's Aide Program. Most of the time she served at the blood bank, but she also assisted nurses at Mercy, St. Joseph's, and St. Luke's Hospitals. Satterfield's work amply filled her days and evenings, ones that would otherwise have been spent

FIGURE 12.2. May Wilkins (*third from right*) thought long and hard before training to become a Red Cross nurse's aide in Fort Collins. *Courtesy*, the Archive at Fort Collins Museum of Discovery, H18029, Fort Collins, CO.

alone. Her husband, an assistant superintendent of the Union Pacific Railroad, was away from home a great deal; her daughter, Lila, was a member of SPAR and her son, William L., died as a young boy in 1934.[66] Similarly, Johnie Herrick, a graduate of the first class of nurse's aides trained by the Denver chapter, spent most of her waking hours as an ARC volunteer. She had always wanted to be a nurse but had not had the chance. World War II and the Red Cross program gave her that opportunity. In 1943 she was made head nurse's aide, personally train-ing all aides at the Red Cross Blood Donor Center at Colorado General Hospital. Although she had a fifteen-year-old son and a husband at home, she worked five days a week, often more than eight hours a day. She credited other Red Cross workers for her success: "Holy Ike, I couldn't do anything without the support of all the other nurse's aides."[67]

Becoming a nurse's aide was not a decision made lightly. May Wilkins, wife of a Fort Collins newspaper editor, wrote to her mother in Iowa in March 1944. She wished she could have talked to her in person and heard her advice about taking nurse's aide training. Wilkins thought it might be wiser to get a part-time job but liked the idea of doing her "bit" for the war. Nurse's aide training and experience would be invaluable. However, she did not like hospitals and uniforms, of which she would have to buy two at a cost of three dollars apiece.[68] In the end, patrio-tism overrode financial considerations. By her last two weeks of training, she felt "pretty important." She had bathed a badly burned man, emptied urinals and bed pans, made beds, delivered food trays, and rubbed patients' backs with alcohol. Her last week in training included learning to give enemas. She told her mother that her husband, Don, bragged that she was a Red Cross nurse.[69]

For other women, being a Red Cross nurse's aide was one way to cope with overwhelming grief. Clara May Morse, a widow who lost her two sons, Francis Jerome and Norman Roi, on the USS *Arizona*, graduated from nurse's aide training at Denver's St. Anthony Hospital eight months after the attack on Pearl Harbor. She wrote in her notebook, "After Pearl Harbor my life was over, or this is the way I felt. But because of good friends and a very strong will, and always the thought before me that my dear sons expected me to carry on . . . I just keep fighting the longing to stop here and go to them, but there is work to do, and I must not give up . . . Time to dress now in my dear little Red Cross uniform, how I love it . . . The Red Cross is a haven of rest, and blessing, to all people." Morse continued her Red Cross volunteer work into the 1950s.[70]

Red Cross chapters often held night classes to accommodate women who worked outside the home or had young children at home and could not attend daytime classes. In Alamosa, Mary Moody, a widow, was the area chairwoman for the ARC. Six women earned their nurse's aide certificates in June 1944 and were ready to assist in the local hospital, where their aid would be "deeply appreciated during the war time shortage of nurses."[71]

By 1945, 7.5 million volunteers and 39,000 paid staff had provided service to the US military. The American public had contributed over $784 million in support of the American Red Cross. Money was donated from the smallest amount of 50 cents to hundreds of dollars. Coloradans contributed their fair share. In 1944, there were sixty-nine American Red Cross chapters across the state. Nearly 300,000 Coloradans were ARC members, contributing more than 8 million hours of volunteer service and nearly $2 million. Through the Home Service program, Colorado chapters assisted 15,100 active service members and their families and 4,700 former service members. Through the Denver Blood Donor Service and its mobile unit, volunteers contributed 84,090 pints of blood to be processed into plasma.[72] Coloradans—and the rest of the nation—had every reason to be proud of their Red Cross contributions.

Home front endeavors, however, did not start and stop with Red Cross activities. Americans spent the war years contending with rationing, participating in recycling efforts, and supporting personnel of the American armed forces who were stationed stateside and overseas. The new 3 Rs—rationing, recycling, and recreation—were as important as civilian nursing efforts.

13

"We All Contributed"[1]

Mary Babnik, the daughter of Slovenian immigrants, quit school when she was twelve years old to help her mother after her father abandoned the family. She first worked as a part-time domestic servant. A year later, she lied about her age and was hired at the National Broom Factory in Pueblo. Although Babnik volunteered at the United Service Organizations (USO) and taught GIs to dance at the Arcadia Ballroom in downtown Pueblo, she wanted to do more for the war effort. She saw her chance in a newspaper advertisement. The government sought women's long blonde hair that had never been treated with chemicals or hot irons. Babnik's hair was so long that she braided and wrapped it around her head, earning her the moniker "the lady with the crown." She had only trimmed her hair through the years, so by 1943 it stretched to her knees when she combed it out. Babnik sent a sample to the government, which immediately requested 22 inches. She shaved off all 34 inches of her hair. She surprised herself by being so upset about the loss of her hair. For months, she wore a bandanna to work at the broom factory. Nevertheless, she turned down the government's offer of war bonds as compensation. In 1943, Babnik only knew that her blonde hair was needed for "meteorological instruments"; over forty years later, she would discover that her hair put the "hair" in the crosshairs of the Norden bombsight.[2]

DOI: 10.5876/9781646420339.c013

RATIONING

As the United States plunged into the war effort, the manufacture of 300 civilian-oriented products was either severely reduced or eliminated entirely. Production of refrigerators, washing machines, beverage cans, and bicycles was discontinued so that factories could produce military vehicles, weapons, and ammunition. The federal government instituted rationing almost immediately. Some items were rationed because they came from areas controlled by the Japanese and others because the troops needed them while items imported were threatened by the navies of the Axis Powers.

In January 1942, the Office of Price Administration (OPA) introduced food rationing to provide an equitable system of distributing scarce goods. Household members were issued ration books containing stamps or coupons that were required along with payment for specific goods. Between 1942 and 1945, four ration books were issued. The government halted all sales of sugar on April 27, 1942. War Ration Book Number One, or the "Sugar Book," was the first of Uniform Coupon Rationing. It was issued on May 4, 1942, through more than 100,000 schoolteachers, PTA groups, and other volunteers. On May 5, 1942, after citizens had received their books, sugar sales resumed. Each person was allotted half a pound per week of sugar, half the normal consumption. Coloradans in Rocky Ford were so worried about getting enough sugar that they swamped the ration office. Even after enlisting two volunteers for filing and interviewing, Margaret Unger was unable to keep up with the stream of people. She closed the office one day and extended Saturday hours.[3]

Sugar rationing was particularly upsetting. It was used by both businesses and Americans in baking, cooking, and canning food. Bakeries, ice cream makers, and other commercial users received rations of about 70 percent of normal usage. Ann Enstrom's father Chet, who started Jones-Enstrom Ice Cream Company in Grand Junction with his partner Harry Jones, was one of those business owners who felt the impact of sugar rationing. One summer, the family traveled to Illinois just to see if Mr. Enstrom could get corn sugar with which to experiment.[4]

For the American public, sugar rationing was a double whammy when the government encouraged people to "Eat what you can. Can what you can't." Canning used sugar. At the end of a visit to her mother in Iowa, May Wilkins packed her car with bushels of walnuts, apples, cabbage, carrots, and turnips. She fretted to her husband, Don, that she would not have enough sugar to can the produce.[5] Americans applied for a special sugar certificate for canning. Contests encouraged and rewarded canning efforts. In August 1944, Edith Stoeber Schmidt, the mother of seven children, won first prize in the annual contest held by members of the home demonstration clubs of Rio Grande County. Mary Collopy of the Colorado Extension Service judged that all twenty-eight exhibits in Monte Vista showed outstanding canning ability.[6]

Red ration stamps were issued for purchasing meats, butter, oil, and cheese; blue stamps were used for canned and bottled foods, frozen fruit and vegetables, and processed foods. Newspaper grocery ads included ration stamp numbers and amounts for the various goods. Each ration stamp had a generic drawing of an airplane, gun, tank, aircraft carrier, fruit, and so on, and a serial number. Some stamps also had alphabetic lettering. The kind and amount of rationed commodities were not specified on most stamps. They were not defined until later when newspapers announced that on a certain date, an airplane stamp (for example) would be required to buy a particular item. The commodity amounts changed from time to time depending on availability. In February 1944, the OPA introduced red and blue tokens. Red and blue stamps were valued at ten points. The colored tokens, approximately the size and thickness of a dime, had a value of one point. They were given to the consumer as change for ration stamps. Likewise, they could be used in place of stamps. For instance, if one bought meat for twenty-five points, the shopper could give the grocer three red stamps at a value of thirty points (in addition to the cash required). In return, the grocer would give the shopper change of five red tokens. Or if the shopper had enough tokens, she could give the grocer two red stamps and five red tokens for the meat valued at twenty-five points.[7]

Signs in Colorado grocery stores announced that one loaf of bread per customer was available only between 9:00 and 10:00 a.m. and 4:00 and 5:00 p.m. For women who worked full-time, those restrictions required strategic planning. "Making do without" became an artform. Informational brochures and cookbooks helped housewives cope with the scarcity of certain foodstuffs by suggesting alternatives. However, there are no substitutes for some foods. Nancy Thompson, a civilian cryptanalyst with the Army Signal Corps, once waited in line for an hour to buy a single banana.[8] "The Kitchen in War Production" was a primer on nutrition, the value of certain foods, and problems causes by particular vitamin deficiencies. The booklet helped homemakers plan nutritious meals given the restrictions imposed by rationing.[9]

Cooking classes taught by food experts were also popular. In the spring of 1942, Arreva French, noted home economist and food lecturer, spoke at the Rialto Theater in Alamosa. During Friday and Saturday morning classes, French emphasized healthy eating, offered shopping hints, and imparted kitchen secrets. A full-page ad in the local newspaper assured participants that "classes will get out promptly at 11:30 so everyone can get home in ample time to get the family's lunch." Nearly 500 women took a second set of classes the following week.[10]

Differential Coupon Rationing, which allowed some people to have more of a particular commodity, was utilized for certain non-food items such as fuel and gasoline. An "A" sticker indicated that a driver was eligible for 3 gallons of gasoline a week. To further conserve the crucial fuel, a "Victory Speed" limit of 35

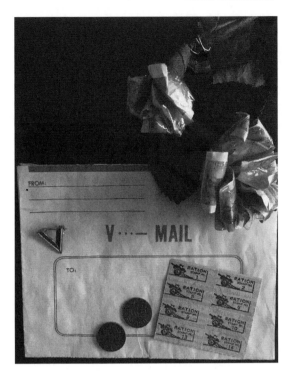

FIGURE 13.1. The demand for weaponry, food, and money to wage World War II wrought changes for Americans on the home front. Citizens participated in metal and rubber scrap drives, wrote letters to loved ones serving overseas on Victory Mail, and proudly wore Victory Pins on their lapels. Americans purchased a variety of food items with ration stamps and received change for stamps in the form of red and blue tokens. War bond stamps—so vital in securing money to win the war—were made into "warsages" to sell at community dances and events. Author's collection.

miles per hour on the highway was enforced. Because May Wilkins drove to her mother's farm each spring, she constantly worried about her allotment. In 1943, she decided to bring her increasingly frail mother to Colorado for the winter. She contacted her mother's physician, who wrote a letter on her behalf for additional gas rations.[11] Don reassured her that she would have enough coupons for her trip home because each one represented 2 gallons of gas, or approximately 30 miles.[12] Had Wilkins had an "essential" wartime job, she may have been eligible for a "B" or "C" sticker, which meant "essential driving, supplemental allowance." The "B" sticker, for 8 gallons of gasoline a week, was generally issued to business owners. Professionals, physicians, nurses, dentists, ministers, priests, farm workers, and construction workers applied for a "C" sticker. Truckers sported a "T" label. An "M" sticker was issued to motorcycle drivers for Western Union and other types of delivery people. Finally, the "X" sticker for an unlimited amount of gasoline was issued to those with high-mileage jobs, such as traveling salespeople. Interestingly, members of Congress included themselves among those who had high-mileage jobs.

Despite gasoline rationing, civilians took it upon themselves to show soldiers stationed in Colorado what a beautiful state it is. Bette Krim, a University of Colorado student during the war, remembered her father using his rations to take several Lowry soldiers on scenic drives every Sunday. His family joined in the excursions in which they stopped along the way, cooked breakfast over a fire, and ate hot dogs for lunch.[13] In contrast, some clubs and organizations, especially in rural areas without public transportation, experienced poor attendance at meetings because of gasoline rationing.[14]

The list of rationed items grew as the war continued. Uniform Coupon Rationing—which began with the Sugar Book—was extended to coffee, shoes, and other items, on the principle that everyone should share alike. In early February 1943, the federal government announced shoe rationing. Purchasing leather or rubber required a special form. Parents with children often sacrificed their new shoes in favor of ones for their children, who rapidly outgrew or wore out their own. The application for a shoe stamp specifically asked if the applicant had a relative with an extra shoe ration and why they could not ask them for that ration instead of applying for a new stamp. Fadonna Carr used her aunt's stamps, but the shoes of synthetic rubber did not last long.[15]

Women's stockings were also a casualty of the war. Silk and nylon were needed for parachutes, medical supplies, and gunpowder bags. One 350-foot-long rope for a glider required 2,400 pairs of nylon.[16] In November 1942, collection centers for worn and discarded stockings were established in hosiery departments. A year later, the Colorado branch of the American Women's Voluntary Services collected 30,743 pounds of nylon and silk stockings in one month.[17] With the entire supply of Japanese raw silk cut off, it was critical that women turn in their used hosiery. Some women resigned themselves to their plight and artificially "colored" their legs with face cream and drew stocking "seams" on the backs of their legs with eyebrow pencils. Screen starlet Kay Bensel demonstrated a gadget designed by Max Factor Jr., a Hollywood makeup man, that helped women paint a straight seam.[18] Other women continued to be on the lookout and rejoiced when they found the rare commodity. In late 1942, Wilkins gleefully reported that she had found three pairs of silk hose.[19] Other women simply did without and chalked up the new stocking-less look to the demands of war. Some women tried wearing rayon stockings, but they sagged unflatteringly at the knees. A 1943 advertisement promised that in time, manufacturers would produce better stockings.[20] When DuPont reintroduced nylon stockings after the war, "Nylon Riots" ensued. In Pueblo, police shut down a department store after 700 women stormed in to buy the first shipment of thirty pairs.[21]

RECYCLING

While civilians struggled with food, clothing, and fuel rationing, recycling and salvaging helped make up for the shortage of strategic raw materials needed for the war. Because scrap metal constituted 50 percent of guns, tanks, submarines, and ships, scrap drives were particularly important. An iron could become two helmets, while a refrigerator provided enough metal to make three machine guns. Four hand grenades could be fashioned from a shovel blade. A 2,000-pound bomb required 12,000 razor blades.[22] Nine months after the attack on Pearl Harbor, the American Industries Salvage Committee gave housewives a list of needed metal items: bedsprings, bathtubs, lawnmowers, kitchen sinks, ash cans, sewing machines, metal fencing, electric fans, washtubs, screens, furnace grates, and golf clubs.[23] Schoolchildren collected smaller items: used lipstick containers, metal hangers, scissors, aluminum foil, pots, pans, and pails. Delta residents turned in the town cannon. Captured from the Germans during World War I, the donation seemed particularly appropriate.[24]

In Logan County, Marie Moyer's only student at Pioneer School was eight-year-old Harold Sheldon. The two of them collected 36,085 pounds of scrap metal. Neighbors helped sift through junk heaps and provided a wagon team and hay rack to haul the scrap. For his efforts, Harold won first place in a statewide contest. Elaine Hansen of Rolling Prairie School in Sedgwick County and Saguache High School student Jearold Freel earned second and third place honors, respectively. Moyer and the three students were rewarded with a trip to the christening of the merchant ship *Chief Ouray* on December 29, 1942, in Richmond, California. Leo Crowley, executive secretary of the Colorado Salvage Committee, joined them on their four-day excursion.[25] At Ship Yard no. 1, Moyer and Elaine were given bouquets of roses. Harold was presented with a silver tray inscribed with his name, the name of the ship, and the date. At the sound of a bell, Jearold released the trigger and Moyer broke a bottle of champagne over the bow of the ship (the teacher had the honor of christening the ship because seamen believe it is bad luck for a male to do so).[26]

Other Colorado businesses and town officials helped children collect scrap metal. In Center, shops closed for a day to help schoolchildren collect 20 tons of scrap metal. Using army trucks, townspeople collected an additional 80 tons of metal by Thanksgiving 1943.[27] Schoolchildren in Silverton collected 100 tons of scrap, and a one-day drive in Grand Junction netted thirty-five truckloads of scrap iron.[28] Other towns used softball games to collect scrap metal. In July 1943, the admission to a Julesburg softball game was a piece of scrap metal. Unfortunately, only 200 pounds were collected. Officials blamed harvest work for the small attendance at the game and said they would try again when farmers were less busy.[29]

Rubber was the second-most-important recyclable resource. In fact, the rationing of gasoline was motivated by the need to conserve rubber as much as by the need to conserve gasoline. Before the war, Africa and the Dutch East Indies provided most of America's rubber. Axis control cut off the US supply. To compensate, Americans donated old tires, garden hoses, and women's bathing caps. One old tire could be converted into eight gasmasks. Other items were girdles, shower caps, gloves, baby pants, plug stoppers, garters, shower curtains, rain-coats, tennis shoes, hot water bottles, and rubber corks.[30]

Fabric was also recycled. After wearing or using items to a threadbare condition, American families were encouraged to turn in vegetable sacks, cotton and wool underwear and dresses, sheets, pillowcases, handkerchiefs, draperies, bed-spreads, towels, and men's shirts. Ropes, clotheslines, curtain cords, hemp rugs, and burlap bags were also needed.[31]

Paper was regularly recycled. One hundred pounds of paper made a carton for thirty-five shells. As much as Americans collected paper and other items, they were exhorted to do more. In spite of the fact that Alamosa had shipped 105,000 pounds of wastepaper to salvage headquarters, a study showed that there were 850,000 tons uncollected in the United States in the month of April 1944. Each family in the San Luis Valley town was told it should be collecting more than 46 pounds of paper a month.[32]

Homemakers were urged to return used kitchen fats and grease to their butcher to be converted to nitroglycerin for use in making explosives. The Office of War Information instructed housewives on how to collect, store, and dispose of the fat.[33] Colorado women responded by saving 87,835 pounds of used cooking fats in June 1943.[34] That November, Don Nelson, War Production Board chairman, announced that the need for 200 million pounds a year of waste fats meant that each American family needed to save 1 pound of fat a month. Interestingly, the Sunrise Club in Sedgwick considered holding a contest to see which member donated the largest amount of fat but found that most women preferred to keep the fat to make soap.[35] Two months later, the Office of Price Administration urged Americans to turn in kitchen fats, pointing out that for every pound received, the local butcher would give housewives four cents and two red points. At the time, one's ration of thirty red points had to last four weeks.[36]

WAR BONDS

In addition to salvaged material, money was critical. War is expensive. To help finance World War II, the government borrowed money from the American people by selling Series E "Defense Bonds," or war bonds. One purchased a $25 war bond for $18.75 and a $50 bond for $37.50. They matured in ten years. Children and others who did not have that much money purchased war bond stamps for 10 or 25 cents each. The stamps were placed in booklets. When the equivalent of $18.70 was purchased, the buyer tossed in the last 5 cents for a war bond. Through the War Finance Program, schools collected more than $1 billion (an average of $21 per child per year). In 1944, that bought 2,900 planes, 33,000 jeeps, 11,600 amphibious jeeps, and 11,690 parachutes.[37] Radio broadcasts, stage appearances, city rallies, and movie theaters promoted bond sales. Actors, actresses, and singers—such as

Bette Davis, Bob Hope, Frank Sinatra, and Kate Smith—headlined the venues. Hedy Lamarr sold kisses for $25,000 in cash, raising $17 million in one day, while Kate Smith's eighteen-hour CBS Radio marathon raised $39 million in bonds.[38] Even cartoon characters—Bugs Bunny and Popeye—promoted sales in comic books and on posters. Eight bond drives were held beginning on November 30, 1941, and ending on December 8, 1945. Nicknamed the Victory Drive, the Eighth War Bond Drive netted more than $21 billion, 192 percent of the original goal. Eighty-five million Americans purchased $185 billion worth of bonds between February 1942 and December 1945.[39]

Defense plants proudly recognized employees who purchased war bonds through payroll deductions. America had scarcely been in the war for eight months when Colorado Fuel & Iron (CF&I) reported that every department had at least 10 percent of its payroll in war savings bonds. In 1944, the local post office in Rio Grande County did the fuel company one better. Its employees invested 44 percent of their January payroll in bonds. In December 1942, CF&I proudly announced that Elsie R. Wood, a key printer in the wire mill department, had bought two $500 war bonds. Equally impressive, she had never missed a day of work.[40]

Women's clubs were equally proud of their members. Women in Brush organized the Women's War Savings Club. Its members came from a variety of women's clubs. A dollar saved a month was the goal for each woman. In December 1942, the club's goal was "a stamp corsage for every woman by Christmas."[41] A stamp corsage, or "warsage," was made by covering war stamps with cellophane, curling them into "petals," grouping them to resemble a rose or other flower, and attaching florist leaves to complete the ensemble. They were sold for dances, church activities, and everyday events. Adams State College female students voted to wear warsages at the annual college guest party. Colorado College students also sported warsages at dances.[42] Others, like Mrs. Frank Wilson of Monte Vista, crafted bouquets of stamps for luncheon centerpieces.[43]

In September 1943, the Colorado Federation of Women's Clubs (CFWC) participated in a novel project—the "Buy a Bomber" campaign. Its goal was to sell enough bonds to add fifty bombers to the air corps. Each heavy bomber, which cost $300,000, would be named after one of the forty-eight states, the District of Columbia, and Alaska. By March 1944, members of the CFWC had sold or purchased $1.7 million in bonds. One heavy bomber was named for the Colorado Federation. In addition, nine pursuit planes (one for each CFWC district), one complete mobile laundry unit, and two motor scooters with side cars were purchased.[44]

War bond finance committees used unique ways to persuade Americans to buy bonds. For the Third War Bond Drive in September 1943, the Rocky Mountain Arsenal displayed two 100-pound incendiary bombs in Colorado towns on the eastern plains. Citizens who bought war bonds wrote a message to the enemy and

FIGURE 13.2. Posters urging Americans to purchase war bonds were common during the war years. *Courtesy*, Prints and Photographs Division, Library of Congress, Washington, DC.

signed their names on the bomb casing before it was returned to the arsenal to be filled with explosives. A bomb casing was also sent west to Mrs. Johnson in Routt County by the "Bomb for Tokyo" finance committee. Her daughter, Jere Johnson, was an office secretary at the arsenal.[45] For the Seventh War Bond Drive, the Julesburg newspaper listed 506 reasons why its townspeople should buy bonds: the area's 11 women and 495 men in the armed forces.[46]

Athletes also promoted war bond sales. In 1945, Babe Didrikson Zaharias, the great female athlete, teamed with a Chicago amateur golfer, Art Doering, to play an eighteen-hole match against Bill Jelliffe of Lakewood and Leonard Ott of Green

Gables. Spectators bought war bonds for the chance to watch. Zaharias bought a $1,000 bond to start the drive. Organizers were hoping to bring in $300,000 in war bonds sales, but bad weather reduced the size of the crowd. However, a quarter of a million dollars was still raised. Zaharias, belting tee shots over 250 yards, and Doering beat the two professional golfers.[47]

Local civic leaders and male athletes were also called upon to promote war bond sales. Gates Rubber Company president Charles Gates, his wife, Hazel, and their teenage daughter, Bernice, survived the attack on Pearl Harbor. After they returned to Colorado, the US Department of the Treasury recruited Hazel Gates for a nationwide speaking tour. In Denver, she joined Jack Dempsey (Colorado native and professional boxer nicknamed the "Manassa Mauler") at a Kiwanis Club meeting before embarking on a trip to five eastern cities. She gave her "Remember Pearl Harbor" speech to over 150 groups, with audience sizes ranging from 5 to 5,000 people. In Colorado she gave forty speeches, one to a crowd of 3,500 Gates Rubber Company employees.[48] Gates spoke in sixteen rural communities. The Sedgwick County Rotary Club asked her to speak at the Ovid High School auditorium. She concluded her speech to the capacity crowd with the plea for Americans to quit complaining about no tires, gasoline rationing, and mere spoonfuls of sugar.[49]

RECREATION

American men and women were important morale boosters for American troops. Women's clubs and organizations were leaders in these efforts. Five members of Mildred Melville's Denver Woman's Press Club (DWPC), founded in 1898, sat on the board of the Soldiers' Recreation Center (located at 1514 Welton Street), and several others served as hostesses at the center. The clubhouse on Logan Street held American Red Cross first aid classes twice a week. Members belonged to the Red Cross Motor Corps and bought over $1,000 in war bonds. DWPC members provided meals and entertainment for soldiers stationed in Denver. Mary Florence Lathrop, one of Colorado's first female attorneys, invited 10 to 20 soldiers to her home for Saturday night dinners. Later, she hosted larger dinner parties at the Cosmopolitan Hotel and Baur's Restaurant. Between 1941 and 1951, she dined with over 12,000 soldiers and sailors. Schoolteacher and author Edwina Fallis opened her home to soldiers who could not find housing in crowded Denver. Gladys Van Vranken Parce and her husband, Yale, entertained hundreds of Chinese airmen who were taking electronics training at Lowry Field. Playwright Mary Coyle Chase lightened everyone's mood with her award-winning play *Harvey*, about an alcoholic and a 6-foot rabbit that only he could see. Another member, Lucille Hastings, wrote publicity for the Red Cross.[50]

E. Atwell Gilman, who later became president of the Central City Opera Association, first met Helen Marie Black, founder of the Denver Symphony Orchestra and DWPC member, when he was a young serviceman waiting in line to buy a ticket to hear the orchestra. Black, the first woman manager of a symphony orchestra in the United States, pulled Gilman from the line and told him that all servicemen and servicewomen were guests and that he should go in and enjoy the concert.[51] As a community of authors, writers, and journalists, one of the unique contributions of the DWPC was its Writers Roundup for soldiers who were writers or interested in writing. The roundup was held at the clubhouse and was jointly sponsored by the Colorado Authors' League and Poetry Fellowship of Colorado.[52]

The Junior League of Denver refurnished a game room at the Service Men's Recreation Center at Fourteenth and California Streets. They sponsored four "Come and Get It" hours, serving Sunday night suppers to nearly 1,000 soldiers each night. Although the league lost one-third of its members during the war as women followed their husbands to military bases and jobs in other cities, its members gave $1,000 to the Red Cross Emergency War Fund, helped register men, participated in Army Day parades, and purchased defense bonds and stamps. The club founded the Preventative Medical Clinic at Colorado General Hospital. In conjunction with the University of Colorado School of Medicine, the clinic examined defense workers to prevent disease and reduce absenteeism. Junior Leaguers helped with admissions, hearing and vision testing, and laboratory work. Individual members worked as Gray Ladies in hospitals and at the Red Cross Blood Bank. The league's Scribblers Club collected over 1,500 books for the reading room at Fitzsimons General Hospital.[53]

Members of the Livermore Woman's Club in northern Colorado bought war bonds, donated boxes of cookies to the USO, and knit afghan squares, sweaters, scarves, and bed socks for the Red Cross. At one meeting, there was a list of the names of men serving in the armed forces. Each member took one name, wrote a letter, and sent cookies to that particular soldier. Pearl Bartels, a member, led the scrap drive. Although she was in her sixties during World War II, she returned to teaching to help relieve the teacher shortage.[54]

The Littleton Woman's Club established the Littleton Service Men's Center in the summer of 1942. Jessie Cozens Shellabarger began writing cards to the mothers and wives of soldiers just before they boarded trains for unknown destinations. Five or six times a week she went to the center and invited men to write their names in her little book. She also asked for the name and address of each man's mother. Every evening, she wrote her cards, including one to the mother of a Denver private: "Dear Mrs. Mosley, We were pleased to entertain Pvt. John W. Mosley enroute from Ft. Logan at our Service Men's Center May 24. He is a fine soldier to be proud of."[55] When the mother did not live too far away, Shellabarger often telephoned her after the train left the station. Mothers were very grateful; some sent donations for the center.[56]

Members of the Colorado Federation of Women's Clubs also gave hundreds of volunteer hours. The Woman's Club of Denver passed a resolution that each member should entertain at least two soldiers a month.[57] Many did that and more. The club offered its building for a soldiers' center; it had served a similar purpose during World War I as the Soldier and Sailor Club. Located at 1437 Glenarm Place, it had a wide vestibule, a charming ballroom, a theater for plays and lectures, a large reception room in the basement, numerous smaller rooms, and an adequate kitchen. A member of the Soldiers Recreation Committee said it would be a place where "nice girls from our best families would be willing to go to meet the boys for an evening of clean fun."[58]

Members of the Twenty-second Avenue Study Club baked more than 110 dozen cookies over the course of two years for the USO "March of Cookies."[59] Zimmie Rupp regularly met servicemen's wives at Union Station and placed servicemen in the private homes of her fellow church and club members. She and her husband, Otto, invited soldiers to their home for Sunday dinners. Their generosity was remembered every Christmas with cards from many of the soldiers long after the war was over.[60]

Members of the So-Ne-Ettes, a social art and needle club founded in 1940 by a group of African American women, also invited soldiers for a home-cooked meal. With many members' husbands serving in the armed forces, they regularly delivered candy, cigarettes, and cookies to patients at Fitzsimons Hospital. In July 1942, the club began participating in the Double V Campaign. Initiated by the *Pittsburgh Courier*, it was inspired by a letter from James G. Thompson of Wichita, Kansas. Thompson advocated for a Double Victory against the enemy overseas and against those who opposed equality, justice, and democracy at home. The idea swept the nation. Clubs gathered material to send to soldiers overseas, met with businessmen about discriminatory practices, and sold war bonds. The So-Ne-Ettes received pins to wear, stickers, and a creed to learn.[61]

The Navy Mothers' Club opened a service club in downtown Denver. Open all day, volunteers answered sailors' questions, served coffee and hot turkey sandwiches, and provided a clean bed for sailors passing through. A similar club was furnished by the Business and Professional Women's Club in Grand Junction. Using a room at the former Civilian Conservation Corps barracks in Lincoln Park, women furnished a recreation room for soldiers at the local Motor Transport School. Several women brought sewing materials and sewing machines to fashion thirty pairs of draperies; some sanded and varnished tables; others painted and re-upholstered chairs. Ladies arranged furniture, hung pictures, and laid out books and magazines for the GIs in the new Enlisted Men's Service Club.[62]

Church auxiliaries provided food, items of clothing, and entertainment for servicemen and servicewomen. The Grand Junction Council of Church Women held an evening of informal entertainment and snacks for the men at the Motor

Transport School and those in the army-navy flight training program at Mesa College. The commanding officer of the transport school asked women to invite a soldier to Sunday dinner because the men were eager to meet community members.[63]

In 1941 the YMCA, YWCA, National Catholic Community Service, Salvation Army, National Jewish Welfare Board, and National Travelers Aid Association met in Washington, DC, and founded the United Service Organizations. Its mission is to serve "the religious, spiritual, welfare, and educational needs of men and women in the Armed Services . . . and, in general, to contribute to the maintenance of morale in American communities and elsewhere."[64] In 1944, the USO operated over 3,000 clubs and canteens that aided 1 million people a day in the United States.[65] While the organization acknowledged the part civilian men played in the success of USO clubs, it readily credited women as its "heart and soul."[66] Senior hostesses, who were in charge of the clubs, were usually married and over the age of thirty-five. They chaperoned events involving junior hostesses and servicemen. Older than most of the GIs, they acted as informal counselors. They sewed insignias on uniforms, baked sweets, and made sandwiches. Junior hostesses, who entertained the men, were generally young women who worked clerical or sales jobs or attended school.[67]

USO-sponsored activities and centers sprang up all over the state. Female students from Adams State College and local girls were brought to a USO dance to be partners for members of the medical corps stationed at Cat Creek near the Alamosa reservoir. The local newspaper emphasized that the young women were "returned to their homes by the county committee at the close of the affair," making it clear that the girls were properly chaperoned.[68] USO dances were held in Clark, north of Steamboat Springs. Glenwood Springs residents donated several hundred hours of volunteer service in January 1944 to create a "home away from home" for servicemen and women. Because the centers were alcohol-free, parents and young women considered them a respectable place where soldiers could safely enjoy female companionship. Both military authorities and town residents hoped the USO centers would draw servicemen away from "amateur prostitutes." Wartime posters warned GIs of the danger of contracting a venereal disease by associating with these "victory girls," "khaki-wackies," or "pickups."[69]

At USO centers, men enjoyed the game room, writing room, library, dance floor, and other club facilities. Another "home away from home" was located in Pueblo. At the club's 1944 anniversary celebration, a number of women were honored for their contributions: Corinne S. Gast, the record holder for the most service hours at the desk; and Maxine Row, one of the record holders for the highest number of hours served by a senior hostess. Eulalia Macy (chair of the Traveler's Aid desk volunteers) and Gladys Dallimore (organizer of USO lounges and installations) were also feted.[70]

FIGURE 13.3. African American GIs and junior hostesses enjoy music at a USO club. *Courtesy*, Western History Collection, Denver Public Library, Z-3062.

To attend USO events, a woman applied to the organization. Leota Broman, a secretary at the Denver Ordnance Plant, filled out an application and was accepted. She and the other USO women were bussed to and from Lowry, Buckley, Fitzsimons Hospital, and Fort Logan for events. They were required to dress nicely, including wearing stockings. On Sunday afternoons, dances were held at the Cosmopolitan Hotel. Army bands played at USO dances while "big bands" played at Lakeside.[71] Fadonna Carr, working in Richmond, California, also loved to dance. A good listener, she found the men were more than eager to talk about their lives before the war.[72] Broman—and other women—found that one had to take some of the men's stories with a grain of salt. They "all had great jobs [before the war] . . . I never had anyone say, 'Oh, I dig ditches.'"[73]

The USO in Denver had two clubs for Black servicemen. Grace Hale, assistant to Fred G. Young at the Glenarm YMCA, was the director of its USO. Hale was the oldest sister of Frances Hale (see chapter 9). Black GIs came from Fort Logan, Lowry Field, Fort Warren in Wyoming, and Fitzsimons Army Hospital to attend dances and mingle with young Black women over refreshments. A 1944 report listed an impressive dossier: 350 junior and senior hostesses had given 50,200 hours of volunteer service; 43 busloads of young women took 34 out-of-town trips to camps and other USOs; 20,000 sandwiches had been served during "snack" hours on Sunday afternoons; overnight lodging in private homes was found for over a thousand GIs and their families who were visiting Denver; at least 30,000 USO envelopes and postcards had been distributed to servicemen; 3,700 religions books and pamphlets had been given out; and Sunday morning religious education classes had been held. In all, the club served a total of 67,000 Black servicemen.[74] In addition, the Sewing Circle of the Shorter A.M.E. Church started a mending service for GIs on the third Thursday of every month at the Service Men's Center.[75]

Another large presence of Black soldiers in Colorado was at Camp Carson south of Colorado Springs. Established in 1942, its facilities housed nearly 37,000 men and 600 nurses. Over 100,000 soldiers trained at the camp over the course of the war. The Haven Club on the base had a PX (post exchange) soda fountain. After wrangling an interview with Johnny James, who managed the post exchange facilities for Blacks, Fannie Mae Duncan was hired on the spot, provided she passed the required Civil Service exam. She did, scoring 99 percent. Duncan's previous jobs had been helping her father, a tenant farmer, run his vegetable stand in Oklahoma and performing domestic service jobs for wealthy residents in the Broadmoor neighborhood in Colorado Springs. James reminded her poignantly that her customers may not be returning from the battlefield. Duncan promised herself that GIs would leave her fountain smiling. She always served her signature treat with a smile, adding, "Here's your banana split, soldier. They're my specialty. Oh, and there's no extra charge for the smile."[76] Soon, the soda fountain was reaping all-time-high profits.

While USO centers abounded for male GIs, servicewomen did not have a multitude of centers available to them. Indeed, the USO portrayed female members of the military as unfeminine and as competition to the junior hostesses. USO authorities argued that servicemen participated in USO events to get away from the military and would not be as likely to attend if WACs or WAVES were present. Of course, that argument holds little substance when one realizes that an individual male GI was joined by hundreds of other male GIs at a USO center and thus was never "away" from a military presence.[77]

Fortunately, not everyone forgot about women in the military. Mary Reed, the widow of Verner Z. Reed, a millionaire businessman, hosted a tea for servicewomen stationed in Denver. Seventy-five army and navy nurses from Lowry, Fitzsimons, Buckley, and Fort Logan were invited to her home. The Denver committee in charge of recruiting military nurses sponsored the event. Wives of Denver's civic and business leaders assisted Reed.[78]

While the home front presented an exciting time and lots of fun dancing with and dating servicemen from around the country, the war years were also bittersweet. Colorado College student Ann Enstrom dated soldiers from the Tenth Mountain Division who came to Colorado Springs on leave. They were "just the nicest boys," but they did not want a serious relationship, knowing there was a good chance they would not return from the battleground. Many of the officers from Camp Hale and Peterson Field to whom she regularly penned letters perished in the mountains of Italy.[79]

Railroad depots, some of the busiest spots in the United States during the war, were scenes of tearful goodbyes and thankful "welcomes home." Trains packed from engine to caboose transported servicemen to the East and West Coasts, where they boarded ships bound for the battlefields of Europe and the Pacific. If civilians could find a spot to sit on their suitcase, they crammed in, too. Volunteers welcomed 4 million servicemen and women at the Union Station canteen in Denver.

An equally important canteen was one in North Platte. Although located in Nebraska, it was heavily supported by communities in northeastern Colorado. In late 1941 Rae Wilson, a store clerk, suggested that the town open a canteen to serve troops as they came through town. She volunteered to run it free of charge. During the war, it was not unusual to have twenty-seven troop trains pass through in a day. Canteen volunteers greeted a total of 6 million, or a daily average of 3,000 to 5,000, military personnel. They served sandwiches, cookies, coffee, milk, and peeled hard-boiled eggs. Young single women placed a slip of paper with their names and addresses in the wrapped popcorn balls they gave to soldiers. The practice resulted in many wartime correspondences.[80]

Thirty communities in Nebraska and eastern Colorado staffed the canteen on a particular day—Julesburg Community Day, Chappell Community Day, and many others. Townspeople in Ovid served at the canteen, while the women of the Sedgwick Sunrise Club donated funds and food.[81] Lee Kizer was a teenager in Julesburg during the war. Twice, he and a friend accompanied his mother, Marie Kizer, to North Platte. She wrapped her homemade sandwiches in wax paper, stowed them in a large washtub, then drove her 1938 Chevy an hour and a half to the Nebraska depot. The three Coloradans spent the day serving soldiers.[82]

Nine women formed the Julesburg Canteen Committee, assisted by representatives from other clubs and church auxiliaries. On November 19, 1943, Albert Smith drove a truck that carried 2,550 buns, 78 loaves of bread, 3,400 cookies, 7 large sheet cakes, 17 birthday cakes, 31 dozen doughnuts, 40 chickens, 12 pounds of meat, 2 baked hams, 10 quarts of mayonnaise, 21 pounds of butter, 20 quarts of cream, 400 half pints of milk (bought in North Platte), 9 pounds of cheese, 32 dozen eggs, 43 pounds of coffee, 9 bushels of apples, 3 dozen oranges, 40 quarts of pickles, 1 quart of peanut butter, 59 cartons of cigarettes, 1 pound of tobacco,

2,900 book matches, 11 decks of cards, and cash donations.[83] Fifteen women and nine men from Julesburg served the food. An estimated 6,000 servicemen on nineteen trains stopped in North Platte that day. For those who could not leave the train and go to the canteen, volunteers placed a large basket of fruit, cookies, cigarettes, and magazines in each coach. In addition to individual donations of cash and fruit, the Rotary Club, Chamber of Commerce, American Legion, fireman's association, Philanthropic Educational Organization, Masonic Lodge, and Order of the Eastern Star gave large sums of money to support the canteen.[84] Small wonder that GIs sang its praises. Lieutenant Francis E. McAllen of Fresno, California, wrote: "It is not only the tasty snacks that mean so much to the travel-weary doughboy. The cheerful, friendly and sincere atmosphere; your smiling and attractive young ladies and other features help make North Platte an oasis that a soldier won't forget."[85]

Just as military bands did their part for the war effort, so did civilian bands of men and women. Many people wrongly assume that the all-girl bands of World War II were founded after male musicians were drafted into the armed forces; in fact, many female bands that entertained civilians and troops during the war years had played professionally since the 1930s. Some of these bands were Ada Leonard's All-American Girl Orchestra, Virgil Whyte's Musical Sweethearts, Dixie Rhythm Girls, and Sweethearts of Rhythm (a Black all-female big band formed in the South that played at the Rossonian Hotel and Lounge in Five Points). In Denver, sixteen-year-old Joy Cayler, a South High School student and trumpet player, formed an all-female big band in 1940. It played locally for private dances and public events at ballrooms, resorts, and military bases.[86]

In 1943, Cayler signed a contract with Music Corp. of America to "go on the road." Joy Cayler's All-Girl Orchestra played at ballrooms, theaters, hotels, and private parties and for servicemen and women at shows throughout the United States. Scarcely older than most of her band members, Cayler—as bandleader, manager, and trumpet soloist—was responsible for the sound of the band, hiring and firing musicians, and fulfilling her promise to band members' parents to keep their daughters safe.[87] The latter expectation—to ensure that women did not get pregnant—was a burden not shared by leaders of male bands.

Cayler's orchestra played in several US cities. In Times Square, Elizabeth Salmon, tenor saxophonist, stood in front of a giant cash register promoting war bonds. Salmon was a sixteen-year-old student at Denver's Holy Family High School when she auditioned for Cayler. Playing at hospital shows, the future Maryknoll nun was deeply moved to see an audience "in head, face or eye bandages, and limbs in slings, with whole groups on crutches or in wheelchairs, and stretchers."[88]

A *Billboard* magazine article called Cayler a "trumpet-tootin' brunette looker." It noted that the band had "a number of surprisingly good musicians, even by male standards."[89] Being initially dismissed as wartime novelties was a common lament among female musicians. Ada Leonard told her band members, "Because you're a girl, people look at you first, then listen to you second."[90] For one of her publicity photographs, Cayler wore a full-length gown that emphasized cleavage. As she told historian Sherrie Tucker, "A few glossies . . . make me look like a stripper . . . but that was the mode of the day."[91] Other women in bands, when told that they played "like men," retorted, "You mean we play like musicians."[92]

The pressure on women to look glamorous—in the military, defense plants, and all-girl bands—was extensive and was glorified as women's patriotic duty. Of course, few people expected male GIs, defense workers, bond salesmen, or musicians to look handsome or to consider them less patriotic if they were not physically attractive. Roberta Ellis (Brower) was a drummer for Joy Cayler's All-Girl Orchestra. Weighing over 200 pounds, Ellis capitalized on the wartime hero Wonder Woman by marketing herself as "Super Woman," effectively sidestepping potential criticism because she was not the shapely pin-up girl adorning the sides of military aircraft.[93]

All bands, male and female, faced obstacles trying to get to gigs. Unless it was with the USO, a band was responsible for its own transportation. Wartime rationing of gasoline and rubber made this difficult. The band sometimes traveled by train, but that presented its own problems. Military officers, enlisted soldiers, wheelchair occupants, and pregnant women were given first priority to board. On one occasion Cayler, realizing that her band was going to miss its performance, grabbed wheelchairs and told two band members to stuff their coats into their pants to pass as pregnant women. The band guiltily boarded the train.[94]

At the end of the war, Joy Cayler's All-Girl Orchestra played overseas for the USO.[95] She attributed her band's longevity in the USO to the fact that she strictly protected her band members' reputations. Following a performance, she allowed only a half-hour party each with officers and with enlisted men. Because Cayler knew GIs had a rougher time of it than officers, if time was short, the officers' party was eliminated.[96] Although the USO handled transportation, that "luxury" did not ensure smooth sailing. In one incident, the plane carrying Cayler's band was hit by lightning over the Pacific Ocean, forcing an emergency landing on what turned out to be Iwo Jima.[97]

Also playing music to entertain servicemen was Jean Ruth, a disc jockey. Under the moniker "Beverly," because it rhymed with "reveille," Ruth's hour-long program, *It's a Date at Reveille*, was broadcast on Denver's KFEL station every weekday at 5:30 a.m. The program was highly successful; she received fan mail from servicemen stationed in Denver and was featured in a *Time* magazine article. After she signed a contract with CBS radio, Ruth moved her show to Los Angeles. The 1943 film *Reveille with Beverly*, starring Ann Miller, was based on her show. It featured Duke Ellington and a young singer, Frank Sinatra, who was appearing in one of his first films.[98]

The "long arm" of World War II that Denver Woman's Press Club member Mildred Melville predicted in 1941 was undoubtedly longer than she imagined. It reached into every home, business, organization, and activity. It reverberated through the social, cultural, economic, and emotional fabric of the United States. No matter where one went, he or she was confronted with the war and the changes it wrought in American society. Americans did what they needed to do—enlist, take a defense job, increase food production, donate blood, buy war bonds, follow rationing rules, or offer aid and solace to servicemen and women. They simply "just did it."

Conclusion

There is no doubt that Americans' lives and work experiences were dramatically changed during World War II. The war required their all-out effort—as military personnel, defense workers, producers of food, and volunteers. As active participants in the war effort, women impacted the war just as they, too, were affected. Over 358,000 American women served in the military during World War II, marking a turning point in the relationship of women to the armed forces.[1] Colorado women served in all the military branches including the merchant marines, one of only a few states able to make that claim.[2] Army and navy nurses followed men into European countries fraught with battle activity and onto Pacific Islands teeming with humidity, insects, and tropical diseases. They administered blood plasma, comforted soldiers, and nursed the wounded in medical evacuation airplanes while battles raged around them. While a majority of women in the WAC, WAVES, SPAR, and marine corps were employed in administrative, clerical, and communications billets—mirroring gender-based divisions in civilian labor—servicewomen were also technicians, mechanics, jeep and truck drivers, code breakers, linguists, air traffic controllers, and instructors.[3] Women Airforce Service Pilots, who encroached the most into "male territory," risked their lives ferrying airplanes, towing gunnery targets, testing new and repaired aircraft, and flying military personnel around the country.[4] Women joined the military for a variety of reasons—excitement, patriotism, family tradition, boredom, and job training. They faced adversity and scandal, coped with boot camp and resentful

DOI: 10.5876/9781646420339.c014   239

FIGURE 14.1. As reluctant as the US military and industries had
been to incorporate women into their services and plants, they were
forced to admit that women more than held their own during the
war years. Unfortunately, such recognition and gratitude did not
translate into postwar opportunities. *Courtesy*, New York, Bressler
Editorial Cartoons, Inc., ca. May 4, 1944, Prints and Photographs
Division, Library of Congress, Washington, DC, LC-DIG-ds-11099.

drill instructors, and received support and admiration from civilians. Although
initially adamant about excluding them, military authorities were pleased with
and proud of the contribution of "their" women.

To be successful, the military required ammunition, weapons, aircraft, ships,
vehicles, and supplies. More than 6 million women entered the labor force during
World War II, joining 14 million working women. Many of these women had not

worked since young adulthood. They took jobs vacated by men, created by the war emergency, or abandoned when women quit to go to work in war factories. In defense plants, female workers became welders, riveters, buckers, technicians, laboratory workers, electricians, and chemists. They made and inspected bombs, bullets, and warships. They shoveled coal and canned fruit. Male supervisors and co-workers grudgingly acknowledged their abilities.[5] The ease with which women adapted to their new responsibilities surprised many.

Because "World War II was fought with typewriters and telephones as much as bombers and bazookas," a third layer in America's war effort was office person-nel.[6] In government, military, and defense plant offices, civilian women handled payroll, completed forms, took dictation, typed letters, and filed reports. Some deliberately made the decision to do clerical work instead of laboring in a defense plant. Although an office job paid less than riveting, its job security was a deciding factor. Defense plant jobs were only going to last as long as the war did. Clerical work, in contrast, continued after the war. It was more "feminine," was physically less tiring, and emphasized interpersonal skills. The jobs rarely required night work and were located in a skyscraper or building on Main Street rather than in a grimy industrial district. In a word, clerical jobs were "classy."[7]

The fourth layer in the war effort provided physical subsistence to the armed forces, defense workers, and civilians. Rural and urban women toiled on farms and ranches. Some participated in the Women's Land Army; others were volunteers or paid workers on their own. They milked cows, fed livestock, branded cattle, and operated farm equipment. Women tended victory gardens and canned produce.

The final layer sustained the morale and underpinnings of American society. One-fourth of American women volunteered their free time to various agencies during the war.[8] This was in addition to their roles as working or stay-at-home mothers. They donated millions of hours to Red Cross activities—manning telephones, assisting servicemen's families, donating blood, driving for the Motor Corps, taking nutrition and first aid classes, and working as nurse's aides. Americans recycled paper, metals, rubber, and kitchen fat. They honored rationing mandates and carpooled to work. For local USO and servicemen's clubs, American civilians furnished recreation rooms and provided home-baked goods. They bought and sold war bonds through their clubs and organizations. They delivered cheer to base hospitals and railroad canteens. In their churches and homes, women sewed pillows for hospitals and knitted sweaters and helmet liners for soldiers.

Then, on September 2, 1945, World War II was officially declared over. The American people were only too glad to leave the war—and all its heartache, loss, and upheaval—behind them. Colorado women who had served in the mil-itary, worked in defense plants and offices, and clocked thousands of volunteer hours turned a happy—but cautious—eye to the future. Laws authorizing the

242COLORADO WOMEN IN WORLD WAR II

wartime WAC, WAVES, SPAR, and Marine Corps Women's Reserve (MCWR) were scheduled to expire six months after the president declared the end of the war. Because of the immense numbers of servicemen and women to be deactivated and the American public's intense desire to do so as quickly as possible, many women—ironically—in all the active branches were retained beyond the six-month period to complete that administrative chore. Once accomplished, the question was, What about women in the military in peacetime? There was never any doubt about the future of the two nursing corps. The need for professional nurses in the military was a foregone conclusion. In 1947, the US Congress passed the Army-Navy Nurse Act, making the nurse corps permanent staff corps in the regular army and navy. Two years later the newly created United States Air Force also established its own nurse corps.[9]

In contrast to the assumed permanence of the Army Nurse Corps (ANC) and the Navy Nurse Corps (NNC), the future of the WAC, WAVES, MCWR, and SPAR was in doubt. Like most servicemen, the vast majority of servicewomen did not have any interest in staying on after the war. Most men and women were all too ready to go home. After the war, most military women were discharged. Nationally, one-third of the former members of the Women's Army Corps began college or made definite plans to enter school shortly after discharge. Fifty percent of all former WACs returned to the workforce immediately after discharge. Of those in the civilian labor force, 40 percent did not return to their previous civilian employment but rather moved into new jobs for which they were trained and developed skills while in the military.[10]

Although many people in the United States opposed having women in the military after the war, a small group of women saw a continuing need for women's military service. On June 2, 1948, after two years of acrimonious debate, Congress passed the Women's Armed Services Integration Act. Signed by President Harry S. Truman, it allowed women to serve as commissioned officers and enlisted members in the permanent regular United States Army, Navy, Marine Corps, and Air Force, as well as the reserves. Although the United States Coast Guard deactivated SPAR, its women could apply for commissioning or enlistment in the other services.[11]

Demobilization also occurred in defense plants. As the war in Europe ended and the war in the Pacific was A-bombed into peacetime, women in the lowest-paying factory jobs quit "at an incredible rate."[12] Women holding jobs in the chemical, rubber, and petroleum industries, which paid well, quit more slowly. Valuable defense workers or not, employers laid off women in heavy industrial sectors. At the beginning of the war, as a recruiting tool, the government and industries had likened many aspects of defense work to women's traditional work. Companies that had convinced women to work in defense plants on the argument that handling acetylene torches was as easy as operating a sewing machine now had no use for those women. The fact that they had proven to be equally adept at both tools was inconsequential. The question as to why a woman could not be hired to handle the same equipment in a peacetime factory was never satisfactorily answered.[13] It did not matter if the same tools were used to make bombs and I-beams for homes; what mattered was the *situation*. Women had been needed in the factories during wartime; they were not needed—at least in the eyes of plant owners and supervisors—during peacetime.[14] Thus the percentage of women in manufacturing industries nearly returned to pre-war levels. In 1940, women comprised 28 percent of the total manufacturing labor force. By 1944, the height of wartime production, that statistic had risen to 36 percent, only to drop to 31 percent by 1946.[15]

Colorado, a "backwater state" in 1940, stood at a precipice in the autumn of 1945.[16] When one looked north to south along the Front Range, war plants and depots dotted the landscape. Just as quickly as they had sprouted in response to the war, they emptied, devoid of the thousands of employees who had "done their part" to win the war. At the site of the former Denver Ordnance Plant, women were re-hired, but they were not attired in overalls and one-piece work clothes or sporting snoods and bandanas. Instead, they looked like the female office workers who had served from 1941 to 1945. They occupied desks and performed clerical and secretarial jobs with federal agencies that moved into the vacated production areas beginning in 1947. The Pueblo Ordnance Plant and Colorado Fuel & Iron (CF&I) retained female clerks, typists, and inspectors while re-hiring male veterans for plant work.

World War II profoundly affected the state of Colorado. Prior to the war, Colorado was an extractive economy dependent on the boom and bust of the mining industry and agriculture. It did not have a substantial manufacturing presence. After the war, Colorado was one of the top states housing government agencies and corporations and factories immersed in the military-industrial complex. It had evolved into a service economy, propelled by massive federal defense expenditures that triggered the need for civilian workers. From 1952 to 1962, one economist estimated that more than 20 percent of the state's income resulted from defense spending, making it one of eight US states most heavily dependent on the national defense budget.[17] This is reflected in the large numbers of Colorado women employed as government workers. By 1950, 76 percent of Colorado women were employed in the census categories of "clerical and kindred workers," "government workers," "service workers," and "professional, technical, and kindred services."[18]

The shift to clerical and office jobs for women occurred across the United States as 3 million women who left wartime jobs were re-hired, mainly in the service sector. These jobs did not pay as well as defense jobs had. Seventy-five percent of the women who had held jobs in war industries were still employed in the postwar years, but 90 percent of them were earning less money.[19] Jobs were also divided according to race. Forty percent of white women worked in clerical positions in contrast to only 5 percent of Black women.[20] By 1950, 60 percent of Black women in the United States were maids in private homes or service workers in institutions. Only 16 percent of white women held similar jobs.

Because of a number of factors, marriage, birth, and divorce rates in the United States fluctuated during the 1940s. In 1942, when it was still possible for a man to receive a draft deferment if he had dependents, the marriage rate peaked. The birthrate jumped from 1941 to 1943. Then, between 1943 and 1945, when US military strength was at its highest levels, there was a decline in the marriage rate and a severe drop in the birthrate. Following V-E and V-J Days and the return of US servicemen and women, the marriage rate experienced a significant spike from 1945 to 1946.[21] Colorado men and women followed this national pattern. Between 1940 and 1950, the percentage of marriages in the state rose from 62 percent to 67 percent. In 1945 there were 23,511 births; in 1946 there were 29,518, an increase of over 20 percent.[22]

Following the trend from 1935 to 1940, divorces increased slightly during the war years. Between 1940 and 1947, however, the divorce rate rose from 2 divorces per 1,000 people to 3.4 per 1,000 people. Women who had profited the most from their wartime economic independence may have also been the most reluctant to cede that independence after the war.[23] Or perhaps the high divorce rate was a result of hasty, ill-advised wartime romances and marriages. It is difficult to judge. In Colorado, divorces among females age fourteen and older increased from 2.3 percent in 1940 to 3 percent in 1950.[24]

Thus, in the postwar era, most women married, had children, and focused on their homes and families, just as they had in the decades preceding the war. On the surface, it appeared that the war had resulted in few lasting changes for women.[25] A typical white middle-class woman was employed as a young adult prior to marriage and then perhaps took a pink- or white-collar job after her children were of school age or no longer living at home. That scenario was not the traditional one for women of color, whose outside-the-home employment was often a necessity for the family to survive. Rather than a blip, the entry of previously unemployed married white women into the workforce during the war was a phenomenon that continues to the present day. Postwar, while individual women faced conflicting pressures to work, a permanent shift had occurred for women as a social group.[26] The presence of married women in the labor force was the most profound change. For that reason, many historians believe the war signaled a permanent shift.[27]

Other historians have been more hesitant to accept "permanent" transformations, noting that very few women seized opportunities for new occupations or that those opportunities even existed.[28] Instead, these historians choose to emphasize the ways the postwar years for female workers were a continuation of pre-war and wartime experiences. Yes, some women riveted and welded during the war, but the vast majority of women did not. In the postwar workplace, women continued to face obstacles. Job and pay inequities were the norm, women were pigeonholed into pink- and "light" blue-collar work, sexual harassment was a real job fear, and childcare facilities that could have eased women's burden of two jobs (home and paid) were practically nonexistent.[29] Pregnancy was also a reason for dismissal. Former Curtiss-Wright engineer Louise Fayram McClain was forced to quit her job as a statistician at Douglas Aircraft when she was three months pregnant. She considered suing the company, but her lawyer told her the effort would be futile.[30] Although they were members of the paid workforce, women strongly identified with and focused on their roles as wives and mothers.[31]

Comparing women's pre-war, wartime, and postwar participation and experiences in the *labor force* tells only part of the story. Several historians acknowledge that women's *military* experience was the most dramatic break with traditional gender roles and forever changed the idea that women could not handle such work.[32] For 358,000 women, their war experience differed from that of female defense workers. Yes, they, too, clustered in mostly administrative and clerical jobs. But living away from home and family in the homogeneous environment of all-female units and serving overseas, military women were doubly impacted by World War II. Female veterans of all branches often remark on the rewards of having served: the camaraderie, meeting people from all walks of life, seeing other parts of the nation and the world, acquiring schooling and skills, the pride in having done something worthwhile outside of family and home, and the increased sense of self-worth.[33] They also—like their male counterparts in the military—experienced harsh conditions, witnessed bloodshed, and saw comrades die in front of them. And like so many GIs, servicewomen often did not and do not talk about that part of their war years.[34] Not only did women gain experience by serving in the military during World War II, but for Coloradans Oleta Crain, Dorothy Starbuck, Maude Fox, Kay Keating, Helen Brecht, and Sue Kumagai, it was the gateway to military and government careers in the postwar years.

During the war years, the American military and American women adapted to one another to a degree that surprised them both. Women proved to be excellent, hardworking, and dedicated soldiers, sailors, marines, and coast guardswomen in whatever job they were assigned.[35] It was women's military record that convinced American military and congressional leaders to make their status in the armed forces permanent.[36] Debates to permanently open the military to women and the question of the proposed Equal Rights Amendment (ERA) sparked the question of the legality and propriety of drafting women into the armed forces as well as their exposure to combat situations. In the end, the ERA was defeated in part because of the fear that it would mandate the drafting of women and having women serve in combat roles.[37] Since then, the establishment of America's all-volunteer army has squashed fears of the possibility of drafting women into the armed forces. In December 2015, Defense Secretary Ashton B. Carter announced that all combat jobs would be open to women.

A grateful US Congress passed the Servicemen's Readjustment Act in 1944. Benefits included payments of tuition and living expenses to attend school, low-cost mortgages, low-interest business loans, and one year of unemployment compensation. White male veterans who took advantage of the GI Bill attained higher median incomes, educational goals, home ownership rates, and net worth than did non-veterans and veterans who did not access the bill. Unfortunately, male veterans of color and female veterans were often shut out of this postwar largesse. Because the GI Bill operated through regulatory agencies at the state level and private institutions such as colleges, banks, and the real estate industry, Blacks doubly experienced racial prejudice whenever they applied for a mortgage or for a job or vocational training.[38] It was also difficult for female veterans to utilize the GI Bill. The veteran status of those who served in the Women's Army Auxiliary Corps and the Women's Army Corps was less than clear. Women Airforce Service Pilots, who had never been militarized prior to deactivation in December 1944, were ineligible for the GI Bill. For women in the other military branches who were eligible, there were a multitude of reasons many did not access the program's benefits. Those who married and had families after the war often did not have the time and energy to go to school; for others, their benefits expired before they had a chance to use them, and unmarried female veterans had to support themselves.[39] In addition, men joined veterans' organizations that counseled them on the benefits of being a veteran. In many cases, women were not integrated into these associations. In the case of the Veterans of Foreign Wars, they were not even accepted into membership. In other cases, female veterans chose to abandon their military identities, believing that because they had not fought in combat, they were not "true" veterans. However, only 27 percent of male veterans were combat veterans.[40] Lastly, some women found that vet status could result in discrimination from potential employers rather than the preference given to male veterans.[41] However, some female veterans, aware that they were eligible, did take advantage of the program.

Among the Army Nurse Corps, the Navy Nurse Corps, and the Cadet Nurse Corps, women's nursing efforts had a lasting and profound effect on individual women, the nursing profession, and nurses in the following decades. As one would expect, wartime nurses from all three corps were very likely to continue as nurses after the war. Those who served in the military were deeply affected by their experiences. Leila Allen Morrison, a veteran of the European Theater of Operations, adamantly believes her time as a member of the Army Nurse Corps made her "a much better American." She believes her strong patriotism is a result of her work in an olive drab shock treatment tent. Rather than making her intolerant of others who may not share her steadfast patriotism, she believes her service made her more tolerant—"They did not see what I saw," so she cannot judge them.[42] Nurses in the Army and Navy Nurse Corps were agents in medical advancements in treating casualties. Flight nurses were pioneers in medical evacuation techniques. Stateside, women in the Cadet Nurse Corps were important agents in the move from traditional nurses' training to the present-day professional course of study, training, and practice. As nurses changed the course of the war, the war years had a "more profound, favorable, and permanent impact upon nurses than upon any other group of working women."[43] The profession would never be the same.

Although women who served in the Women Airforce Service Pilots were never part of the military during World War II, they, too, transformed their wartime experience into postwar careers. As women whose World War II service was the most significant break from women's traditional roles, those who served as WASPs also had the least opportunity to continue in their chosen field of aviation. Several Colorado WASPs never again piloted an airplane. Ruth Humphreys Brown spent the rest of her life in Aspen as a noted philanthropist. A member of the Aspen Hall of Fame, Brown died only nine months after being awarded the Congressional Gold Medal for her WASP service. Dori Marland returned to Denver after WASP deactivation and took a job modeling designer fashions. After two marriages, she earned her real estate license. Peggy Moynihan McCaffrey raised her four daughters and one son, earned her teaching certificate, and taught for several years before starting the homebound program for the Montrose School District. Another teacher was Jane Dunbar Tedeschi, who taught high school biology in Connecticut public schools.[44] Doris Bristol opened a Gamble's store in La Veta with her family. Intending to stay only until the shop was up and running, she met and married Julian Tracy, which changed her plans to relocate. While raising two daughters, she was active in the PTA and served on the Board of Directors of the Francisco Fort Museum. A memorial honoring Tracy stands in the courtyard between the public library and the courthouse in La Veta. One larger-than-life bronze sculpture depicts a WASP in flight gear; the other is of a young girl holding an airplane. Both are by La Veta artist Joan Hanley.[45] Millicent Peterson Young was a social worker for twenty-one years in El Paso County.[46] Gerry Ashwell tried to continue to fly after deactivation. Seeing a need for fresh lobster to be flown from Maine to New York City restaurants, she diligently studied the crustaceans to determine their reaction to altitude. Her idea never got off the ground, however, because the monoplane she was going to use caught fire and burned. Using her WASP nickname "Gerry" on an application for American Airlines, she was granted an interview. But the vice president, believing the public was not ready for a woman pilot, offered her a job as a stewardess. She refused the offer and eventually returned to her job as a botanist. In 1946 she married Wladimir "Bill" Lotowycz and replaced her WASP nickname with Betty, after her given middle name Elizabeth. Betty established and curated the herbarium at Planting Field Arboretum New York State Park, where she worked for over twenty years. At age eighty-eight, she coauthored the *Illustrated Field Guide to Shrubs and Woody Vines of Long Island.*[47]

After World War II, Lucile Doll married Robert W. Wise and raised two children. She was instrumental in the campaign to obtain military recognition and veteran's benefits for WASP members. Within the WASP organization, she served in numerous roles, including regional director, by-laws chair, scholarship chair, and president.

Although facing discrimination and doubts about their abilities to fly, other WASPs successfully pursued a career in aviation. Elizabeth "Betty" Haas accepted a job as a stewardess flying for Pan-American Airlines. She raced airplanes, learned to fly a helicopter, founded the Snowmass Balloon Races, organized the Pitkin County Air Rescue, and successfully lobbied for a heliport at the Aspen Valley Hospital and the construction of a control tower at Sardy Field.[48] Ann Brothers Frink taught at two aviation schools in Pueblo. She also owned her own aircraft sales company and a flight school.[49] Betty J. Clark, born in Rifle, worked at Denver's Vest Aircraft before moving to Glenwood Springs to be a charter and instructor pilot. It was there that she started crop dusting. She bought Rader Flight Service and operated a Fixed Base Operation at Rifle. She and former WASP Patricia J. Sullivan ran Mile High Aviation. Sullivan handled the business end while Clark handled flight operations. Sullivan also flew Civil Air Patrol search and rescue missions, did aerial game counts for the Fish and Game Division, and conducted aerial fire patrols and hunting area surveys.[50]

The wartime efforts of millions of volunteers basically ended with the surrender of Japan. Historian D'Ann Campbell has asserted that women's volunteer work, especially some American Red Cross activities, was only simple morale building—the woman doing the work wanted to feel like she was contributing to the war effort and to the return of her loved ones from military service, as well as helping society at large.[51] In contrast, Meghan Winchell points out that women who volunteered during the war continued doing volunteer work for the rest of their lives.[52]

Concentrating on women's postwar labor force participation does not do justice to the other ways World War II affected American women. On the surface, it may at first appear that neither American women as a whole nor Colorado women as a piece of the nation experienced any great and lasting changes because of World War II. But they did. One component of the war's legacy is women's attitudinal and internal changes. As has often been argued, individual experiences and perceptions, as well as social changes, are difficult to measure. But in both direct and indirect ways, World War II had an important impact on millions of American women, on gender roles and norms, and on the emergence of postwar feminism.[53]

Sherna Gluck notes that while social change is difficult to measure, oral histories of women from the era revealed the "often private and subtle way in which the individual women were changed by their wartime experiences." She points out that it is in fact the changes individuals experience that both push for and support social transformations. Although "there is a lag with ideas preceding practice . . . women's wartime experience played a vital role in the process of redefinition."[54] Even those Americans who returned home and married the boy or girl next door carried something of their faraway experiences with them. At dinner tables and in workplaces, "Their new ideas and new ways unsettled local knowledge." Even within the culture of conformity that dominated the postwar era, "One can also see a people negotiating the cultural dislocations of war and its aftermath."[55]

For African American women, their wartime experiences extended a bridge on which the modern civil rights movement progressed. Nationally, the war accelerated the drive for equality. Blacks who fled the repressive South for defense jobs often found less restrictive situations in Northern and California cities. Colorado's Black population, in contrast, remained relatively constant during the war. There was no mass exodus from or migration to Colorado; instead, most female Coloradans of color remained in the state. Those who did leave for war jobs generally found themselves in more restrictive situations than those in Colorado. Frances Hale and Jennie Walker faced segregated transportation and dining establishments in Washington, DC. Both women returned to Colorado, earned college degrees, and became professionals working for their community. Just as she had entered and eaten lunch in the House of Representatives basement, initially defied a white bus driver's demand that she sit in the back of the bus, and later ordered whites to "sit in the front" so she could have a seat, Hale did not let societal prejudices dictate her life. After earning a teaching degree, she boldly told the Denver Public Schools that they had already denied her two older sisters teaching positions; she herself refused to settle for that. She was hired and spent her career as a teacher and social worker in the district.[56] Similarly, Jennie Walker Rucker continued to break barriers as she navigated Denver's de facto segregation. She became an educator and a librarian, one of the founding faculty members of the Community College of Denver, and a philanthropist.[57] Oleta Crain spent twenty years in the army, attaining the rank of major. She parlayed that experience into a long career with the US Department of Labor, focusing on the labor rights of all women.[58]

Would Currin, Rucker, and Crain have accomplished so much if it had not been for their wartime experiences? One cannot know. But one can point to continued efforts for and advancements in civil rights in Colorado after the war. In the late 1940s and early 1950s, barriers were broken down. Women teachers of color were hired in public schools, segregated movie theaters were forced to change their policies, and restrictive real estate covenants were gradually removed from the books. Similar advancements in civil rights after World War II were seen in other parts of the country.[59]

For Colorado women, military, labor force, and volunteer experiences changed the way they saw themselves and viewed others; the experiences opened doors previously closed to them. While some of those doors were slammed shut after 1945, women had seen a glimpse of the possibilities and felt within themselves a sense of capability and power. Over and over again, women of the era emphasized the importance of the war years on their lives. Female veterans regularly noted that their time in the military was the best time of their lives and the most important thing they had done.[60] They had met, mingled, and worked with people from diverse backgrounds, many of whom became their lifelong friends. Their experiences changed the way they raised their own children. WAVE Elaine Watkins Brennan believed she raised her two daughters differently because of her time in the Naval Reserve. Unlike her mother who did not support her enlistment, Brennan encouraged her older daughter to join the air force; her younger daughter became a rocket scientist.[61] Female military personnel met the loves of their lives. They saw other parts of the world and witnessed the disparity between their lives and those of others. Female defense workers earned their own pay, made their own decisions, played the role of two parents, and dealt with sexual harassment and inequities in the workplace. It was no small achievement. In the words of one female war worker, "You must tell your children, putting modesty aside, that without us, without women there would have been no spring in 1945."[62] Colorado women's service in the military, in defense plants, in office buildings, on farms and ranches, and in voluntary organizations planted the seeds for their own future lives and for the civil rights and feminist movements. Their legacy was not just an end to World War II; it was also a new beginning.

List of Abbreviations

DOP: Denver Ordnance Plant

DP: *Denver Post*

PC: *Pueblo Chieftain* (Pueblo, CO)

PPLD: Special Collections 1905, Carnegie Library, Pikes Peak Library District, Colorado Springs, CO

PSJSC: *Pueblo Star Journal and Sunday Chieftain* (Pueblo, CO)

RG156: Denver Ordnance Plant History, Record Group 156: Records of the Chief of Ordnance, National Archives at Denver, CO

RMN: *Rocky Mountain News* (Denver, CO)

SCW: Steelworks Center of the West, Pueblo, CO

TWU: Texas Woman's University. Denton

UNCG: University of North Carolina at Greensboro, Betty H. Carter Women Veterans Historical Project

VHP: Veterans History Project, American Folklore Center, Library of Congress, Washington, DC

Notes

INTRODUCTION

1. Over the past several years, interviewees Elaine Watkins Brennan, Frances Hale Currin, Edna Guise Doyle, Bette Krim Kamlet, Dorothy Bowen Kennedy, Grace "Betty" Ashwell Lotowycz, John McCaffrey, Thelma Morey Robinson, Marie Jansen Rugg, and Lucile Doll Wise have passed away.

2. Cle Cervi and Nancy M. Peterson, *The Women Who Made the Headlines: Denver Woman's Club, the First Hundred Years* (Lakewood, CO: Western Guideways, 1998), 49.

3. Elaine Tyler May, "Pushing the Limits, 1940–1961," in Nancy F. Cott, ed., *No Small Courage: A History of Women in the United States* (Oxford: Oxford University Press, 2000), 476.

4. Carl Abbott, Stephen J. Leonard, and Thomas J. Noel, *Colorado: A History of the Centennial State*, 5th ed. (Boulder: University Press of Colorado, 2013), 299.

5. US Department of Commerce, Bureau of the Census, *Fifteenth Census of the United States: 1930: Statistical Abstract of the United States 1930* (Washington, DC: US Government Printing Office, 1930): "No. 50 Females Ten Years of Age and Older Engaged in Each Group of Gainful Occupations, by States, 1920"; US Department of Commerce, Bureau of the Census, *Sixteenth Census of the United States: 1940. Statistical Abstract of the United States 1940* (Washington, DC: US Government Printing Office, 1940): "No. 52 Gainful Workers Ten Years of Age and Older, by Sex, by Occupational Groups, by States: 1930."

6. US Department of Commerce, Bureau of the Census, *Fifteenth Census of the United States*; US Department of Commerce, Bureau of the Census, *Sixteenth Census of the United States.*

7. US Department of Commerce, Bureau of the Census, *Fifteenth Census of the United States*; Quintard Taylor, *In Search of the Racial Frontier: African Americans in the American West, 1528–1990* (New York: W. W. Norton, 1998), 262.

8. Abbott, Leonard, and Noel, *Colorado*, 301.

9. Douglas Brinkley, ed., *The World War II Memorial: A Grateful Nation Remembers* (Washington, DC: New Voyage Communications, 2004), 205.

10. "Work of the Red Cross in Colorado," *Eagle Valley Enterprise* (Eagle, CO), March 9, 1945, www.RedCross.org.

11. Margaret Culkin Banning, *Women for Defense* (New York: Duell, Sloan, and Pearce, 1942), ix. A 1912 graduate of Vassar College, Banning wrote 36 novels and over 400 essays and short stories. During World War II, she served with the British Information Services. *Women for Defense* insisted that all women in the United States should get jobs, participate in civilian defense, maintain the country's morale, and follow government policies related to the war effort.

12. William Henry Chafe, *The American Woman: Her Changing Social, Economic, and Political Roles, 1920–1970* (New York: Oxford University Press, 1972), 142.

13. Seymour L. Wolfbein, "Postwar Trends in Negro Employment," *Monthly Labor Review* 65 (December 1947): 664, quoted in Julia Brock, Jennifer W. Dickey, Richard J.W. Harker, and Catherine M. Lewis, *Beyond Rosie: A Documentary History of Women and World War II* (Fayetteville: University of Arkansas Press, 2015), 57.

14. Chafe, *American Woman*, 142–144; John W. Jeffries, *Wartime America: The World War II Home Front* (Chicago: Ivan R. Dee, 1996), 94. Labor unions such as the United Automobile Workers and the United Electrical Workers gained thousands of new female members under the "maintenance of membership" agreements with industry. The vast majority of those new unionists worked in the Midwest and coastal aircraft and shipbuilding industries. Ruth Milkman, "American Women and Industrial Unionism during World War II," in Margaret Randolph Higonnet, Jane Jenson, Sonya Michel, and Margaret Collins Weitz, eds., *Behind the Lines: Gender and the Two World Wars* (New Haven, CT: Yale University Press, 1987), 169.

15. I classified women as "Colorado women" if they met one of three criteria: they were living in Colorado at the time of America's involvement, they had trained or were stationed at Colorado military bases, or they, like many of us, were transplants from other states—arriving in Colorado after 1945—but were active in wartime activities elsewhere.

16. Quote from anonymous female war worker at the Rosie the Riveter Memorial Park, Rosie the Riveter World War II Home Front National Historic Park, National Park Service, Richmond, California. The principal component of the memorial is a walkway inscribed with a time line about the home front and quotes from women workers sandblasted into white granite.

17. William M. Tuttle Jr. *"Daddy's Gone to War": The Second World War in the Lives of American Children* (New York: Oxford University Press, 1993), 31.

18. Margaret Regis, *When Our Mothers Went to War: An Illustrated History of Women in World War II* (Seattle: Navpublishing, 2008), 85.

19. Clark Secrest, "The Day Clara May Morse Died: Pearl Harbor and One Mother's Heartbreak," *Colorado Heritage* (Autumn 1991): 36–44.

20. Mark Jonathan, Franklin D. Mitchell, and Steven J. Schechter, *The Home Front: America during World War II* (New York: G. P. Putnam's Sons, 1984), 253.

21. Tuttle, *"Daddy's Gone,"* 31.

22. Tuttle, *"Daddy's Gone,"* 53–54.

23. Tuttle, *"Daddy's Gone,"* 36.

24. "Before and After 1940: Change in Population Density," www.census.gov.

CHAPTER 1: THE ARMY NURSE CORPS

1. Jeanne Holm, Major General, USAF (Ret'd.), ed., *In Defense of a Nation: Servicewomen in World War II* (Washington, DC: Military Women's Press, 1998), 143. Major General (USAF Ret'd) Holm estimates the number as close to 400,000 women while others, including the National World War II Museum in New Orleans, give the number of women serving in the US military during World War II as 358,074.

2. Section 8 is a category of discharge from the US military indicating that the member is mentally unfit for service. Leila Allen Morrison, interview by author, November 25, 2014, Windsor, CO.

3. Eleanor Roosevelt, "The Time Is Now!" *American Journal of Nursing* (August 1942): 924.

4. Kathi Jackson, *They Called Them Angels: American Military Nurses of World War II* (Westport, CT: Praeger, 2000), 3.

5. "Pueblo Nurses Must Enlist or Be Drafted," *PC*, July 5, 1942; "All Nurses in District to Register on December 29," *PC*, December 23, 1942; "Forty-Three Registered Nurses from Region in Military Service," *PC*, August 10, 1944.

6. Brad Hoopes, *Reflections of Our Gentle Warriors: Personal Stories of World War II Veterans* (Bradenton, FL: BookLocker.com, 2015), 249.

7. Helen I. Hyatt DeKorp, interview at med-dept.com/veterans-testimonies/veterans-testimony-helen-i-hyatt-dekorp.

8. DeKorp, interview.

9. "News of Our Men and Women in Uniform," *Julesburg Grit-Advocate,* September 30, 1943; "News of Our Men and Women in Uniform," *Julesburg Grit-Advocate,* August 17, 1944.

10. Interview letter from Wells, February 19, 1980, to Barbara Brooks Tomblin, *G.I. Nightingales: The Army Nurse Corps in World War II* (Lexington: University Press of Kentucky, 1996).

11. Tomblin, *G.I. Nightingales*, 107.

12. Tomblin, *G.I. Nightingales*, 107.

13. Tomblin, *G.I. Nightingales,* 108.

14. Evelyn M. Monahan and Rosemary Neidel-Greenlee, *All This Hell: U.S. Nurses Imprisoned by the Japanese* (Lexington: University Press of Kentucky, 2000), 231.

15. Janet A. Bachmeyer, Veterans History Project, AFC/2001/001/57409, American Folklife Center, Library of Congress, Washington, DC. Bachmeyer was scheduled to be sent to the Pacific Theater of Operations, but the war ended before she was transferred. She was discharged but went back on active duty during the Korean War and the Vietnam War. By the time she left the service for good, she had risen to the rank of lieutenant colonel.

16. "WWII Committee Member Wartime Biographies," littletongov.org.

17. Lille Steinmetz Magette, interview, November 8 and 15, 2005, Call number 2005.216.1000, Archives and Local History at Douglas County Libraries, Castle Rock, CO.

18. "Witness to War," *Daily Sentinel* (Grand Junction, CO), November 8, 1998.

19. Eileen Ella Bradley Paine Collection, Veterans History Project, AFC/2001/001/11230, American Folklife Center, Library of Congress, Washington, DC.

20. Magette, interview. As early as 1941 the United Kingdom was running out of prison camp space and asked the United States for help with housing German prisoners of war. Between 1942 and 1945, over 400,000 POWs, mostly Germans, were housed in 500 camps in the United States. Colorado was home to 8 camps. At the end of the war, the United States began repatriating the prisoners to their home countries. This was accomplished by the end of 1946.

21. Morrison, interview.

22. Morrison, interview.

23. Morrison, interview.

24. Nancy Caldwell Sorel, *The Women Who Wrote the War* (New York: Arcade, 1999), 247.

25. John C. McManus, *Hell before Their Very Eyes: American Soldiers Liberate Concentration Camps in Germany April 1945* (Baltimore: Johns Hopkins University Press, 2015), 25, 33, 50–51, 57. Buchenwald was established in 1937. Its prisoners were criminals, political opponents, Polish citizens, and Jewish prisoners from Germany and countries overrun by the Nazis. In 1945, Nazis began evacuating prisoners from the camp. On April 11, US troops liberated the remaining 21,000 prisoners, including about 1,000 children and youth. One teenage survivor was novelist Elie Wiesel, who had been marched from Auschwitz to Buchenwald.

26. Quoted in Regis, *When Our Mothers Went to War*; Sorel, *Women Who Wrote the War*, 347–350.

27. Judith A. Bellafaire, *The Army Nurse Corps* (Washington, DC: US Army Center of Military History, 1993), 20.

28. Elizabeth M. Norman, *We Band of Angels: The Untold Story of the American Women Trapped on Bataan* (New York: Random House Trade Paperbacks, 2013), 4.

29. "Transcript of Josephine Nesbit Davis interview," interview by Major Susan Graski, April 9, 1983, 2–3. Transcript and audiotapes on file at the Department of the Army, Center for Military History, Washington, DC.

30. "Transcript of Josephine Nesbit Davis interview," 2–3. Two groups of navy nurses were held as prisoners of war by the Japanese during World War II. Chief nurse Marion Olds and four nurses were taken prisoner on Guam shortly after the attack on Pearl Harbor and incarcerated in Japan. They were repatriated in August 1942. Chief nurse Laura Cobb and eleven nurses were captured in 1942 and imprisoned in the Los Banos internment camp until their liberation by American forces in February 1945. These nurses, part of the "Angels of Bataan," served in the prison camp alongside captured army nurses. See Emilie Le Beau Lucchesi's *This Is Really War: The Incredible True Story of a Navy Nurse POW in the Occupied Philippines* (Chicago: Chicago Review Press, 2019).

31. Vern L. Bullough, *American Nursing: A Biographical Dictionary*, vol. 3 (New York: Springer, 2000), 215–218.

32. Elizabeth M. Norman, *We Band of Angels: The Untold Story of the American Women Trapped on Bataan* (New York: Random House Trade Paperbacks, 2013), 86–87.

33. Norman, *We Band of Angels*, 106.

34. Norman, *We Band of Angels*, 134.

35. Monahan and Neidel-Greenlee, *All This Hell*, 190–191.

36. Norman, *We Band of Angels*, 186–187.

37. Norman, *We Band of Angels,* 187.

38. Gail M. Beaton. *Colorado Women: A History* (Boulder: University Press of Colorado, 2012), 263.

39. Althea Williams, interview, November 30, 1994, the Archive at Fort Collins Museum of Discovery, Fort Collins, CO.

40. Agnes Turnovec Thornton, interview by Beth Smith, December 5, 2003, gunnisonld.marmot.org.

41. Wilma Vanden Hoek Broekstra Collection, Veterans History Project, AFC/2001/001/33388, American Folklife Center, Library of Congress, Washington, DC.

42. Broekstra Collection.

43. Williams, interview.

44. Quoted in Jeanne Manning, *A Time to Speak* (Paducah, KY: Turner, 1999), 253.

45. Quoted in Manning, *A Time to Speak*, 254.

46. Thomas J. Noel, *Colorado: A Historical Atlas* (Norman: University of Oklahoma Press, 2015), 200–202.

47. Melissa Connor and James Schneck, *Fort Carson in World War II: The Old Hospital Complex* (Lincoln, NE: National Park Service, 1997), 24.

48. "Helen Kuhns in Pacific," *PC*, November 11, 1943. After her Camp Carson stint, Lieutenant Kuhns wrote to her parents telling them she was "somewhere in the Pacific."

49. Beaton, *Colorado Women*, 254–255.

50. Betty Berry Godin, interview by Eric Elliott, June 19, 1999, Betty H. Carter Women Veterans Historical Project, Hodges Special Collections and University Archives, UNCG University Libraries, University of North Carolina at Greensboro.

51. Judith Barger, *Beyond the Call of Duty: Army Flight Nursing in World War II* (Kent, OH: Kent State University Press, 2013), 55.

52. Barger, *Beyond the Call*, 66–67.

53. This is especially ironic since her commanding officer, Morris Kaplan, had earlier stated that the training at Bowman Field, which included bivouacs, procurement, and preparation of equipment and supplies for overseas shipment, was "an opportunity to weed the boys [the medical technicians] from the men and the crocheter from the real women." Barger, *Beyond the Call*, 65.

54. Godin, interview.

55. Barger, *Beyond the Call*, 78–80.

56. Godin, interview. Berry returned to flying status after V-J Day. Her new routes were from Manila to Tokyo, Guam, Kwajalein, and Johnson Island. She also tended to patients on flights into what is now Travis Air Force Base outside San Francisco.

57. Edy Parsons, "Women's Nursing Corps, Army," in Lisa Tendrich Frank, ed., *An Encyclopedia of American Women at War: From the Home Front to the Battlefields*, vol. 2: *M–Z* (Santa Barbara, CA: ABC-CLIO, 2013), 652.

58. "Anna M. Pritekel, Local War Nurse, Called by Death," *PC*, December 25, 1942.

59. Morrison, interview.

60. Jackson, *They Called Them Angels*, 14.

61. Holm, *Women in the Military*, 92. *Stars and Stripes* is an American newspaper that reports on matters affecting members of the US armed forces. During World War II it was printed in dozens of editions in several theaters of operation. One hundred percent of the US women in the military were volunteers, and less than 39 percent of US men serving were volunteers; the rest were draftees. Thus the serviceman's statement, "We are here because we have to be." "US Military by the Numbers," www.nationalww2museum.org.

62. Eleanor Roosevelt, "The Time Is Now!" *American Journal of Nursing* (August 1942): 924.

63. Morrison, interview; Magette, interview.

64. Morrison, interview.

65. Jeanne Holm, Major General, USAF (Ret'd.), *Women in the Military: An Unfinished Revolution* (Novato, CA: Presidio, 1992), 91.

CHAPTER 2: THE NAVY NURSE CORPS

1. Jackie Jacquet Melvin, interview by author, August 8, 2017, Lafayette, CO.

2. Susan H. Godson, *Serving Proudly: A History of Women in the U.S. Navy* (Annapolis, MD: Naval Institute Press, 2001), 133.

3. Ruth Banning Lewis Papers, MSS 0109, Box 4, "Papers, [1906]–1953," Folder 3, "Volunteer Nurse's Aide Corps, Letterbook 1-R, Undated," Special Collections 1905, Carnegie Library, Pikes Peak Library District, Colorado Springs, CO.

4. Godson. *Serving Proudly*, 139. In contrast, the Army Nurse Corps' numbers exceeded 57,000.

5. Godson, *Serving Proudly*, 139. Ruth Catherine Ostergaard, who spent her childhood in the San Luis Valley, had perhaps one of the shortest stints in the NNC. A graduate of the Minnequa School of Nursing at Corwin Hospital (Pueblo), she enlisted in November 1941 and married Walter Tammen on December 31, 1941, which led to her discharge from the NNC as it did not allow married women to serve at that time. Ruth Catherine Ostergaard Tammen Collection, Biography by Cathy Tammen, July 1, 2016, Steelworks Center of the West, Archives, Pueblo, CO.

6. Godson, *Serving Proudly*, 142.

7. Godson, *Serving Proudly*, 141.

8. Melvin, interview.

9. "Battle Casualties Recovering at Famous Hotel Colorado," *RMN*, May 14, 1944.

10. "Colorado Hotel at Glenwood Joins Navy," *RMN*, February 21, 1943.

11. Doris Weatherford, *American Women during World War II: An Encyclopedia* (New York: Routledge, 2010), 315.

12. "Battle Casualties Recovering."

13. "Battle Casualties Recovering."

14. Godson, *Serving Proudly*, 135.

15. Godson, *Serving Proudly*, 149–150.

16. Godson, *Serving Proudly*, 150.

17. Margaret Gates Gravdahl, interview by Linda Bell, December 15, 1994, the Archive at Fort Collins Museum of Discovery, Fort Collins, CO.

18. "Mary Edith 'Meg' Goldcamp," Landlocked Navy Nurse Association, www.facebook.com /llnnca.

19. med.navy.mil.

20. med.navy.mil.

21. Melvin, interview.

22. Melvin, interview.

23. Melvin, interview; Maureen Christopher (daughter), phone conversation with author, July 22, 2018.

24. Godson, *Serving Proudly*, 150.

25. "Yanks Find Nothing Good about Jap Island," *Brush Tribune,* September 6, 1945.

26. Melvin, interview.

27. Melvin, interview.

28. Melvin, interview.

29. Melvin, interview.

30. Melvin, interview.

31. Melvin, interview. Chili Williams became a popular pin-up girl after posing for *Life* magazine in a polka-dot bikini.

32. "World War II 'Angels' Get Their Due," *RMN*, May 14, 2008.

33. "World War II 'Angels' Get Their Due."

34. www.navy.mil.

35. Godson, *Serving Proudly*, 146.

36. Landlocked Navy Nurse Corps Association, www.facebook.com/llnnca.

37. Melvin, interview; "WWII Flight Nurse One of a Noble Few," *RMN,* May 14, 2008.

38. Godson, *Serving Proudly*, 139.

39. See chapter 1 for the ordeal of army and navy nurses interned by the Japanese.

40. Godson, *Serving Proudly*, 133.

41. Godson, *Serving Proudly*, 134.

CHAPTER 3: THE WOMEN'S ARMY AUXILIARY
CORPS AND THE WOMEN'S ARMY CORPS

1. "Retired Army Major Fought, Lived through Bias," *DP*, November 22, 2007; Oleta Lawanda Crain, oral interview for *Colorado Reflections* (Denver: University of Colorado at Denver, Office of Public Information, 1984); Jeanne Varnell, *Women of Consequence: The Colorado Women's Hall of Fame* (Boulder: Johnson Books, 1999), 165. Band 1 was formed at Fort Des Moines in July 1942. It played for graduations, in military parades known as pass in reviews, at war bond rallies, and in military hospitals throughout the United States. The group escorted troops to class and bugled "Reveille" and "Taps." Ultimately, five WAC bands were formed, including a Black band in September 1943. It was later designated the 404th (cld), with the initials indicating it was a

"colored" unit. Jill M. Sullivan, *Bands of Sisters: U.S. Women's Military Bands during World War II* (Lanham, MD: Scarecrow, 2011), 17, 30–32.

2. Mattie E. Treadwell, *The Women's Army Corps*, United States Army in World War II Special Studies (Washington, DC: Office of the Chief of Military History, Department of the Army, 1954), 20.

3. Anne Bosanko Green, *One Woman's War: Letters Home from the Women's Army Corps, 1944–1946* (St. Paul: Minnesota Historical Society Press, 1989), x.

4. Doris Weatherford, *American Women during World War II: An Encyclopedia* (New York: Routledge, 2010), 497–498.

5. "Makes Self Over to Qualify as Wac," *PC*, April 27, 1944.

6. "Our Denver Girls as W.A.A.C.," *Denver Star*, December 26, 1942.

7. Varnell, *Women of Consequence*, 166. While a sergeant, Crain was one of a cadre of six African American WAACs serving under the command of Charity Adams, who later led the first contingent of Black WACs to Europe. Charity Adams Earley, *One Woman's Army: A Black Officer Remembers the WAC* (College Station: Texas A&M University Press, 1989), 85.

8. Varnell, *Women of Consequence*, 166–167. Ironically, Crain later served a regimental office that had control of WAC bands. She also played "Taps" at a military funeral for an "Ann" in Kentucky.

9. Martha S. Putney, *When the Nation Was in Need: Blacks in the Women's Army Corps during World War II* (Metuchen, NJ: Scarecrow, 1992), 168–169. Lemoore is presently a naval air station.

10. www.msudenver.edu/camphale/interviews/emilycollinsworth.

11. Bernice Moran Miller, interview by Eric Elliott, October 13, 1999, Bernice Moran Miller Papers, Betty H. Carter Women Veterans Historical Project, Hodges Special Collections and University Archives, WV 0104.5.001, UNCG University Libraries, University of North Carolina at Greensboro.

12. May, interview.

13. Doris Weatherford, *American Women and World War II: An Encyclopedia* (New York: Facts on File, 1990), 51–52.

14. Manning, *A Time to Speak*, 248–249.

15. Letter to Topsy, January 11, 1943, Anne Elizabeth Heyer Collection, Betty H. Carter Women Veterans Historical Project, Hodges Special Collections and University Archives, UNCG University Libraries, University of North Carolina at Greensboro. Two months earlier the recruit wrote that there were three recruits named Betty on the train from California to Daytona Beach. One "became" Beth, the other "Mickey," and she remained, to her liking, Betty. Topsy was her younger sister, Harriet. Letter to Topsy, December 11, 1943.

16. "Denver Office Swears in 31 WAAC Recruits," *DP*, November 24, 1942.

17. May, interview.

18. Miller, interview.

19. "Scott Carpenter NASA Astronaut," www.jsc.nasa.gov. Alice's sister, Florence Noxon Carpenter, was back in Colorado from New York City with her son, Malcolm Scott Carpenter, because she was suffering from tuberculosis. Malcolm, the nephew of Alice Noxon, is famous as Scott Carpenter, Aurora 7 astronaut.

20. National Cemetery Administration. *U.S. Veterans' Gravesites, ca. 1775–2006* (Provo, UT: Ancestry.com Operations, Inc., 2006).

21. "Join Brothers in Service," *PC*, February 18, 1944.

22. "WAC Instructor," *PC*, August 15, 1945; "Husband of Former Alamosan Killed in Plane Crash," *PC*, November 22, 1944.

23. "First WAAC," *The Blast,* February 12, 1943.

24. "WAC Says to Keep Passing the Steel," *The Blast,* April 13, 1945.

25. Victoria Miller (museum curator, Steelworks Center of the West, Pueblo, CO), phone conversation with author, August 14, 2018.

26. "All-Out for the War Effort," *The Blast,* February 25, 1944.

27. "Lieutenant," *The Blast,* March 3, 1944.

28. *Men and Women in the Armed Forces from Montrose County* (Oklahoma City: Western Publishing, 1946).

29. "Our Boys in Armed Forces," *Julesburg Grit-Advocate,* May 20, 1943; "News of Our Men and Women in Uniform," *Julesburg Grit-Advocate,* December 23, 1943; "With Monte Vista Boys in Service," *Monte Vista Journal,* March 24, 1943; "With Monte Vista Boys and Girls in Service," *Monte Vista Journal,* December 8, 1944.

30. Holm, *Women in the Military,* 40.

31. Earley, *One Woman's Army,* 57; Manning, *A Time to Speak,* 249.

32. May, interview. Low pay, however, was not a deterrent for Detweiler, a teacher earning $1,440 a year when she enlisted. Her mother thought she was out of her mind to quit for a private's pay of $21 a month. But she asked, as a WAC, what did she need money for? Manning, *A Time to Speak,* 248.

33. Emily Nydigger Collinsworth, interview by Monys Hagen, March 20, 1996, Nampa, ID, https://msudenver.edu/camphale/resoures/interviews/emilycollinsworth; David R. Witte, *World War II at Camp Hale: Blazing a New Trail in the Rockies* (Charleston, SC: History Press, 2015), 139.

34. Weatherford, *American Women and World War II,* 84–85; Dorothy Schooley Amato obituary, ancestry.com.

35. "Air-Wac Life," Boulder Historical Society, A. A. Paddock Collection, World War II, 1939–1945, W–X, BHS 328, Box 255, Folder 9, Boulder Carnegie Library for Local History, Boulder, CO.

36. "Most of Your Friends Away?" *Brush Tribune,* January 20, 1944.

37. "100 Women Are Needed as Technicians," *Brush Tribune,* March 22, 1945.

38. Letter to Topsy, March 20, 1944, Anne Heyer Collection.

39. Treadwell, *Women's Army Corps,* 198.

40. Weatherford, *American Women and World War II,* 201.

41. Mary Kelles Stone, interview by Monys Hagen, May 22, 1997, Waterford, CT, https://msudenver.edu/camphale/resoures/interviews/marystone.

42. Varnell, *Women of Consequence,* 167.

43. Treadwell, *Women's Army Corps,* 206.

44. Miller, interview.

45. Weatherford, *American Women and World War II,* 206.

46. "A Service Command WAC Officer Says," *Camp Hale Ski-Zette,* November 5, 1943.

47. Allan Berube. *Coming Out under Fire: The History of Gay Men and Women in World War II* (Chapel Hill: University of North Carolina Press, 2010), 14–18.

48. Leisa D. Meyer, *Creating GI Jane: Sexuality and Power in the Women's Army Corps during World War II* (New York: Columbia University Press, 1996), 156–160. Women in other branches of the military were also discharged as "undesirable" for homosexual offenses. In her 1945 report on the women reservists of the United States Marine Corps, Director Ruth Streeter reported that twenty reservists had been discharged for such offenses between July 1, 1944, and July 1, 1945. Peter A. Soderbergh, *Women Marines: The World War II Era* (Westport, CT: Praeger, 1992), 141.

49. Weatherford, *American Women during World War II,* 269.

50. Berube, *Coming Out,* 30.

51. Berube, *Coming Out,* 4.

52. Jacquelyn Beyer, interview, December 2, 1984, GLBT Historical Society Museum and Archives, San Francisco, CA. Beyer served until 1948 (and later in the reserves). Serving in Germany beginning in 1946, she knew lesbian couples in the army but never knew of anyone who suddenly disappeared. She suspected there was a network of information and support that allowed lesbians to remain "under the radar" while serving in the United States Army.

53. Weatherford, *American Women during World War II*, 270.

54. Berube, *Coming Out*, 31–32.

55. Earley, *One Woman's Army*, 180–181.

56. "Denver Y Officer Joins the WAAC in Des Moines," *Denver Star*, April 24, 1943; "WAAC at Walla Walla Air Field," *Denver Star*, August 18, 1943. Like other women who joined the military, Fant had a brother who was also a member of the army during World War II. "Our Denver Girls," *Denver Star*, September 25, 1943.

57. "Another Denver Girl Making Good in Des Moines," *Denver Star*, May 8, 1943.

58. "These WAACs Will Serve as WIRES," *PC*, January 14, 1943.

59. "Fifty WAACs Arrive at Lowry Field," *RMN*, January 29, 1943.

60. "Lowry Graduates Class of WAACS in Photography," *RMN*, April 25, 1943.

61. Weatherford, *American Women and World War II*, 65.

62. Treadwell, *Women's Army Corps*, 770.

63. Richard K. Young, *The Ute Indians of Colorado in the Twentieth Century* (Norman: University of Oklahoma Press, 1997), 144. After the war, Sunshine Cloud Smith became a member of the tribal council. She was instrumental in establishing the Southern Ute Head Start Program and was a member of the Ute Language Committee that was responsible for writing the first Ute Language Dictionary. Nationwide, one third of all able-bodied American Indian men and perhaps as many as 800 American Indian women served in the armed forces during World War II. Grace Mary Gouveia, "We Also Serve: American Indian Women's Role in World War II," *Michigan Historical Review* 20, no. 2 (Fall 1994): 159.

64. Lorelei Cloud, phone conversation with author, August 29, 2018; vasouthernute-nsn.gov, Southern Ute Veterans Association. Secretary of War Henry Stimson ordered Indians integrated into white military units. Gouveia, "We Also Serve," 157.

65. www.msudenver.edu/camphale/resources/interviews/emilycollinsworth.

66. "Monte Vista Girl WAC of the Week at Camp Slocum," *Monte Vista Journal*, August 11, 1944.

67. Nell Brown Propst, *Those Strenuous Dames of the Eastern Plains* (Boulder: Pruett, 1982), 242.

68. Propst, *Those Strenuous Dames*, 243.

69. Propst, *Those Strenuous Dames*, 243.

70. Noonie Fortin, *Women at Risk: We Also Served* (Lincoln, NE: Writers Press Club, 2002), 46.

71. Shirley Sears Melvin, interview by Brad Hoopes, July 16, 2009.

72. Treadwell, *Women's Army Corps*, 460.

73. Manning, *A Time to Speak*, 138–139.

74. "GI Amazons Join Warriors in Normandy," *Stars and Stripes*, New York, London, France edition, July 17, 1944.

75. "Confident Denver Woman Was a 'Born Sergeant,'" *DP*, August 10, 2003.

76. "Mom Mum about Medal," *DP*, November 4, 2018.

77. Regis, *When Our Mothers Went to War*, 92.

78. Holm, *Women in the Military*, 84.

79. Holm, *Women in the Military*, 84.

80. Treadwell, *Women's Army Corps*, 95–96.

81. Letter to Topsy, March 20, 1944; April 3, 1944; April 17, 1945, Anne Heyer Collection.

82. Letter to Topsy, July 4, 1944; August 5, 1945, Anne Heyer Collection.

83. Brenda L. Moore. *Serving Our Country: Japanese American Women in the Military during World War II* (New Brunswick, NJ: Rutgers University Press, 2003), 14. Some released internees worked in Colorado in defense and non-defense jobs alike. Masako Toyama rewound truck armatures at Thompson Auto Supply Company in Denver, while Yoshiye Abe was employed at the Flag and Decorating Company on Lawrence Street. Her husband was originally released in October to work in the sugar beet fields in the Longmont area. By 1943, he was a houseman at the Albany

Hotel. Mary Higuchi voluntarily evacuated from San Pedro, California; in 1943, she separated eggs at Toner's Egg Company in Denver. Ninety percent of the eggs were for the United States Army or the Lend-Lease.

84. Beginning in 1944, the regiment fought primarily in Italy, southern France, and Germany. It was the most decorated unit for its size and length of service in the history of American warfare. In total, about 14,000 men served in the regiment.

85. Moore, *Serving Our Country*, 14, 19.

86. Moore, *Serving Our Country*, 96–97.

87. Moore, *Serving Our Country*, 95, 98.

88. Kisa Noguchi Sasaki Collection, Box 1, Folder 1, Guide to Japanese Americans in Northeastern Colorado, Special Collection 40, University of Northern Colorado, Greeley.

89. "Vest-Pocket Nisei WAC Joins Pharmacy Staff of Army Hospital," *Pacific Citizen*, February 10, 1945, 3; quoted in Moore, *Serving Our Country*, 112.

90. Moore, *Serving Our Country*, 49.

91. Moore, *Serving Our Country*, 21–22.

92. Moore, *Serving Our Country*, 25–26.

93. Trudy Oda Hirowaka Photograph Collection, #Ph00526, History Colorado, Denver.

94. Holm, *Women in the Military*, 100.

95. Holm, *Women in the Military*, 95.

96. Godson, *Serving Proudly*, 108.

CHAPTER 4: THE WOMEN ACCEPTED FOR VOLUNTEER EMERGENCY SERVICE (WAVES)

1. Her diary entry of December 1, 1942, reveals a woman unsatisfied with her life and questioning her choice of careers. Her personal angst is woven throughout her diaries from 1942 through the 1950s. Her happiest moment is her service in the WAVES. Martha Scott Trimble Collection, Box MT 1-17, diary entry, December 14, 1942; letter to her mother and father, February 16, 1943, Box MT-9, Diary, "My Life in the Service," the Archive at Fort Collins Museum of Discovery, Fort Collins, CO. Colorado State College became Colorado State University in 1957.

2. Godson, *Serving Proudly*, 108.

3. Godson, *Serving Proudly*, 111–112.

4. Godson, *Serving Proudly*, 112.

5. Godson, *Serving Proudly*, 117.

6. "Sixty-One Puebloans Enter Waves since Unit Founded," *PC*, July 30, 1944.

7. Doris June Rew Kirkwood, Veterans History Project, AFC/2001/001/52457, American Folklore Center, Library of Congress, Washington, DC.

8. Kathryn Chittenden Haines, interview, undated, Call number 2010.007.1000, Archives and Local History at Douglas County Libraries, Castle Rock, CO.

9. Godson, *Serving Proudly*, 121.

10. Louise Nash Dorsett, interview by Hermann J. Trojanowski, January 18, 1999, Betty H. Carter Women Veterans Historical Project, Hodges Special Collections and University Archives, UNCG University Libraries, University of North Carolina at Greensboro.

11. "News," *Steamboat Pilot*, February 25, 1943.

12. "Yoeman [*sic*] Second Class Virginia Haynes," *Julesburg Grit-Advocate*, April 27, 1944. A yoeman's duty is clerical in nature. Her duties "include stenography and typewriting, preparation of reports, operation of duplication machines, use of navy file systems, keeping personnel records, recording and filing correspondence, and handling routine details of enlistments, discharges,

transfers, promotions, transportation, and travel." Mary V. Harris, *Guide Right: A Handbook for WAVES and SPARs* (New York: Macmillan, 1994), xxiii.

13. Mary Devlin Barry Collection, Veterans History Project, AFC/2001/001/26642, American Folklife Center, Library of Congress, Washington, DC.

14. Edna Guise Doyle, interview by author, June 16, 2016, Denver, CO; Edna Guise Doyle Papers, courtesy of her daughter Diana Doyle, June 13, 2016, Aurora, CO. According to Jeanne Holm, military historian, today's women in the United States Navy wear this same uniform with only minor modifications. Holm, *Women in the Military* (1992), 42.

15. "Bananas Did the Trick," *DP*, April 14, 1943; "New Faces in the *Post* Hall of Fame," *DP*, April 17, 1943. Sadly, George Weidenfeller was killed in action in the battle for Okinawa on May 14, 1945. Ancestry.com., "World War II Navy, Marine Corps, and Coast Guard Casualties, 1941–1945."

16. "Ensign Anderson and Lt. Moyers Married in East Last Week," *Alamosa Daily Courier*, March 27, 1943.

17. Barry Collection.

18. Guise, letter to parents, August 26, 1944.

19. Trimble Collection, Box MT 1-17, diary entries, December 21, 1942; February 18, 1943; March 24, 1943, Box MT-9, Diary, "My Life in the Service."

20. "Coloradans in the War," *RMN*, August 28, 1943.

21. Mildred Doherty Zupon Collection, Veterans History Project, AFC/2001/001/65177, American Folklife Center, Library of Congress, Washington, DC.

22. Virginia Moore, interview, January 17, 1995, World War II Oral History Project, the Archive at Fort Collins Museum of Discovery, Fort Collins, CO.

23. Natalie O'Brien Jones, interview by Linda Bell, December 13, 1994, Veterans of World War II Project, the Archive at Fort Collins Museum of Discovery, Fort Collins, CO.

24. Haines, interview.

25. Dorsett, interview.

26. Wright became a renowned architect in her own right. After settling in Colorado Springs with her husband, Gordon Ingraham, she designed over 100 buildings in the city, including the Vista Grande Community Church (1987), the first building in the state to use Thermomass, making it innovatively "green." She founded the Wright-Ingraham Institute in 1970 to encourage and develop opportunities contributing to the conservation, preservation, and wise use of human and natural resources. "Famed Colorado Springs Architect Elizabeth Wright Ingraham Dies at Age 91," *Gazette-Telegraph*, September 24, 2013.

27. Ina Elizabeth Renkel Winger obituary, findagrave.com.

28. Godson, *Serving Proudly*, 119.

29. Virginia Hudson Schmidt, interview, August 29, 2009, Call number 2007.027.1000, Archives and Local History at Douglas County Libraries, Castle Rock, CO.

30. Guise, letter to parents, August 26, 1944.

31. Dorsett, interview.

32. "Our Men and Women in Uniform," *Julesburg Grit-Advocate,* November 11, 1943.

33. "News of Our Men and Women in Uniform," *Julesburg Grit-Advocate,* November 11, 1943; US Census Bureau, 1940 Census.

34. Bobbie Carlton, ed., *WAVES of Colorado: US Navy Memories of World War II* ([without place of publication]: Bobbie Carlton, 2009), 26.

35. Doyle, interview.

36. Doyle, interview.

37. "Juanita Joseph Taylor" obituary, *Costilla County Free Press* (San Luis, CO), August 11, 2016.

38. Lillian Mae Bainbridge Green Collection, Veterans History Project, AFC/2001/001/62658, American Folklife Center, Library of Congress, Washington, DC.

39. "WAVE Promoted," *PC*, July 27, 1944; "News," *Steamboat Pilot,* February 25, 1943.

40. Sylvia Pettem, "Boulder History: Gahm Sisters Served Their Country during WWII," *Boulder Daily Camera*, May 24, 2012.

41. Elaine Watkins Brennan, interview by author, December 4, 2018, Centennial, CO.

42. "Coloradan Broke Navy Barriers," *DP*, June 7, 2009; Katherine Keating Collection, Veterans History Project, AFC/2001/001/10522, American Folklife Center, Library of Congress, Washington, DC.

43. Jones, interview.

44. Captain Wyman H. Packard, USN (ret'd), *A Century of U.S. Naval Intelligence* (Washington, DC: Naval Intelligence and the Naval Historical Center, Department of the Navy, 1996), 366–367; Roger Dingham, *Deciphering the Rising Sun: Navy and Marine Corps Codebreakers, Translators, and Interpreters in the Pacific War* (Annapolis, MD: Naval Institute, 2009), 10–12.

45. Dingham, *Deciphering the Rising Sun*, 11–16.

46. "Elizabeth McKinnon Carr, 1918–2013," Japanese Language School Newsletter #140, February 1, 2008. http://cublibraries.colorado.edu/archives.

47. "Kimiko Miyamoto JLS/OLS Faculty," Japanese Language School Newsletter #111, May 1, 2007. http://cublibraries.colorado.edu/archives.

48. Kaya Kitagawa Sugiyama, "Relocation," the *Interpreter* #129, November 1, 2008, 4.

49. Sugiyama, "Relocation," the *Interpreter* #131, January 1, 2009, 2.

50. Sugiyama, "Relocation," 2–3.

51. Ruth Halverson Craig File, US Navy Japanese/Oriental Language School Archival Project, Norlin Library, Archives, University of Colorado Boulder.

52. Barbara Shuey File, US Navy Japanese/Oriental Language School Archival Project, Norlin Library, Archives, University of Colorado Boulder.

53. Nancy Rebecca Pearce (Helmbold) File, US Navy Japanese/Oriental Language School Archival Project, Norlin Library, Archives, University of Colorado Boulder.

54. Marie Edwards, Veterans History Project, AFC 2001/001.000280, American Folklife Center, Library of Congress, Washington, DC. It must have been the right question because 90 percent of the women he selected graduated from the Japanese Language School in Boulder. Dingham, *Deciphering the Rising Sun,* 54.

55. Sugiyama, "Relocation (2)," the *Interpreter* #132, February 1, 2009, 4.

56. Evelyn "Betty" Knecht Hansen File, US Navy Japanese/Oriental Language School Archival Project, Norlin Library, Archives, University of Colorado Boulder.

57. Abby Jane White Bakony File, US Navy Japanese/Oriental Language School Archival Project, Norlin Library, Archives, University of Colorado Boulder; Dingham, *Deciphering the Rising Sun*, 55. White later served as a US Supreme Court Justice from 1962 to 1993. White's wife, Marion Lloyd Stearns, daughter of CU president Robert P. Stearns, was a World War II WAVE. They married in 1946.

58. Margaret Dilley File, US Navy Japanese/Oriental Language School Archival Project, Norlin Library, Archives, University of Colorado Boulder.

59. Dingham, *Deciphering the Rising Sun*, 32.

60. Mary Lou Siegfried Williams File, US Navy Japanese/Oriental Language School Archival Project, Norlin Library, Archives, University of Colorado Boulder. While WAVES could not board ships, they could launch them. In January 1944, Seaman Second Class Carol June Barnhart of Pueblo was the first WAVE to sponsor a naval vessel on the West Coast. In Richmond, California, the site of many naval shipyards, Barnhart smashed a bottle of champagne on the hull of the USS *Pueblo*, officially launching the battleship. "Pueblo WAVE Launches USS Pueblo in Fight versus Axis," *PC*, January 23, 1944.

61. Hansen file.

62. The iris farm was probably Long's Gardens, established in 1905 in what was then north of Boulder. Irene Slaninka Thiel Collection, US Navy Japanese/Oriental Language School Archival Project, Norlin Library, Archives, University of Colorado Boulder.

63. Mary Lou Siegfried Williams, the *Interpreter* #59, January 1, 2000; #117, November 1, 2007; US Navy Japanese Language School/Oriental Language School Archival Project, Norlin Library, Archives, University of Colorado Boulder.

64. Pearce file.

65. "Kay Hoeriger Clauset," Japanese Language School Newsletter #105a, November 15, 2006, Norlin Library, Archives, University of Colorado Boulder.

66. Dingham, *Deciphering the Rising Sun*, 130.

67. Shuey file.

68. Blanche Y. Belitz, the *Interpreter* #87a, May 15, 2005; Margaret Dilley, #136, June 1, 2009; Evelyn (Betty) Knecht Hansen, #95, January 1, 2006; Avis Pick Waring, #133, March 1, 2009.

69. Liza Mundy, *Code Girls: The Untold Story of the American Women Code Breakers of World War II* (New York: Hachette Books, 2017), 19; Mary Jane Konold Carroll, WAVE, Japanese Language School, WAVE JLS Reunion Book #122 (April 1, 2008), US Navy Japanese/Oriental Language School Archival Project, Norlin Library, Archives, University of Colorado Boulder.

70. Mundy, *Code Girls*, 19.

71. Mundy, *Code Girls*, 19–20, 300.

72. Mundy, *Code Girls*, 172.

73. Mundy, *Code Girls*, 193.

74. Ida Mae Olson Brueske obituary, 2016.

75. Hazel Marie Hester Miller Collection, Veterans History Project, AFC/2001/001/42192, American Folklore Center, Library of Congress, Washington, DC.

76. Manning, *A Time to Speak*, 247.

77. Kirkwood Collection.

CHAPTER 5: WOMEN AIRFORCE SERVICE PILOTS

1. "Women WWII Pilots Finally Finding Recognition," *Montrose Daily Press*, February 28, 2002; John McCaffrey, interview by author, April 16, 2015, Montrose, CO.

2. Karen Zeinert, *Those Incredible Women of World War II* (Brookfield, CT: Millbrook, 1994), 20–21.

3. In the early 1930s, Cochran (1906–1980) took flying lessons; within two years she obtained her commercial license. At the time of her death, no other pilot in aviation history held more speed, distance, or altitude records.

4. Eleanor Roosevelt, "My Day," September 1, 1942, United Feature Syndicate, Inc.

5. Nancy Harkness Love (1914–1976) earned her pilot's license at age sixteen. By the end of her freshman year in college, she had earned her commercial license. She competed in air races in 1937 and 1938 before becoming a test pilot.

6. Sara Bryn Rickman, *Nancy Love and the WASP Ferry Pilots of World War II* (Denton: University of North Texas Press, 2008), 95–96.

7. Zeinert, *Those Incredible Women*, 25, 27; Sara Bryn Rickman, *WASPs of the Ferry Command: Women Pilots, Uncommon Deeds* (Denton: University of North Texas Press, 2016), 33, 146.

8. Rickman, *Nancy Love*, 117, 119.

9. Quoted in Emily Yellin, *Our Mothers' War: American Women at Home and at the Front during World War II* (New York: Free Press, 2004), 158.

10. The designation refers to the year, "W" indicating women, and the class. Up to ten classes were held a year.

11. www.wingsacrossamerica.us/wasp/stats.

12. "Woman Soared as WWII Flier," *DP*, April 11, 2004.

13. "Mary Elizabeth Trebing," Placard, National WASP World War II Museum, Sweetwater, TX. 43-W-4 indicates that Trebing graduated in the fourth class of women in 1943.

14. "Love at First Flight: Former WASP Still Living Life at Full Throttle," http://airportjournals .com/love-at-first-flight-former-wasp-still-living-life-at-full-throttle.

15. "Anna Mae Petteys," WASP Archive, Texas Women's University, Denton.

16. "Female WWII WASP Pilot Shares Her Pioneering Story," http://ksmu.org/post/female -wwii-wsp-pilot-shares-her-pioneering-story.

17. Lucile Doll Wise, interview by author, December 2, 2014, Arvada, CO.

18. "WASP Final Flight," http://waspfinalflight.blogspot.com/2013/05/dori-marland-martin-43 -w-8.

19. Jane Dyde Miller Collection, Veterans History Project, AFC/2001/001/78137, American Folklife Center, Library of Congress, Washington, DC.

20. Marianne Verges, On Silver Wings: Women Airforce Service Pilots of World War II, 1942–1944 (New York: Ballantine Books, 1991), 154.

21. "WASP Gayle Snell, 44-9," WASP Final Flight, http://waspfinalflight.blogspot.com/2009/08/ wasp-gayle-snell-44-9.

22. Wise, interview.

23. "Colorado Women Honored with Congressional Gold Medal," DP, March 11, 2010; Betty Ashwell Lotowycz, interview by author, September 24, 2015, Louisville, CO. Her given name was Grace Elizabeth Ashwell. During her stint as a WASP, Ashwell went by the nickname "Gerry." After marriage, she went by Betty (for her middle name, Elizabeth) Lotowycz.

24. Vera S. Williams, WASPs: Women Airforce Service Pilots of World War II (Honolulu: Pacific Historic Parks, 1994), 94.

25. Lotowycz, interview.

26. Wise, interview.

27. Jean Hascall Cole, Women Pilots of World War II (Salt Lake City: University of Utah Press, 1992), 27.

28. Cornelia Fort, "At the Twilight's Last Gleaming," Woman's Home Companion (July 1943): 19.

29. "Colorado Girl Passes Test to Join WASP: Marion Carlstrom Is State's First Member of Woman's Air Service," DP, September 14, 1943.

30. "Betty [Haas] Pfister, Aspen Hall of Fame Inductee," http://www.aspenhalloffame.org/betty _pfister.

31. Miller Collection.

32. "Remembering My Sister, Mary," http://www.wingsacrossamerica.org/Trebing.

33. June A. Willenz, Women Veterans: America's Forgotten Heroines (New York: Continuum, 1983), 26.

34. "Betty [Haas] Pfister, Aspen Hall of Fame Inductee."

35. Quoted in Cole, Women Pilots, 99.

36. Lotowycz, interview.

37. "Love at First Flight."

38. Verges, On Silver Wings, 131. In a later reminiscence Cochran revealed, "We did have seven girls killed by sabotage." Harriet Sigerman, ed., The Columbia Documentary History of American Women since 1941 (New York: Columbia University Press, 2003), 79.

39. "Women WWII Pilots Finally Finding Recognition," DP, February 28, 2002.

40. Gayle Mildred Snell obituary, Gazette-Telegraph, August 30, 2009.

41. "Woman Made Revolutionary WWII Flights," DP, May 29, 2017.

42. Doris Bristol letters to mother, October 3, 1944, December 5, 1944. Originals in possession of Julie Tracy Geiser, daughter of WASP Doris V. Bristol Tracy, Alamosa, CO; copies in possession of author.

43. "Ann Brothers Is WASP Graduate," PC, April 21, 1944.

44. Quoted in Cole, *Women Pilots*, 104–105.

45. Wise, interview.

46. Wise, interview.

47. Quoted in Amy Goodpaster Strebe, *Flying for Her Country: The American and Soviet Women Military Pilots of World War II* (Westport, CT: Praeger Security International, 2007), 66.

48. "Address by H. H. Arnold, Commanding General, Army Air Forces, before WASP Ceremony, Sweetwater, TX, Thursday, December 7, 1944," Press Release, Department of War, Bureau of Public Relations Press Branch, DC.

49. General "Hap" Arnold, letter to WASPs, October 1, 1944, in the possession of Julie Tracy Geiser, daughter of WASP Doris V. Bristol Tracy, Alamosa, CO.

50. "The WASP in the 2014 Rose Parade," Smithsonian National Air and Space Museum blog, December 29, 2013.

51. Wise, interview.

52. "Colorado Women Honored with Congressional Gold Medal," *DP*, March 11, 2010. The WASP official archive is located in the Blagg-Huey Library, Texas Woman's University (TWC) in Denton. It lists thirteen women who considered Colorado home when they enlisted: Jane C. Dyde Miller, Anna Mae Petteys Pattee, Marion Carlstrom, Betty J. Clark, Anna Hopkins Dance, Ruth A. Humphreys Brown, Doris M. Marland Martin, Doris I. Moffat Long, Janice E. Norton Kaufman, Carmel LaTorra Seidenberg, Anna Bartholf Rawlings, Peggy Moynihan McCaffrey, and Ann M. Brothers Frink. A similar list, excluding Dance, Long, and Rawlings, exists at the WASP Museum in Sweetwater, Texas. It includes five others not on the TWU list: Mary E. Trebing, Eleanore Bryant Folk, Bernice M. Dannefer Pickerton (or Pinkerton as she is listed on the TWU site), Jean D. Downey Harman, and Phyllis Lee Hitner. Trick, Brown, Clark, Frink, and McCaffrey were born, lived, and died in Colorado. Pattee was born and lived in Colorado but passed away in California. Robinson, Snell, Sullivan, Gunderson, Lotowycz, Moss, Pfister, Tracy, and Wise lived in Colorado after the war and died there. Young moved to Colorado years after deactivation. Harman and Kaufman were born in Colorado, but I did not find more information about them. Because of the paucity of information, I did not include Seidenberg, Josephine Pitz Egan, and Rosina Lewis Todd who died in Colorado. Another woman with Colorado ties was Dorothy Lamb Young, who was honored by the Colorado Aviation Historical Society for her work in aviation. As a member of WASP Class 43-W-1, she trained in Houston. The unmarried Dorothy Lamb lived in Sterling in the 1920s and 1930s, marrying Paul E. Young in 1936. In 1940, he was a flying instructor and she was listed as a secretary for an aviation company. Records indicate that she enlisted on November 16, 1942, and was released in September 1943, after having trained and served as a WASP for ten months.

CHAPTER 6: WOMEN OF THE COAST GUARD, THE MERCHANT MARINE CORPS, AND THE MARINE CORPS WOMEN'S RESERVE

1. "Survey," Jane Silverstein Ries Papers, WH 1785, Box 31, Folder #34, Western History Collection, Denver Public Library, Denver, CO.

2. www.uscg.mil.

3. Manning, *A Time to Speak*, 242–243.

4. Manning, *A Time to Speak*, 244.

5. "Accepted by SPARs for War Service," *PC*, January 1, 1943.

6. "General Requirements for SPARs," "Application Women's Reserve," "Physical Examination Report," and "Sample Aptitude Test," www.uscglivinghistory.com.

7. "SPARS to Be Here Friday and Saturday," *Julesburg Grit-Advocate*, May 4, 1944.

8. "SPAR Recruiters to Visit Alamosa Soon," *Alamosa Daily Courier*, June 8, 1944.

9. "Procurement Board in District February 27," *Steamboat Pilot*, February 8, 1943.

10. "Vision Requirements Changed for WAVES and SPARs," *Steamboat Pilot*, June 24, 1943.

11. "Our Boys in the Armed Forces," *Steamboat Pilot*, November 4, 1943.

12. "News," *Steamboat Pilot*, August 23, 1945.

13. Dolores Plested, *Some Reminiscences along the Way* (Denver: Dolores Plested, 2002), 106.

14. Sullivan, *Bands of Sisters*, 67.

15. Sullivan, *Bands of Sisters*, 72–73.

16. Sullivan, *Bands of Sisters*, 74.

17. Sullivan, *Bands of Sisters*, 79.

18. Dorothy Jeanne Gleason, "My Experiences as a SPAR during World War II (February 1943–June 1946)," in Paula Nassen Poulos, ed., *A Woman's War Too: US Women in the Military in World War II* (Washington, DC: National Archives and Records Administration, 1996), 123.

19. "Our Boys and Girls Soldiers," *Palisade Tribune,* July 9, 1943; "Societies and Clubs," *Palisade Tribune,* September 21, 1945.

20. "SPARS End Training," *RMN*, January 7, 1945.

21. Harriet Butler Martin, interview by Brad Hoopes, June 12, 2015 (part of the Northern Colorado Veterans History Project). DVD in author's possession, courtesy of Brad Hoopes.

22. "Our Men and Women in the War," *RMN,* January 4, 1945.

23. "Survey," Ries Papers.

24. "War Housing Project," Ries Papers, Box 31, Folder #52.

25. "Survey," Ries Papers.

26. "Survey," Ries Papers.

27. Gleason, "My Experiences," 125.

28. Manning, *A Time to Speak*, 244.

29. American women served as stewardesses aboard United States Merchant Marine ships prior to World War II and in the first few months after Pearl Harbor. Several were on ships attacked by the enemy. After December 7, 1941, they were required to quit their jobs as soon as their ships reported to port. www.USMM.org.

30. Mary Allen Converse, *Captain Mary: The Biography of Mary Parker Converse, Captain U.S. Merchant Marine* (King's Point, NY: American Merchant Marine Museum, 1987).

31. Converse, *Captain Mary*, 184.

32. "Naval Recruiting Staff Is Aided by Woman Captain: Defense Society Matron Aids National Defense by Nautical Knowledge," *DP*, April 3, 1941.

33. "Women Marines," *Life Magazine*, March 27, 1944, 81.

34. "Geraldine C. Bower Lannon in the US Marine Corps Muster Rolls, 1798–1958," ancestry .com (Provo, UT: ancestry.com Operations, Inc., 2007).

35. Colonel Mary V. Stremlow (USMC ret'd.), *Free a Marine to Fight: Women Marines in World War II*. Marines in World War II Commemorative Series (Washington, DC: Marine Corps Historical Center, 1994), 5.

36. Soderbergh, *Women Marines*, 26.

37. Rice, interview.

38. Shirley Elizabeth Gunston Brown Collection, Veterans History Project, AFC/2001/001/34261, Veterans History Project, American Folklife Center, Library of Congress, Washington, DC (subsequent citations VHP).

39. Betty Lee Leist Megenity Collection, AFC/2001/001/09094, VHP.

40. Velma C. Comstock Brooke Collection, AFC/2001/001/56220, VHP.

41. LaVerne Marie Novak Sarber Collection, AFC/200/001/665191, VHP.

42. *Men and Women in the Armed Forces from Montrose County* (Oklahoma City: Western Publishing, 1946).

43. "Mary Morgan in the U.S. Department of Veterans Affairs BIRLS Death File, 1850–2010," ancestry.com (Provo, UT: ancestry.com Operations, Inc., 2011).

44. Jeanne E. Barrenche Hackler Collection, AFC/200/001/57276, VHP.

45. "Our Men and Women in Uniforms," *Julesburg Grit-Advocate,* June 20, 1944; May 10, 1945.

46. Stremlow, "Free a Marine," 8.

47. Megenity Collection.

48. Phyllis Ilgen Smith, interview by Lieutenant Colonel Dick Merritt, n.d., Roaring Fork Veterans History Project, Aspen Historical Society, Aspen, CO.

49. Marie Jansen Rugg, interview by author, August 30, 2017, Littleton, CO.

50. Soderbergh, *Women Marines,* 40.

51. Megenity Collection.

52. Stremlow, "Free a Marine," n.p.

53. Rugg, interview.

54. Soderbergh, *Women Marines,* 49.

55. Weatherford, *American Women and World War II,* 54.

56. "Whoa—Easy Does It!" *Brush Tribune,* July 8, 1943.

57. Stremlow, "Free a Marine," n.p.

58. Patricia Jane Irvine Whiting interview, AFC/2001/001/21227, VHP.

59. Rugg, interview.

60. Rice, interview.

61. Rice, interview.

62. Barbara L. Kees Meeks Collection, AFC/2001/001/57220, VHP.

63. Rice, interview.

64. Hackler Collection.

65. Brown Collection.

66. Pauline E. Parker, ed., *Women of the Homefront: World War II Recollections of 55 Americans* (Jefferson, NC: McFarland and Company, 2002), 130.

67. Marie Jansen Rugg, telephone conversation with author, September 15, 2017.

68. Sylvia Pettem, "Boulder History: Gahm Sisters Served Their Country during WWII," *Boulder Daily Camera,* May 24, 2012.

69. Marjorie Arlene Alexander obituary, *DP,* September 30, 2018; Megenity Collection.

70. Stremlow, "Free a Marine," n.p.; "Mary Lou A. Gillan in the US Marine Corps Muster Rolls, 1798–1958," ancestry.com (Provo, UT: ancestry.com Operations, Inc., 2007).

71. Whiting, interview.

72. Rice Collection. Also see USO center in chapter 13, Meghan H. Winchell, *Good Girls, Good Food, Good Fun: The Story of the USO Hostesses during World War II* (Chapel Hill: University of North Carolina Press, 2008), 60–62.

73. Rugg, interview.

74. Marguerite Moore Hauser Collection, AFC/2001/001/69276, VHP.

75. Sarber Collection.

76. Rugg, interview.

77. Smith, interview.

78. Stremlow, "Free a Marine," n.p.

79. Stremlow, "Free a Marine," n.p.

80. Stremlow, "Free a Marine," n.p.

81. Rice Collection.

82. Stremlow, "Free a Marine," n.p.

83. Rugg, telephone conversation with author, September 15, 2017.

84. Brown, interview.

85. "Sisters Join Marines," *PC,* July 22, 1945.

86. Stremlow, "Free a Marine," n.p.

87. "Women Marines Faithful to the Core," *DP*, April 8, 2002.

CHAPTER 7: WOW! WOMEN ORDNANCE WORKERS

1. Colorado Fuel & Iron Company Collection; "Something New Has Been Added," *The Blast*, February 19, 1943.

2. Chafe, *American Woman*, 148; Leila J. Rupp, *Mobilizing Women for War: German and American Propaganda, 1939–1945* (Princeton, NJ: Princeton University Press, 1978), 75.

3. Jeffries, *Wartime America*, 94–95.

4. Chafe, *American Woman*, 140.

5. US Department of Commerce, Bureau of the Census, *Sixteenth Census of the United States 1940: Characteristics of the Population*, "Table 20—Persons 14 Years Old and over in the Labor Force, 1940, and Gainful Workers 14 Years and over, 1900 to 1930, by Race and Sex, for the State"; *Seventeen Census of the United States 1950: Characteristics of the Population*.

6. Abbott, Leonard, and Noel, *Colorado*, 487.

7. Alice Trott Baker, interview, June 4, 2008, Call number 2008.028.1000, Archives and Local History at Douglas County Libraries, Castle Rock, CO.

8. Christine Pfaff, "Bullets for the Yanks: Colorado's World War II Ammunition Factory," *Colorado Heritage* (Summer 1992): 43.

9. Pfaff, "Bullets for the Yanks," 39–40.

10. Pfaff, "Bullets for the Yanks," 40.

11. "DOP History Supplement 1, 1 January 1943–30 September 1943," 80, Box 1, Folder 1, Reports and Historical Narratives, 1940–1945, RG156.

12. "DOP History Sixth Supplement, 1 April 1945–31 December 1945," Box 1, Folder 2, Reports and Historical Narratives, 1940–1945, RG156.

13. "Army-Navy 'E' Flag Presented Builders of Arsenal Here," *RMN*, April 18, 1943. The United States Army and Navy awarded "E" pennants and pins for "Excellence in Production."

14. John F. Hoffecker, *Twenty-Seven Square Miles: Landscape and History at Rocky Mountain Arsenal National Wildlife Refuge* (Washington, DC: US Fish and Wildlife Service, Rocky Mountain Arsenal National Wildlife Refuge, 2001), 59.

15. Lee Scamehorn, *Mill and Mine: The CF&I in the 20th Century* (Lincoln: University of Nebraska Press, 1992), 197–198.

16. Scamehorn, *Mill and Mine*, 154.

17. "Great Tonnage Handled at Pueblo's Ordnance Depot," *PSJSC*, August 19, 1945; "Pueblo Depot Tops in Efficiency toward Handling Mountains of Victory Materiel," *PSJSC*, May 8, 1945.

18. "Women Assured Fair Treatment in Depot Set-Up," *PC*, January 1, 1943.

19. "Gadget Manufacturer Now Making Armor Piercing Projectiles at Littleton Plant," *RMN*, January 25, 1945.

20. Chafe, *American Woman*, 142–143.

21. Bureau of the Census, *Sixteenth Census of the United States, 1940*, Census Place: *Longmont, Boulder, Colorado*, Roll: *m-t0627-00457*, Page: *14B*, Enumeration District: *7-49B*.

22. Chafe, *American Woman*, 142.

23. *Polk's Pueblo City Directory, 1943* (Salt Lake City: R. L. Polk, 1943); Master Copy CF&I Company—Auditing Payroll Mill Time Payroll, December 1944, Original #3546, SCW.

24. *Polk's Pueblo City Directory, 1943*.

25. Master Copy CF&I Company—Auditing Payroll Mill Time Payroll, December 1944; US Department of Commerce, Bureau of the Census, *Sixteenth Census of the United States 1940: Population*.

26. "News of Our Neighbors," *Steamboat Pilot*, January 29, 1942; "Local News," *Eagle Valley Enterprise* (Eagle, CO), February 27, 1942; "Mt. Harris," *Steamboat Pilot*, February 17, 1942.

27. "Women in Boulder Defense Classes Laugh at Idea That Work Is 'Terribly Hard,'" *Boulder Daily Camera*, 1942, news clipping in A. A. Paddock Collection, "World War II, 1939–1945, W–X," BHS 328, Box 255, Boulder Carnegie Library for Local History, Boulder, CO.

28. "Women in Boulder Defense Classes Laugh at Idea That Work Is 'Terribly Hard.'"

29. Quoted in Herbert Burstein, *Women in War: A Complete Guide to Service in the Armed Forces and War Industries* (New York: Service Publishing, 1943), 103.

30. American War Manpower Poster.

31. Alice Kessler-Harris, *Out to Work: A History of Wage-Earning Women in the United States* (New York: Oxford University Press, 2003), 288.

32. "Women in Boulder Defense Classes Laugh."

33. Master Copy CF&I Company—Auditing Payroll Mill Time Payroll, December 1944.

34. "Edith Daugherty Joins Cadet Nurses," Steamboat Pilot, December 23, 1943.

35. US Department of Commerce, Bureau of the Census, *Sixteenth Census of the United States 1940: Population.*

36. Fadonna Carr Hurban Papers, RORI 718, National Park Service Museum Collections, Rosie the Riveter WWII National Home Front Historical Park, Richmond, CA.

37. Chafe, *American Woman*, 142.

38. Oleta Crain, oral interview for *Colorado Reflections* (Denver: University of Colorado at Denver, Office of Public Information, 1984).

39. Transcript of YWCA Leadership Meeting, testimony of Oleta Crain, June 9, 1942, Employed Girls Group, Box 17, Folder 416, YWCA Collection, History Colorado, Denver.

40. "Denver Citizens Grow [a] Bit Anxious about Our Girls Being Employed on Same Basis at Munition Plant," *Denver Star*, February 21, 1942.

41. Transcript of YWCA Leadership Meeting, testimony of Oleta Crain.

42. Moya Hansen, "'Try Being a Black Woman!' Jobs in Denver, 1900–1970," in Quintard Taylor and Shirley Ann Wilson Moore, eds., *African American Women Confront the West, 1600–2000* (Norman: University of Oklahoma Press, 2003), 214.

43. "DOP History Supplement #5," 1, Reports and Historical Narratives, 1940–1945, RG156.

44. "Women Ordnance Workers Win Praise from Army," *PSJSC*, June 13, 1943.

45. US Department of Commerce, Bureau of the Census, *Sixteenth Census of the United States 1940: Population.*

46. "DOP History Supplement #652," 133–134, Box 1, Folder 1, Reports and Historical Narratives, 1940–1945, RG156.

47. "DOP History Supplement #652," 130.

48. "On the Home Front, Magdalen Lampman Made Sure the Ammo Worked during World War II," *Plain Dealer* (Cleveland, OH), March 10, 2010.

49. Pfaff, "Bullets," 43.

50. US Department of Commerce, Bureau of the Census, *Sixteenth Census of the United States 1940: Population;* Master Copy CF&I Company—Auditing Payroll Mill Time Payroll, December 1944; Colorado, Steelworks Employment Records, 1887–1979, SCW.

51. "Ordnance Depot to Hire Women as Carpenters," *PC*, October 16, 1942; "Ordnance Depot Checkers Wanted," *PC*, November 26, 1942.

52. "Mighty Shells and Bombs Manufactured," *RMN*, January 11, 1945.

53. "DOP History Sixth Supplement."

54. "DOP History Supplement #652," 130.

55. "DOP Organizational Charts and Personnel, 1 July 1945–1 June 1946," Box 1, Folder 2, Reports and Historical Narratives, 1940–1945, RG156.

56. "Tons of Grinding Balls," *The Blast*, February 19, 1943.

57. "CF&I Workers 'Pass the Ammunition,'" *The Blast*, January 29, 1945.

58. "We Proudly Present Our Record-Making Workers at the Forge Shop," *The Blast*, April 13, 1945, 6–7.

59. "Keep Their Caps On," *The Blast*, January 19, 1945.

60. Chafe, *American Woman*, 140.

61. Hoffecker, *Twenty-Seven Square Miles*, 63.

62. "Gates Rubber Co. War Goods Go to Every Front," *RMN*, January 19, 1945.

63. "Twenty Stenographers Needed on War Program's New Plant," *PC*, July 18, 1942; "Ordnance Depot Seeks Women as Auto Mechanics," *PC*, April 13, 1943; "Women Ordnance Workers Needed," *PC*, March 30, 1944.

64. "Women Ordnance Workers Win Praise from Army."

65. "Women Ordnance Workers Win Praise from Army."

66. "Ordnance Depot Seeks Women as Auto Mechanics"; "Women Ordnance Workers Win Praise from Army."

67. "Women Ordnance Workers Win Praise from Army."

68. "Women Ordnance Workers Win Praise from Army."

69. Master Copy CF&I Company—Auditing Payroll Mill Time Payroll, December 1944.

70. "Reta Copeland Collaborates with Husband at Main Chemistry Laboratory," *The Blast*, December 17, 1943.

71. "Drafts (Wo)Man," *The Blast*, April 1943.

72. "Women Ordnance Workers Win Praise from Army."

73. Stephen M. Voynick, "The Rise of Climax Molybdenum," *Colorado Central Magazine* (November 1, 1994), coloradocentralmagazine.com.

74. "World War II Mattie Cora Custus Lee Simpson," Rosie Stories, rosietheriveter.net, posted September 29, 2015.

75. Brenda Ralph Lewis, *Women at War: The Women of World War II — At Home, at Work, on the Front Line* (Pleasantville, NY: Reader's Digest Association, 2002), 32.

76. "Santa Clause Will Visit Eagle," *Eagle Valley Enterprise* (Eagle, CO), December 14, 1945.

77. "Getting Underground," minesmagazine.com. Betty Gibbs, a 1969 mining engineering graduate of Colorado School of Mines, was the first woman to work underground at Climax.

78. "DOP History Supplement 1," 10–11.

79. "Ordnance Employe [*sic*] Recreation Group Is Now Organized," *PC*, August 2, 1942.

80. "Depot Chooses Rodeo Jean-Queen," *PSJSC*, June 3, 1945; "Some Kisser!" *PC*, July 3, 1945.

81. "Many More Houses Are Needed Here," *PC*, October 8, 1942.

82. "Ordnance Depot Bus Plan Stands Despite Protest," *PSJSC*, July 11, 1943; "Ordnance Workers Urged to Pool More Car Rides," *PC*, August 4, 1943.

83. Marcia Goldstein, "We Can Wear the Pants, Too! Denver's Women Ordnance Workers, 1941–1945," unpublished paper in author's possession, 1996. 16.

84. Tuttle, *"Daddy's Gone to War,"* 83–84.

85. Cott, *No Small Courage*, 479.

86. "Child Care Unit Is Established," *Denver Ordnance Bulletin*, July 15, 1943.

87. "War Plant Workers Take Notice," *Denver Star*, June 12, 1943. The forty cent a day fee was less than that paid by a worker on the West Coast, who generally paid fifty cents a day for care, lunch, and two snacks for a child between the ages of two and five. Tuttle, *"Daddy's Gone to War,"* 80.

88. Goldstein, "We Can," 17.

89. Baker, interview.

90. "Women Ordnance Workers Win Praise from Army."

91. Regis, *When Our Mothers Went to War*, 66.

92. Hoffecker, *Twenty-Seven Square Miles*, 66.

93. Hurban Collection.

94. Pfaff, "Bullets," 43.

95. "Women Employes [*sic*] Fall in Line and Help out Men Thinkers," *The Blast*, April 21, 1944.

96. "Signal Honor," *The Blast*, August 31, 1945.

97. "Women Ordnance Workers Win Praise from Army."

98. Chafe, *American Woman*, 184.

99. Master Copy CF&I Company—Auditing Payroll Mill Time Payroll, December 1944.

100. Chafe, *American Woman*, 155–156.

101. "CF&I Women of WWII," http://scalar.usc.edu/works/cfi-women-of-wwii.

102. Regis, *When Our Mothers Went to War*, 71.

103. Cott, *No Small Courage*, 477, 479.

104. Goldstein, "We Can," 20.

105. Baker, interview.

106. "On the Home Front."

107. Cott, *No Small Courage*, 476.

108. Chafe, *American Woman*, 139.

109. "Workers at Ordnance Plant Now Are One-Fourth Women," *PC*, July 27, 1943.

110. "Workers at Ordnance Plant Now Are One-Fourth Women."

111. Ruth Milkman, *Gender at Work: The Dynamics of Job Segregation by Sex during World War II* (Urbana: University of Illinois Press, 1987), 17.

112. From "You're Going to Hire Women" (Washington, DC: Government Printing Office, 1943), quoted in Lester W. Gregory, *Women in Defense Work during World War II: An Analysis of the Labor Problem and Women's Rights* (New York: Exposition, 1974), 12.

113. "Ordnance Depot Will Have 60 Per Cent Women Workers," *PSJSC*, May 9, 1943; June 13, 1943.

114. "Women Ordnance Workers Win Praise from Army"; US Census, 1940. A former sharecropper with her husband, Ulmon (who worked at CF&I), Andrews returned to her previous line of work after the war. In the 1950s and 1960s, she was a janitor or charwoman for a department store and a fabric store. *Pueblo City Directory*, 1945, 1948, 1950, 1962, 1963.

115. "DOP History Supplement #652 Appendix," 110.

116. D'Ann Campbell, *Women at War with America: Private Lives in a Patriotic Era* (Boston: Harvard University Press, 1984), 115.

117. For a full discussion of this topic, see Melissa A. McEuen, *Making War, Making Women: Femininity and Duty on the Home Front, 1941–1945* (Athens: University of Georgia Press, 2011); Marilyn E. Hegarty, *Victory Girls, Khaki Wackies, and Patriotutes: The Regulation of Female Sexuality during World War II* (New York: New York University Press, 2008).

118. *Transportation*, July 1943, quoted in the *Gazette-Telegraph* (Colorado Springs), April 29, 2001.

119. "Something New Has Been Added," *The Blast*, February 19, 1943.

120. "Mighty Shells and Bombs Manufactured," *RMN*, January 11, 1945.

121. "Our Victory Is But Half Won," *RMN*, May 13, 1945.

122. "Food Branch of War Plant Closes Down," *DP*, August 14, 1945.

123. Susan M. Hartmann, *The Home Front and Beyond: American Women in the 1940s* (Boston: Twayne, 1982), 90.

124. "Women to Demand Equality in Peacetime Working World," *DP*, January 14, 1945. A bill in the Colorado General Assembly to prohibit discrimination in personnel hiring and retention died.

125. Pfaff, "Bullets," 45.

126. "Fifty Jobs Open for Veterans at Ordnance Plant," *PC*, February 1, 1946; "Depot Needs More Women Laborers," *PC*, March 6, 1946.

127. "Veterans," *The Blast*, August 10, 1945.

CHAPTER 8: COLORADO WOMEN IN THE AIRCRAFT
AND SHIPBUILDING INDUSTRIES

1. Barbara Mae Byron Papers, RORI 4053, National Park Service Museum Collections, Rosie the Riveter WWII Home Front National Historical Park, Richmond, CA.

2. Cott, ed., *No Small Courage*, 476; Regis, *When Our Mothers Went to War*, 65.

3. "We'll Pay You a Salary and Teach You Aircraft Drafting," *RMN*, April 25, 1943, original emphasis.

4. Debra Faulkner, *Touching Tomorrow: The Emily Griffith Story* (Palmer Lake, CO: Filter, 2005), 97.

5. Elinor Bluemel, *The Opportunity School and Emily Griffith, Its Founder* (Denver: Green Mountain, 1970), 64.

6. "Opportunity School Like Real War Plant Nowadays," *RMN*, September 26, 1943.

7. "Denver Modification Center Checks America's War Birds," *DP*, September 20, 1942.

8. W. David Lewis, ed., *Airline Executives and Federal Regulation: Case Studies in American Enterprise from the Airmail Era to the Dawn of the Jet Age* (Columbus: Ohio State University Press, 2000), 182.

9. Tucker Collection.

10. Tucker Collection.

11. "New Fighter Planes Passing through Denver Modification Center," *DP*, January 16, 1944.

12. Bert Bemis, "There Go the Gun Girls," article in company newsletter, undated.

13. Lois Ann Altman Collection, RORI 2414, National Park Service Museum Collections, Rosie the Riveter WWII Home Front National Historical Park, Richmond, CA.

14. "Denver War Mothers Join Sons in Fight for Victory," *RMN*, September 26, 1943.

15. "Modification Center Women's Counselor Pioneering in Work," *DP*, March 4, 1945.

16. "Bombers Given Radar Device at Denver Center," *DP*, March 20, 1945.

17. "Denver Modification Center Will Finish Its Work by September 1," *RMN*, July 8, 1945.

18. "Denver Modification Center's War Time Roles Are Revealed," *DP*, August 31, 1945.

19. Tucker Collection.

20. Virginia Wilson Horn, telephone interview by author, August 11, 2017.

21. "Props to Colorado Springs' Own 'Rosie the Riveter,'" www.peterson.af.mil/news, March 26, 2013.

22. Viola "Vonny" Strutzel O'Leary, interview by author, Lakewood, CO, June 9, 2017.

23. Manning, *A Time to Speak*, 232–233.

24. "Women Needed," *DP*, April 4, 1943.

25. Manning, *A Time to Speak,* 229.

26. Quoted in Manning, *A Time to Speak*, 230.

27. Quoted in Manning, *A Time to Speak*, 229–230; Turza Gene Briscoe Pflug obituary.

28. Quoted in Manning, *A Time to Speak*, 232.

29. Manning, *A Time to Speak*, 227–228.

30. Regis, *When Our Mothers Went to War*, 65.

31. Ruth Johnson Mullis, interview by author, October 13, 2014, Littleton, CO.

32. Mullis, interview.

33. Mullis, interview.

34. Laura Micheletti Puaca, *Searching for Scientific Womanpower: Technocratic Feminism and the Politics of National Security, 1940–1980* (Chapel Hill: University of North Carolina Press, 2014), 30.

35. Jean-Vi Lenthe, *Flying into Yesterday: My Search for the Curtiss-Wright Aeronautical Engineering Cadettes* (El Prado, NM: Wild Hare, 2011), 51.

36. Lenthe, *Flying into Yesterday*, 48–49.

37. Louise Fayram McClain, "Rosie the Riveter: World War II American Home Front Oral History Project," interview by Sam Redman, 2011, Oral History Center, Bancroft Library, University of California–Berkeley.

38. Lenthe, *Flying into Yesterday*, 53.

39. "Curtiss Cadettes Take Crash Course," Aerospace Engineering and Mechanics, University of Minnesota, http://www.umn.edu.

40. "Curtiss Cadettes Take Crash Course."

41. "Curtiss Cadettes Take Crash Course."

42. "Accepts Position with Curtiss-Wright Firm," *Julesburg Grit-Advocate*, February 18, 1943. This article (and her obituary in 2008) spelled her name as "Sara," while the documents at the University of Minnesota spelled her name "Sarah."

43. "War Training Programs: World War II, Curtiss-Wright Engineering Cadette Training Program, Volume A 1," 2–4, Aerospace Engineering and Mechanics, www.aem.umn.edu.

44. "War Training Programs," 49; Lenthe, *Flying into Yesterday*, 35, 173.

45. Lenthe, *Flying into Yesterday*, 54; "War Training Programs," 54.

46. "War Training Programs," 54. Two days after leaving Curtiss-Wright, Johnson married her first husband in Baltimore, MD. Four years later she married Henry Schoellhorn.

47. Thomas J. Noel and Kevin E. Rucker, *Eaton Metal Products: The First 80 Years—a Story of Vision and Commitment* (Denver: A. B. Hirschfield, 1998), 46.

48. "Projects—Shipbuilding c1942–1944," Series II, Box 2, ff13a, Midwest Steel and Iron Company Collection, Ph 00587, MSS 03096, History Colorado, Denver.

49. Byron Papers.

50. "World War II Shipbuilding in the San Francisco Bay Area," www.nps.gov/nr/travel/wwii bayarea/shipbuilding.htm.

51. "World War II Shipbuilding in the San Francisco Bay Area."

52. Byron Papers.

53. Byron Papers.

54. Noel and Rucker, *Eaton Metal Products*, 43.

55. "History of Midwest Steel and Iron Works, 1894–1969," Series I, Box 1, ff1, Midwest Steel and Iron Company Collection, Ph 00587, Mss 03096, History Colorado, Denver.

56. "Project—Shipbuilding Army and Navy 'E' Award."

57. "Coveted 'E' for Shipyards in the Rockies," *RMN*, April 26, 1943.

58. "Bouquets for One of Denver's Busiest Women," *RMN*, April 27, 1943.

59. Tom Lytle, "Shipbuilding on a 'Mountaintop': World War II's Rocky Mountain Fleet," *Colorado Heritage* (Summer 1998): 22.

60. "War Smashes Ahead on Pontoons Built Here," *RMN*, January 9, 1945.

61. Olson and McQuilkin quoted in Lytle, "Shipbuilding," 22.

62. Mullis, interview; Tucker Collection; Byron Papers; Manning, *A Time to Speak*, 231.

63. Margaret Amick, interview, Call number 2013.016.1000, August 6, 2013, Archives and Local History at Douglas County Libraries, Castle Rock, CO.

64. Quoted in Manning, *A Time to Speak*, 232–233.

65. Manning, *A Time to Speak*, 230–231.

66. Mullis, interview.

67. "Denver War Mothers Join Sons in Fight for Victory," *RMN*, September 26, 1943.

68. Quoted in Manning, *A Time To Speak*, 227–228.

69. McClain, interview.

70. "An army marches . . ." has been attributed to both Napoleon Bonaparte and Frederick the Great.

CHAPTER 9: OFFICE WORKERS AND OTHER
NON-INDUSTRIAL WORKERS

1. Frances Hale Currin, interview by author, September 16, 2016, Denver, CO.

2. Jeffries, *Wartime America*, 97.

3. "More Typists Needed to Speed War Effort Says Civil Service," *Alamosa Daily Courier*, April 11, 1942.

4. Moya Hansen, "Try Being a Black Woman!' Jobs in Denver, 1900–1970," in Taylor and Moore, eds., *African American Women Confront the West*, 212.

5. The Federal Council of Negro Affairs—the so-called Black Cabinet—served as an advisory board to the Roosevelt administration on issues facing Blacks in America. The group met regularly in Bethune's office or apartment.

6. Hansen, "Try Being a Black Woman," 218. After the war, Walker married George Rucker with whom she owned Rucker's Drug Store across from Whittier School. The school principal hired Mrs. Rucker as the first Black secretary of the Denver Public Schools. She earned bachelor's and master's degrees from the University of Denver before earning her doctorate in education at the University of Northern Colorado. Dr. Rucker was a founding faculty member at the Community College of Denver and the first librarian at the Pauline Robinson Branch Library. Gwen Ashbaugh, "The Widow's Mite: The Story of Dr. Jennie Rucker," *Colorado Heritage* (May–June 2010): 5, back cover.

7. Campbell, *Women at War with America*, 75.

8. Currin, interview.

9. Currin, interview.

10. Currin, interview.

11. Currin, interview.

12. Currin, interview.

13. Mundy, *Code Girls*, 27, 51–52.

14. Nancy Muir Thompson Tipton, interview by author, November 16, 2018, Centennial, CO. Although the army initially hired civilian women beginning in May 1942, it also utilized WAACs/WACs as code breakers.

15. Nancy Tipton, "Memoirs of a Cryptographer, 1944–1946," February 20, 2006, copy in author's possession.

16. Tipton, interview.

17. Tipton, interview.

18. Tipton, "Memoirs."

19. Tipton, "Memoirs." In 1947, Thompson married John K. (Jack) Tipton, a fourth-generation Coloradan who served with the 503rd Airborne in World War II. Her brother served as a Japanese code breaker during the war and received a Congressional Medal of Honor. Nancy was feted at a "Code Girl" reunion in March 2019 sponsored by the Library of Congress and Liza Mundy, author of the book *Code Girls*. Telephone conversation with Tipton, June 27, 2019.

20. "NYA Seeks Girls to Train as Typists," *Steamboat Pilot,* October 8, 1942. I was unable to ascertain how many young women from the northwest corner of the state signed up for the program, but the newspaper later published various articles listing women who were working at the plant. Dorothy Angle, Bertha Wanamaker, Thelma Horton, and Annabelle Brock were all reported to be at the plant after Pollard's recruiting visit. *Steamboat Pilot*, December 31, 1942; April 29, 1943; May 13, 1943; April 20, 1944.

21. "Clay Family Has Proud Service Record," *Steamboat Pilot*, March 18, 1943.

22. "Pin-Up Girl Former Oak Creek Resident," *Steamboat Pilot*, April 20, 1944.

23. Leota Broman Hettinger, interview by author, October 13, 2016, Lakewood, CO.

24. Charlene Grainger O'Leary, interview by author, May 23, 2017, Lafayette, CO. Charlene is the daughter of Roberta Grainger.

25. "Organization Charts and Personnel, 24 December 1942, 25 March 1943, 1 January 1944, May 1944," Box 1, Folder 7, Reports and Historical Narratives, 1940–1945; "Denver Ordnance Plant History Supplement III, 1 April 1944–30 September 1944"; "Report of Contract Termination," Box 1, Folder 1, Reports and Historical Narratives, 1940–1945, RG156.

26. "Shops Men Are Calm as Women 'Invade' Mill," *The Blast*, May 22, 1942.

27. Douglas Nelson, *Heart Mountain: The History of an American Concentration Camp* (Madison: University of Wisconsin Press, 1976), 10.

28. Robert Harvey, *Amache: The Story of Japanese Internment in Colorado during World War II* (Lanham, MD: Taylor Trade, 2003), 31–32.

29. Kara Mariko Miyagishima, "Colorado's *Nikkei* Pioneers: Japanese Americans in Twentieth Century Colorado," MA thesis, University of Colorado–Denver, 2007.

30. Abbott, Leonard, and Noel, *Colorado*, 306.

31. Beaton, *Colorado Women*, 33, 39–40.

32. Miyagishima, "Colorado's *Nikkei* Pioneers," 136.

33. Melyn Johnson, "At Home in Amache," *Colorado Heritage* (1989): 7.

34. Amache Collection, MSS 1269, Box 1, Folder 86, History Colorado, Denver.

35. "Amache Directory January 1943," Amache Collection, MSS 1269, Box 1, Folders 27, 29.

36. "Japanese See Their Evacuation as Part of America's War Effort," *Lamar Daily News*, September 19, 1942, in Amache Collection, MSS 1269, Box 1, Folder 27.

37. Amache Collection, MSS 1269, Box 1, Folders 26, 29.

38. "Masculine Traditions Totter—Denver Woman Gets He-Man Job," *DP*, April 9, 1942.

39. Beaton, *Colorado Women*, 192.

40. "Both Are at Battle Stations," *Center Post-Dispatch* (Center, CO), May 21, 1943.

41. Betty Lou Dale Summers, interview, OH0902, Maria Rogers Oral History Program, June 19, 1997, Boulder Carnegie Library for Local History, Boulder, CO.

42. Summers, interview.

43. Elizabeth "Bette" Gilbert Saunders, interview, Call number 1993.003, March 7, 1992, Archives and Local History at Douglas County Libraries, Castle Rock, CO.

44. Saunders, interview.

45. "Directing Air Traffic Keeps Denver Girl Busy," *RMN*, September 14, 1943.

46. "Personal View of Dorothy Hurd Chambers," Women in the Weather Bureau during World War II, *NOAA History: A Science Odyssey*, http://www.history.noaa.gov.

47. "Personal View of Dorothy Hurd Chambers."

48. "Personal View of G. Fay Dickerson," Women in the Weather Bureau during World War II, *NOAA History: A Science Odyssey*, http://www.history.noaa.gov.

49. "Personal View of G. Fay Dickerson."

50. "Personal View of G. Fay Dickerson."

51. Helen Morgan Harris, interview by author, July 31, 2017, Windsor, CO.

52. Harris, interview.

53. Elsie Virginia Mann Kinkel, interview, Call number 2014.034.1000, October 29, 2014, Archives and Local History at Douglas County Libraries, Castle Rock, CO.

54. Kinkel, interview.

55. Kinkel, interview.

56. Mary Ann Gallegos Ceminski, Rosie the Riveter World War II Homefront Oral History Project: An Oral History with Mary Ann Ceminski conducted by Esther Ehrlich, 2003, Regional Oral History Office, Bancroft Library, University of California, Berkeley, 2007.

57. McEuen, *Making War, Making Women*, 102–103, 107–108.

58. Currin, interview.

59. Currin, interview.

60. Currin, interview. Lucy Diggs Slowe, the first African American woman to win a national championship (in tennis) in any sport, made her mark as an educator. A graduate of Howard University, she was its first dean of women. She established a women's campus at Howard and helped organize and served as the first president of the National Association of College Women (NACW), an organization dedicated to raising the standards in colleges for Black women, developing women faculty, and securing scholarships.

61. Hettinger, interview.

62. O'Leary, interview.

63. Harris, interview.

64. Kinkel, interview.

65. Ceminski, interview.

CHAPTER 10: "FOOD FOR VICTORY": COLORADO FARMS, RANCHES, AND VICTORY GARDENS

1. Ann Enstrom Scott, interview by author, January 15, 2015, Windsor, CO.

2. Jacob J. Kaufman, "Farm Labor during World War II," *Journal of Farm Economics* (February 1949): 131.

3. Clark Secrest, "Vitamins for Victory," *Colorado Heritage* (1995): 26.

4. "U.S. Will Ask for Bigger Crops in Colorado," *DP*, October 12, 1941.

5. R. Douglas Hurt, *The Great Plains during World War II* (Lincoln: University of Nebraska Press, 2008), 169.

6. "Western Farmers Are Told to Solve Labor Problems," *DP*, May 21, 1942.

7. Cindy Hamilton, *Footprints in the Sugar: A History of the Great Western Sugar Company* (Ontario, OR: Hamilton Bates, 2009), 358.

8. "Harvest Complete," *Brush Tribune*, November 11, 1943.

9. Hurt, *Great Plains*, 308.

10. "Farmers Urged to Apply Early for Labor," *Brush Tribune*, January 28, 1943.

11. William Wei, "The Strangest City in Colorado: The Amache Concentration Camp," *Colorado Heritage* (Winter 2005): 11.

12. Wei, "Strangest City in Colorado."

13. Miyagishima, "Colorado's *Nikkei* Pioneers," 138.

14. Deborah Cohen, *Braceros: Migrant Citizens and Transnational Subjects in the Postwar United States and Mexico* (Chapel Hill: University of North Carolina Press, 2011), 22.

15. Cohen, *Braceros*, 30.

16. Cohen, *Braceros*, 30.

17. Cohen, *Braceros*, 115; Ana Elizabeth Rosas, *Abrazando el Espiritu: Bracero Families Confront the US-Mexico Border* (Oakland: University of California Press, 2014), 216.

18. "180 Farm-Deferred Morgan Youth to Report," *Brush Tribune*, January 1, 1944.

19. "What Fort Morgan Farmers Are Doing," *Brush Tribune*, February 17, 1944.

20. "State Asks for 10,000 Mexicans for Farms," *Eagle Valley Enterprise*, March 10, 1944. There are a number of studies of the bracero program. Most concentrate on the male workers; a few document the experiences of women and children left behind in Mexico as male relatives worked in the United States. For the latter, see Ana Elizabeth Rosas, "Breaking the Silence: Mexican Children and Women's Confrontation of Bracero Family Separation, 1942–1964," *Gender and History* 23, no. 2 (August 2011): 382–400; Rosas, *Abrazando el Espiritu*; Mayra Lizette Avila, "La Pena Negra: Mexican Women, Gender, and Labor during the Bracero Program, 1942–1964," PhD dissertation, University of Texas at El Paso, 2018. Unfortunately, none of these works discuss Mexican

women who entered the United States during World War II as an illegal component of the bracero program.

21. "Beet Growers Will Get $25,175,000," *Brush Tribune*, November 16, 1944.

22. "Farm Produce of Valley Hit All-Time High This Season," *Alamosa Daily Courier*, April 3, 1943; "County Potato Growers['] Best Season in History," *Brush Tribune*, November 16, 1944; "Most Successful Potato Year in History of San Luis Valley Drawing to a Close," *Alamosa Daily Courier*, April 4, 1944; "War Prisoners Help Harvest Big Spud Crop," *Saguache Crescent*, October 14, 1943.

23. "Canning Factory Contracting for Tomato Yield," *Daily Sentinel* (Grand Junction), March 2, 1942; "D&RG Estimates Bumper Valley Vegetable Crop in 1942," *Alamosa Daily Courier*, June 26, 1942.

24. "To Feed Fewer Lambs," *Brush Tribune*, October 14, 1943.

25. "Extension Service Places More than 8,000 Workers," *Record Journal of Douglas County* (Castle Rock, CO), July 23, 1943.

26. "Colorado Harvests One of Greatest Grain Crops," *DP*, September 5, 1943.

27. "Grand Junction Schools Will Open September 8; High School May Be Later; Announce New Instructors," *Daily Sentinel* (Grand Junction), August 12, 1942; "Opening Dates of Mesa County Schools Decided; Teacher Lists Near Completion," *Daily Sentinel*, September 3, 1944.

28. "On Food Line of Defense," *DP*, April 19, 1945.

29. "Farmers Being Trained to Fix Own Machines," *Alamosa Daily Courier*, March 6, 1944.

30. Cecilia Gowdy-Wygant, *Cultivating Victory: The Women's Land Army and the Victory Garden Movement* (Pittsburgh: University of Pittsburgh Press, 2013), 117.

31. Gowdy-Wygant, *Cultivating Victory*, 118.

32. Hurt, *Great Plains*, 362.

33. Stephanie A. Carpenter, *On the Farm Front: The Women's Land Army in World War II* (DeKalb: Northern Illinois University Press, 2003), 5.

34. "Women's Land Army Offers Help for Ranches in State," *Steamboat Pilot*, June 29, 1944.

35. Judy Barrett Litoff and David C. Smith, eds., *American Women in a World at War: Contemporary Accounts from World War II* (Wilmington, DE: Scholarly Resources, 2001), 208.

36. Litoff and Smith, *American Women in a World at War*, 206–207.

37. Hurt, *Great Plains*, 230.

38. "Women's Land Army Is Doing Big Job in State," *DP*, September 28, 1944.

39. Judy Barrett Litoff and David C. Smith, "To the Rescue: The Women's Land Army during World War II," *Prologue* 25, no. 4 (Winter 1993): 10.

40. "Gals Get in the Saddle as Cowboys Go to War," *Daily Sentinel* (Grand Junction), July 12, 1942.

41. "Gals Get in the Saddle."

42. "Women Assume New Responsibilities," *Palisade Tribune*, March 24, 1944.

43. "Beers Sisters," Littleton Historical Museum, Littleton, CO. The sisters retired in 1945.

44. "Women Profit by Raising Poultry," *Steamboat Pilot*, November 9, 1944.

45. Hurt, *Great Plains*, 229.

46. "NYA Canning to Start This Week," *Daily Sentinel* (Grand Junction), August 26, 1942; "Canning Plants of Valley Ready for Operations," *Daily Sentinel*, August 30, 1942; "Negotiate for 250 Mexican Nationals for Peach Harvest," *Daily Sentinel*, July 30, 1944.

47. "This Is War Work, Too!" *Palisade Tribune*, July 16, 1943.

48. "7 Out of 10 Peaches Go to Fighting Men," advertisement, *Daily Sentinel* (Grand Junction), August 20, 1944; "Your Help Will Be Needed," advertisement, *Daily Sentinel*, August 20, 1944; "Peak Tomato Canning Season in Valley Expected This Week; More Help Is Needed," *Daily Sentinel*, September 24, 1944.

49. Marles Humphrey, *Lilies of Our Valley: Stories of Routt County Women* (Steamboat Springs, CO: Michael James Publishing, 2006), 9.

50. Lewis Kemry Letter to Harriet Kemry, April 9, 1944, Eunice Kemry Dorr Collection, Tread of Pioneers Museum, Steamboat Springs, CO.

51. Harriet Kemry Aspegren, interview by Katie Adams, curator, Tread of Pioneers Museum, Steamboat Springs, CO, August 2007.

52. Lewis Kemry Letter to Harriet Kemry, November 1, 1944, Eunice Kemry Dorr Collection, Tread of Pioneers Museum, Steamboat Springs, CO.

53. "Farm Women Meet War Shortages with Ingenuity," *Steamboat Pilot*, June 8, 1944.

54. "Musings of a Farm Wife," *Brush Tribune*, June 17, 1943.

55. "Brush Woman Keeps Busy Caring for Dozen Jobs," *Brush Tribune*, August 10, 1944.

56. "Packers Need More Workers," *RMN*, January 14, 1945.

57. "Packers Need More Workers."

58. Jody Lopez and Gabriel Lopez, with Peggy A. Ford, *White Gold Laborers: The Story of Greeley's Spanish Colony* (Bloomington, IN: AuthorHouse, 2007), 66–67.

59. Scott, interview.

60. Gowdy-Wygant, *Cultivating Victory*, 135.

61. Gowdy-Wygant, *Cultivating Victory*, 136.

62. Faulkner, *Touching Tomorrow*, 97.

63. "Victory Garden School Will Start Monday Evening at Alamosa High School Building," *Alamosa Daily Courier*, March 3, 1943.

64. "Victory Garden Circular Ready," *Ledger News* (Antonito), May 5, 1944.

65. "Fruita Canning Center Open House Thursday," *Daily Sentinel* (Grand Junction), July 26, 1944; "Out-of-County People Patronize Canning Center More than Locals," *Daily Sentinel*, September 18, 1944.

66. "Your Victory Garden," *The Blast*, 1942–1945, Colorado Fuel & Iron, Pueblo.

67. Secrest, "Vitamins for Victory," 27.

68. Secrest, "Vitamins for Victory," 27.

69. Secrest, "Vitamins for Victory," 28.

70. Secrest, "Vitamins for Victory," 27.

CHAPTER 11: THE CADET NURSE CORPS

1. Jay Alire, interview by author, April 8, 2019, Lakewood, CO. Mother Cabrini opened the orphanage in 1904. It closed in 1969.

2. Heather Willever, "The Cadet Nurse Corps, 1943–1948," *PHS* [Public Health Service] *Chronicles* 109, no. 3 (May–June 1994): 455–457.

3. Thelma Morey Robinson and Pauline M. Perry, *Cadet Nurse Stories: The Call for and Response of Women during World War II* (Indianapolis: Center Nursing Press, 2001), 2007; Thelma Morey Robinson, telephone conversation with author, August 21, 2018.

4. Thelma Morey Robinson, interview by author, May 27, 2015, Boulder, CO.

5. Robinson, interview; Robinson and Perry, *Cadet Nurse Stories*, 5.

6. Robinson and Perry, *Cadet Nurse Stories*, 37. The US population in 1940 was over 132 million.

7. "Wanted: 125,000 Student Nurses," *Del Norte Prospector*, September 1, 1944.

8. Manning, *A Time to Speak*, 237. Based on a book written by Juanita Hipps, one of the "Angels of Bataan" who was rescued before the other nurses were captured by the Japanese, the movie infuriated nurses because of its inaccurate portrayal of their work and lives in the Philippines. Hipp tried to convince director and producer Mark Sandrich to more faithfully follow her book, but he did not. Hipp was reviled by her sister nurses for her part in the story.

9. Quoted in Robinson and Perry, *Cadet Nurse Stories*, 72.

10. Robinson and Perry, *Cadet Nurse Stories*, 70.

11. Robinson, interview.

12. Robinson and Perry, *Cadet Nurse Stories*, 73; Morrison, interview.

13. Robinson, interview; Thelma Morey Robinson, telephone conversation with author, August 21, 2018.

14. Dorothy Bowen Kennedy, interview by author, June 15, 2017, Lakewood, CO.

15. Kennedy, interview.

16. Robinson and Perry, *Cadet Nurse Stories*, 49–50.

17. Robinson and Perry, *Cadet Nurse Stories*, 95–96.

18. Diane B. Hamilton, *Becoming a Presence within Nursing: The History of the University of Colorado School of Nursing, 1898–1998* (Denver: University of Colorado School of Nursing, 1999), 56–57.

19. Thelma Morey Robinson, *Nisei Cadet Nurse of World War II: Patriotism in Spite of Prejudice* (Boulder: Black Swan Mill, 2005), 114.

20. Robinson, *Nisei Cadet Nurse,* 50–53.

21. Robinson, *Nisei Cadet Nurse*, 101–102.

22. Robinson, *Nisei Cadet Nurse*, 100–103.

23. Robinson, *Nisei Cadet Nurse*, 20–22.

24. Moore, *Serving Our Country*, 143.

25. Robinson, *Nisei Cadet Nurse*, 12–14.

26. Robinson, *Nisei Cadet Nurse*, 148–152.

27. Robinson, interview.

28. "Bonnie June Smith Newitt," www.uscadetnurse.org.

29. Mable Evelyn Kitsmiller Hubert, Bonnie June Hewitt, and Margaret Kathryn Featherstone McDuff obituaries at uscadetnursecorps.org and *U.S. World War II Cadet Nursing Corps Card File, 1942–1948*, Box 174, Cadet Nursing Corps Files, compiled 1943–1948, documenting the period 1942–1948, National Archives and Records Administration, Washington, DC; Dorothy A. Zabrusky obituary, *Gazette-Telegraph* (Colorado Springs), February 5, 2014; Mabel Alvina "Peggy" Meyer Bishop obituary, *U.S. Find a Grave Index, 1600s–Current*, Ancestry.com.

30. Sylvia Pettem, "Boulder History: Gahm Sisters Served Their Country during WWII," *Boulder Daily Camera*, May 24, 2012; Robinson and Perry, *Cadet Nurse Stories*, 35.

31. Quoted in Robinson and Perry, *Cadet Nurse Stories*, 170.

32. http://cadetnurse.com/Welcome.html.

33. Thelma Morey Robinson, *Cadet Nurse Corps: Your Country Needs You* (Bloomington, IN: XLibris, 2009), 234–235.

34. "Estelle Dracon," *U.S., World War II Cadet Nursing Corps Card File, 1942–1948; Denver City Directory* (The Gazetteer Company, Denver: 1964, 1970).

35. "Sister Pauline Apodaca Focused on Welfare of Migrant Workers," *RMN*, June 17, 2000; "Nun Helped Improve Migrants' Lives," *Cincinnati Enquirer*, June 18, 2000.

CHAPTER 12: THE AMERICAN RED CROSS

1. Eva Christensen, "Doughnut Girl," *Ladies Home Journal* (September 1944): 166.

2. "Boulder Women during 1942 Give All-Out Cooperation to War Effort," *Boulder Daily Camera*, January 9, 1943. The article points out that Boulder women's work for the Red Cross had started before the attack on Pearl Harbor.

3. "Report of the Chairman Conejos County Red Cross," *La Jara Gazette*, December 25, 1941.

4. "World War II and the American Red Cross," RedCross.org.

5. "Former Sedgwick Girl Is Recreation Worker," *Julesburg Grit-Advocate*, May 18, 1943; June 21, 1945; August 9, 1945.

6. "Denver Woman Serves Negro Troops in Britain," *RMN*, January 1, 1943.

7. Jeannette McGrath Albersheim, interview, Call number 2012.012.1000, March 2, 2012, Archives and Local History at Douglas County Libraries, Castle Rock, CO; "Red Cross at War," Jeannette Albersheim Blog, 2011, www.blogs.va.gov.

8. Albersheim, interview.

9. Albersheim, interview.

10. Albersheim, interview.

11. Albersheim, interview.

12. Albersheim, interview.

13. Albersheim, interview.

14. Albersheim, interview.

15. Albersheim, interview.

16. Albersheim, interview.

17. Albersheim, interview.

18. Yellin, *Our Mothers' War*, 178.

19. "World War II and the American Red Cross," RedCross.org.

20. "Newsettes," *Brush Tribune*, June 8, 1944; Christensen, "Doughnut Girl," 4–5, 166.

21. Christensen, "Doughnut Girl," 4.

22. Christensen, "Doughnut Girl," 5.

23. Eva Christensen did not give last names for her instructor or her co-workers in her article for the *Ladies Home Journal*.

24. Christensen, "Doughnut Girl," 4.

25. Christensen, "Doughnut Girl," 5.

26. Christensen, "Doughnut Girl," 4.

27. Christensen, "Doughnut Girl," 4, 166.

28. Christensen, "Doughnut Girl," 166.

29. Christensen, "Doughnut Girl," 166.

30. "Going Places," *Brush Tribune*, June 29, 1944.

31. Quoted in Yellin, *Our Mothers' War*, 178–179.

32. McCaffrey, interview.

33. "Something New about the Red Cross," *Camp Hale Ski-Zette*, November 5, 1943.

34. "Red Cross Annual Report," *Brush Tribune*, May 4, 1944.

35. Ellen Kingman Fisher, *Junior League of Denver* (Denver: Colorado Historical Society, 1993), 80.

36. "World War II and the American Red Cross," 15, www.redcross.org.

37. "Minutes, 1940–1946," Box LWC-3, 81, Livermore Woman's Club Collection, the Archive at the Fort Collins Museum of Discovery, Fort Collins, CO.

38. "Brush Joins in Blood Service," *Brush Tribune*, April 1, 1943.

39. "Blood Plasma to Save Wounded Is Big Red Cross Move," *Aspen Daily Times*, January 7, 1943; "Oak Creek Woman Gives Blood Four Times," *Oak Creek Times*, September 30, 1943; no heading, *Steamboat Pilot*, January 13, 1944; "Woman's Club Has First Meeting," *Steamboat Pilot*, September 16, 1943; "Red Cross Sponsors Blood Donor Program," *Eagle Valley Enterprise*, March 10, 1944.

40. "Red Cross Sponsors Blood Donor Program."

41. "Louisville Has 44 Regular Donors," *Louisville Times*, July 22, 1943.

42. "Time to Prepare for Visit of Blood Bank," *Colorado Transcript* (Golden), August 3, 1944; "Pueblo's No. One Blood Donor Mother of Three in Marines," *PC*, July 23, 1943.

43. "Steel Women Aid Red Cross," *The Blast*, October 2, 1942.

44. "Victory Book Campaign Will Start January 12," *Craig Empire Courier*, January 7, 1942; "Maybell," *Craig Empire Courier*, February 11, 1942.

45. Fisher, *Junior League*, 24.

46. "World War II and the Red Cross," RedCross.org.

47. "Canteen Corps Report by Anne Cheney Merrill, Chairman," Ruth Banning Lewis Papers, [1906]–1953, Box 4, Folder 16, "Volunteer Nurse's Aide Corps, Letterbook 2-R, 1943," PPLD.

48. "Wrenches, Hammers, and Coveralls," *Boulder Daily Camera*, April 24, 1942.

49. Lewis Papers, [1906]–1953, Box 4, Folder 1, "Volunteer Nurse's Aide Corps, Letterbook 1-N-O, 1942–1943," and Folder 16, "Volunteer Nurse's Aide Corps, Letterbook 2-R, 1943."

50. "World War II and the American Red Cross," 13, redcross.org.

51. Lewis Papers, [1906]–1953, Box 4, Folder 16.

52. "Work Finished for Red Cross in Display," *Craig Empire Courier*, January 7, 1942.

53. "North Side Woman's Club Yearbooks, 1942–1943," Western History Collection, Denver Public Library, Denver, CO.

54. Lucile Kling, "History of the Twenty-second Avenue Study Club, 1943–1944," MS 965, History Colorado, Denver.

55. "Woman's Club Opens Commodity Exchange and Bandage Center," *DP*, August 9, 1942.

56. "Work Finished for Red Cross in Display," *Craig Empire Courier*, January 7, 1942.

57. "Local Red Cross Production Immense According to Report Given to Kiwanians," *Center Post-Dispatch*, March 12, 1943.

58. "Red Cross at Work Here," *Daily Sentinel* (Grand Junction), January 11, 1942; "Need Volunteers for Evening Work at Gauze Room," *Daily Sentinel*, September 11, 1942.

59. "Steel Women Aid Red Cross," *The Blast*, October 2, 1942.

60. "Maybell," *Craig Empire Courier*, February 11, 1942; "Saguache County's Red Cross War Fund Drive Gets More than Quota," *Center Post-Dispatch*, April 16, 1943.

61. Cheryl Dong, "Red Cross Volunteer Nurse's Aide Corps," in Lisa Tendrich Frank, ed., *An Encyclopedia of American Women at War: From the Home Front to the Battlefields,* vol. 2: *M–Z* (Santa Barbara, CA: ABC-CLIO, 2013), 463.

62. "Nurses Aid[e] to Train April 1," *Brush Tribune*, March 18, 1943.

63. Lewis Papers, [1906]–1953, Box 3, Folder 15, "Volunteer Nurse's Aide Corps, Letterbook 1-E, 1942 and undated."

64. Bernice Broadstreet, interview by author, September 5, 2017, Denver, CO.

65. Lewis Papers, [1906]–1953, Box 4, Folder 16, "Volunteer Nurse's Aide Corps, Letterbook 1-F, 1941–1942 and undated."

66. "Women on the Home Front: Mrs. W. C. Satterfield," *RMN*, January 3, 1945.

67. "Mrs. Johnie Herrick Is Head Nurse's Aide," *RMN*, August 30, 1943.

68. Letter from May Wilkins to her mother, March 25, 1944, May Wilkins Collection, Box 4, Folder 53, the Archive at Fort Collins Museum of Discovery, Fort Collins, CO.

69. Letter from May Wilkins to her mother, May 5, 1944, Wilkins Collection.

70. Clark Secrest, "The Day Clara May Morse Died: Pearl Harbor and One Mother's Heartbreak," *Colorado Heritage* (Autumn 1991): 36–44.

71. "Night Class of Red Cross Nurses Aides Given Certificates," *Alamosa Daily Courier*, June 1, 1944.

72. "Work of the Red Cross in Colorado," *Eagle Valley Enterprise*, March 9, 1945.

CHAPTER 13: "WE ALL CONTRIBUTED"

1. Scott, interview.

2. "Woman Donated Hair for War Effort," *Gazette Telegraph* (Colorado Springs), June 8, 1987; "Hair Triggered Development of Bombsight—Pueblo Woman Cut Her Long Locks for War,"

Gazette Telegraph, November 18, 1990. Sometime after 1944, Babnik married Carl Brown. She worked at the National Broom Factory for forty-two years. In 1947, she became the first female vice president of the State Federation of Labor. In 1987, Brown finally found out why the government wanted her long tresses. The army air force had tried different materials for the crosshairs of the Norden bombsight. Used in the B-24 Liberator, the B-29 Superfortress, and the B-17 Flying Fortress, the Norden bombsight was so secret that crews were ordered to destroy it if their bomber ran the risk of falling into enemy hands. At altitudes as high as 20,000 feet, crosshairs were subjected to freezing temperatures and rapid changes in humidity. Black widow spider webs were tried originally but were too fragile and scarce. In 1990, Babnik was honored with a special achievement award from the Colorado Aviation Historical Society. "Two Puebloans Earn Colorado Aviation Hall of Fame," *PC*, November 11, 1990.

3. "Applicants for Canning Sugar Swamp Rocky Ford Ration Force," *PC*, May 21, 1942.

4. Scott, interview. By 1960, the almond toffee that Chet Enstrom and his wife, Vernie, made for family and friends was so popular that they founded Enstrom Candies.

5. Letter from May Wilkins to Don Wilkins, October 17, 1942, Box 3, Folder 51, Wilkins Collection.

6. "Mrs. Frank Schmidt Winner in Canning Contest in M.V.," *Alamosa Daily Courier*, August 24, 1944.

7. "Here's the Dope on New Ration Tokens," *Brush Tribune*, February 24, 1944.

8. Tipton, interview.

9. "The Kitchen in War Production," Public Affairs Pamphlet no. 82, 1943, Box 255, Folder 6, Paddock Collection.

10. "Friday Is the Big Day for Courier's Cooking School," *Alamosa Daily Courier*, April 6, 1942; "Nearly 500 Women Enjoyed Second Cooking Class," *Alamosa Daily Courier*, April 11, 1942.

11. Letter from J. M. Lloyd, MD, to May Wilkins, October 27, 1943, Box 5, Folder 63, Wilkins Collection.

12. Letter from Don Wilkins to May Wilkins, November 12, 1943, Box 3, Folder 51, Wilkins Collection.

13. Bette Krim Kamlet, interview by author, June 7, 2016, Denver, CO.

14. "Scrapbook, 1936–1967," Sunrise Club Collection, Fort Sedgwick Historical Society, Julesburg, CO.

15. Hurban Papers.

16. Silent Wings Museum, Lubbock, TX.

17. Weatherford, *American Women during World War II*, 99.

18. "How to Paint That Seam Straight," *Daily Sentinel* (Grand Junction), August 17, 1942.

19. Letter from May Wilkins to Don Wilkins, October 17, 1942, Box 7, Folder 90, Wilkins Collection.

20. "How to Get the Most From Your Rayon Stockings," *Julesburg Grit-Advocate*, February 4, 1943.

21. McEuen, *Making War, Making Women*, 171.

22. Lewis, *Women at War*, 52.

23. "Every Housewife to Be Given List of Needed Scrap Items," *DP*, September 20, 1942.

24. "Old Cannon from Delta Park Goes into Scrap Pile," *Daily Sentinel* (Grand Junction), October 2, 1942.

25. Marie Moyer and Dolores Nelson, "War Effort Came from Smallest of Schools," in Bud Wells, ed., *Logan County, Better by 100 Years: A Centennial History of Logan County, Colorado, 1887–1987* (Raleigh, NC: Curtis Media, 1982), 114.

26. Moyer and Nelson, "War Effort," 114.

27. "Estimated 100 Tons [of] Scrap Iron Were Collected," *Center Post-Dispatch*, November 26, 1943.

28. "Silverton Kids Collect 100 Tons of Scrap," *Aspen Daily Times*, July 9, 1942; "News of Our Neighbors," *Steamboat Pilot*, March 19, 1942.

29. "Scrap Metal Drive Will Be Benefited by Softball Games," *Julesburg Grit-Advocate*, July 23, 1942; "Softball Fans Give Scrap Iron," *Julesburg Grit-Advocate*, July 30, 1942.

30. "Every Housewife to Be Given List of Needed Scrap Items."

31. "Every Housewife to Be Given List of Needed Scrap Items."

32. "Tons of Paper Uncollected in Spite of Monthly Donations," *Alamosa Daily Courier*, June 1, 1944.

33. Office of War Information Press Release, July 10, 1942, "World War II: Office of War Information, War Production Board, Press Releases, 1942," Box 255, Folder 4, Paddock Collection.

34. Weatherford, *American Women during World War II*, 99.

35. "Waste Fats Make Munitions and Medicine; Need 200 Million Pounds a Year," *Alamosa Daily Courier*, November 18, 1943; "Scrapbook, 1936–1967," Sunrise Club Collection.

36. Quoted in Julia Brock, Jennifer W. Dickey, Richard J.W. Harker, and Catherine M. Lewis, *Beyond Rosie: A Documentary History of Women and World War II* (Fayetteville: University of Arkansas Press, 2015), 170.

37. "1941—Home Front—1945," Poster. Author's collection.

38. Regis, *When Our Mothers Went to War*, 47.

39. Regis, *When Our Mothers Went to War*, 47.

40. "A Plaque for Perfection," *The Blast*, August 7, 1942; "This County Reaches 87 Percent of Bond Drive Quota," *Monte Vista Journal*, February 4, 1944; "Helping the Sixth," *The Blast*, December 1, 1944.

41. "Woman's War Savings Club Is Organized in Brush," *Brush Tribune*, December 3, 1942.

42. "Adams State Coeds Go All Out for Victory: To Wear Defense Stamps Instead of Posies," *Alamosa Daily Courier*, January 17, 1942; Scott, interview. I would like to thank Ann for first telling me about the warsages, as I had not come across them before in any research or interviews.

43. "Defense Stamps Used for Table Decorations," *Monte Vista Journal*, February 2, 1944.

44. "$1,700,010,085 in War Bonds Sold or Purchased by CFWC Members," *Boulder Daily Camera*, March 44, 1944; Jeanette Bain, *History and Chronology of the Colorado State Federation of Women's Clubs, 1895–1955* (Denver: Colorado Federation of Women's Clubs, 1955), 81–82.

45. "Incendiary Bombs Are on Display," *Julesburg Grit-Advocate*, September 9, 1943; "Mt. Harris," *Steamboat Pilot*, September 9, 1943.

46. "To the People of Sedgwick County: Our Quota in the 7th War Loan Is $225,000.00," *Julesburg Grit-Advocate*, May 10, 1945; "506 Reasons Why You Should Buy War Bonds Today," *Julesburg Grit-Advocate*, November 23, 1944.

47. "Babe Didrikson Zaharias to Compete in War Bond Match at Lakewood June 3," *RMN*, May 20, 1945; "Babe Zaharias to Feature War Bond Golf Match Today," *RMN*, June 3, 1945; "Babe Zaharias and Doering Beat Jelliffe and Ott, 2–1," *RMN*, June 4, 1945.

48. Randall C. Teeuwen, *Growing Up Gates: A Family History* (Greenwoood Village, CO: Bear Creek, 2002), 159.

49. "Speaker to Tell of Pearl Harbor," *Julesburg Grit-Advocate*, June 18, 1942; "Pearl Harbor Talk Thrills Audience," *Julesbug Grit-Advocate*, July 2, 1942.

50. Cervi and Peterson, *Women Who Made the Headlines*, 49–50.

51. Plested, *Some Reminiscences along the Way*, 109.

52. Cervi and Peterson, *Women Who Made the Headlines*, 49–50, 56.

53. Fisher, *Junior League of Denver*, 24–25, 30.

54. "Minutes 1940–1946," Livermore Woman's Club Collection.

55. Jessie Cozens Shellabarger Postcard to Mrs. Mosley, John W. Mosley Papers, MSS-ARL 6, Boxes 1 and 2, Blair-Caldwell Research Library, Denver, CO. John Mosley, the first African

American to play football in the defunct Big Seven Conference, continued to serve his country as a civilian employee of the US Department of Health and Human Services. In 1945 John married Edna Wilson. Edna Mosley, a civil rights activist, worked for the Colorado Civil Rights Commission and as the state affirmative action director. She was also a founding member of the Women's Bank and the first African American city council member in Aurora.

56. "Cozens Family." www.littletongov.org.

57. *Yearbook of the Woman's Club of Denver, 1942–1943*, Yearbooks of the Woman's Club of Denver, 1895–1943, Western History Collection, Denver Public Library, Denver, CO.

58. "Woman's Club Building Will Be Used for Soldiers' Center: WPA Contributes $15,000 for Improvements," *DP*, August 28, 1941.

59. Lucile Kling, "History of the Twenty-second Avenue Study Club, 1944-45"; Dorothy W. Fallon, "History of the Twenty-second Avenue Study Club, 1945-1946," MSS 965, History Colorado, Denver.

60. Zimmie Rupp, interview by author, October 15, 1986, Denver, CO.

61. "Denver Federation of Colored Women's Clubs," MSS 340, Box 9, Item 10, History Colorado, Denver.

62. "Sailors Find Haven in Denver," *RMN*, January 7, 1945; "Service Club for Enlisted Men of Local Motor Transport School Furnished by Business and Professional Women's Club," *Daily Sentinel* (Grand Junction), September 29, 1942.

63. "Service Men to Be Guests at Party Next Saturday," *Daily Sentinel* (Grand Junction), November 8, 1942; "Want to Invite a Soldier to Sunday Dinner?" *Daily Sentinel*, October 21, 1942.

64. Judy Barrett Litoff and David C. Smith, eds., *American Women in a World at War: Contemporary Accounts from World War II* (Wilmington, DE: Scholarly Resources, 2001), 98.

65. Winchell, *Good Girls, Good Food, Good Fun*, 2.

66. Winchell, *Good Girls, Good Food, Good Fun*, 3.

67. Winchell, *Good Girls, Good Food, Good Fun*, 12, 48–49.

68. "Servicemen at Cat Creek Camp Guests Here at USO Dance," *Alamosa Daily Courier*, October 16, 1943.

69. Winchell, *Good Girl, Good Food, Good Fun*, 78, 110.

70. "Clark Again Makes Success of Drive," *Steamboat Pilot*, September 24, 1942; "Aspen Women Praised for USO Donations," *Aspen Daily Times*, March 2, 1944; "The USO 'Home Away from Home' in Pueblo," *PC*, February 2, 1944.

71. Hettinger, interview; Winchell, *Good Girls, Good Food, Good Fun*, 70.

72. Hurban Papers.

73. Hettinger, interview.

74. Joan Reese, "Two Enemies to Fight: Blacks Battle for Equality in Two World Wars," *Colorado Heritage* (1990): 13.

75. "The Service Men's Center," *Denver Star*, June 14, 1944.

76. Kathleen F. Esmiol, "Chasing the American Dream: Fannie Mae Duncan and the Cotton Club" in Ted Blevins et al., eds., *Enterprise and Innovation in the Pikes Peak Region* (Colorado Springs: Clausen Books, 2011), 305–306.

77. Winchell, *Good Girls, Good Food, Good Fun*, 60–62.

78. "Tea Is Held by Mrs. Reed," *RMN*, April 29, 1943.

79. Scott, interview.

80. Bob Greene, *Once upon a Town: The Miracle of the North Platte Canteen* (New York: William Morrow/John Deadline Enterprises, 2002). The North Platte Canteen operated until 1973 when passenger train service through North Platte was terminated.

81. "Julesburg Community Will Serve North Platte Canteen Nov. 19," *Julesburg Grit-Advocate*, November 4, 1943; "Minutes, 1945," Sunrise Club Collection.

82. Lee Kizer, interview by author, October 12, 2017, Julesburg, CO. Lee confessed that he and his friend Jerry Brown helped themselves to a sandwich or two on the ride.

83. "Julesburg Community Will Serve North Platte Canteen Nov. 19"; "Julesburg Day at North Platte a Great Success," *Julesburg Grit-Advocate*, November 25, 1943.

84. "Julesburg Day at North Platte a Great Success."

85. "Minutes, 1945," Sunrise Club Collection.

86. Sherrie Tucker, *Swing Shift: "All Girl" Bands of the 1940s* (Durham, NC: Duke University Press, 2000), 48–49, 65.

87. Tucker, *Swing Shift*, 65.

88. "All-Girl Band Brought Swing to WWII Troops," *DP*, May 23, 2015.

89. "All-Girl Band Brought Swing to WWII Troops."

90. Quoted in Tucker, *Swing Shift*, 49.

91. Quoted in Tucker, *Swing Shift*, 58–59.

92. Quoted in Tucker, *Swing Shift*, 68.

93. Tucker, *Swing Shift*, 61.

94. Tucker, *Swing Shift*, 66–67.

95. "All-Girl Band Brought Swing to WWII Troops"; Joy Cayler Obituary, *DP*, September 24, 2014.

96. Tucker, *Swing Shift*, 247.

97. Tucker, *Swing Shift*, 64.

98. Yellin, *Our Mothers' War*, 75–76.

CONCLUSION

1. Holm, *In Defense of a Nation*, 143. Major General (USAF Ret'd) Holm states that the number is close to 400,000, while the National World War II Museum in New Orleans places the number serving in the US military at 358,074 women.

2. American women served as stewardesses aboard United States Merchant Marine ships prior to World War II. After December 7, 1941, they were required to quit their jobs as soon as their ships reported to port. www.USMM.org.

3. Cott, *No Small Courage*, 486.

4. Donna B. Knaff, *Beyond Rosie the Riveter: Women of World War II in American Popular Graphic Art* (Lawrence: University Press of Kansas, 2012), 148.

5. Alice Kessler-Harris, *Out to Work: A History of Wage-Earning Women in the United States* (New York: Oxford University Press, 2003), 299.

6. Campbell, *Women at War with America*, 104.

7. Campbell, *Women at War with America*, 108.

8. Winchell, *Good Girls, Good Food, Good Fun*, 15.

9. Holm, *In Defense of a Nation*, 148.

10. Meyer, *Creating GI Jane*, 182.

11. Holm, *In Defense of a Nation*, 149.

12. Kessler-Harris, *Out to Work*, 286.

13. Chafe, *American Woman*, 138.

14. Margaret Randolph Higonnet and Patricia L.-R. Higonnet, "The Double Helix," in Higonnet et al., *Behind the Lines*, 35–36.

15. Milkman, *Gender at Work*, table 3.

16. Abbott, Leonard, and Noel, *Colorado*, 299.

17. Abbott, Leonard, and Noel, *Colorado*, 318.

18. Geospatial and Statistical Data Center, http://fisher.lib.virginia.edu.

19. Cott, *No Small Courage*, 493.

20. Cott, *No Small Courage*, 494.

21. US Department of Commerce, Bureau of the Census, *A Statistical Abstract of the United States 1950* (Washington, DC: US Government Printing Office, 1950).

22. *Statistical Abstract of the United States 1950*.

23. Jonathan, Mitchell, and Schechter, *The Homefront*, 239.

24. *Statistical Abstract of the United States 1950*.

25. Joan W. Scott, "Rewriting History," in Higonnet et al., *Behind the Lines*, 25; Kessler-Harris, *Out to Work*, 299.

26. Chafe, *American Women*, 188; Milkman, *Gender at Work*, 99.

27. William Chafe asserted that "within the existing set of values, the economic role of women had been dramatically and permanently transformed." Chafe, *American Woman*, 194. Ruth Milkman, acknowledging that individual women faced conflicting pressures in the postwar years, echoed him when she declared that the war "was a watershed period that left women's relationship to work permanently changed." Milkman, *Gender at Work*, 100.

28. Campbell, *Women at War*, 236.

29. Kessler-Harris, *Out to Work*, 299.

30. Louise Fayram McClain interview, "Rosie the Riveter: World War II American Home Front Oral History Project," conducted by Sam Redman in 2011, University of California–Berkeley, 2012.

31. Campbell, *Women at War*, 97–98, 104, 236.

32. D'Ann Campbell quoted in Anne Bosanko Green, *One Woman's War: Letters Home from the Women's Army Corps, 1944–1946* (St. Paul: Minnesota Historical Society Press, 1989), xi; Jonathan, Mitchell, and Schechter, *The Homefront*, 266; Knaff, *Beyond Rosie the Riveter*, 7; Tawnya J. Adkins, *Manipulating Images: World War II Mobilization of Women through Magazine Advertising* (Lanham, MD: Lexington Books, 2011), 151.

33. Willenz, *Women Veterans*, 47.

34. Since we met in 2014, I have had many conversations with Leila Morrison and have also heard her speak to groups a number of times. But it was not until her daughter sent me a particular photograph that I knew Leila had been injured during the war when the vehicle in which she was riding overturned. Her driver died. When I asked her about it and why she had not mentioned the incident before, her simple answer was that she did not want to dwell on the bad. The war had been tragic enough at the time. She preferred to concentrate on American fortitude, heroism, stoicism, and effort.

35. Holm, *In Defense of a Nation*, 146.

36. Holm, *In Defense of a Nation*, 1.

37. David E. Kyvig, "Historical Misunderstandings and the Defeat of the Equal Rights Amendment," *Public Historian* 18, no. 1 (Winter 1996): 51, 62.

38. Lizabeth Cohen, *A Consumer's Republic: The Politics of Mass Consumption in Postwar America* (New York: Vintage Books, 2003), 138, 166.

39. Willenz, *Women Veterans*, 50. Willenz is the former executive director of the American Veterans Committee.

40. Michael C.C. Adams, *The Best War Ever: America and World War II* (Baltimore: Johns Hopkins University Press, 1994), 11.

41. Cohen, *Consumer's Republic*, 138–139. Over 7 million eligible veterans took advantage of the education benefits of the GI Bill. During World War II, with so many men in the military or working in defense plants, women had enjoyed a larger role in campus affairs. In a cruel twist of fate, college enrollment of male veterans shoved women applicants to the back of the pack. Their overwhelming presence on campuses also pushed women away from college leadership positions with campus newspapers and governance bodies they had held during the war.

42. Morrison, interview.

43. Campbell, *Women at War*, 104.

44. "Woman Made Revolutionary WWII Flights," *DP*, May 29, 2017.

45. "WASP Final Flight—WASP Doris Bristol Tracy," http://waspfinalflight; Julie Tracy Geiser, interview with author, November 11, 2016, Denver, CO.

46. "Recognition Finally Arriving for Millicent Young, Other Women Pilots in WWII WASP Program," January 7, 2015, westsidepioneer.com.

47. Grace "Betty" Ashwell Lotowycz, interview by author, September 24, 2015, Louisville, CO.

48. Elizabeth Haas Pfister obituary, *Aspen Times*, November 22, 2011.

49. "Ann Brothers Frink," http://www.coloradoaviationhistoricalsociety.org.

50. "Betty J. Clark" and "Patricia J. Sullivan," http://www.coloradoaviationhistoricalsociety.org.

51. Campbell, *Women at War*, 71.

52. Winchell, *Good Girls, Good Food, Good Fun*, 103.

53. Jeffries, *Wartime America*, 106.

54. Sherna Berger Gluck, *Rosie the Riveter Revisited: Women, the War, and Social Change* (Boston: Twayne, 1987), 270.

55. Beth Bailey, *Sex in the Heartland* (Cambridge, MA: Harvard University Press, 1999), 16.

56. Currin, interview. Frances Hale married Windsor Marcellus Currin in 1950.

57. Ashbaugh, "The Widow's Mite," inside back cover. Jennie Walker married George Rucker after the war.

58. Crain Papers.

59. See Megan Taylor Shockley, *"We, Too, Are Americans": African American Women in Detroit and Richmond, 1940–54* (Urbana: University of Illinois Press, 2004).

60. Meeks Collection; Manning, *A Time to Speak*, 247; Kirkwood Collection; Brenda L. Moore, *Serving Our Country: Japanese American Women in the Military during World War II* (New Brunswick, NJ: Rutgers University Press, 2003), 96–97.

61. Brennan, interview.

62. Quote from anonymous woman war worker at Rosie the Riveter Memorial Park, Rosie the Riveter World War II Home Front National Historic Park, National Park Service, Richmond, CA. The principal component of the memorial is a walkway inscribed with a time line about the home front and quotes from women workers sandblasted into white granite.

Sources

PRIMARY SOURCES

Adams State University, Nielsen Library, Alamosa, CO
    Alamosa Daily Courier
    Center Post-Dispatch
    Costilla County Free Press
    Del Norte Prospector
    La Jara Gazette
    Ledger News (Antonito)
    Monte Vista Journal
    Saguache Crescent
    San Luis News
The Archive at Fort Collins Museum of Discovery, Fort Collins, CO
    Margaret Gates Gravdahl interview
    Natalie O'Brien Jones interview
    Livermore Woman's Club Collection
    Virginia Moore interview
    Martha Scott Trimble Collection
    May Wilkins Collection
    Althea Williams interview

Archives and Local History at Douglas County Libraries, Castle Rock, CO
    Jeanette McGrath Albersheim, Call number 2012.012.1000
    Margaret Amick, Call number 2013.016.1000
    Alice Trott Baker, Call number 2008.028.1000
    Kathryn Chittenden Haines, Call number 2010.007.1000
    Elsie Virginia Mann Kinkel, Call number 2014.034.1000
    Lille Steinmetz Magette, Call number 2005.216.1000
    Elizabeth "Bette" Saunders, Call number 1993.003
    Virginia Hudson Schmidt, Call number 2007.027.1000
    Jeanne A. Wells, Call number 2005.208.1000
Author's Interviews
    Jay Alire (nephew of Pauline Apodaca)
    Elaine Watkins Brennan
    Bernice Broadstreet
    Maureen Christopher (daughter of Jackie Jacquet Melvin)
    Lorelei Cloud (granddaughter of Sunshine Cloud Smith)
    Frances Hale Currin
    Edna Guise Doyle
    Julie Tracy Geiser (daughter of Doris Bristol Tracy)
    Helen Morgan Harris
    Leota Broman Hettinger
    Virginia Wilson Horn
    Julie Jensen (daughter of Omilio Halder Jensen)
    Bette Krim Kamlet
    Dorothy Bowen Kennedy
    Lee Kizer (son of Marie Kizer)
    Grace "Betty" Ashwell Lotowycz
    John McCaffrey (husband of Peggy Moynihan McCaffrey)
    Jackie Jacquet Melvin
    Leila Allen Morrison
    Ruth Wall Johnson Mullis
    Charlene Grainger O'Leary (daughter of Roberta Grainger)
    Viola "Vonny" Strutzel O'Leary
    Thelma Morey Robinson
    Marie Jansen Rugg
    Ann Enstrom Scott
    Nancy Muir Thompson Tipton
    Lucile Doll Wise
Blair-Caldwell African American Research Library, Denver Public Library, Denver, CO
    Oleta Lawanda Crain Papers, C MSS-ARL 48

John W. Mosley Papers, C MSS-ARL 6 Boulder Carnegie Library for Local History, Boulder, CO

    A. A. Paddock Collection, World War II, 1939–1945, W–X, BHS 328, Box 255, Folder 9

    Boulder Daily Camera

    Marie Rogers Oral History Program, Betty Lou Summers interview, OH 0902

Colorado College, Tutt Library, Colorado Springs, CO

Amache Camp, MS 0299 Denver Public Library, Western History Collection, Denver, CO

    Denver Ordnance Plant Bulletins

    Denver Post

    Denver Star

    Jane Silverstein Ries Papers, WH 1785

    Rocky Mountain News

    Yearbook of the Woman's Club of Denver, 1942–1943

    Yearbooks of the Woman's Club of Denver, 1895–1943

East Morgan County Library District, Brush, CO

    Brush Tribune

Fort Sedgwick Historical Society, Julesburg, CO

    Julesburg Grit-Advocate

    Sunrise Club Collection

GLBT Historical Society Museum and Archives, San Francisco, CA

    World War II Project Papers Series 2, Oral History Interviews, Jacquelyn Beyer Collection #1995-16

Glenwood Springs Historical Society and Frontier Museum, Glenwood Springs, CO

Naval Convalescent Hospital file Guide to Japanese Americans in Northeastern Colorado, University of Northern Colorado, Greeley

Kisa Noguchi Sasaki Collection, Special Collection 40

Historic Colorado Newspapers (online source)

    Aspen Daily Times

    Camp Hale Ski-Zette

    Colorado Transcript (Golden)

    Craig Empire Courier

    Eagle Valley Enterprise

    Golden Transcript

    Lamar Daily News

    Louisville Times

    Oak Creek Times

    Palisade Tribune

    Record Journal of Douglas County

    Steamboat Pilot

History Colorado, Denver

    Amache Collection, MSS 1269

    Denver Federation of Colored Women's Clubs, MSS 304

    Trudy Oda Hirowaka Photograph Collection, Ph 00526

    Midwest Steel and Iron Company Collection, Ph 005887, MSS 03096

    Relocation Center: Lest We Forget by Enola Kjeldgaard, Folio Box 24

    Twenty-second Avenue Study Club Collection, MS 965

YWCA Collection, MSS 1254 Metropolitan State University, Denver, CO

    Emily Nydigger Collinsworth interview

    https://www.msudenver.edu/camphale/resources/interviews

    Mary Andrea Kelles Stone interview

Museums of Western Colorado, Grand Junction

    Daily Sentinel

National Archives, Denver/Broomfield, CO

    Denver Ordnance Plant, RG 156 and 160

National Archives, Washington, DC

    Cadet Nursing Corps files

National Park Service Museum Collections, Rosie the Riveter WWII Home Front
  Historical National Park, Richmond, CA

    Lois Ann Altman Collection, RORI 2414

    Barbara Mae Byron Papers, RORI 4053

    Fadonna Carr Hurban Papers, RORI 718

    Helen Louise Warren Tucker Collection, RORI 2679

Northern Colorado Veterans History Project (Brad Hoopes), Fort Collins

    Harriet Butler Martin interview

    Shirley Sears Melvin interview

    Leila Allen Morrison interview

Oral History Center, Bancroft Library, University of California–Berkeley

    Mary Ann Gallegos Ceminski interview

    Louise Fayram McClain interview

Pikes Peak Library District, Colorado Springs, CO

    Rosemae Wells Campbell Papers, 1904–1991, MSS 0429

    Gazette-Telegraph

    Ruth Banning Lewis Papers, MSS 0109

    Penrose–St. Francis Hospital Collection, MSS 0290

Rawlings Library, Pueblo, CO

    John Korber Collection of the *Pueblo Chieftain* and the *Pueblo Star Journal*: The
      Pueblo Ordnance Depot, Volumes I and II

    Pueblo Chieftain

    Pueblo Star Journal

She's a WOW: Women Ordnance Workers in Pueblo, CO, 1942–1945, exhibit by
Lauren Knight and Alyssa Vargas Lopez, March 29–April 25, 2018
Roaring Fork Veterans History Project, Aspen Historical Society, Aspen, CO
June Rew Kirkwood interview
Phyllis Ilgen Smith interview
Steelworks Center of the West, Archives, Pueblo, CO
The Blast
Colorado Fuel & Iron Company Collection
Ruth Catherine Ostergaard Tammen Collection
Texas Woman's University, Denton
WASP Archive
Tread of Pioneers Museum, Steamboat Springs, CO
Harriet Kemry Aspegren interview
Eunice Kemry Dorr Collection
University of Colorado Boulder, Norlin Library, Archives, Boulder
US Navy Japanese/Oriental Language School Archival Project
University of North Carolina at Greensboro, Betty H. Carter Women Veterans
Historical Project, Hodges Special Collections and University Archives, UNCG
University Libraries, Greensboro
Louise Nash Dorsett interview, WV0017
Betty Berry Godin interview, WV0096
Anne Elizabeth Heyer Collection, WV0320
Mary Haynsworth Mathew Collection, WV0119
Alice Starr May interview, WV0595
Bernice Moran Miller Collection, WV0104
Dorothy Griffin Rice interview, WV0112
Veterans History Project, American Folklife Center, Library of Congress,
Washington, DC
Janet A. Bachmeyer Collection, AFC/2001/001/57409
Mary Devlin Barry Collection, AFC/2001/001/26642
Wilma Vanden Hoek Broekstra Collection, AFC/2001/001/33388
Velma C. Comstock Brooke Collection, AFC/2001/001/56220
Shirley Elizabeth Gunston Brown Collection, AFC/2001/001/34261
Marie Edwards Collection, AFC 2001/001/000280
Lillian Mae Bainbridge Green Collection, AFC/2001/001/62658
Jeanne E. Barrenche Hackler Collection, AFC/200/001/57276
Katherine Keating Collection, AFC/2001/001/10522
Doris June Rew Kirkwood Collection, AFC/2001/001/52457
Barbara L. Kees Meeks Collection, AFC/2001/001/57220
Betty Lee Leist Megenity Collection, AFC/2001/001/09094
Hazel Marie Hester Miller Collection, AFC/2001/001/42192

Jane Dyde Miller Collection, AFC/2001/001/78137

Eileen Bradley Paine Collection, AFC/2001/001/11230

LaVerne Marie Novak Sarber Collection, AFC/2001/001/665191

Patricia Jane Irvine Whiting interview, AFC/2001/001/21227

Mildred Doherty Zupon Collection, AFC/2001/001/65177

WASP Museum, Sweetwater, TX

Women in Military Service for America Memorial, Arlington, VA

SECONDARY SOURCES

Abbott, Carl, Stephen J. Leonard, and Thomas J. Noel. *Colorado: A History of the Centennial State*. 5th ed. Boulder: University Press of Colorado, 2013.

Addams, Michael C.C. *The Best War Ever: America and World War II*. Baltimore: Johns Hopkins University Press, 1994.

Anderson, Karen. *Wartime Women: Sex Roles, Family Relations, and the Status of Women during World War II*. Westport, CT: Greenwood, 1981.

Ashbaugh, Gwen. "The Widow's Mite: The Story of Dr. Jennie Rucker." *Colorado Heritage* (May–June 2010): 5, inside back cover.

Avila, Mayra Lizette. "La Pena Negra: Mexican Women, Gender, and Labor during the Bracero Program, 1942–1964." PhD dissertation, University of Texas at El Paso, 2018.

Bailey, Beth. *Sex in the Heartland*. Cambridge, MA: Harvard University Press, 1999.

Bain, Jeanette. *History and Chronology of the Colorado State Federation of Women's Clubs, 1895–1955*. Denver: Colorado Federation of Women's Clubs, 1955.

Banning, Margaret Culkin. *Women for Defense*. New York: Duell, Sloan, and Pearce, 1942.

Barger, Judith. *Beyond the Call of Duty: Army Flight Nursing in World War II*. Kent, OH: Kent State University Press, 2013.

Beaton, Gail M. *Colorado Women: A History*. Boulder: University Press of Colorado, 2012.

Bellafaire, Judith A. *The Army Nurse Corps*. Washington, DC: US Army Center of Military History, 1993.

Berube, Allan. *Coming Out under Fire: The History of Gay Men and Women in World War II*. Chapel Hill: University of North Carolina Press, 2010.

Bluemel, Elinor. *The Opportunity School and Emily Griffith, Its Founder*. Denver: Green Mountain, 1970.

Brinkley, Douglas, ed. *The World War II Memorial: A Grateful Nation Remembers*. Washington, DC: New Voyage Communications, 2004.

Brock, Julia, Jennifer W. Dickey, Richard J.W. Harker, and Catherine M. Lewis. *Beyond Rosie: A Documentary History of Women and World War II*. Fayetteville: University of Arkansas Press, 2015.

Bullough, Vern L. *American Nursing: A Biographical Dictionary*, vol. 3 (New York: Springer, 2000).

Burstein, Herbert. *Women in War: A Complete Guide to Service in the Armed Forces and War Industries*. New York: Service Publishing, 1943.

Campbell, D'Ann. *Women at War with America: Private Lives in a Patriotic Era*. Boston: Harvard University Press, 1984.

Carlton, Bobbie, ed. *WAVES of Colorado: US Navy Memories of World War II*. [no place of publication]: Bobbie Carlton, 2009.

Carpenter, Stephanie A. *On the Farm Front: The Women's Land Army in World War II*. DeKalb: Northern Illinois University Press, 2003.

Cervi, Cle, and Nancy M. Peterson. *The Women Who Made the Headlines: Denver Woman's Club, the First Hundred Years.* Lakewood, CO: Western Guideways, 1998.

Chafe, William Henry. *The American Woman: Her Changing Social, Economic, and Political Roles, 1920–1970.* New York: Oxford University Press, 1972.

Cohen, Deborah. *Braceros: Migrant Citizens and Transnational Subjects in the Postwar United States and Mexico.* Chapel Hill: University of North Carolina Press, 2011.

Cohen, Lizabeth. *A Consumer's Republic: The Politics of Mass Consumption in Postwar America.* New York: Vintage Books, 2003.

Cole, Jean Hascall. *Women Pilots of World War II.* Salt Lake City: University of Utah Press, 1992.

Connor, Melissa, and James Schneck. *Fort Carson in World War II: The Old Hospital Complex.* Lincoln, NE: National Park Service, 1997.

Converse, Mary Allen. *Captain Mary: The Biography of Mary Parker Converse, Captain U.S. Merchant Marine.* King's Point, NY: American Merchant Marine Museum, 1987.

Cott, Nancy F., ed. *No Small Courage: A History of Women in the United States.* Oxford: Oxford University Press, 2000.

Dingham, Roger. *Deciphering the Rising Sun: Navy and Marine Corps Codebreakers, Translators, and Interpreters in the Pacific War.* Annapolis, MD: Naval Institute, 2009.

Dong, Cheryl. "Red Cross Volunteer Nurse's Aide Corps." In Lisa Tendrich Frank, ed., *An Encyclopedia of American Women at War: From the Home Front to the Battlefields,* vol. 2: *M–Z* 462-464. Santa Barbara, CA: ABC-CLIO, 2013.

Earley, Charity Adams. *One Woman's Army: A Black Officer Remembers the WAC.* College Station: Texas A&M Press, 1989.

Esmiol, Kathleen F. "Chasing the American Dream: Fannie Mae Duncan and the Cotton Club." In Ted Blevins, Dennis Daily, Sydne Dean, Chris Nicholl, and Michael L. Olsen, eds., *Enterprise and Innovation in the Pikes Peak Region,* 296–335. Colorado Springs: Clausen Books, 2011.

Faulkner, Debra. *Touching Tomorrow: The Emily Griffith Story.* Palmer Lake, CO: Filter Press, 2005.

Fessler, Diane Burke. *No Time for Fear: Voices of American Military Nurses in World War II.* East Lansing: Michigan State University Press, 1997.

Fisher, Ellen Kingman. *Junior League of Denver.* Denver: Colorado Historical Society, 1993.

Fortin, Noonie. *Women at Risk: We Also Served.* Lincoln, NE: Writers Press Club, 2002.

Gilliland, Shirley, ed. *World War II: The People and Events of Morgan County, Colorado.* Raleigh, NC: Curtis Media, 1995.

Gluck, Sherna Berger. *Rosie the Riveter Revisited: Women, the War, and Social Change.* Boston: Twayne, 1987.

Godson, Susan H. *Serving Proudly: A History of Women in the U.S. Navy.* Annapolis, MD: Naval Institute Press, 20001.

Goldstein, Marcia. "We Can Wear the Pants, Too! Denver's Women Ordnance Workers, 1941–1945." Unpublished paper, 1996.

Gouveia, Grace Mary. "We Also Serve: American Indian Women's Role in World War II." *Michigan Historical Review* 20, no. 2 (Fall 1994): 153–182.

Gowdy-Wygant, Cecilia. *Cultivating Victory: The Women's Land Army and the Victory Garden Movement.* Pittsburgh: University of Pittsburgh Press, 2013.

Green, Anne Bosanko. *One Woman's War: Letters Home from the Women's Army Corps, 1944–1946.* St. Paul: Minnesota Historical Society Press, 1989.

Greene, Bob. *Once Upon a Town: The Miracle of the North Platte Canteen.* New York: William Morrow/John Deadline Enterprises, 2002.

Gregory, Lester W. *Women in Defense Work during World War II: An Analysis of the Labor Problem and Women's Rights*. New York: Exposition, 1974.

Hamilton, Cindy. *Footprints in the Sugar: A History of the Great Western Sugar Company*. Ontario, OR: Hamilton Bates, 2009.

Hamilton, Diane B. *Becoming a Presence within Nursing: The History of the University of Colorado School of Nursing, 1898–1998*. Denver: University of Colorado School of Nursing, 1999.

Harris, Mary V. *Guide Right: A Handbook for WAVES and SPARS*. New York: Macmillan, 1994.

Hartmann, Susan M. *The Home Front and Beyond: American Women in the 1940s*. Boston: Twayne, 1982.

Harvey, Robert. *Amache: The Story of Japanese Internment in Colorado during World War II*. Lanham, MD: Taylor Trade, 2003.

Hegarty, Marilyn E. *Victory Girls, Khaki Wackies, and Patriotutes: The Regulation of Female Sexuality during World War II*. New York: New York University Press, 2008.

Higonnet, Margaret Randolph, Jane Jenson, Sonya Michel, and Margaret Collins Weitz, eds. *Behind the Lines: Gender and the Two World Wars*. New Haven, CT: Yale University Press, 1987.

Hoffecker, John F. *Twenty-seven Square Miles: Landscape and History at Rocky Mountain Arsenal National Wildlife Refuge*. Washington, DC: US Fish and Wildlife Service, Rocky Mountain Arsenal National Wildlife Refuge, 2001.

Holm, Jeanne, Major General, USAF (Ret'd.), ed. *In Defense of a Nation: Servicewomen in World War II*. Washington, DC: Military Women's Press, 1998.

Holm, Jeanne, Major General, USAF (Ret'd.). *Women in the Military: An Unfinished Revolution*. Novato, CA: Presidio, 1992.

Hoopes, Brad. *Reflections of Our Gentle Warriors: Personal Stories of World War II Veterans*. Bradenton, FL: BookLocker.com, 2015.

Humphrey, Marles. *Lilies of Our Valley: Stories of Routt County Women*. Steamboat Springs, CO: Michael James Publishing, 2006.

Hurt, R. Douglas. *The Great Plains during World War II*. Lincoln: University of Nebraska Press, 2008.

Jackson, Kathi. *They Called Them Angels: American Military Nurses of World War II*. Westport, CT: Praeger, 2000.

Jeffries, John W. *Wartime America: The World War II Home Front*. Chicago: Ivan R. Dee, 1996.

Johnson, Melyn. "At Home in Amache." *Colorado Heritage* (1989): 2–11.

Jonathan, Mark, Franklin D. Mitchell, and Steven J. Schechter. *The Homefront: America during World War II*. New York: G. P. Putnam's Sons, 1984.

Kaufman, Jacob J. "Farm Labor during World War II." *Journal of Farm Economics* (February 1949): 131–142.

Kessler-Harris, Alice. *Out to Work: A History of Wage-Earning Women in the United States*. New York: Oxford University Press, 2003.

Kirstein, Peter N. *Anglo over Bracero: A History of the Mexican Worker in the United States from Roosevelt to Nixon*. Saratoga, CA: R and E Research Associates, 1977.

Knaff, Donna B. *Beyond Rosie the Riveter: Women of World War II in American Popular Graphic Art*. Lawrence: University Press of Kansas, 2012.

Kyvig, David E. "Historical Misunderstandings and the Defeat of the Equal Rights Amendment." *Public Historian* 18, no.1 (Winter 1996): 45–63.

Lenthe, Jean-Vi. *Flying into Yesterday: My Search for the Curtiss-Wright Aeronautical Engineering Cadettes*. El Prado, NM: Wild Hare, 2011.

Lewis, Barbara Ralph. *Women at War: The Women of World War II —at Home, at Work, on the Front Line*. Pleasantville, NY: Reader's Digest Association, 2002.

Lewis, W. David, *Airline Executives and Federal Regulation: Case Studies in American Enterprise from the Airmail Era to the Dawn of the Jet Age*. Columbus: Ohio State University Press, 2000.

Litoff, Judy Barrett, and David C. Smith, eds. *American Women in a World at War: Contemporary Accounts from World War II*. Wilmington, DE: Scholarly Resources, 2001.

Litoff, Judy Barett, and David C. Smith. "To the Rescue: The Women's Land Army during World War II." *Prologue* 25, no. 4 (Winter 1993): 9–22.

Lopez, Jody, and Gabriel Lopez, with Peggy A. Ford. *White Gold Laborers: The Story of Greeley's Spanish Colony*. Bloomington, IN: AuthorHouse, 2007.

Lucchesi, Emilie Le Beau. This Is Really War: The Incredible True Story of a Navy Nurse POW in the Occupied Philippines. Chicago: Chicago Review Press, 2019.

Lytle, Tom. "Shipbuilding on a 'Mountaintop': World War II's Rocky Mountain Fleet." *Colorado Heritage* (Summer 1998): 14–24.

Manning, Jeanne. *A Time to Speak*. Paducah, KY: Turner, 1999.

McEuen, Melissa A. *Making War, Making Women: Femininity and Duty on the American Home Front, 1941–1945*. Athens: University of Georgia Press, 2011.

McManus, John C. *Hell before Their Very Eyes: American Soldiers Liberate Concentration Camps in Germany April 1945*. Baltimore: Johns Hopkins University Press, 2015.

McNaughton, James C. *Nisei Linguists: Japanese Americans in the Military Intelligence Service during World War II*. Washington, DC: Department of the Navy, 2006.

Men and Women in the Armed Forces from Montrose County. Oklahoma City: Western Publishing, 1946.

Meyer, Leisa D. *Creating GI Jane: Sexuality and Power in the Women's Army Corps during World War II*. New York: Columbia University Press, 1996.

Milkman, Ruth. *Gender at Work: The Dynamics of Job Segregation by Sex during World War II*. Urbana: University of Illinois Press, 1987.

Miyagishima, Kara Mariko. "Colorado's *Nikkei* Pioneers: Japanese Americans in Twentieth Century Colorado." MA thesis, University of Colorado–Denver, 2007.

Monahan, Evelyn M., and Rosemary Neidel-Greenlee. *All This Hell: U.S. Nurses Imprisoned by the Japanese*. Lexington: University Press of Kentucky, 2000.

Moore, Brenda L. *Serving Our Country: Japanese American Women in the Military during World War II*. New Brunswick, NJ: Rutgers University Press, 2003.

Moore, Brenda L. *To Serve My Country, to Serve My Race: The Story of the Only African-American Wacs Stationed Overseas during World War II*. New York: New York University Press, 1996.

Moyer, Marie, and Dolores Nelson. "War Effort Came from Smallest of Schools." In Bud Wells, ed., *Logan County, Better by 100 Years: A Centennial History of Logan County, Colorado, 1887–1987*. Raleigh, NC: Curtis Media, 1982.

Mundy, Liza. *Code Girls: The Untold Story of the American Women Code Breakers of World War II*. New York: Hatchette Books, 2017.

Noel, Thomas J. *Colorado: A Historical Atlas*. Norman: University of Oklahoma Press, 2015.

Noel, Thomas J., and Kevin E. Rucker. *Eaton Metal Products: The First 80 Years—a Story of Vision and Commitment*. Denver: A. B. Hirschfield, 1998.

Norman, Elizabeth M. *We Band of Angels: The Untold Story of the American Women Trapped on Bataan*. New York: Random House Trade Paperbacks, 2013.

Parker, Pauline E., ed. *Women of the Homefront: World War II Recollections of 55 Americans*. Jefferson, NC: McFarland, 2002.

Parsons, Edy. "Women's Nursing Corps, Army." In Lisa Tendrich Frank, ed., *An Encyclopedia of American Women at War: From the Home Front to the Battlefields*, vol. 2: *M–Z* 651-653. Santa Barbara, CA: ABC-CLIO, 2013.

Pfaff, Christine. "Bullets for the Yankees: Colorado's World War II Ammunition Factory." *Colorado Heritage* (Summer 1992): 33–45.

Plested, Dolores. *Some Reminiscences along the Way*. Denver: Author, 2002.

Poulos, Paula Nassen, ed. *A Woman's War Too: U.S. Women in the Military in World War II*. Washington, DC: National Archives and Records Administration, 1996.

Propst, Nell Brown. *Those Strenuous Dames of the Eastern Plains*. Boulder: Pruett, 1982.

Puaca, Laura Micheletti. *Searching for Scientific Womanpower: Technocratic Feminism and the Politics of National Security, 1940–1980*. Chapel Hill: University of North Carolina Press, 2014.

Reese, Joan. "Two Enemies to Fight: Blacks Battle for Equality in Two World Wars." *Colorado Heritage* (1990): 2–17.

Regis, Margaret. *When Our Mothers Went to War: An Illustrated History of Women in World War II*. Seattle: Navpublishing, 2008.

Rickman, Sarah Bryn. *Nancy Love and the WASP Ferry Pilots of World War II*. Denton: University of North Texas Press, 2008.

Rickman, Sarah Bryn. *WASPs of the Ferry Command: Women Pilots, Uncommon Deeds*. Denton: University of North Texas Press, 2016.

Robinson, Thelma Morey. *Cadet Nurse Corps: Your Country Needs You*. Bloomington, IN: XLibris, 2009.

Robinson, Thelma Morey. *Nisei Cadet Nurse of World War II: Patriotism in Spite of Prejudice*. Boulder: Black Swan Mill, 2005.

Robinson, Thelma Morey, and Pauline M. Perry. *Cadet Nurse Stories: The Call for and Response of Women during World War II*. Indianapolis: Center Nursing Press, 2001.

Rosas, Ana Elizabeth. *Abrazando el Espíritu: Bracero Families Confront the US-Mexico Border*. Oakland: University of California Press, 2014.

Rosas, Ana Elizabeth. "Breaking the Silence: Mexican Children and Women's Confrontation of Bracero Family Separation, 1942–64." *Gender and History* 23, no. 2 (August 2011): 382–400.

Rupp, Leila J. *Mobilizing Women for War: German and American Propaganda, 1939–1945*. Princeton, NJ: Princeton University Press, 1978.

Scamehorn, Lee. *Mill and Mine: The CF&I in the 20th Century*. Lincoln: University of Nebraska Press, 1992.

Secrest, Clark. "The Day Clara May Morse Died: Pearl Harbor and One Mother's Heartbreak." *Colorado Heritage* (Autumn 1991): 36–44.

Secrest, Clark. "Vitamins for Victory." *Colorado Heritage* (Winter 1995): 25–27.

Shockley, Megan Taylor. *"We, Too, Are Americans": African American Women in Detroit and Richmond, 1940–54*. Urbana: University of Illinois Press, 2004.

Sigerman, Harriet, ed. *The Columbia Documentary History of American Women since 1941*. New York: Columbia University Press, 2003.

Soderbergh, Peter A. *Women Marines: The World War II Era*. Westport, CT: Praeger, 1992.

Sorel, Nancy Caldwell. *The Women Who Wrote the War*. New York: Arcade, 1999.

Strebe, Amy Goodpaster. *Flying for Her Country: The American and Soviet Women Military Pilots of World War II*. Westport, CT: Praeger Security International, 2007.

Stremlow, Mary V., Colonel, USMC (Ret'd). *Free a Marine to Fight: Women Marines in World War II*. Marines in World War II Commemorative Series. Washington, DC: Marine Corps Historical Center, 1994.

Sullivan, Jill M. *Bands of Sisters: U.S. Women's Military Bands during World War II*. Lanham, MD: Scarecrow, 2011.

Taylor, Quintard. *In Search of the Racial Frontier: African Americans in the American West, 1528–1990*. New York: W. W. Norton, 1998.

Taylor, Quintard, and Shirley Ann Wilson Moore, eds. *African American Women Confront the West, 1600–2000*. Norman: University of Oklahoma Press, 2003.

Teeuwen, Randall C. *Growing Up Gates: A Family History*. Greenwood Village, CO: Bear Creek, 2002.

Tomblin, Barbara Brooks. *G.I. Nightingales: The Army Nurse Corps in World War II*. Lexington: University Press of Kentucky, 1996.

Treadwell, Mattie E. *The Women's Army Corps*. United States Army in World War II Special Studies. Washington, DC: Office of the Chief of Military History, Department of the Army, 1954.

Tucker, Sherrie. *Swing Shift: "All Girl" Bands of the 1940s*. Durham, NC: Duke University Press, 2000.

Tuttle, William M., Jr. *"Daddy's Gone to War": The Second World War in the Lives of American Children*. New York: Oxford University Press, 1993.

Varnell, Jeanne. *Women of Consequence: The Colorado Women's Hall of Fame*. Boulder: Johnson Books, 1999.

Verges, Marianne. *On Silver Wings: Women Airforce Service Pilots of World War II, 1942–1944*. New York: Ballantine Books, 1991.

Weatherford, Doris. *American Women and World War II*. New York: Facts on File, 1990.

Weatherford, Doris. *American Women during World War II: An Encyclopedia*. New York: Routledge, 2010.

Wei, William. "The Strangest City in Colorado: The Amache Concentration Camp." *Colorado Heritage* (Winter 2005): 2–17.

Willenz, June A. *Women Veterans: America's Forgotten Heroines*. New York: Continuum, 1983.

Willever, Heather. "The Cadet Nurse Corps, 1943–1948." *PHS* [Public Health Service] *Chronicles* 109, no. 3 (May–June 1994): 455–457.

Williams, Vera S. *WASPs: Women Airforce Service Pilots of World War II*. Honolulu: Pacific Historic Parks, 1994.

Winchell, Meghan H. *Good Girls, Good Food, Good Fun: The Story of the USO Hostesses during World War II*. Chapel Hill: University of North Carolina Press, 2008.

Witte, David R. *World War II at Camp Hale: Blazing a New Trail in the Rockies*. Charleston, SC: History Press, 2015.

Yellin, Emily. *Our Mothers' War: American Women at Home and at the Front during World War II*. New York: Free Press, 2004.

Young, Richard K. *The Ute Indians of Colorado in the Twentieth Century*. Norman: University of Oklahoma Press, 1997.

Zeinert, Karen. *Those Incredible Women of World War II*. Brookfield, CT: Millbrook, 1994.

Index

Page numbers in italics indicate illustrations.